Tim Ferris
08-04-2010

Retirement Success

Retirement Success

A Complete Instruction Guide
for Plan Sponsors
and Their Advisors

Dr. Gregory W. Kasten

Unified Trust Company, NA

Lexington, Kentucky

Contents

Acknowledgments

No book could be considered complete without a word of thanks to the many people who helped make it happen. First and foremost, I would like to thank my wonderful wife, Jan, who has supported me in my efforts to compile nearly two decades of experience into something that will help others. She endured many nights and weekends as I reviewed articles, studies, and other materials that went into this book.

Second, I would like to thank the excellent employees of Unified Trust Company, NA, who helped review this book and offered many important suggestions. I would particularly like to thank Michele Hardesty, Pete Swisher, Natalie Wyatt, Melody Townsend, Angela Bryant, Rob Williams, Jamie Eads, Richard Holt, Alan Veal, Norm Golibersuch, Kim Blanton, and David Roberts.

About the Author

Dr. Kasten and his wife, Jan, have three children. They reside in Lexington, Kentucky, and are active at Southern Acres Christian Church, Lexington Christian Academy and Habitat for Humanity. Dr. Kasten serves as a member on the boards of directors of several charitable foundations.

For more than twenty years, Dr. Kasten has devoted the major part of each working day to helping employees successfully define and meet their retirement goals.

Dr. Kasten is a board certified anesthesiologist with thirteen years of practice experience. Following graduation from Southern Illinois University School of Medicine in 1980, he completed an internal medicine internship and anesthesiology residency at the University of Kentucky Medical Center.

In addition to serving as a teaching physician, Dr. Kasten received a master of business administration degree with an emphasis on finance and investment management from the University of Kentucky College of Business Graduate School. Following substantial success with his personal investments, he retired from active medical practice to pursue investment management on a full-time basis.

From his early days of interacting with physicians and nurses, Dr. Kasten became interested in improving the outcome of retirement plan participants. He constantly observed the difficulty that both highly compensated and rank-and-file workers faced in trying to build a successful retirement program. Dr. Kasten found it puzzling that most retirement programs and investment recommendations are not analyzed for outcome effectiveness.

He likened it to a physician's prescribing a medicine with no data to support whether or not it worked.

Dr. Kasten found that most of what passes for retirement advice and investment analysis makes little, if any, difference in improving outcomes. Most plan sponsors have been unable to determine what helps and what hurts, as most of what is presented to them is a "sales pitch."

Dr. Kasten set out to apply the same rigorous outcome analysis used in medicine to investing and retirement planning. Many plan sponsors were using "back-tested" information. Often, they had little, if any, data that what they were doing made any meaningful difference after they implemented it. In the financial world, back-tested information seldom tells the client anything about tomorrow.

Dr. Kasten's rule of thumb was simple: "If it doesn't make a difference *after* you use it, don't use it!" He set out to offer an approach that utilized only those factors that were shown to make a positive difference in outcomes—after they were put to use. He believed that most individuals would not meet their retirement objectives and that they required professional help. He developed a comprehensive program to accurately measure and predict success outcomes. He also developed a program to monitor plan-participant activity and to improve success likelihood.

Dr. Kasten has published numerous original mutual-fund research papers and has developed the Unified Fiduciary Monitoring Index® as a method of measuring mutual fund and predictive performance factors when observed from a fiduciary standpoint. The Denver College of Financial Planning awarded Dr. Kasten the Certified Financial Planner designation after his completion of its two-year program. The American Society of Pension Actuaries awarded him the Certified Pension Consultant designation after his completion of its two-year program.

x

Dr. Kasten has published more than forty-five papers on financial planning and investment-related topics in various financial and business journals. Many of these articles have been widely quoted in the United States in both academic and business circles.

Specific areas were improving participant outcomes, measuring mutual-fund predictive factors, defining and measuring Monte Carlo outcome success, fiduciary liability management, fiduciary monitoring, portfolio analysis, investment management, retirement plan design, financial planning, and reducing portfolio risk.

In recent years, he has spoken each year at national pension society meetings on developing a comprehensive written trust-investment policy. Dr. Kasten has appeared on several national public television programs dealing with investment topics. His published article, "The Changing Relative Risk between Stocks and Bonds" has been widely quoted in the United States in both academic and business circles.

In 1985, Dr. Kasten started a registered investment advisory firm, Health Financial Inc., to provide money management and retirement plan consultations to individuals and plan sponsors.

In 1993, he started First Lexington Trust Company. In 2000, First Lexington Trust became Unified Trust Company, N.A.; Dr. Kasten serves as the trust company's CEO and president. Unified Trust Company specializes in both wealth management and consulting with and managing 401(k) and other employee benefit plans.

A unique feature of the trust company is a service guarantee, in which every investment fund entering a client's account is in the top 25 percent of its peer group, based upon the Unified Fiduciary Monitoring Index® created by Dr. Kasten. This process is patent-pending.

Unified Trust Company, provides complete fiduciary and trustee services and currently employs a staff of more than forty professionals. More than 350 retirement plans are administered, with assets under management in excess of $700 million. Unified Trust Company is located at 2353 Alexandria Drive, Suite 100, Lexington, KY 40504. The phone number is (859) 296-4407, and the fax number is (859) 296-0880. You may contact Dr. Kasten by e-mail at greg.kasten@unifiedtrust.com.

Introduction

This book is written for plan sponsors and their advisors. The advisor could be your human resources department, your retirement committee, your board of directors, or certain key employee groups, or you may employ an outside advisor. The book is designed to allow Ockham's Razor to be put to good use:

Ockham's Razor

"What can be done with fewer assumptions is done in vain with more."

William of Ockham (1285-1349), English theologian and philosopher, is given credit for Ockham's Razor (also spelled Occam's Razor, pronounced AHK-uhmz).

Ockham's Razor is the idea that, in trying to understand something, getting unnecessary information out of the way is the fastest way to the truth or to the best explanation.

My goal is simple: To put into simple language the specific processes proven to help improve the outcome success probability of plan participants.

This book will help you optimize the Three A's that are essential for a successful retirement: Adequate Savings, Asset Allocation Advice, and Asset Quality. I further simplify this into the combination of savings rate and real rate of investment return (SR+RR Index) needed for success. Adequate Savings is determined by the savings rate. Asset Allocation and Asset Quality determine the real rate of investment return.

For more than two decades, I have devoted the major part of every working day to helping employees retire successfully. Over that time, we have seen 401(k) plans become nearly universal and defined benefit plans diminish in importance. We have seen all types of neat innovations, such as participant-directed accounts; Internet account information with trading, mutual-fund subscription services like Morningstar; and the publication of dozens of self-help books on investing and retirement.

Yet with all this help (or is it noise?), the average worker is less likely to have a successful retirement plan today than twenty years ago. The average 401(k) participant has a 20% likelihood of meeting his retirement needs. This is true for doctors and lawyers, as well as rank-and-file workers. What can we do to raise that possibility to 50% or, even better, 80%?

Chart I-1: Improving the Success/Failure Ratio

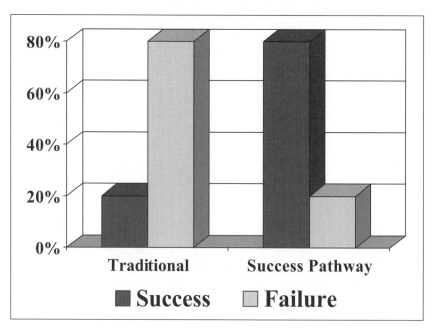

The major reason for poor outcomes is that most of what is emphasized to the plan sponsor is in the form of a sales pitch. The plan sponsor is not being sold tried-and-true processes that are proven to improve outcomes—after implementation. Usually the plan sponsor has no data showing whether a certain idea or features makes any meaningful difference. I have always found it amazing that most retirement programs, self-directed brokerage accounts, mutual-fund subscription and ratings services, and investment recommendations are not analyzed for outcome effectiveness. In other words, no one ever looks after the service is introduced to see whether or not it has helped.

There are many well-written "technical" books about the Employee Retirement Income Security Act (ERISA) and the myriad rules and regulations about retirement plans. This book assumes that the plan sponsor has competent ERISA legal advice, as well as a competent plan administration group. The highly technical topics of plan administration and ERISA rules are not covered here. Likewise, this book is not a "CYA" approach to fiduciary liability. There is no question that ERISA fiduciary liability is a huge issue. However, I focus on improving success rates among plan participants. In other words, my approach is more pragmatic than legalistic.

Some financial planning and investment books have a chapter or two on retirement planning and Social Security, but none of these really help the plan sponsor. They tend to be oversimplified and are often too optimistic. Universally, they contain advice that has not been proven to work after it is implemented by either the plan sponsor or the individual participant.

I liken the approach that many plans' sponsors take to selecting and managing their retirement plan to a professional golfer who is playing in the most important round of golf in his career. Imagine if the professional only played one round of golf once every five years! I don't think he would win often. Yet that's just what we do with retirement plans. Every three to five years, the human resources people or the chief financial officer solicits proposals and picks a new vendor. They usually miss most of the important details, and they almost never make their decision based upon processes that are proven to work *after* implementation. They collect most of their information from the salesperson (the "pension consultant"), who has a vested interest in telling them whatever they want to hear to close the sale. The plan sponsors go from vendor to vendor and wonder why they never improve the outcomes of their participants. All too often they do not even know that the outcomes are poor.

This book will help you optimize the Three A's essential for a successful retirement: Adequate Savings, Asset Allocation Advice, and Asset Quality. Without sufficient savings, there is little chance of a successful retirement. Once the proper amount of savings has been put into place through the innovative programs described in this book, the plan participant must obtain a higher real rate of return (after inflation) than most are receiving today. Obtaining a higher real rate of return depends upon the proper asset allocation and on maintaining a high level of asset quality.

Chart I-2: "Three A's" of Retirement Success

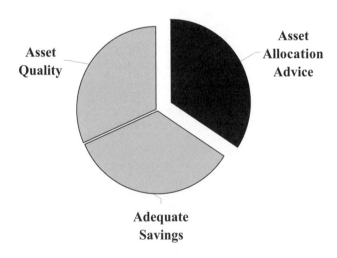

An example of success/failure research can be seen in Chart I-3. It is the result of more than 500,000 retirement simulations of a thirty-year-old worker needing to replace 70% of his after-tax current income over his life expectancy in retirement. The worker can expect to receive some Social Security benefit, albeit reduced, and the rest must come from his retirement plan. Is he saving enough? Is he earning a high enough real (after inflation) rate of return? "Success" is defined as a 75% probability that the plan will work.

Keep in mind that the median worker saves 6% to 7% and earns an effective real rate of return of between -1% and +1% . The X shows where the worker falls in the "Failure Region" part of the chart.

Chart I-3: Savings Rate and Real Rate of Return Define Success or Failure Regions

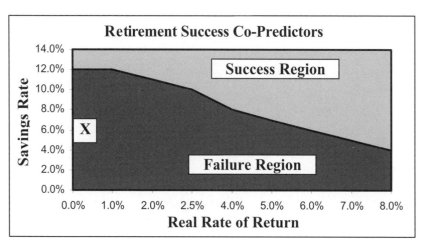

So, how do we help a worker move into the Success Region? How do we raise his savings rate and his real rate of return? We will guide you in putting together proven processes that can make a significant difference in improving outcomes. In addition, we have developed and perfected the fiduciary monitoring process that gathers asset information and combines it with data on the asset quality of the funds by using our patent-pending

Unified Fiduciary Monitoring Index®. Finally, in chapter 19, we describe the Unified Success Pathway™ for improved participant success, and in chapter 20 we demonstrate how to objectively review several proposals for ERISA services based upon outcome improvement factors using the Unified Proposal Evaluation System^SM.

This takes into account everything discussed in this book to dramatically improve the plan participant's probability of retirement success. I trust that this will help you put together a sound program to allow your employees to successfully prepare for retirement.

Thank you.

Gregory W. Kasten, M.D., MBA, CFP, CPC
President
Unified Trust Company, N.A.

Chapter 1

Most Employees Will Face Retirement Crisis

Chapter Summary

Only about two in ten Americans is on track for retirement success. Why? They are not saving enough money, and their real investment returns are consistently suboptimal. In a nutshell, they are not following any of the time-tested and successful management techniques followed by sophisticated defined benefit plans.

We define "retirement success" as an adequate combination of savings rate and real rate of investment return that produces a 75% or better probability that plan participants will have sufficient inflation-adjusted replacement income throughout their life expectancy in retirement to maintain their standard of living.

National data reveal that the savings rate for plan participants averages about one-half that needed for adequate income replacement—assuming that they are earning "normal" real investment returns.

In addition to low savings hurting their chances for successful retirement, aggregate data reveal that investors earned minimal returns even during favorable market conditions over the two decades before the market downturn of 2000–2002. The returns incurred by the average equity-fund investor have averaged just 2.7% per year, compared with the S&P 500 return of 12.0%. With even "mild" inflation of 3.0%, this translates into a negative real rate of return after inflation.

Available Money Will Not Be Sufficient

Starting now and running through the next three decades, America is launching an entire generation into retirement without sufficient financial resources to support them. These retirees can expect to live longer, retire earlier, and endure inflation longer than any of the generations that preceded them.

For some years now, there has been general consensus that baby boomers will be worse off than their parents during their retirement years. Through the years, study after study has shown that boomers save less than their parents. During the 1980s, boomers' participation in retirement programs lessened significantly. The mid-1980s began a trend away from employer-sponsored defined benefit plans and toward less costly defined contributions plans, especially 401(k) plans. The stock market boom from 1991 to 1999 offered higher-than-normal equity investment returns, and many thought this would offset a lower savings rate.

Chart 1-1: Percentage of Workers Covered by Defined Benefit and Defined Contribution Plans, 1981–2001

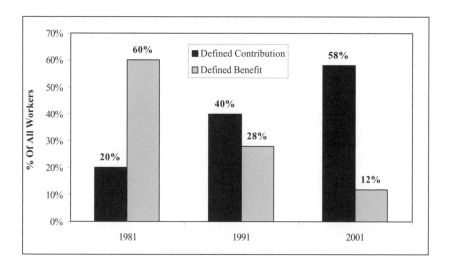

The switch from defined benefit to defined contribution plans has major implications for retirement success and national policy. To illustrate, we can examine two major differences between the plans: 1) the nature of the benefit and 2) the reliability of the payments.

Traditional defined benefit plans offer an annuity—that is, a stream of payments for life—while defined contribution plans typically pay a lump sum. Individuals may perceive an expected flow of income for life differently than they do a lump sum of equal value, contrary to traditional economic theory. For example, individuals may be reluctant to spend their 401(k) balances in the hope of leaving sizable bequests.

Others may spend down their wealth too slowly in order to ensure that they do not exhaust their assets before they die. For these reasons, when pension payments are in the form of a lump sum rather than an annuity, individuals may desire higher levels of wealth in retirement in order to maintain equivalent levels of consumption. Therefore, we might expect to see an increase in the retirement age due to the increase in lump-sum distributions associated with defined contribution plans.

Second, some individuals may react differently to levels of retirement wealth, depending on their sense of the reliability of the amount. For example, it is possible for 401(k) balances to change dramatically in a short period, which can make it difficult for individuals to reliably predict how much income they can expect to receive from the account.

In addition, upon receiving a lump sum at retirement, individuals must decide how to invest the money and then estimate the interest they will receive on their investments. The presence of this investment uncertainty may cause some individuals to err on the side of caution and stay in the workforce longer than if they had a more predictable income stream from a defined benefit plan.

Lost in a ocean of too much information, defined contribution participants float and drift here and there, reaping predictably poor results. Using either no strategy or fatally flawed strategies, most place their meager and hard-earned savings in the wrong markets and then fail to even come close to a market return.

Of course, if the stock market can generate a 20% annual return, lagging by -5% or -10% is not such a big deal. However, the huge decline in the S&P 500 from March 2000 to October 2002 changed the retirement success landscape considerably. Between 1999 and 2002, the total value of assets in 401(k) plans dropped from $1.9 trillion to $1.5 trillion (including new contributions). This plunge spurred a renewed interest in retirement savings plans by both the government and employers. Even old-fashioned annuities and defined benefit pension plans, which were previously considered "out of date," have started to look attractive again.

Defined contribution plans place the burden of obtaining good investment results squarely on the shoulders of plan participants. As we will see later in the chapter, most 401(k) plan participants and individual investors miss the lion's share of investment return. Many studies have shown that they typically lag a diversified stock-and-bond portfolio by -5% to -9% per year and earn real rates of return (after inflation) near zero.

The main problem is that, in effect, defined contribution plan participants must function as their own actuaries, funding assessment specialists, Pension Benefit Guaranty Corporation (PBGC), investment managers selection-and-retention-evaluation consultants, asset allocation specialists, mutual-fund evaluation specialists, plan consultants and trustees (see Chart 1-2). In a defined benefit plan, the plan sponsor hires numerous and expensive specialists, many of whom are national firms, in order to provide these complex services, because even the most sophisticated plan sponsors cannot competently perform such services themselves and have successful outcomes.

Chart 1-2: Specialists Needed for Success in Defined Benefit Plans

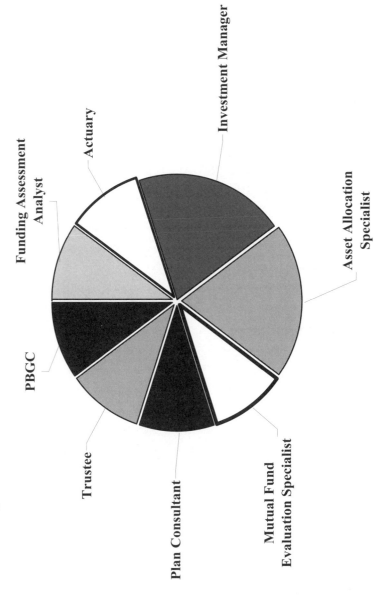

Over the last twenty years, many plan sponsors have switched from defined benefit to defined contribution plans to eliminate the costly specialists and funding risks to the plan sponsor. But, if a $200 million plan had trouble with these issues, how can anyone expect individual participants with $20,000 account balances to solve these complex problems?

For practical effects geared toward participant success, there really are no "defined contribution" plans. Every 401(k) plan must be operated as a series of tiny defined benefit plans, one for each plan participant. This means that actuarial calculations, periodic review and assessment of adequate funding, ongoing mutual-fund evaluation, investment manager reviews, and so forth must be provided to individual participants, as they cannot do it themselves.

Sometimes, even with the best efforts of multiple specialists, the defined benefit plan still fails. In 1974, recognizing this risk, Congress established the Pension Benefit Guaranty Corporation (PBGC) as part of ERISA to provide a mechanism to ensure and pay benefits to plan participants of failed defined benefit plans. There is no fail-safe provision for defined contribution participants, even though the odds of failure are many times higher. Yet, in defined contribution plans, the participant is expected to do it all.

Almost all the financial powerhouses have agendas opposed to the best interests of investors. Wall Street wants them to keep buying expensive in-house proprietary products. The media is out to sell magazines, newspapers, or airtime; any useful information they might pass on in the process is almost an accidental byproduct. Fund companies and managers naturally resist the idea that they are not likely to add value through their vaunted skills in either market timing or individual stock selection.

Table 1-1: Key Differences in Savings Rates between Defined Benefit Plans and Defined Contribution Plans

PARAMETER	DEFINED BENEFIT	DEFINED CONTRIBUTION
Actuarial Funding Calculation	Yes	No
Awareness of Funding Level to Meet Need	Yes	No
Annual Review of Success Probability	Yes	No
Commitment to Meeting Funding Need	Yes	No
IRS Penalty if Account Underfunded	Yes	No
Required Funding	Yes	No
Successful Outcome Goals Orientation	Yes	No
Likelihood of Success	Very High	Usually Low
Options after Failure	PBGC Benefit Guarantee	No

Table 1-2: Key Management Differences between Defined Benefit Plans and Defined Contribution Plans

PARAMETER	DEFINED BENEFIT	DEFINED CONTRIBUTION
Plan Sponsor Fiduciary Liability Awareness	Yes	Rarely
Board of Directors Fiduciary Documentation	Yes	No
Discretionary Trustee	Usually	Rarely
Investment Policy Statement	Present	Usually Missing
Regularly Review Investment Policy Statement	Yes	No
Written Asset Allocation Strategy	Yes	No
Regular Asset Allocation Monitoring	Yes	No
Diversification Reviews	Yes	No
Investment Decision Makers	Specialists	Employees
Expert Investment Performance Monitoring	Yes	No
Market Timing in Response to Adverse News	Rare	Often
Investment Time Horizon	Usually Long Term	Short Term Focus
Risk Tolerance	Moderate	Often Low
Overall Plan Performance	Usually Near Benchmark	Usually Below Benchmark
Real Rate of Investment Return	Higher	Lower

In the succeeding chapters, we will discuss in detail the two key factors for successful retirement: the savings rate and the real rate of investment return. The purpose of this chapter is to provide an understanding that most employees are falling behind on both counts.

Many workers believe that they are making sufficient progress and have accumulated some retirement savings. In most cases, the current account balance they have accumulated combined with their savings rate and real rate of investment return is woefully short of the cash account balance they will need at retirement.

Consider a forty-year-old worker earning $60,000 per year. She has one year's gross pay ($60,000) in her 401(k) and contributes $3,000 (5%) to her plan. She is earning a real rate of return over time of 1%. This worker has a virtually zero probability that she will be able to successfully retire on 70% of her after-tax income, even with some Social Security benefits. (See the X on the chart below.)

Chart 1-3: Real Rate of Return vs. Savings Rate for 75%
Success Probability
(40-Year-Old Worker with One Year Gross Pay Saved)

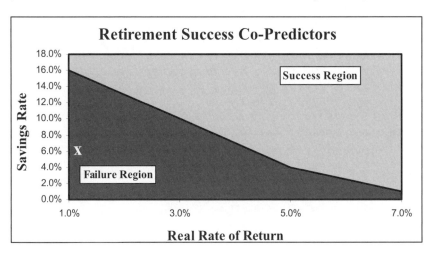

Problem No. 1
The Savings Rate Is Far Too Low

One way to gauge how well people are preparing for retirement is simply asking them, as several surveys have done. The Retirement Confidence Survey, for instance, gauges the views and attitudes of workers regarding their preparations for retirement. One important step in the retirement planning process is determining how much retirement savings is needed. In 2001, 46% of workers reported that they had at least tried, although not necessarily successfully, to determine how much money they will need to save for retirement, a decline from the previous year's finding but still up from 29% in 1996. As we will point out in subsequent chapters, often the retirement savings calculators are too simplistic and too optimistic.

Although this overall trend, possibly attributable to increased financial education, is encouraging, half of all workers have yet to determine how much they will need to save. Who buys a car not knowing what it will cost? Yet this is exactly what most workers do for their retirement—even though the financial impact is greater than that of any car.

Some 60% of the surveyed workers felt that they were behind schedule for planning and saving for retirement. Only 5% felt that they were ahead of schedule. Finally, although the percentages of individuals who say they are saving and planning for retirement have generally increased in recent years, they declined between 2000 and 2001, possibly reflecting recent economic uncertainty and the decline in the stock market. Paradoxically, people responded to the falling market returns by putting less money in the 401(k) plans, instead of more to make up the shortfall. Workers who have done a retirement-needs calculation are more likely to feel confident that they will have enough money to live comfortably throughout retirement and are less likely to feel behind schedule in retirement planning.

A number of papers have shown that employees who report saving too little actually do have low 401(k) saving rates. In other words, at least some of the employees are in trouble and know it. However, almost none who report intending to raise their savings rates in the next two months do so.

At any point in time, employees are likely to do whatever requires the least effort. Almost always, the easiest thing to do is nothing whatsoever, a phenomenon called "passive decision-making." Inertia is a behavioral phenomenon that must be turned around and used to the employee's advantage.

Such passive decision-making implies that employers have a great deal of influence over the savings outcomes of their employees. For example, employer choices of default savings rates, automatic annual savings increases (SMarT^{TM} programs—"Save More Tomorrow"), and default investment funds strongly influence employee savings levels. Even though employees can opt out of such defaults, few do so.

Solutions to the passive decision-making problem require innovative programs to help employees. As an example, it has been shown that automatic enrollment in a 401(k) plan dramatically raises participation rates but that the vast majority of employees accept the automatic-enrollment default contribution rate for their investment allocation. By contrast, before automatic enrollment was instituted, few employees chose to invest at these default rates. Such automatic programs must be designed to keep employee savings on track over long periods.

Finally, employer match rates and the employer match thresholds (the maximum employee contributions that the employer matches) have marked effects on savings outcomes. The match threshold is an important focal point in the selection of employee contribution rates.

Problem No. 2
The Real Rate of Investment Return Is Almost Nil

The recent stock market decline seemed to awaken investors to the struggle they face with their investment decisions, although most investors have struggled for decades, not just over the past couple of years. Large-scale aggregate data from mutual-fund cash flows reveal that investors earned minimal returns, even during favorable market conditions over the two decades before the market downturn.

Investors seem unaware of the substantial gap between rates of return on stock, bond, and money market funds and those of the markets in which they invest and, even worse, how far they lag the average fund. While the S&P 500 Stock Index has risen at a 12.2% average annual rate since 1984, for example, the average equity fund has grown at a 9.3% rate. Much worse is the actual performance of the typical investor. The returns incurred by the average equity-fund investor since 1984 have averaged just 2.7% per year. The real (after-inflation) return was near zero.

Chart 1-4: Total Earnings Generated on $1,000 Invested during 1984–2002

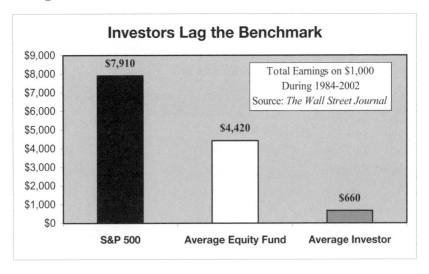

Table 1-3: Historical Real Rates of Return for Various Asset Allocation Mixes

| | S&P 500 | Bonds | Money Market | \-\-\-Asset Allocation Mixes (Stocks/Bonds)\-\-\- | | | | |
				80/20	60/40	40/60	20/80
Pre-Inflation Return	10.8%	5.3%	3.8%	9.7%	8.6%	7.5%	6.4%
Inflation	3.1%	3.1%	3.1%	3.1%	3.1%	3.1%	3.1%
Real Return	7.7%	2.2%	0.7%	6.6%	5.5%	4.4%	3.3%

Source: Ibbotson Associates; Stocks, Bonds, Bills and Inflation (1926-2002 Data)

We calculate the actual return of a retirement plan and then compare the plan's return to that of an equally weighted benchmark. We then know how far the plan is lagging a benchmark and can estimate the plan's long-term real rate of return. For example, assume that a plan's asset allocation is 60% stocks and 40% fixed income. Over a three-year period, the plan lagged the 60/40 benchmark by 4.1%. Looking at the Ibbotson data for a 60/40 mix, we find the long-term real return to be 5.5%. The plan's long-term real return is calculated as follows:

Plan Real Rate of Return % = 5.5% (Benchmark) – 4.1% (Plan Lag) = 1.4%

The bewildering array of choices among nearly 14,000 mutual funds has ill-served investors. Most mutual-fund rating services have been unable to help investors and plan sponsors correctly select the best funds for their accounts. Recent data suggest that some retirement plan sponsors are recognizing this and reducing the number of choices for plan participants in an effort to improve their outcomes.

Investment success requires both asset allocation and asset quality. We use the Unified Fiduciary Monitoring Index® to measure and maintain asset quality. The investor must receive generally accepted investment advice to ensure effective asset allocation. However, education is not advice. Advice is much more specific and helps individual investors build portfolios for their particular situations.

Plan sponsors and plan participants make buy or sell decisions based upon advertised "time-weighted" returns, but they can only spend "dollar-weighted" returns. What is the difference?

Time-weighted returns are the average annual return earned by the mutual-fund or investment manager and assume that cash was invested consistently throughout the measurement period. Time-weighted returns provide for standardized comparison between various investments; however, they tell plan participants virtually nothing about how their money is doing.

On the contrary, dollar-weighted returns are the profits earned by the investor on the total number of dollars invested in a fund. The only scenario where dollar-weighted and time-weighted returns are the same is when a single investment has no additions or withdrawals. This simplistic scenario almost never happens. Dollar-weighted returns are greatly affected by investor timing and are often much less than published time-weighted returns.

Table 1-4: Dollar-Weighted vs. Time-Weighted Returns with a Single Cash Flow

Year	1	2	3	4
Beginning Balance	$0	$159,300	$175,230	$140,184
Cash Flow	$135,000	$0	$0	$0
Earnings	$24,300	$15,930	-$35,046	$8,411
Ending Balance	$159,300	$175,230	$140,184	$148,595
Time Wt Return	18.0%	10.0%	-20.0%	6.0%
Dollar Wt. Return	18.0%	10.0%	-20.0%	6.0%

Table 1-5: Dollar-Weighted vs. Time-Weighted Returns with Multiple Cash Flows

Year	1	2	3	4
Beginning Balance	$0	$11,800	$38,054	$113,277
Cash Flow	$10,000	$25,000	$100,000	$0
Earnings	$1,800	$1,254	-$24,777	$6,797
Ending Balance	$11,800	$38,054	$113,277	$120,074
Time Wt. Return	18.0%	10.0%	-20.0%	6.0%
Dollar Wt. Return	Dollar Weighted = -11.05%			

In Table 1-4, the four-year time- and dollar-weighted returns are the same. With the single investment of $135,000, our plan participant has an ending balance of $148,595. He has earned 10.02% cumulative over four years.

In the example shown in Table 1-5, our plan participant has also invested a total of $135,000 in the fund, but he staggered his purchases. Perhaps he held most of his money in a bond fund during years one and two, and decided to put more money in the stock fund in year three—just before a market downturn. His ending balance is $120,074, and he lost money over the four years ($135,000 - $120,074 = $14,926 loss). Even though the time-weighted return is positive, he only has $120,074 to spend in retirement, which is less than he invested.

Recent Past Does Not Predict the Future

In 1900, a blue-ribbon panel identified key issues needing to be addressed to keep New York City vibrant and healthy twenty-five years hence. Their number-one issue? Being able to grow and transport enough hay to feed the projected growth in the horse population. Likewise, employees who try to connect the historical dots to predict or manage their retirement programs find that it is fraught with uncertainty.

Investor behavior is so perverse and returns so dismal that a whole branch of economics is devoted to finding out what makes investors tick. One recent study of investors found that no matter what they tell you about thinking long-term, most investors' perceptions and expectations are heavily influenced by their experience of the last eleven months.

If the markets have been doing poorly for the previous year, investors begin to believe that they will continue to do poorly forever. They begin to sell. If they have been doing well, investors become euphoric and begin to believe "that this time it is different." The higher the market price goes, the more they want to buy. You needn't be a rocket scientist to see how this leads to self-defeating behavior.

In some investment situations, more choice can be downright dangerous. Two finance professors once studied the performance of 66,465 households with discount brokerage accounts. Households that traded infrequently received an 18% return on their investments, while the return for the households that traded most actively was 11.3%.

In later work, these financial economists investigated who it was that traded too much. They found that one important determinant of excessive trading was gender. Psychologists consistently find that men tend to have excessive confidence in their own abilities, a fact that will come as no surprise to most women.

A national study of 1.5 million 401(k) plan participant accounts found that trades between stock funds and bond funds correlated only to recent past performance. When stock funds were doing well, investors sold bonds and bought stocks. When the opposite occurred, investors sold stocks and bought bonds. The study could find no correlation between the trading activity and future performance.

There is a huge discrepancy between the fund's return and the return of the average investor in that fund. This gets back to the difference we explained earlier between time-weighted returns and dollar-weighted returns. Not long ago, legendary money manager Peter Lynch, the retired manager of Fidelity's Magellan Fund, disclosed that a shocking percentage of his fund's investors lost money. Now, no fund in the entire history of the universe has been more successful than Magellan during the time Peter Lynch managed the fund.

However, Magellan has been volatile, and the swings have alternately attracted investors and then frightened them off—just at the wrong times! The only thing Magellan (or most equity fund) investors needed to do to achieve truly great returns was just stay invested. But, a surprising number of them just couldn't make themselves do the right thing.

Investors who are seeking the best buy among mutual funds should be cautious about how they use the Morningstar rating system in selecting their purchases. Many investors look to Morningstar, one of the most widely used mutual-fund rating services, to predict which funds are the highest performers and best investments. Morningstar uses a five-star system to rate a fund's performance, with one star being the worst and five the best.

Investors are misguided if they use Morningstar ratings for picking funds that are going to have superior performance in the future. Morningstar ratings should be viewed as achievement marks from past performance, not predictors of the future.

A number of studies have attempted to determine how well Morningstar did at predicting future fund performance. (In almost all of its publications, Morningstar states that its star ratings are not predictors of future performance.) However, many funds advertise their Morningstar ratings, and investors tend to pour their money into five-star funds, which they expect to be the most profitable. The studies found little if any correlation between the star rating and the fund's future performance.

A five-star rating has a large effect on fund flow, whether as an initial rating or as a rating upgrade. An initial five-star rating yields a seven-month cash flow of 53% above-normal expected flow. Other rating categories elicit smaller but economically and statistically significant flow responses that are remarkably consistent in sign, positive for upgrades and negative for downgrades. The flow response is immediate and detectable at the same time that Morningstar releases new ratings.

Table 1-6: How Star Rating Drives Fund Cash Flow

MORNINGSTAR STAR RATING ATTRACTS CASH FLOW

Investor cash flows to highly rated funds (Four or Five Star) dwarfed those of funds with weak ratings. Figures in billions of dollars.

Fund Categories	Four- and Five-Stars	One-, Two-, Three-Stars
Equity	$79.6	-$108.2
Fixed Income	$64.6	$28.8
Total	$144.2	-$79.4

Source: Financial Research Corp. 2002 mutual fund data.

For Further Reading

Agnew, J., "Inefficient Choices in 401(k) Plans: Evidence from Individual Level Data," 2002, Fourth Annual Joint Conference for the Retirement Research Consortium, (May 2002).

Choi, J., Laibson, D., Madrian, B. and Metrick, A. "Defined Contribution Pensions: Plan Rules, Participant Decisions, and the Path of Least Resistance.", Tax Policy and the Economy, Harvard Press, (November 2001).

Guercio, D. "Star Power: The Effect of Morningstar Ratings on Mutual Fund Flows." Federal Reserve Bank of Atlanta Conference, (May 2002).

Jackson, R. "The Global Retirement Crisis, the Threat to World Stability, and What to Do about It," Center for Strategic and International Studies, (2002).

Jacobius, W. "Retirement Assets Huge Drop over the Past Two Years." *Pensions & Investments*, (June 10, 2002).

Kasten, G. "Do Most 'Do It Yourself' Investors Really Make Any Money in Stock Funds?" Unified Trust Company, NA, (July 2002).

McDonald, I. "Mutual-Fund Ratings Come under Fire. *Wall Street Journal*, (January 15, 2003).

Quill, G. "Investors Behaving Badly: An Analysis of Investor Trading Patterns in Mutual Funds." *Journal of Financial Planning* (11), (2001).

Uccello, C. "Are Americans Saving Enough?" Center for Retirement Research, no. 7, (July 2001).

Chapter 2

Social Security: Past, Present, and Future

Chapter Summary

For its first 150 years, the philosophy of the American government was that responsibility for the care of the aged was a private matter. When the Social Security Act became law in 1935, responsibility for the aged was transferred from the individual family to society. The Social Security program was founded on three overlapping promises:

- Everyone who paid into the system would benefit.
- General tax revenues would never finance the program.
- Social Security was a supplement to retirement income.

Today, the Social Security program has become an integral part of the American economic system. Every day, the Social Security system pays benefits of more than $1 billion.

The number of workers supporting each retiree has steadily declined. During the 1940s, some fifty workers paid into Social Security for every person collecting benefits. By 2040, only two workers will be paying in for every person collecting benefits. The trust fund is expected to be exhausted in 2032–2040. Workers today should expect higher taxes and reduced benefits in the future. The average worker will see the share of total required retirement income replaced by Social Security decline from 35% today to less than 25% in the future.

The History of Social Security

The idea of providing retirement plans for every older worker was mostly a European concept. Other than pensions paid to veterans of the Civil War, the philosophy of the American government from inception until 1935 was that responsibility for the care of the poor and the aged was a private matter and one that belonged to the family. State and local communities did help on occasion, but only in cases of dire need. Chancellor Otto von Bismarck made retirement insurance compulsory in Germany in 1889. Germany required that working people, employers, and the government all contribute to a retirement program. By the early 1920s, retirement programs were prevalent across most of Europe.

In the early 1930s, the devastating aftermath of the Great Depression changed the American public's view. After President Franklin D. Roosevelt signed the Social Security Act into law in August 1935, responsibility for the aged was transferred from the individual family to society. This was a giant step forward for the United States, taken long after the industrial nations of Europe had adopted some form of retirement benefits for their citizens.

The early retirees discovered Social Security to be a windfall program. In the early days, many more workers were paying into the system than the number of retirees taking money out, and the program seemed to make sense. The first Social Security recipient was Mrs. Ida Fuller of Ludlow, Vermont. After turning sixty-five, Mrs. Fuller received her first check in January 1940. She lived to be ninety-nine and collected a total of $22,889. She paid in a mere $24 in total Social Security taxes to collect this benefit.

The Social Security program has been expanded many times since 1935. In 1939, supplemental benefits were added for spouses and children. In 1951, coverage was again expanded to include self-employed workers. Health insurance through the Medicare program was added in 1965.

The Three Promises of Social Security

The Social Security program was founded on three overlapping promises:

- It belonged to everyone who paid into the system.
- It would never be financed by general tax revenues.
- It was intended to supplement retirement income.

When first passed, Social Security was not intended to be means testing or a complete source of retirement income for the elderly. Anyone doubting that means testing was not intended should read the speech given by A.J. Altmeyer, a member of the Social Security Board, on September 3, 1935:

"I appreciate this opportunity to discuss briefly the Social Security Act which has just gone into effect because I believe that it is the most important act of the many important acts passed by the Congress that has just adjourned. Even though it will vitally affect the daily lives of the industrial workers of this country its specific provisions are as yet little known, nor are its full implications thoroughly understood. . . .

. . . State old age pensions are paid only to persons who can establish they had no adequate means of support, but the benefits that will be paid under the Federal old age insurance system will be paid as a matter of right to qualified individuals who have been paying their contributions into the Federal Treasury. It is most important to again emphasize that these payments will be made as a matter of right and not on the basis of a showing of need. That is to say, qualified individuals will receive these benefits regardless of the amount of property or income they possess, just as they would receive benefits from a private insurance company to which they had paid premiums."

Critics of Franklin Delano Roosevelt have said that 1935 was the optimal time to introduce social security legislation in the United States, but FDR failed to seize the day.

To FDR's disappointment, the bill faced a long and bumpy road; passage took seven months of struggle. There was little initial support for FDR's bill even from Democratic politicians; farmers and businessmen lined up against it. Even some labor unions were lukewarm, because they feared social security would weaken the incentives for workers to join unions to get pensions and welfare benefits.

The consummate politician, Roosevelt saw where the social security parade was headed and jumped out in front to lead it, steering it as far to the right as possible. The result was a modest piece of legislation. A less conservative chief executive would have, and could have, pushed legislation through Congress to establish a much more comprehensive and generous social security program, one that included old-age insurance, survivors insurance, disability insurance, unemployment insurance, and a national health-insurance plan.

The one thing Roosevelt was completely sure of was that the program would never be funded with general tax revenues. His treasury secretary, Henry Morgenthau Jr., had originally endorsed the Economic Security Bill, but later changed his mind over two key issues. First, Morgenthau objected to the accruing of huge unfunded obligations by the old-age insurance system while it paid higher-than-justified benefits to the early retirees. Furthermore, he objected to promising that a future Congress would meet those obligations with an injection of general revenues.

To win his treasury secretary's support of the bill, Roosevelt endorsed a higher payroll tax rate and lower benefits for the first retirees. Roosevelt also insisted that old-age insurance receive no funds—ever—from general revenues.

Roosevelt believed—and time has proven him correct—that workers who contributed to a social insurance program that used no general revenues established a moral right to future benefits, a right that future Congresses would be reluctant to tamper with. Roosevelt also believed that the social insurance program should set a floor of retirement income rather than be the only source of income for retirees.

Social Security Administration officials echo this view even today. In a recent speech in 2002, James B. Lockhart, deputy commissioner of Social Security, said:

"Planning and saving for retirement is an individual responsibility. Unfortunately, many Americans mistakenly believe that Social Security alone will guarantee their financial future. The reality is Social Security was never intended to be the sole source of income in our retirement years. Only half of today's retirees have a private pension. And too few Americans save as much as they should."

Social Security was never meant to be a complete program of retirement income. Instead, it was meant to provide a foundation upon which people could plan for their financial well-being. Financial planning has often been compared to a three-legged stool. One leg represents Social Security. The second leg represents pensions provided by an employer or 401(k) plans for employees and the self-employed. The third leg represents savings and other investments. The stool will not work with only one or two legs, but it is solid enough to stand on with all three legs.

Concerned that Americans are not saving enough for retirement and other important needs, the Social Security Administration launched the "Save for your Future" campaign in 2002. This campaign was designed to inform Americans of how vital it is to save for retirement and other life stages.

Social Security Today

Today, the Social Security program has become an integral part of the American economic system. Every day the Social Security system pays benefits of more than $1 billion. The average Social Security monthly benefit for a retired worker is now $870. It is estimated that nearly 90% of all American households with someone over sixty-five receive benefits. In 2002, 45.6 million people received benefits. Overall, 43% of beneficiaries are men, and 57% are women.

Without Social Security, 50% of all the elderly would live below the poverty level. But with the program, today only 8% of elderly Americans live below the poverty line. The program contains some internal redistribution in the sense that returns on contributed payroll taxes are higher for low-wage workers than for high-wage workers.

These higher returns, reflected in relatively higher benefit payments for lower-wage retirees, largely explain why the program has been responsible for so much reduction of poverty among the aged and partly explain why Social Security accounts for such a high share of the retirement income received by lower-income retirees. See Charts 2-7 and 2-8 for more information on income replacement.

Social Security provides monthly income to retired workers (and their spouses) based on their period of employment and earnings. It works like an annuity in that the beneficiary receives a fixed monthly payment and the total received depends on how long the beneficiary lives. It does not work like a regular retirement savings plan that pays the beneficiary a lump sum upon retirement based on how much was contributed.

This federal program provides comprehensive benefits for the average American family that would otherwise be unaffordable for many. Taxing the earnings of working people derives payments for benefits. This package includes retirement, disability, and survivors' benefits.

Supplemental Security Income, a fourth program funded out of general revenues, is payable to the blind, disabled, and people age sixty-five or older whose principal sources of income are insufficient to provide a minimum standard of living. Medicare, a fifth program, provides hospitalization and medical expense benefits to those sixty-five or older. Under the Old Age, Survivors, and Disability Insurance program, the Social Security system provides the following benefits:

- Monthly benefits to retirees and their spouses
- Monthly benefits for the survivors of deceased workers
- Monthly benefits for disabled workers and their dependents
- A lump-sum death benefit payment for certain insured workers

Chart 2-1 shows the total annual Social Security taxes paid by the upper-income worker (including the employer portion). The program is now collecting more money than needed for payments to current retirees, and the federal government borrows the surpluses to balance its budget.

Chart 2-1: Annual Social Security Taxes Paid by Upper-Income Workers

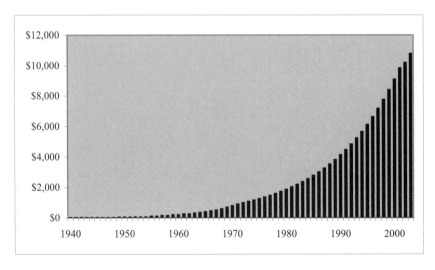

The amount of money collected by the Social Security system depends on two factors: the tax rate and the maximum taxable wage base. Table 2-1 shows the current tax rates and maximum taxable amounts.

Table 2-1: Social Security Taxes and Benefits

Taxable Year	2004
Maximum Taxable Wages	$87,900
Employee Withholding Tax	7.65%
Employer Payroll Tax	7.65%
Self- Employed	15.30%
Maximum Earnings While Receiving Benefits	
Age 62--64	$11,640
Age 65 or Higher	No Limit
Quarters of Coverage Required	40
Lump Sum Death Benefit	$255
Average Monthly Benefit	$870

The system will collect more funds than needed to pay benefits until around 2020–2025. After that point, the surplus will rapidly become exhausted. The Social Security trust fund is expected to become insolvent between 2032 and 2040. Benefits will then be paid by current Social Security taxes, and benefits will average 50–70% of the current level.

Chart 2-2: Social Security Trust Fund Surplus (in billions of dollars)

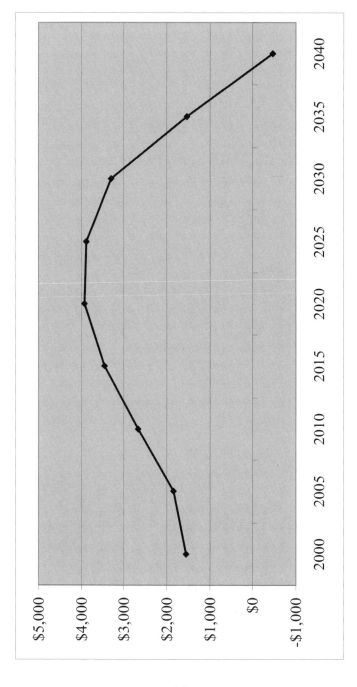

Social Security Soundness

When Social Security was first established, average life expectancy was the same as the retirement age. Life expectancy has steadily increased, causing benefits to be paid longer. For instance, in 1940, only 54% of males survived to collect Social Security benefits. By 1990, more than 72% did so. To fund the rising benefits, Congress raised both the tax rate and the amount of income subject to Social Security tax numerous times.

Chart 2-3: Historical Social Security Tax Rates

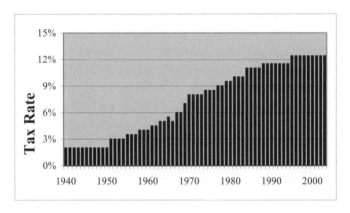

Chart 2-4: Likely Future Social Security Tax Rates

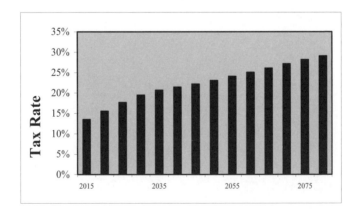

U.S. demographics have changed over time. In 1950, for instance, there were 7.3 Americans aged twenty to sixty-four for each American aged sixty-five and over. That ratio has now dropped to under 5:1, and by 2025, it will dip below 3:1.

During the 1940s, some fifty workers paid into Social Security for every person collecting benefits. In 1950, there were sixteen workers paying Social Security taxes for every beneficiary collecting; today there are only three. By 2040, there will be only two workers paying in for every person collecting benefits.

Chart 2-5: Number of Covered Workers per Social Security Beneficiary

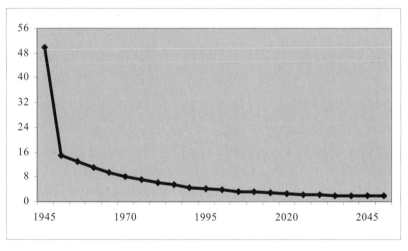

Beginning around 2025–2030, it will not be possible to pay full benefits. Taking into consideration the workers and retirees now in the Social Security system, the "present value" of the unfunded liability (measured by the amount in today's dollars of extra money beyond payroll taxes that would be needed today to pay benefits) would be as much as $12 trillion. There is no guarantee that this massive unfunded liability will not become worse.

The unreliability of the government's estimates is evident in Social Security policy over the past twenty-five years. A benefit increase in 1972 was accompanied by promises that the system would be solvent for another seventy-five years. Five years later, President Jimmy Carter signed a record payroll-tax increase that was supposed to guarantee that the Social Security system would be solvent for fifty years.

After only five years, the system was in crisis again. The result: further payroll-tax hikes, increases in the retirement age, and some trimming in the growth of benefits, all accompanied by still more promises that the system would be financially secure for another seventy-five years.

The primary reason that the Social Security cost rate will increase rapidly between 2010 and 2030 is that, as the large baby-boomer generation, born in 1946 through 1964, retires, the number of beneficiaries will increase much more rapidly than the number of workers. (See Chart 2-5 for more information.) In 2002, there were about 3.3 workers for every beneficiary.

The baby boomer generation will have largely retired by 2030, and the projected ratio of workers to beneficiaries will be only 2.2 at that time. Baby boomer retirements coupled with increased lifespans have meant that the beneficiary population will skyrocket in coming decades. Thereafter, the number of workers per beneficiary will slowly decline, and the Social Security cost rate will continue to increase. The retirement age has been gradually increased from sixty-five to sixty-seven and may need to be raised again.

Still another important way to look at Social Security's future is to view its cost as a share of the U.S. economy. Social Security's cost as a percentage of Gross Domestic Product (GDP) will grow 1.6 times, from 4.4% in 2002 to 7.0% in 2077. Over the same period, the estimated cost of Social Security, expressed as a percentage of taxable payroll, will also dramatically grow.

Chart 2-6: Social Security as a Percentage of GDP

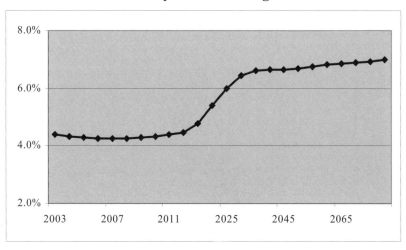

Income Replacement Issues

Today, Social Security replaces 25% of a highly paid worker's income, 35% of an average-paid worker's income, and 50% of a low-paid worker's income. (See Chart 2-7.) Most retirement experts calculate that workers should replace 60–80% of preretirement income in order to enjoy standards of living in retirement close to what they enjoyed before retirement.

By 2025, it is estimated that Social Security will replace only 10-20% of a highly paid worker's income, 20-30% of an average-paid worker's income and 40% of a low-paid worker's income. (See Chart 2-8.)

In part, the low replacement stems from the low rate of return a taxpayer "earns" on Social Security taxes. A married couple with two children and a single earner fares best, receiving 2.6% if the earner was born in 1966. An average-earning single male born after 1966 can expect to receive an annualized real rate of return of less than 0.5% (less than 0.5%) on lifetime payroll taxes.

Chart 2-7: Social Security Income Replacement (2004)

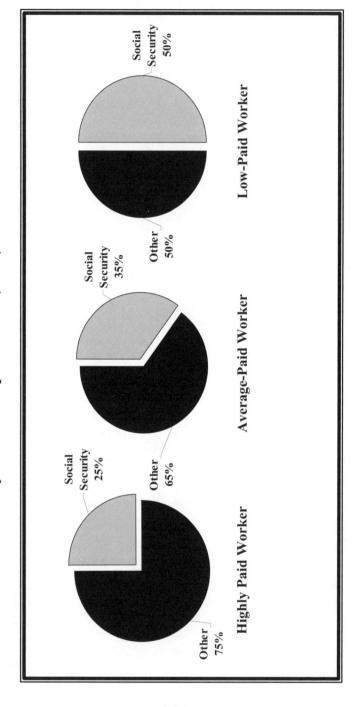

Social Security 50%

Other 50%

Low-Paid Worker

Social Security 35%

Other 65%

Average-Paid Worker

Social Security 25%

Other 75%

Highly Paid Worker

Chart 2-8: Social Security Income Replacement (2025)

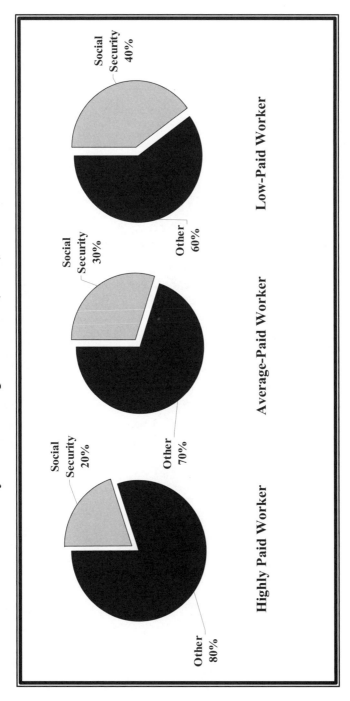

The Future of Social Security

All of the gloom and doom about Social Security has many people expressing doubt about the future of the program. One poll found that more college students believe in space aliens and UFOs than believe in the long-term viability of the Social Security program.

It is important to keep in mind that even when the trust fund is "insolvent" in 2030–2040, some benefits will be paid. After insolvency, benefits will be paid from current Social Security tax collections. It is likely, however, that Social Security taxes will be higher and benefits much lower in the future. Therefore, a prudent person would plan retirements by assuming that Social Security will replace less income than it does today. At the extreme, a very prudent person might plan on receiving no benefits from Social Security; however, it is likely that most people will receive something.

Various proposals have been put forward to reform Social Security. Some encourage the "privatization" of the program, allowing taxpayers to invest some or all of the taxes collected from both the employee and the employer. The downside to privatization is that the money diverted from the program may be needed to fund benefits, and it is likely that many people will invest poorly, as we have seen in 401(k) plans.

For Further Reading

Beach, W., et al. "Social Security: Improving Retirement for All Americans." © Heritage Foundation (1998).

Berheim, D., and Shoven, J. "Pension Funding and Saving." *Pensions in the U.S. Economy*. Chicago: University of Chicago Press, (1988).

Colie, C. and Gruber, J. "Fiscal Effects of Social Security Reform in the United States." CRR WP 2003-05, Center for Retirement Research at Boston College, (2003).

Feldstein, M. "Social Security and the Distribution of Wealth." *Journal of the American Statistical Association* : 90–93, (December 1976).

Mathews, M. "No Risky Scheme: Retirement Savings Accounts That Are Personal and Safe." IPI Policy Report No. 163, (January 11, 2002).

Moffit, R. "Reforming Social Security: Understanding the Council's Proposals." © Heritage Foundation (1997).

Robbins, A. "Social Security Reform and Tax Reform—Is One Possible without the Other?" IPI Policy Report No. 172, Institute for Policy Innovation, (February 2002).

Rust, J., and Phelan, C. "How Social Security and Medicare Affect Retirement Behavior in a World of Incomplete Markets." *Econometrica* 65(4): 781–831, (1999).

"The 2003 Annual Report of the Board of Trustees of the Federal Old-Age and Survivors Insurance and Disability Insurance Trust Funds." U.S. Government Printing Office, (March 17, 2003).

Chapter 3

Retirement Success: Defining, Measuring, and Predicting

Chapter Summary

"Retirement success" can be defined as holding a sufficient level of assets at the beginning of retirement to give a 75% or higher probability that an appropriate lifestyle can be maintained in retirement.

Retirement plan sponsors and participants have little idea of whether their courses of action will succeed in producing the retirement income they need. Most illustrations are too optimistic and do not take into account "real world" events that significantly alter outcomes. Monte Carlo Simulation is a process that uses the brute force of computers to create multiple scenarios based upon the independent probability of each event. Research using Monte Carlo Simulation has introduced a scientific rigor into the process of measuring retirement success by accounting for millions of possible financial outcomes based upon different combinations of probable events.

The two most important factors of retirement success are savings rate and real rate of investment return.

We combined the savings rate and the real rate of investment return into the SR+RR Index. We show how using the SR+RR Index can accurately predict and improve retirement success rates for participants of all ages.

The Retirement Income Guessing Game

Plan participants can easily project how big their nest eggs will be and how long they will last by crunching numbers on a calculator. Although the math may be correct, the conclusions could be terribly wrong.

The weakest link in retirement planning is the inevitable error introduced by the numerous assumptions used in the planning process. Errors are introduced in both the savings, or accumulation, phase and in the withdrawal, or spending, phases. Usually, the assumptions are too optimistic and result in illustrations that look much better than those likely to actually occur. Assumptions based upon long-term averages of inflation, stock and bond-market returns, life expectancy, and so forth are almost always too optimistic when the real world intervenes.

Put another way, the only certainty in retirement planning is that nothing is certain. This cartoon, published in October 2000 by the *San Jose Mercury News*, shows the fallacy of trusting "average" values.

Figure 3-1: "Average" Depth Three Feet

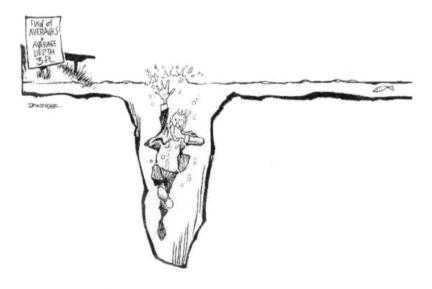

Predicting market performance is amazingly difficult. Not knowing what else to do, many retirees determine their yearly withdrawal rates based upon historic investment average performances. Basing a withdrawal strategy on projected average rates of return can be perilous. The key idea to keep in mind is that retirement spending is the opposite of accumulation. This translates into the phenomenon of reverse dollar cost averaging. In retirement, the effect of spending the same number of dollars in a down market is that more shares must be sold. So the portfolio depletes itself faster than anticipated.

Let's look at a real-world example to illustrate the problem of relying upon average values. Suppose a plan participant is ready to retire with a $250,000 account balance. She decides to invest her retirement fund in the Standard & Poor's 500 index in such a way that her withdrawals will last twenty years. How much can she withdraw per year? The return of the S&P 500 has varied over the years but has averaged about 12% per year over the last thirty years from 1973 to 2003. Using an annuity spreadsheet program, our participant learns that she can withdraw $33,469 each year and have the money last twenty years.

Chart 3-1: Theoretical Smooth Retirement Withdrawals

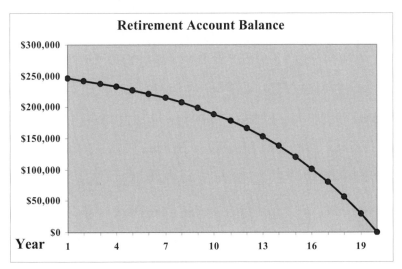

-41-

The exceptions to the averages create troubles for retirees. A retiree who is forced to regularly draw down savings during such times doesn't have the luxury of sitting investments for decades like a thirty-year-old investor, who can weather the storm.

Given typical levels of stock market volatility or variability, there are only slim odds that the fund will survive the full time. Chart 3-2 shows that if the investor retired in 1973, her fund would have lasted only about seven years. If she retired in 1975, her fund would have lasted twenty years. Even if the return fluctuated in the future, as long as it averaged 12% per year, her retirement fund would last twenty years, right? Wrong! It seems likely that the same outcome will occur for plan participants who retired in 1999, just before the three-year stock market decline during 2000–2002.

Chart 3-2: 1973–1980 Retirement Withdrawals

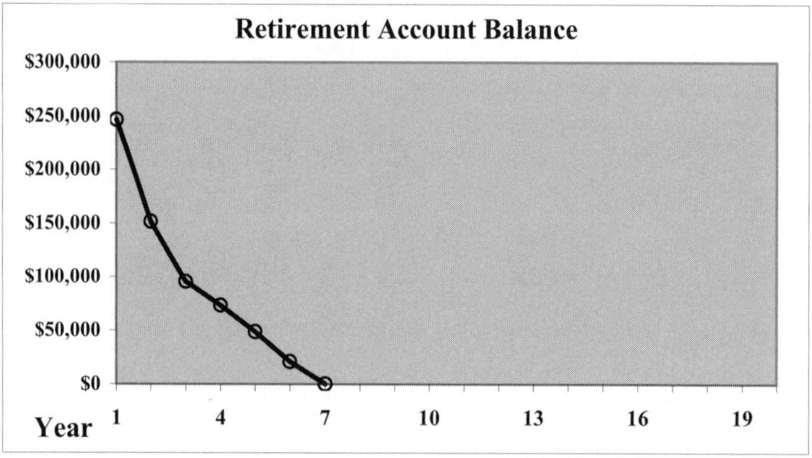

Plan participants' confidence can be greatly increased by borrowing some important concepts from the arcane world of probability theory. Using this theory to solve real-world problems is known as Monte Carlo Simulation.

Monte Carlo Simulation

Monte Carlo Simulation was named for Monte Carlo, Monaco, where the primary attractions are casinos containing games of chance. Games of chance, such as roulette wheels, dice, and slot machines, exhibit random behavior. When we use the word "simulation," we refer to any analytical method meant to imitate a real-life system, especially when other analyses are too mathematically complex or too difficult to reproduce.

Monte Carlo Simulation is not gambling, but rather a large number of mathematical probabilities. You can trace its history back to the 1940s, when scientists involved in the top-secret Manhattan Project used the calculations to help find solutions to otherwise insolvable problems.

The expression "Monte Carlo Simulation" is general. The Monte Carlo process relies on the use of random numbers and probability statistics to investigate problems. Monte Carlo is used in everything from economics to nuclear physics to regulating the flow of traffic. A Monte Carlo Simulation program allows us to use the brute force of computers to create multiple scenarios. For example, for the illustrations later in this chapter, we performed more than 1 billion simulations.

Research using Monte Carlo simulations has introduced scientific rigor into the process of spending retirement savings by accounting for thousands of possible financial variables that could occur during a retirement period. Such scenarios, for instance, include the possibility that interest rates will be either high or low for certain stretches of someone's retirement or throughout the entire period.

Once we know the various spending outcomes, we can then apply the same logic to determine the various accumulation, or savings, outcomes. In solving retirement income problems, the spending phase of the problem must be solved first. Once the spending problem is solved, we can then solve the savings-phase, or accumulation-phase, problem.

A dizzying number of possibilities about investment returns for stocks, bonds, and cash are also plugged into the equation. One scenario might have stocks treading water for an entire decade; another could have inflation raging at double digits for several years. Obviously, some outcomes are more likely than others. The simulation model follows its own bell curve, with the largest group of possibilities clustered near the bulging middle and far fewer at either end. The software runs all these random scenarios thousands or even millions of times.

If we continue to focus on the withdrawal strategy, we will finally need to answer the question "What should the withdrawal rate be?" Most plan participants, even those sitting on nest eggs of $1 million or more, are stunned by the modest amounts of money that Monte Carlo Simulations say they can prudently withdraw without jeopardizing their portfolios.

Traditional wisdom holds that retirees can earn 10% a year on their investments, take out 7% annually, and pretty much guarantee that they will die with an impressive chunk of money left behind in a brokerage account. But Monte Carlo proves that this traditional wisdom doesn't always wash and illustrates that withdrawal rates of 4% are more likely to be sustainable.

Many aggressive investors who remain fiercely loyal to stocks no doubt figure that such a modest withdrawal rate does not have to apply to them. In their view, a portfolio that is all stocks can grow fast enough to take bigger withdrawal hits. But remaining aggressively committed to stocks can catapult even the brightest investor into trouble. Investors are trained to think that if they invest aggressively and remain disciplined over time, they'll do well. But that strategy works only in the accumulation phase, not in the spending phase. An aggressive portfolio with a modestly higher average rate of return is more likely to fail than a more conservative balanced portfolio with a slightly lower long-term average rate of return.

Using Monte Carlo Simulation to Predict Retirement Spending Success Rates

Later in this chapter, we will examine key factors affecting the probability of success in both the accumulation phase and the spending phase. Because two phases are involved, the calculations are more complex, and a greater number of variables must be introduced.

To begin with simpler illustrations, we can examine the amount of money that must be accumulated at the beginning of retirement to support a retiree. We can express this as various multiples of gross pay saved by retirement and then study the success in retirement related to each multiple of pay.

We assume that the worker will need to receive 70% of his preretirement after-tax, inflation-adjusted income from both his 401(k) and Social Security. We assume that Social Security will replace about 20% of his income. This is a lower replacement fraction than today but highly likely given the projected funding problems that Social Security faces, as explained in chapter two.

Monte Carlo Simulation produces an accurate predictive effect when used to carefully examine retirement spending needs. Note that this approach shortcuts the uncertainty of the savings period. It simply looks at the withdrawal period uncertainty. Expressing all dollars in today's dollars also factors out inflation uncertainty.

The real rate of return is the net total portfolio return after inflation and fees achieved by the retiree. As an example, if the gross portfolio return is 6.0%, fees are 1.5%, and inflation is 2.5%, the real rate of return is 2.0%. As we described in chapter 1, typical investors earn real rates of return of between –2% and 0% on their invested dollars over long periods.

Chart 3-3: Required Savings at Retirement Age Expressed as a Multiple of Gross Pay

(1% Real Rate of Return in Retirement)

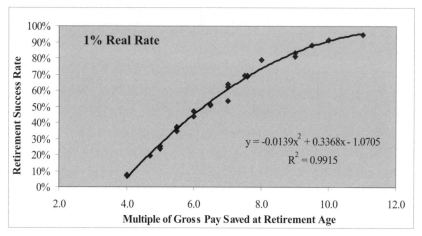

Monte Carlo analysis tells us both the likelihood of success in the savings, or accumulation, phase during preretirement and the likelihood of success in the withdrawal, or spending, phase in actual retirement.

Let us look at three simple illustrations. In these we can examine various multiples of gross pay saved by retirement and then study the success in retirement related to each multiple of pay.

Chart 3-3 shows the highly predictive effect of success related to the size of the final account balance as a multiple of gross pay. In this illustration, the real rate of return in retirement is 1%. The success rate can be calculated using the following equation, where x is the multiple of gross pay saved by retirement:

Success % = $-0.0139x^2 + 0.3368x - 1.0705$

Chart 3-4: Required Savings at Retirement Age Expressed as a Multiple of Gross Pay

(3% Real Rate of Return in Retirement)

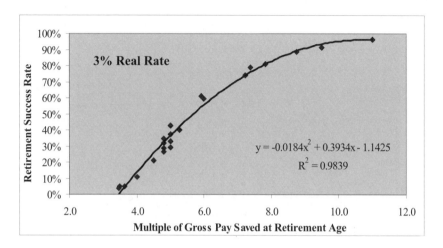

With a 3% real rate of return in retirement, the success rate can be calculated using the following equation, where x is the multiple of gross pay saved at the time of retirement:

Success % = -0.0184x² + 0.3934x − 1.1425

At a 3% real rate of return, the multiple of savings needed in retirement is smaller. For example, assume that a retirement plan participant is seeking a 75% probability that his 401(k) account balance will provide for his retirement needs and that he will also receive a Social Security benefit.

Based upon Chart 3-3, showing a real rate of return in retirement of 1%, the participant would need an account balance equal to 8.1 times his gross pay. According to Chart 3-4, if he can earn 3% real rate of return, he would only need an account balance equal to 7.2 times his gross pay.

Note that in all three illustrations, the dollars are current (inflation-adjusted) dollars and have constant purchasing power.

Chart 3-5: Required Savings at Retirement Age Expressed as a Multiple of Gross Pay

(5% Real Rate of Return in Retirement)

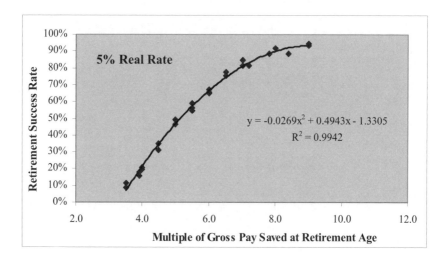

At a 5% real rate of return in retirement, our plan participant can enjoy probable success with an even smaller account balance. With a 5% real rate of return, the success rate can be calculated using the following equation, where x is the multiple of gross pay saved at the time of retirement:

Success % = -0.0269x² + 0.4943x – 1.3305

Chart 3-5 demonstrates that if plan participants can earn a 5% real rate of return in retirement, they would only need an account balance equal to 6.5 times their gross pay, assuming again a Social Security benefit. This is significantly less than the 8.1 times pay needed when the real rate is

1% and the 7.2 times pay when the real rate is 3% (all at the 75% probability level).

Finally, you should also observe the high correlation between each calculated value and the best fit line. The R^2 correlations are very high at 0.9915, 0.9839, and 0.9942. For you who are not statistics buffs, an R^2 of 1.00 is a perfect fit, a 0.00 is no fit, and a –1.00 is a negative fit.

Chart 3-6: Required Savings at Retirement Age Expressed as a Multiple of Gross Pay

(1, 3 or 5% Real Rate of Return in Retirement)

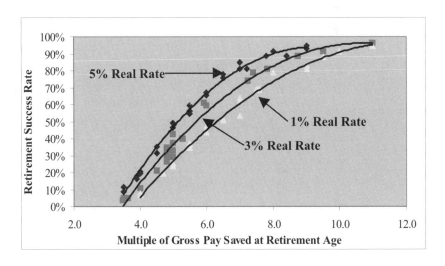

Chart 3-6 shows the likelihood of retirement success for all three real rates of return. As the real rate of return improves, the curve shifts to the left.

During retirement, the participant does not have the ability to substantially alter their account balance with more contributions. Thus the investment return is the single most important factor that explains their success or failure.

Using Monte Carlo Simulation to Predict Lifetime Accumulation and Retirement Spending Success Rates

For the remainder of this chapter, we will focus on the two key variables that determine accumulation and spending success rates: savings rate and real rate of return.

The savings rate is the total percentage of pay that is contributed to the plan on behalf of the participant. This can come from employee deferrals, matching contributions, and general employer contributions. The real rate of return is the net total portfolio return after inflation and fees achieved by the participant.

As described earlier, if the gross portfolio return is 6.0%, fees are 1.5%, and inflation is 2.5%, the real rate of return is 2.0%. Here we will examine the effects of real rates of return of 1%, 3%, 5%, and 7%. As we proved in chapter 1, typical investors earn real rates of return of between -2% and 0% on their invested dollars over long periods.

Focusing on real rate of return is important. It allows simplification of the simulation models without diminishing of the result. It does not require assuming any set return of stock or bonds, and it does not require any particular asset allocation mix. The purpose of this calculation is simple: to determine the mix of savings and real rate of return that must be achieved in order for the plan participant to have a certain probability for retirement income success.

In later chapters, we will explore methods to produce the higher real rates of return typically needed by plan participants. Real rates of return are influenced by both asset allocation policy and the maintenance of high asset quality with good fiduciary monitoring.

In running the more than 1 billion simulations to produce our outcome success charts, we assumed that the retirement plan participant would retire at age sixty-five, that he needed 70% of his after-tax income, and that he was in the 25% tax bracket. We assumed that he would receive a Social Security benefit in the future but at a reduced amount from today.

The annual income and savings during the accumulation phase and the annual retirement spending are adjusted for inflation so that purchasing power is preserved over time. In the three scenarios with Social Security, we assumed that the retirement income replacement ratio from Social Security would be 20% of total retirement income needs. We assumed a traditional amount of stock- and bond-market volatility, or standard deviation.

We did not assume any set stock- or bond-market average investment return or asset allocation mix. Instead, we sampled what real rates of return are needed with various savings rates to give a 75% or better success rate in retirement spending. "Failure" was defined as running out of money before the end of life expectancy for the plan participant.

We combined the savings rate and real rate of return into the SR+RR Index. This is the combination of savings rate and real rate of return at each point on the curve that gave a 75% or better success rate.

We looked at four possible scenarios, at ages thirty, forty, and fifty.

- No current account balance, no Social Security
- No current account balance, Social Security benefit
- One-year gross-pay current account balance, Social Security benefit
- Two-year gross-pay current account balance, Social Security benefit

Table 3-1: SR+RR Index Requirements for 75% Success

Age	Social Security Benefit?	Current Savings?	SR+RR INDEX >75% Success Formula
30	No	No	13.3
30	Yes	No	11.3
30	Yes	1 Yr Gross Salary	8.3
30	Yes	2 Yr Gross Salary	6.0
40	No	No	20.0
40	Yes	No	16.8
40	Yes	1 Yr Gross Salary	11.8
40	Yes	2 Yr Gross Salary	8.5
50	No	No	27.8
50	Yes	No	27.0
50	Yes	1 Yr Gross Salary	20.5
50	Yes	2 Yr Gross Salary	14.3

Chart 3-7: Real Rate of Return vs. Savings Rates for 75% Success for a 30-Year-Old Worker
(No Current Savings with Social Security)

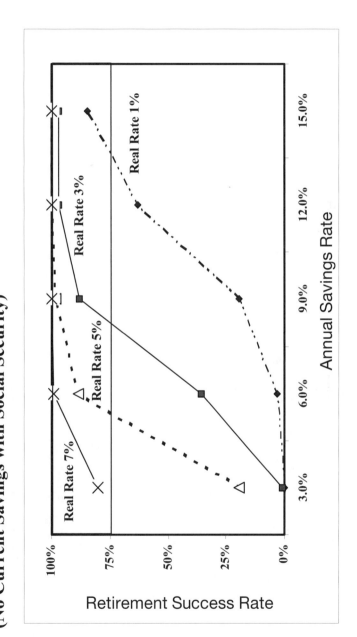

Chart 3-8: Real Rate of Return vs. Savings Rates for 75% Success for a 40-Year-Old Worker (No Current Savings with Social Security)

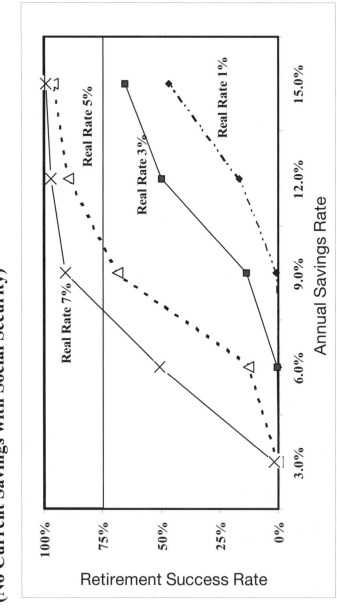

Chart 3-9: Real Rate of Return vs. Savings Rates for 75% Success for a 40-Year-Old Worker (One Year Gross Pay Savings with Social Security)

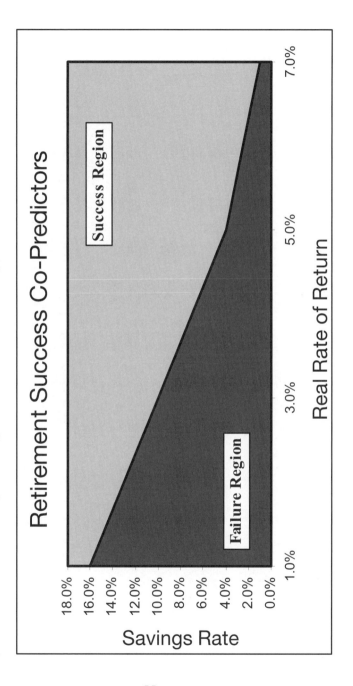

Retirement Success Co-Predictors

Success Region

Failure Region

Savings Rate

Real Rate of Return

Chart 3-10: Real Rate of Return vs. Savings Rates for 75% Success for a 50-Year-Old Worker
(Two Years Gross Pay Savings with Social Security)

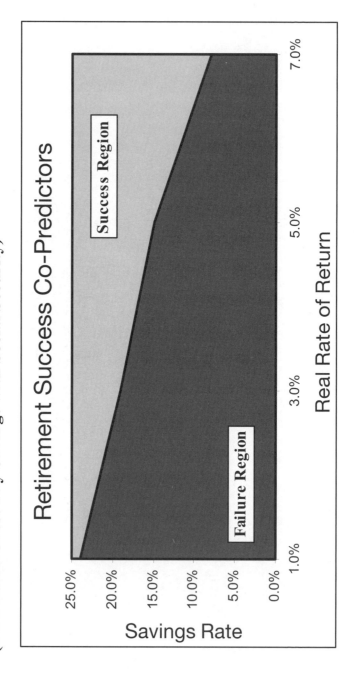

Retirement Success Co-Predictors

Success Region

Failure Region

Savings Rate

25.0% 20.0% 15.0% 10.0% 5.0% 0.0%

1.0% 3.0% 5.0% 7.0%

Real Rate of Return

Chart 3-11: SR+RR Index (Log Scale) for 75% Success for Workers Ages 20–60 (No Current Savings and No Social Security Benefit)

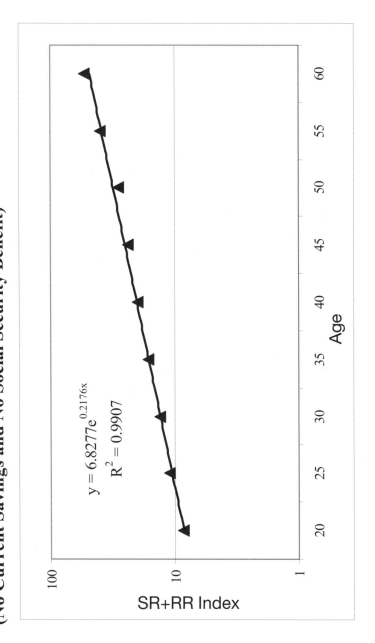

$y = 6.8277e^{0.2176x}$
$R^2 = 0.9907$

Chart 3-12: SR+RR Index (Log Scale) for 75% Success for Workers Ages 20–60 (No Current Savings with Social Security Benefit)

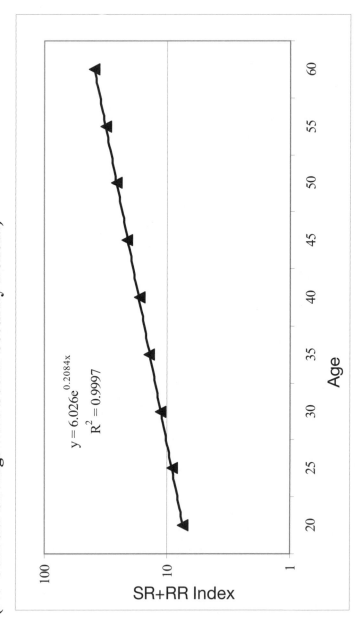

$$y = 6.026e^{0.2084x}$$
$$R^2 = 0.9997$$

SR+RR Index

Age

Chart 3-13: SR+RR INDEX VALUES (LOG SCALE)
For 75% Success for Workers Ages 20–60
(One Year Gross Pay Current Savings with Social Security)

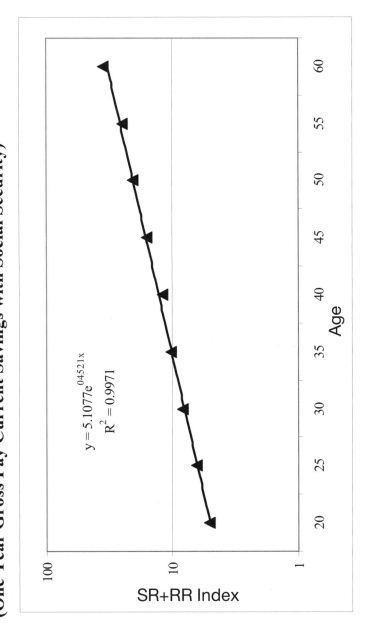

$y = 5.1077e^{.04521x}$

$R^2 = 0.9971$

Chart 3-14: SR+RR Index Values (Log Scale)
For 75% Success for Workers Ages 20–60
(Two Years Gross Pay Current Savings with Social Security)

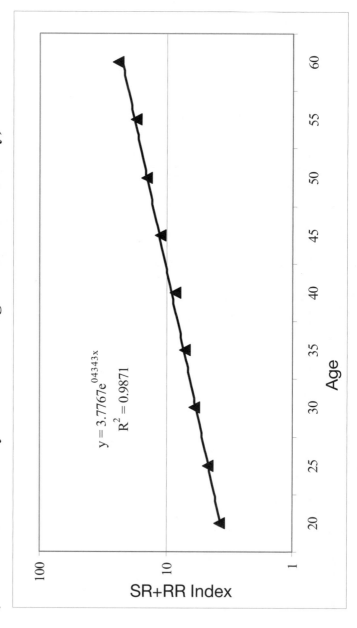

$y = 3.7767e^{.04343x}$
$R^2 = 0.9871$

SR+RR Index

Age

Using SR+RR Index Information to Increase Participant Success

Table 3-1 shows the various SR+RR Index amounts needed for a 75% probability of retirement success. Let's take a closer look at a forty-year-old worker as illustrated in Table 3-2.

Table 3-2: SR+RR Index Levels Needed for a 40-Year-Old Worker

Social Security Benefit	Current Savings?	SR+RR INDEX >75% Success Formula
No	No	20.0
Yes	No	16.8
Yes	1 Yr Gross Salary	11.8
Yes	2 Yr Gross Salary	8.5

Assuming that the worker has one year's gross pay already saved and that he will receive a Social Security benefit, she needs an SR+RR Index score of 11.8 for a 75% chance for retirement success. That means his combination of savings and real rate of return must be 11.8 or higher. If he is the typical worker saving 6% of pay and earning a long-term real rate of return of 0%, he has virtually no probability of successful retirement.

Focusing on both his real rate of return and savings rate will enhance his chance for success. Today, far too many "advice" solutions focus on minor changes in asset allocation and the success probability does not improve.

In most cases, the savings rate is the more certain way to increase the SR+RR Index. After all, the savings rate is within the participant's control; the stock market is not.

To see how the SR+RR Index makes this easier, let's take a closer look at a fifty-year-old worker, as illustrated in Table 3-3. We assume that the worker has two years' gross pay saved so far.

Table 3-3: SR+RR Index Levels Needed for a 50-Year-Old Worker

Social Security Benefit	Current Savings?	SR+RR INDEX >75% Success Formula
No	No	28.1
Yes	No	26.0
Yes	1 Yr Gross Salary	20.5
Yes	2 Yr Gross Salary	14.3

The table shows that if this worker has two years' gross pay already saved and if he will receive a Social Security benefit, he needs an SR+RR Index score of 14.3 for a 75% chance for retirement success.

That means his combination of savings and real rate of return must be 14.3 or higher. If he is the typical worker saving 6% of pay and earning a long-term real rate of return of 0%, he has only a 10% probability of successful retirement. This is failure, not success.

Again focusing on both his real rate of return and savings rate will enhance his success. If he can enter a long-term program to raise his savings rate from 6% to 11%, then he only needs to earn 3.3% on a real basis for a high probability of success. As outlined earlier, in most cases, the savings rate is the more certain way to increase the SR+RR Index.

How to Create Monte Carlo Scenarios

Unified Trust Company has developed the Unified Retirement Counselor^{SM} online advice and retirement planning tool, which we make available free of charge to all our retirement plan clients. The purpose of this Web site is to help plan participants improve their retirement success probabilities. It allows participants to easily create Monte Carlo Simulations. The Web address is www.unifiedtrust.com.

This online advice site helps participants optimize the Three A's that are essential for a successful retirement: Adequate Savings, Asset Allocation Advice and Asset Quality. The Three A's determine the participant's SR+RR Index score. Enhancing either the savings rate or the real rate of return or preferably both at the same time can improve their success probabilities.

Chart 3-15: Unified Retirement Counselor[SM]

-64-

Chart 3-16: Unified Retirement Counselor^{SM}

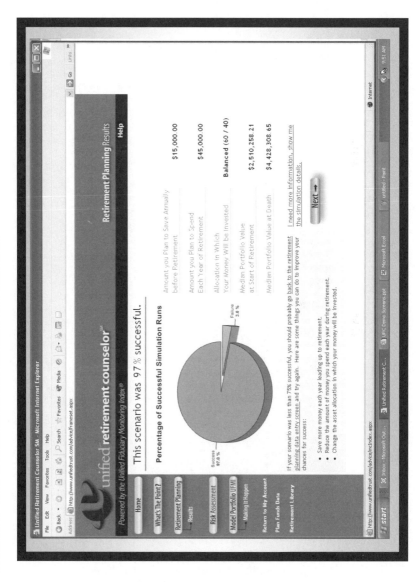

Chart 3-17: Retirement Success Calculation for Full Plan

Retirement Success Probability Analysis Summary

Current Situation Success Analysis

Savings Rate	6.06%
Real Rate Of Investment Return	2.00%
SR+RR Index	8.06%
Current Success Probability	21%

Target Outcomes For Improved Success

Savings Rate	11.06%
Real Rate Of Investment Return	4.50%
SR+RR Index	15.56%
Target Success Probability	71%

unified trust
COMPANY, N.A.

Chart 3-18: Retirement Success Calculation per Participant

Current Situation Retirement Success Probability For Each Plan Participant

Participant	Current $ Balance	Plan Real Rate of Inv Return	Savings Rate	SR+RR Index	Annual $ Savings	Years Left Until 65	Projected Balance	Ending Multiple of Pay	Success %
A	$45,000	2.00%	7.00%	9.00%	$3,920	28	$223,587	3.99	25%
B	$12,000	2.00%	10.00%	12.00%	$3,500	29	$157,083	4.49	37%
C	$45,000	2.00%	7.00%	9.00%	$1,470	10	$70,951	3.38	17%
D	$125,000	2.00%	11.00%	13.00%	$11,000	23	$514,407	5.14	42%
E	$250,000	2.00%	5.00%	7.00%	$4,700	7	$322,113	3.43	1%
F	$125,000	2.00%	7.00%	9.00%	$2,576	11	$186,768	5.08	50%
G	$12,000	2.00%	5.00%	7.00%	$2,100	32	$115,491	2.75	0%
H	$575,500	2.00%	10.00%	12.00%	$20,000	10	$920,526	4.60	30%
I	$10,000	2.00%	5.00%	7.00%	$2,000	41	$147,742	3.69	17%
J	$45,000	2.00%	7.00%	9.00%	$2,800	9	$81,092	2.03	0%

Projected Retirement Success Probability For Each Plan Participant

Participant	Current $ Balance	Plan Real Rate of Inv Return	Savings Rate	SR+RR Index	Annual $ Savings	Years Left Until 65	Projected Balance	Ending Multiple of Pay	Success %
A	$45,000	4.50%	10.60%	15.10%	$6,720	28	$517,172	9.24	94%
B	$12,000	4.50%	13.60%	18.10%	$5,250	29	$344,479	9.84	94%
C	$45,000	4.50%	10.60%	15.10%	$2,520	10	$100,850	4.80	64%
D	$125,000	4.50%	14.60%	19.10%	$16,000	23	$967,013	9.67	94%
E	$250,000	4.50%	8.60%	13.10%	$9,400	7	$415,595	4.42	35%
F	$125,000	4.50%	10.60%	15.10%	$4,416	11	$263,979	7.17	90%
G	$12,000	4.50%	8.60%	13.10%	$4,200	32	$337,478	8.04	94%
H	$575,500	4.50%	13.60%	18.10%	$30,000	10	$1,262,380	6.31	74%
I	$10,000	4.50%	8.60%	13.10%	$2,562	41	$512,168	12.80	94%
J	$45,000	4.50%	10.60%	15.10%	$3,688	9	$118,724	2.97	2%

unified trust
COMPANY, N.A.

For Further Reading

Alexander, C. *Risk Management and Analysis: Measuring and Modeling Financial Risk.* West Sussex, England: Wiley Press, (1998).

Bell, H., and Raul, R. "The Full Monte." *Journal of Financial Planning* (June 2002).

Bratley, B.L., Fox, L, and Schrage E.L. *A Guide To Simulation.*"New York, NY Springer, (1983).

Holden, S, and van der Hei, J. "Can 401(k) Accumulations Generate Significant Income for Future Retirees?" Investment Company Institute, vol. 8, no. 3 (November 2002).

Jackel, P. *Monte Carlo Methods in Finance.* West Sussex, England: Wiley Press, (2002).

Samwick, A., and Skinner, J. "How Will 401(k) Plans Affect Retirement Income?" *NBER Journal* (July 2003).

Wright, J. *Monte Carlo Risk Analysis and Due Diligence of New Business Ventures.* New York, NY McGraw Hill University Press, (2002).

Chapter 4

Explaining Plan Participant Actions with Behavioral Finance Research

Chapter Summary

The switch from defined benefit plans to defined contribution plans requires plan participants to function as their own actuaries, investment managers, asset allocation specialists, and plan consultants. In a defined benefit plan, the plan sponsor hires specialists to provide these complex services. Yet in defined contribution plans, participants are expected to do it all. Because they are so overwhelmed, plan participants engage in several distinct behaviors that are detrimental to successful outcomes.

Detrimental behaviors include inertia, decision framing, anchoring, aversion to choice overload, and procrastination. Investment decisions are driven by recent performance and peer group actions, both of which result in poor outcomes. These collective behaviors reduce participants' saving rates and their real rates of return below the combined minimum level needed for success. Awareness of their impending retirement failure is not transformed into meaningful actions to solve the problem.

Thus, merely offering an educational program to demonstrate these problems seldom improves outcomes. Specific programs must be incorporated into the defined contribution plans that take such behaviors into account and direct them into solutions. The programs can result in dramatically improved success for participants.

401(k) Plans Are Really Mini Defined Benefit Plans

There is no doubt that participant-directed defined contribution plans have become the cornerstone of the private-sector retirement system around the world. In the United States, participant choice has spread not only to pensions but also to a great many other aspects of employee benefit packages, such as health care plans, flexible benefit programs, and time-off arrangements. The trend toward giving participants more choice also underlies recent proposals to reform Social Security by adding personal accounts and Medicare proposals to permit seniors to choose between a public or a privately managed health-care plan.

Underlying this choice-driven movement is an assumption about behavior: that the participant to whom the responsibility of choice has been handed is a well-informed economic agent who acts rationally to maximize his self-interest. To this end, it is assumed that he can interpret and weigh sometimes conflicting information presented regarding options offered by employers and governments, appropriately evaluate and balance these choices, and then make an informed decision based on a weighing of the alternatives.

Recently, however, a different perspective has emerged regarding how "real" people make economic decisions, one developed by leading social scientists working at the interface of economics, finance, and psychology. This perspective is consistent with the fundamental economic proposition that people try to maximize their self-interest, but it also recognizes that such decisions are often made with less-than perfect outcomes.

As mentioned above, too many decisions are thrust upon defined contribution plan participants that are simply too complex for these individuals to master on their own. Individuals have the right intentions and beliefs, but they lack the willpower to carry out the appropriate changes in behavior. These new notions of how people make decisions have spurred the rapidly growing fields of behavioral economics and finance.

The central question addressed by this research is how markets work and how consumers make decisions when some, or even many, people labor under such mental or emotional constraints and complications. This research can have a profound impact on the way analysts now view varied aspects of economic and financial life, including the ways in which we understand how people decide to save, invest, and consume.

Why Do Plan Participants Save?

Understanding why plan participants save and what they invest in are questions of central import to economists and government policy makers. With the growth of defined contribution savings plans in the United States and around the world, especially plans with 401(k) or employee contributory features, it is clear that having a meaningful retirement benefit depends increasingly on participants' decisions to save and invest in their retirement plans. As will be discussed in subsequent chapters, without an adequate savings rate, there is little possibility of retirement success.

Traditional economic theory depicts current savings as the result of people trading current consumption for future consumption. Thus, households are thought to compare the benefit gained from consuming their income today with the benefits of deferring some of that income into the future. This is what is thought to drive contributions to 401(k) or individual retirement accounts, with the goal saving for retirement.

The life-cycle model of saving assumes that individuals are rational planners of their consumption and their saving needs over their lifetimes who, at the same time, take into account the interests of their heirs. During their younger years, workers tend to be negative savers, borrowing from the future by means of debt to boost current consumption. At middle-age, individuals become net savers and purchasers of financial assets and enter an accumulation phase, during which they stockpile financial assets for their final, retired phase of life.

In retirement, labor-driven earnings decline or disappear, and people then spend their financial assets to finance old-age consumption. According to this life-cycle theory, people will logically develop assets for retirement that will be sufficient to protect them from unexpected declines in their standard of living in old age. Of course, it assumes that people can accurately project these needs several decades in advance.

On balance, the life-cycle theory is thought to do a reasonable job of explaining patterns of household saving behavior. Saving generally rises with income and age, and it is positively associated with education and total wealth. Young households generally have more debt than assets, and prime-aged households do appear to begin saving more and accumulating financial holdings. Finally, in retirement, people tend to consume portions of their financial assets as they age.

However, some saving behavior clearly appears to be at odds with this theory. The first question is, how good are households at calculating an appropriate saving goal for retirement? Arguably, if the life-cycle analysis is true, households should have some demonstrated skill at estimating their needs for retirement, and analysis of actual saving behavior should demonstrate some reasonably widespread competency at the task. Keep in mind that a sophisticated defined benefit plan requires many specialists to calculate these numbers and that the numbers must be revised each year.

Calculating the appropriate retirement savings rate requires accurate estimates of uncertain future processes, including lifetime earnings, asset returns, investment risk, tax rates, family and health statuses, and longevity. To solve this problem, the human brain as a calculating machine would need to have the capacity to solve many variables simultaneously, independent of one another. The calculations would need to take into account decades-long time-value-of-money problems and with massive uncertainties as to specific cash flows and their overall timing.

Survey and empirical research suggest that individuals are not particularly good at the retirement savings problem. Relatively few people feel able to plan effectively for retirement. Surveys repeatedly find that fewer than 35% of U.S. workers have calculated how much they will need to retire, 30% have not saved anything for retirement, and only 15-20% percent feel very confident about having enough money to live comfortably in retirement. Other studies have shown that even in the group feeling "very confident," about half have used incorrect assumptions and have overestimated the amount of money they will likely have, as well as their success rate probability.

Furthermore, the empirical evidence suggests that failing to save enough also has serious negative consequences. A recent study of postretirement consumption patterns indicates that most workers experience an unexpected decline in their standard of living after retirement. Other research suggests that only 30% of preretirees are fully prepared for retirement at age sixty-five. Of the remaining group, another 30% have a reasonable chance to close the savings gap by age sixty-five. Finally, fully 40% appear unlikely to achieve a reasonable standard of replacement income by age sixty-five. The results are even worse if retirement is planned for age sixty-two, which is the median age an American retires.

Behavioral economists would not find it surprising that people struggle with retirement saving in view of the problem's complexity. Many would take it as prima facie evidence that large groups of workers do not "get the saving problem right," contrary to the assumption of rationality and wise planning underlying the life-cycle model. Behaviorists tend to rely on a straightforward psychological explanation called "lack of willpower." People try to save for retirement, but they too often prove to be limited in their capacity or desire to execute intentions.

In a sense, saving for retirement requires behavior similar to that undertaken in other behavior-modification programs, such as exercising, dieting, quitting smoking, or following through on New Year's resolutions. It would seem that although people intellectually understand the benefits of a specific behavior—and they may even have some idea of how to get started—they have difficulty implementing their intentions.

Numerous studies have identified that the problem of self-control may be an important deterrent to saving for retirement. Individuals make tradeoffs regarding risk and time. Psychologists have shown that peoples' near-term discount rates are much higher than their long-term discount rates. People confronting long-term decisions can exhibit high levels of patience. For instance, they might say, "If I can receive an apple in 100 days and two apples in 101 days, I'll be happy to wait the extra day for another apple." But when the decision shifts to the present, their patience wears thin, and they think, "I'd rather have an apple today than wait for two tomorrow."

In standard time-value-of-money calculations, discount rates are postulated to remain constant over time so they do not vary today, tomorrow, or a year from now. Given this assumption, one dollar saved today would be perceived to grow steadily in value over time. But when individuals are hyperbolic discounters, they apply high discount rates to the near term and lower discount rates to the future. In this case, one dollar's worth of saving today is perceived as growing more rapidly in the short run and less in the longer run. The hyperbolic discounters place a lower value on future benefits and overvalue the present. The application to retirement is clear: they will overconsume today and undersave because of self-control problems.

Decision theorists working along this line try to understand the self-control problem in a more detailed way. The processing of emotions typically involves gauging risk in terms of two components: dread risk, or the potential for near-term catastrophe, and uncertainty risk, a generalized fear of the unknown or the new. Many plan participants rate retirement risks low along both dimensions: few people have a palpable fear of impending disaster or of great uncertainty in their retirement planning, as compared with other risks in their lives.

Awareness Does Not Produce Action

Whether viewed from an economics or a decision theoretic perspective, the self-control problem supports the view of a wide divergence between individuals' desires and their actual behaviors. For example, a survey of 10,000 employees at one company found that 68% of participants said their retirement savings rate was "too low." These workers reported that they should be saving 14% of earnings, whereas, in fact, they were only saving about 6%. Interestingly, only 1% of all workers felt they were saving too much. After a six month follow up virtually none of the low savers increased their 401(k) saving rate on their own.

Most retirement plan participants reported that they knew they were saving less than they should. In other words, a key obstacle to saving more is not necessarily lack of awareness; rather it is the ability to take action on the knowledge. The difficult task is to overcome hyperbolic discounting, in which plan participants place a lower value on future benefits and overvalue the present.

In recognizing such problems, people often seek to protect themselves through the use of mechanisms that help foster desirable changes in behavior. Commitment devices for saving may be an analogue of the fad diet: one way of imposing some degree of discipline on one's wayward behavior is to create some seemingly arbitrary rules about what one can and cannot eat.

For example, financial planners use "Pay yourself first" as a standard commitment device to encourage disciplined saving and budgeting; it is also the principle underlying U.S. payroll-deduction 401(k) plans. These plans are one of the most successful commitment devices in current use, and they are formulated such that contributions are automatically deducted from workers' pay before the money can be spent. Participation rates in 401(k)-type plans, where payroll deduction is the norm, is at least four times as high as for Individual Retirement Accounts (IRAs), where structured payroll deductions are uncommon.

This is the same logic applied by the federal government in collecting income taxes though payroll deduction, rather than waiting for people to send in their checks on April 15. According to 1997 tax return data, some 27% of workers contributed to workplace savings plans, compared with just 6% contributing to an IRA. Withdrawal restrictions on IRAs and 401(k)s and other retirement plans are also commitment devices: once the money is allocated to these plans, a psychological and financial hurdle is imposed on accessing the money, helping to counteract lapses in personal willpower.

Other evidence that individuals vary in their capacity for self-control and financial discipline comes from industry surveys of workers' saving and planning behaviors. Workers' desire to plan has strong positive influence on retirement wealth accumulation. However, studies reveal that as many as half of pension participants are uninterested in the financial and retirement planning activities thought necessary to plan successful retirement.

A "planner" paradigm, where the individual consciously pursues retirement saving and investment goals in a disciplined, systematic way, appears to apply to only about half of the retirement plan population. In many of these cases, the plan participant makes incorrect calculations. The other half appears unable to impose the self-control needed to try to solve this problem.

Framing and Default Choices

Many individuals deviate from standard economic theory in another important way: they can be easily influenced by what is called "decision framing." Rational economic agents would not be expected to vary their responses to a question based on how it is asked. But in practice, many people do exactly that, in both the saving and investment areas. An example of decision framing arises with automatic enrollment in retirement saving plans. Under the traditional (nonautomatic) approach, the employee makes a positive election to join the 401(k) plan. By contrast, with automatic enrollment, the employee is signed up by the employer for the plan at a given percentage contribution rate, and the employee retains the right to opt out of this decision.

This simple rephrasing of the saving question from negative to positive elicits a tremendously different response in overall plan-participation rates. When workers are required to opt in, the default decision (or the nondecision) is to save nothing; by dramatic contrast, with automatic enrollment, the default decision proves to be that people save at the rate specified by the employer. For one large U.S. firm, plan participation rates jumped from 37% to 86% percent for new hires after automatic enrollment was introduced. What this suggests, in the end, is that many workers do not have particularly firm convictions about their desired saving behavior. In other words, they seem to go with the flow. By merely rephrasing the question, their preferences can be changed from not saving to saving.

The impact of automatic enrollment is also part of a broader behavioral phenomenon, the power of the default option and its influence on decision-making. When confronted with difficult decisions, individuals tend to adopt shortcuts to simplify the complex problems they face. One simple shortcut is to accept the available default option (with the implicit assumption that it must be "reasonable" or it wouldn't be the default). So for 401(k) enrollment, the simplest default is the nondecision: do nothing.

An emerging literature indicates that individual behavior is easily swayed by default choices. Although automatic enrollment boosts the number of individuals participating in a retirement plan, it may not actually increase total plan savings. The reason is that when they are automatically enrolled, people who would have voluntarily enrolled in the plan at higher contribution rates or who would have chosen more aggressive investments decide to stick with the lower saving rate and the conservative investment option set by their employer.

The positive effect is that saving rises for people who formerly did not participate, but an unexpected negative result is that saving falls for those who would have enrolled at higher deferral rates and in more aggressive investment options but instead elected to adopt the employer's defaults. On net, it appears that these two effects largely offset one another.

The Inertia and Procrastination Factors

Evidence on automatic enrollment has also revealed another anomaly about individuals and their saving behavior: the impact that inertia or procrastination has on decision-making. In one analysis of automatic enrollment, the benefit of higher plan-participation rates appeared to be offset by a profound level of inertia.

Most participants remained at the default saving and conservative investment choices set for them by their employer. Once enrolled, participants made few active changes to the contribution rates or investment mixes selected for them by their employers; rather, they simply stayed with what was assigned to them.

Another analysis explored how inertia and default behavior influenced several other defined-contribution-plan activities: eligibility, enrollment, the employer match level, cash distributions at termination, and the effect of education. It was found that most plan participants followed the path of least resistance in their decision-making. They often were heavily influenced by coworker decisions. In other words, they tended to make the easiest, rather than the best, decision.

Again, the persistence of inertia and what might be called a passive approach to decision-making are both indicative of individuals' being somewhat imperfect rational economic agents in their retirement and saving decisions.

Desire versus Action

Even after education invokes in the plan participant a desire to change, there is seldom any meaningful action to produce change. An illustration of this compares workers' attitudes expressed after having attended an employee education seminar with actual behavioral changes recorded on company administrative data systems.

Immediately following a seminar, for example, 100% of workers not participating in a firm's 401(k) plan indicated in a survey that they would join the plan. However, over the next six months, only 14% actually did so. A similar though smaller gap between desire and action was true for other behaviors, including intentions to boost saving, change existing portfolio allocations, and change the mix of future contributions.

In addition, the number and quality of investment choices, along with peer group pressure, can change saving rates. One tenet of contemporary economics is that more choice is better. At Unified Trust Company, we have always maintained that quality is better than quantity. Studies have found that offering workers too many investment choices can produce choice overload. In this case, plan participants become overwhelmed with the complexity of the decision, and as a result, pension plan participation is reduced. Faced with complex investment choices, some participants may elect to simplify the decision by following the default shortcut, which is not to decide and not to join the plan.

Saving decisions can be strongly influenced by peers. Studies have found that people with virtually identical demographic characteristics can have dramatically different saving rates, depending on whether their peers save for retirement or not. They also demonstrate that communications directed to individuals can influence not only the saving behaviors of those individuals but also the behaviors of others in their work groups. As a corollary, the work group can strongly influence individuals as well.

Automatic Savings Increases

Taking the automatic enrollment idea one step further incorporates automatic deferral escalators into an ongoing program. The behavioral activities we previously described that affect saving behavior have been incorporated into an effective program called the Save More Tomorrow (SMarT™) program developed by professors Richard H. Thaler and Shlomo Benartzi. Under this program, plan participants indicate that they wish to increase their pension saving rates on regularly scheduled dates. For example, they may wish to increase their savings 2% a year on each anniversary of their employment, which might also correspond with merit or cost-of-living raises.

The Thaler and Benartzi program is designed to address several behavioral anomalies. First, it recognizes that individuals have self-control problems and that they benefit from committing to a retirement saving solution. Second, it exploits inertia, as people tend to sign up initially and the program is automatically carried out in the future. Third, it recognizes the possibility of hyperbolic discounting; that is, people tend to be averse to saving today, but they are willing to push off their commitment to the future—or promise to "save more tomorrow." As hyperbolic discounters, they significantly underestimate the impact of such commitment. Last, the program exploits money illusion. Thus, participants often think only in terms of nominal take-home pay, so if the savings increase is designed to coincide with pay raises, they tend to believe that the savings increase had little or no cost, even though their real current consumption may have declined by small amounts. If their pay increases 4% and they put 2% more in the plan, they are still "ahead."

In the initial study, the SMarT™ program was offered to employees at a 300-person firm. Employees were given the option of financial counseling; most signed up for the counseling, and received the advice that they should boost their saving rates by an average of 5%. Nearly 80 workers took that advice; many more, just over 160, signed up for the SMarT™ plan instead, which required annual increases of 3%. After three years, the individuals who signed up for SMarT™ experienced dramatic increases in their savings rates—from 3.5% before the plan began to 13.6% by the fourth anniversary.

Chart 4-2: Impact of SMarT™ Program on Deferral Rates over Time

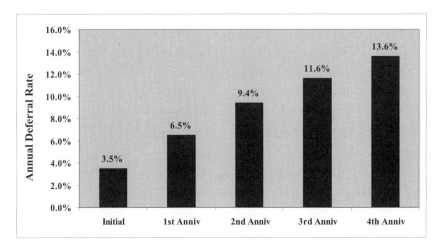

The success of the Thaler and Benartzi SMarT™ program provides further evidence of the divergence between real-world behavior of employees versus the rational agents that many economic theorists assumed the actions of employees to follow. Many people attempt to save for retirement and even appear to know when they are not doing as well as they should, but they struggle with exercising the right degree of self-control or willpower.

Reframing the saving decision to include defaults with automatically higher saving rates and using commitment devices, procrastination, inertia, and money illusion to address the self-control problems of hyperbolic discounters are useful approaches to addressing the practical problems associated with the saving decision.

Making Investment Decisions

As in the case of the saving problem, the question of how to invest one's money during the accumulation phase has been explored through widely accepted models of investment decision-making. Such principles are at the heart of investment decision-making, both in employer-directed defined benefit plans and employee-directed defined contribution plans. Keep in mind the many specialists whom the plan sponsor must hire to run the defined benefit plan to help with decisions concerning strategic asset allocation, ongoing investment, and performance attribution for investment managers. In the defined contribution plan, plan participants are expected to have such expertise—which they don't.

Rational investors should seek efficient combinations of securities that optimize risk and return. A given portfolio is on the "efficient frontier" if it offers the highest return for a given level of risk. Institutions select from the array of portfolio choices on the efficient frontier based on their expected utility. In their utility preferences, individuals are presumed to be risk-averse, meaning that they penalize, or demand higher compensation for, riskier investments.

One of the important predictions of this modern portfolio theory is that investors will be inadequately compensated for assuming the risks of investing in an individual security. In other words, an efficient capital market will compensate investors only for the aggregate market risk they endure, so there will be no single-stock investments on the efficient frontier. The individual stock risk is called "nonsystem" risk, while the total stock market risk is called "system" risk. Consequently, rational investors will seek to maximize portfolio diversification and eliminate all stock-specific nonsystem risk in the pursuit of optimal portfolio solutions. This principle has been at the foundation of the growth of low-cost indexed strategies as an investment management style in many retirement plans.

Another implication of this theory of time diversification is that the closer one is to an anticipated investment goal where spending from the portfolio begins (such as retirement), the less risky will be the investment portfolio. In practice, many financial planners propose time diversification as a popular investment principle, suggesting that people invest something like 100%, or 110%, minus their age in stocks. Thus, a fifty-year-old worker should hold something like 50–60% of his account in stocks. The time diversification view is also the basis for most defined-contribution education and advisory services, which suggest that older investors should hold more conservative portfolios than younger investors.

As with saving theory, behavioral economics asks a fundamental question about investors in general and plan participants in particular: How good are they at actually understanding and acting on the predictions of mean-variance theory?

In theory, a rational investor should do a reasonable job of constructing portfolios that are mean-variance efficient, so there should be some evidence of widespread competency at these types of investment decisions. Of all American households who own stocks, the median family owns only two stock positions, and even the most affluent households hold a median of fifteen. These low levels of diversification fall well short of the number of positions thought to represent a well-diversified portfolio.

It appears that for many investors, diversification is more akin to holding a variety of assets rather than the construction of a well-diversified portfolio. A related diversification puzzle is why, in defined-contribution retirement plans, do so many participants overinvest in their employer's stock? A recent study estimated that more than eleven million participants held more than 20% of their 401(k) account in their employer's stock; of that group, five million participants had 60% or more of their account in company stock. The amount of nonsystem risk these participants take is alarmingly high.

Plan Participants Have Weak Preferences for Their Investment Portfolios

The studies we discussed earlier on automatic enrollment illustrate that many workers lack firm preferences for saving. By merely rephrasing the question from a positive to a negative election, workers who weren't planning to save suddenly find themselves saving—and workers who would have saved at higher savings rates find themselves saving at the defaults set by their employers. A similar lack of strong preferences appears to affect investment decisions. Arguably, if investors were completely rational, we would expect them to have well-defined preferences over their portfolios. Theoretically, the portfolios they select represent their unique expectations of risk and return and are tailored to their own needs and preferences.

However, retirement plan participants appear to have relatively weak preferences for the portfolios they elect. Studies have demonstrated that where workers were given choices between holding their own portfolios, the portfolios of median participants in their plan, or the portfolios of average participants, 79% preferred the medians to their own. Only 21% continued to prefer the portfolios they initially selected. Furthermore, many found the average portfolios to be quite satisfactory. In other words, participants seemed to be just as satisfied with portfolios constructed at the statistical averages of their coworkers' behavior as with the portfolios they themselves constructed.

These findings are supported by various studies regarding preference reversals. When individuals do not arrive at decisions with firm preferences in mind, their preferences do not appear to be strongly ingrained. Rather, individual preferences tend to be situational and emerge when the decisions are made, based on the conditions and information surrounding those decisions.

Choice Overload

Recent research has conclusively shown that offering an ever-increasing number of investment options hurts, rather than helps, the plan participant. Psychologist and behavioral economists generally believe that more choice is better. Numerous experiments and performance data from many retirement plans reveal that people in extensive choice environments enjoy the idea of choice, but have trouble effectively selecting the right choice for their situation. Participants seem to become unsure of themselves as their choices expand. Perhaps this is reasonable given their weak preferences for most investments portfolios.

Data reveal that participants are no better off, and are often in worse shape, by being able to select their own portfolios. In general, this is due to the fact that most participants are unable to do a particularly good job of matching risk and return to their individual situation. Thus the preponderance of recent studies makes clear that most participants are not better off with more choices. In fact, too many choices can be demoralizing and reduce plan participation significantly.

Framing the Investment Decision

Just as saving choices can be affected by how they are presented (framing), so too can investment decisions be influenced, sometimes strongly, by framing effects. Much of the research in this area has investigated the effect of investment-menu design on participant investment choices in defined-contribution retirement plans.

Research has demonstrated that the menu design is a more powerful influence on participant decision-making than the underlying risk and return characteristics of the investments being offered. The investment menu is far too complex to allow most participants to completely and rationally digest the underlying risk and return characteristics of their investments. Many participants appear to have weak convictions regarding risk and return, and they can easily be swayed in their decisions by the framing effects of an investment menu.

In one experiment, participants were given two fund offerings and asked to select an investment mix for their retirement plans. Some participants were presented with a stock fund and a bond fund, others with a stock fund and a balanced fund, and a third group with a bond fund and a balanced fund. In all three cases, a common strategy was to choose a 50/50 mix of the two funds offered, although many participants did select different weightings. What was striking in the data was that radically different underlying asset allocations ensued, given the different choices offered.

For an illustration of the various asset allocation results, see Chart 4-3 on the next page. For people given the choice of an equity fund and a bond fund, the average allocation to equities was 54%. For those offered two equity-oriented portfolios, a balanced fund and an equity fund, the average allocation to equities was 73%. And for those offered a balanced fund and a bond fund, the average allocation to equities was only 35%.

Chart 4-3: Participant Asset Allocation Is Dependant on Underlying Fund Choices

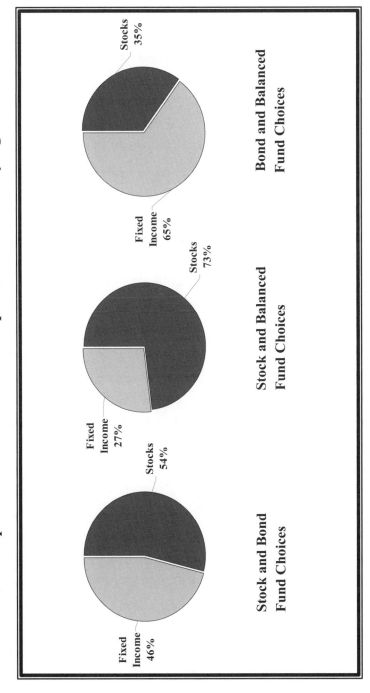

Stocks 35%

Fixed Income 65%

Bond and Balanced Fund Choices

Stocks 73%

Fixed Income 27%

Stock and Balanced Fund Choices

Stocks 54%

Fixed Income 46%

Stock and Bond Fund Choices

In a related experiment using investment menus with five funds, the asset allocations chosen by participants were again strongly influenced by menu design. If the plan offered several equity funds, participants invested more in equities; when it included more fixed income funds, they chose fixed income options instead.

A different study also asked plan participants to select investments from three different menus. The investments allowed ranged from A (low risk) to D (high risk). The first menu offered included options A, B, and C; the second menu, just options B and C; and the third menu, options B, C, and D. Comparing options B and C, which were in all three menus, 29% of the participants preferred C over B in the first menu; 39% in the second menu; and 54% in the third menu.

In summary, in the first menu, where an investment option C was at the extreme, it was liked least; in the third menu, where option C was the middle choice, it was liked most. As with the asset allocation experiment above, this shows that participants appeared to use a decision tree shortcut to avoid extremes and picked the middle option rather than maintaining a consistent set of well-ordered risk preferences.

Related research indicates that beyond these menu effects, even simple changes in the way information is presented can influence asset allocation decisions. In one experiment, plan participants were asked to make investment decisions based on reviewing the one-year return profile of U.S. common stocks; in a second experiment, they made decisions based on a thirty-year return profile.

When looking at the one-year stock returns, the average allocation to equities was 63%, but when looking at thirty-year returns, the equity allocation was 81%. These findings underscore the powerful influence of framing effects on decision-making in retirement plans, as many plan participants seem to lack well-formed investment preferences.

Inertia and Procrastination Relating to Investment Decisions

As with savings behavior, inertia also plays a large role in investment decision-making. Studies have shown high levels of inertia in the investment decision-making of plan participants. As an example, look at Chart 4-4. Vanguard examined how their 2.3 million plan participants at the Vanguard Group allocated their new contributions accounts as of June 30, 2003. First, they found that fewer than 10% of plan participants changed their contribution allocations each year. Further, participants who enrolled in their plans near the top of the bull market in 1999 allocated about 70% of new contributions to equities in June 2003, notwithstanding the huge market drop sustained over the preceding three-year period. Meanwhile, participants who enrolled during the first six months of 2003, after the three-year fall in stock prices, allocated only 48% of new monies to equities.

Chart 4-4: Current Stock Market Conditions Affect Participant Investment Decisions

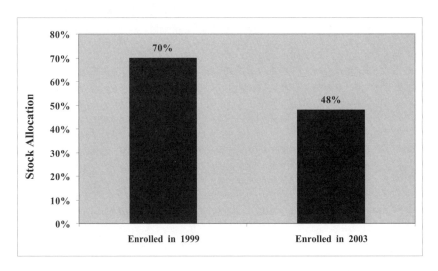

These data illustrate how sensitive participant investment decisions at enrollment are to then-current market conditions; it also demonstrates the power of inertia. It seems unlikely that participants enrolled in 1999 would have dramatically different risk preferences than those who enrolled in 2003, yet recent enrollees were presumably making active choices based on then-current information, whereas earlier enrollees did not react so dramatically to market news.

Finally, this also explains the anchoring effects for pension investors. Anchoring refers to the notion that decision-making is strongly influenced by starting values, no matter how arbitrary they may be. Among participants, it appears that the relevant anchor is their initial allocation decision, and subsequent portfolio changes tend to be made with reference to that initial value, rather than on some absolute basis.

Employer Stock Issues

Following the Enron and World-Com debacles, the use of company stock within a defined contribution plan raises important issues of risk and return. The conventional economic explanation for this phenomenon is that employers and stockholders seek to promote employee productivity through stock ownership, so they encourage or mandate large employee holdings of company stock. As rational agents, however, employees who are aware of the risks they are being required to assume should demand compensation in some other form, such as higher wages.

There is some support for the rational-agent view of workers holding company stock. This is because concentrated company stock positions are most common for large firms, and such firms typically pay higher wages and benefits to their employees. Yet from a behavioral perspective, there is also evidence that concentrated stock positions are not solely due to incentive effects; rather, it seems that computational or behavioral errors on the part of participants also explain the phenomenon.

Studies have demonstrated evidence of risk myopia regarding employer stock; many participants rate their employers' stock as safer than diversified equity funds. Another survey found that even after the post-Enron publicity surrounding company stock, 67% of participants rated their employers' stock as safer than, or as safe as, a diversified portfolio of many stocks. Only 33% said it was more risky.

What is striking about these results is the comparison between participant risk perceptions and the actual return and volatility of their employers' stock. Looking at the risk ratings first, it is natural to conclude that at least two-thirds of participants are not good investment managers when it comes to company stock. They rate stock as safer than or as safe as a diversified portfolio, despite its greater volatility than a broad market index: a clear-cut "error" under modern portfolio theory. It is likely that participants do not base their risk perceptions on volatility, because their participants' risk ratings are well correlated with the historic relative returns of their employers' stock.

The conclusion that plan participants overlook volatility and focus on returns is supported by studies of pension investments in employer stock. Participant allocations were based on extrapolations of the company's historic stock performance. More often than not, participants who over-rated their employers' stock based on good past performance found that those stocks subsequently generated below-average performances. Conversely, those participants who under-rated their employers' stock due to poor past performance typically later saw the stock becoming above-average performers.

The Endorsement Effect

Participants' allocations were also influenced by whether their employers provided matches in company stock, a phenomenon named the "endorsement effect." The conclusion is that, just as menu design influences participant investment decisions, so too do employers' plan-design decisions. Because offering matches in company stock encourages participants to hold more in stock, workers whose companies offer matches in company stock hold more than workers whose employers do not offer matches. Other researchers have also argued that past performance, rather than risk, drives participants' portfolio decisions.

Investors Rely on Past Performance to Make Investment Decisions

Investors tend to see patterns in small series of randomly drawn numbers, and when making decisions, people attempt to impose order or structure on the information they see. This is particularly true when they are presented with conflicting information. For example, a mutual fund investor might identify a fund manager with three years of top performance and conclude that the manager has unusual skill, rather than view it as a random process. Of course, viewed across the universe of thousands of investment managers, a given manager's three-year track record is just as likely an indication of chance as of skill. As a result, a random outcome may appear to be logical sequence.

A second issue is that many people appear to be subject to what has been called an "availability shortcut." When faced with difficult decisions, they tend to rely on readily available information. Investors may rely on past performance because that information is cheaply available. In some case, they rely upon Morningstar ratings, even though most studies have shown that the star rating system does not offer valid predictive help.

Plan participants are aware that retirement plans and investment companies generate huge amounts of past-performance data that is available in statements, on Web sites, in enrollment materials, and in newsletter updates. Past performance is also pervasive in the media, but few report systematically on expected returns.

Of course, in the United States and elsewhere, reports on past investment performance are often accompanied by the legal disclaimer that "past performance is no guarantee of future results." Yet one need only compare the size of that disclaimer to the volume of past-performance data to understand its limitations in the face of the availability shortcut. At Unified Trust Company, we have developed the Unified Fiduciary Monitoring Index® to help with investment decision-making.

In terms of risk and return, individuals will experience losses more acutely than gains. The experimental evidence suggested that the index of loss-aversion is about 2.5. In other words, when evaluating risky gambles, individuals will report that losses are 2.5 times as painful as the equivalent dollar value of gains. For example, if someone were presented with a 50% chance of losing $1,000 or a 50% chance of gaining an unknown amount x, evidence suggests that many people would not entertain this gamble until the value x is on the order of $2,500 or so.

In addition, actual behavior will depend on the exact sequence of gains and losses and how the individual has incorporated prior gains and losses into current perceptions. For example, suppose an individual wins $100. If offered a reasonable chance to win more money or lose the $100, many people would decline the additional gamble because of the risk of forfeiting the $100 sure gain. But if offered a choice to win more money while preserving a meaningful part of the $100 gain, many people take the risk. This is known as the "house money" effect: while people are generally risk-averse in the domain of gains, if they feel they are risking someone else's money (e.g. accumulated earnings from prior bets), they become more risk-seeking.

On the loss side of the equation, after losing $100, many people will accept a gamble that entails losing significantly more than $100 in an effort to recoup the $100 loss. This represents both the element of risk-seeking in the domain of losses and the break-even effect. Faced with the realization of a certain loss, many people seek additional risk in an effort to recoup their investment, contrary to the conventional economic notion that sunk costs are sunk costs. This approach offers an explanation for why investors have difficulty realizing losses on their investments (a strong desire to avoid loss realization and break even). It also might help explain why they sometimes increase risk taking in risk equity markets (existing gains appear to be locked in and are house money, which can be gambled) and in falling markets (existing losses appear temporary, and extra risk-taking will help recoup those losses).

Overconfidence Abounds

In the domain of gains, one of the important findings of psychology and behavioral economics is that people often forecast their futures with overconfidence and excessive optimism. Such overconfidence may be partly because of an inability to understand accurately the role of random chance in determining the future. Most plan participants are notoriously poor statisticians, and they find patterns and trends in data that could just as easily be explained by random chance.

Individuals appear to significantly underestimate the impact of random chance on their lives and, in hindsight, overemphasize the degree of control they have over outcomes. Lack of objectivity might help explain self-evaluations: Individuals generally perceive themselves as better than others and have better views of themselves than others do. There is also a gender element at work, as men tend to be more overconfident than women.

Overconfidence leads to investing behaviors that are less than optimal most of the time. For instance, overconfidence helps explain the high levels of trading activity in equity markets. One study calculated that trading is typically hazardous to one's wealth, with active traders earning 11.4% over a five-year period, while the market returned 17.9%, and low-turnover accounts, 18.5%. That study also reported that men trade 77% (versus 53% for women) and that men earn lower rates of return because of their trading. For more information on brokerage accounts, see chapter 14.

Loss Aversion

If overconfidence helps explain behavior on the upside of the prospect theory ledger, then the downside is dominated by aversion to loss realization. This plays out in interesting ways. For instance, as noted above, people are inclined to take a gamble if confronted with the choice of realizing an incurred loss versus taking the gamble in which they might break even or lose more. Particularly if there is a reasonable prospect of breaking even and avoiding a loss, many people take the gamble and risk losing even more money.

In the investment setting, plan participants who invest in stocks appear to rush to realize gains too quickly: they try to lock in or make certain the gains that they have already realized. However, they also appear to have trouble cutting their losses, that is, they hold on to loss-making stocks too long in the hope of recovering the investment.

The effect on brokerage account investors is not small. One study found that investors who sold winning stocks saw those stocks outperform the market by 2% in the subsequent year, and investors who kept their losing stocks saw those stocks underperform the market by 1% over the same period.

The net impact of selling winners too quickly while holding losers cost investors 3% per year in terms of portfolio returns. These results also validate the notion of overconfidence in investment decisions: people continued to hold and sell the wrong stocks, leading to lower returns, despite actual results.

Estimating Retirement Risks

The last phase of financial decision-making for retirement happens during the retirement, or spending, period. This is likely to occur during later middle age and beyond, and it is the period when most people decide how they will spend down their accumulated assets. Of course, if there were no uncertainty, the rational life-cycle investor would plan to spend down retirement assets to ensure optimal retirement consumption and protect bequest motives.

In practice, of course, people confront many sources of risk during the retirement period. The most important of these concern longevity, inflation, health (leading to unexpected expenses and costs), and the capital market. All or a combination of these risks can contribute to experiencing consumption shortfalls during retirement—or simply running out of money. Again, this is why plan sponsors who run defined benefit plans must hire many specialists to calculate these multiple risks.

So many fundamental uncertainties, further complicated by the psychological considerations discussed above, combine to make it quite difficult for retirees to deftly manage the drawdown process for retirement accounts in old age. In this section, accordingly, we first summarize available evidence on how people deal with longevity risk, then turn to a discussion of inflation risk, and finally, conclude with a brief discussion of how to manage capital market risk during the withdrawal period.

Longevity Risk. Because people do not know precisely how long they will live, they run the risk of exhausting their assets before dying. Such risk exposure can be reduced by consuming less per year during retirement, but of course, this simply elevates the chances that a retiree might die with "too much" wealth left.

One way to offset longevity risk is to buy an annuity with all or part of one's retirement assets. Single-premium lifelong annuities are relatively appealing, because they continue to pay benefits as long as the retiree lives, irrespective of whether the retiree outlives the life tables. Some studies have found that retirees holding annuities are more satisfied with their retirements, holding other things constant. Consequently, the implication is that holding at least some annuities may provide the peace of mind associated with longevity protection.

Notwithstanding the substantial theoretical appeal of annuities, however, relatively little retirement money is today devoted to the purchase of annuities. For instance, life annuity purchases in the United States amounted to more than $120 billion in 1999, but the majority of sales were for variable annuities, which are used mainly in the accumulation process, rather than for decumulation products that pay lifetime benefits. One large life-insurance company reported that virtually none of its annuity holders annuitized (taking lifetime income) their contracts.

In terms of national policy, there is growing attention to this issue. Previously, defined benefit plans normally paid either single or joint and survivor life annuities as a matter of course, and rarely was any sort of lump sum option available in lieu of the lifetime benefit stream. In recent years, many plans have begun offering lump sum distributions to their retirees. As a result, workers reaching retirement age with pension coverage are increasingly unlikely to take their benefits as lifetime annuities. A recent study found that 75% of company pension distributions are now paid as lump sum cash-outs rather than as lifetime annuity payments. In this sense, fewer and fewer retirement plans are providing longevity insurance in the form of lifetime insured annuity benefits.

Several explanations for the declining demand for annuities in retirement have been offered. One factor is that people may be poorly informed regarding their remaining life expectancies, tending to underestimate the risk of outliving one's income. For instance, a recent industry survey reported that only one-third of the respondents knew that someone who attained the age of sixty-five had a substantial chance of living beyond his life expectancy. Other surveys have reported that the expected survival patterns of retirees track actuarial tables relatively closely, and retirement asset shortfalls are uncorrelated to people expecting to die soon in retirement. Another factor discouraging annuity purchase is that retirees often have strong bequest motives, and many retirees expect to have to pay for long-term care. In such cases, they might elect to hold on to their funds rather than holding them as annuities on retirement.

Several other explanations may provide insights into why annuity purchases are low despite the fact that baby boomers are moving into retirement age. First is an interest-rate factor. The decision to purchase annuities at a given point in time represents an irreversible decision to lock in then-current yields (which underlie the contract pricing). However, the interest rate effect is less a factor on payment size as age increases. This is because the mortality factor becomes greater with increasing age and can dominate the assumed interest rate.

Below is shown how much annual income plan participants would receive if they invested $100,000 in an immediate fixed annuity from a well-known national life-insurance company:

Age at Purchase	Male	Female
65	$7,740	$7,296
70	$8,712	$8,148
75	$10,068	$9,396
80	$11,964	$11,292
85	$14,688	$14,172

A second reason that annuity purchases are low is the cost factor: retirees sometimes see insured products as uncompetitive with pure investments due to the loads levied by the insurance providers. Yet the loads have decreased substantially over time, and evidence indicates that retirees can expect high money's worth for annuity products from many companies. Consequently the respectable returns, combined with the insurance protection, should induce more interest in this payout structure as the baby boomer generation moves into the retirement years.

The other main reason that lump sums are attractive is that regulations now permit workers to take a relatively large lump sum computed with a transitorily depressed discount rate, and in many cases, this is more economically profitable than leaving the funds in the plan to grow.

Behavioral factors, especially loss aversion, may also explain the low demand for annuities in retirement. Some retirees may worry about potential losses to heirs if they die "early," as the holding of annuities typically eliminates the possibility of bequeathing these funds. Adding to the problem is that retirees may heavily discount future benefit coverage in the event that they live a long time in retirement. Such a valuation could enhance the probability of retirees' taking their pension accruals as a lump sum rather than buying life annuities and may explain why some argue that locking up one's assets in annuities boosts, rather than reduces, risk. In many cases, the best solution will be a combination of a fixed annuity and a managed portfolio. Employers wishing to help workers with their self-control problem might offer annuities as the default option at retirement, rather than making the lump sum the standard choice.

Nonetheless, it appears that many people fundamentally undervalue the appeal of a lifetime annuity—sometimes at substantial, if not overwhelming, cost. One example was a study of behavior with regard to annuities for personnel at the U.S. Department of Defense (DOD). In 1992, about 65,000 officers and enlisted personnel were involved in a program to reduce staffing at the DOD. They were offered payments from their retirement plan in the form of an annuity or a lump sum. The internal rate of return on the annuity ranged from 17.5% to 19.8% at a time when government bond rates were around 7%. Economists estimated that all of the officers and half of the enlisted personnel would take the annuity. In the end, contrary to expectations, 52% of the officers and 92% of the enlisted personnel took the lump sum. In total, the DOD employees forfeited a total of $1.7 billion in economic value by electing the lump sum over the annuity.

The risk of inflation and capital market risk is substantial during the retirement period. It is somewhat well known that the common worker is rather poorly informed about volatility in asset returns and inflation rates. For instance, from the late 1970s to the late 1990s, the United States had a relatively low rate of inflation and rising stock prices that contributed to a widespread belief that equities serve as a good hedge for inflation. But this is not accurate. During the 1970s, inflation moved into double digits, yet stock prices fell by over half in a short two-year jolt (1974-5).

The fact that workers take lump sums from their pensions rather than have their funds continue to be managed by the pension fund itself may also be of concern for several other reasons. One possible explanation is overconfidence: many people believe that they can live well on relatively small asset pools during retirement, yet after leaving work, they then find they run out of money, sometimes within a few months of retirement. This is exacerbated by the lump sum benefit, which is often "framed" in a way that induces them to overvalue the lump sum and to undervalue the annuity. Offering a retiree a lump sum of $100,000 while offering a joint and survivor annuity of $600 per month for life tends to highlight the "massive sum" as opposed to the longevity protection. Finally, many retirees are poorly equipped to manage their investments in old age, perhaps because they never were particularly financially literate or because they suffer diminished faculties due to poor health. Remember that most young people have problems with the calculations as well.

Plan Design Issues and Solutions

Behavioral research challenges the notion that workers are rational, autonomous, precise calculators who exercise independent and unbiased judgment when it comes to their workplace retirement plans. The evidence suggests that people do strive to maximize their self-interest, but for a variety of reasons outlined here, they often fail to act in accordance with the expectations of rational economic and financial theory, in both the accumulation and decumulation phases.

Some people have self-control problems when it comes to saving; such individuals could benefit from commitment devices. Others simply undervalue the future and overvalue the present; such people could benefit from automatic savings programs. Still others might be unduly influenced by defaults and inertia: as a result, their attitudes and actions diverge—they want to save more for retirement, but they do not. Also, some individuals do not appear to evaluate their investment portfolios in rational terms, and past performance and risk errors cloud their judgment. They are overconfident about the future and have trouble cutting their losses. Some trade too much, think too small in terms of gains and losses, and take lump sums when, in fact, all of these behaviors increase, rather than reduce, risk.

Behavioral finance and economics also challenge the notion that pension plan design is a neutral vehicle within which participants make their own choices independently. Because of default, framing, and inertia effects, the design of a retirement system or plan profoundly affects participant investment and saving decisions. Sponsors and policymakers can alter behavior in fundamental ways by choosing different default structures. In particular, the design decisions to set up automatic enrollment, automatic saving, or default investment programs, which makes some saving and investment decisions automatic, are particularly critical.

Using traditional policy and plan design language, defined contribution plans are "employee directed," with employees seen as the active agents, while the employer is thought to play a minimal decision-making role. In some sense, this is a libertarian decision-making model, where independent agents can act to maximize their personal welfare within the constraints of the system.

But behavioral research demonstrates a far different picture of many workers. These are people with weak or uncertain preferences about such basic questions as how much to save or how much risk to take. Plan design decisions then emit powerful signals about "appropriate" employee behavior, and employer/policymaker design specifications trump independent decision-making. The paternalistic elements of retirement plan design play a powerful role in shaping the choices offered.

The standard approach taken in most contemporary defined contribution plans may be counterproductive to encouraging retirement saving. Generally, participants are told that (1) saving for retirement is optional (as joining the plan is discretionary), (2) the need to increase saving over time is optional (it requires a voluntary election by the worker), and (3) investing for retirement should focus on principal stability rather than taking on risk or balancing the portfolio (as the default fund in most retirement savings plans is a conservative fixed-income option).

It is interesting that employers and policymakers rely on a model of voluntary choice by the worker in retirement saving plans, although they do not do so in other components of workplace benefits programs. No health care plan is run like a 401(k) plan, which the workers must run themselves without professional help. In a sense, the 401(k) plan today is equivalent to telling workers, "Here is a scalpel and bottle of pills. Now you figure out your health care plan yourselves."

The growth of participant-directed defined contribution plans has been followed by an expansion in the provision of workplace education. Much of the educational effort has been motivated by nondiscrimination testing—employers have an incentive to encourage plan use among lower-paid employees and to allow highly paid employees greater ability to contribute to the plan. Other motivations have been employers' desires to promote a popular saving benefit and to minimize fiduciary liability for participant investment decisions.

The current educational model tends to emphasize communication and education activities, both of which are aimed at producing behavioral change (e.g., joining the plan, boosting saving, investing more effectively). Yet the behavioral literature suggests that for many workers, this model is limited in its applicability. There is the problem of inertia, which we have described as the divergence between desire and effective action. There is also the notion that only part of the workforce is motivated to learn about personal finances or interested in using financial education. Contemporary education practices assume that most workers are rational agents and planners, but the published studies strongly suggest that large numbers of workers simply are not.

The desired behavior must be brought to fruition with or without education. Mechanisms must be found, whether through plan defaults or delegation to a third party, where workers begin practicing the right behaviors at the outset. Education then can play an ancillary role, explaining the rationale for the defaults and alternative courses of future action.

In effect, behavioral economics suggests a reversal in the causality of education, a shift from education's driving behavioral change to initial behavioral change preceding education. These broad themes—imperfect investors and savers, the critical role of system design, a new model for education—suggest that a number of policy and plan design choices deserve prominent attention.

The Default Contribution Setup Is Critical

One way to exploit the findings of this rich new behavioral literature would be to alter the nature of default decision-making in participant-directed retirement plans. Inertia, procrastination, and lack of decision-making willpower can be exploited to encourage more retirement saving. An "auto-pilot" 401(k) is one possibility. Others are automatic enrollment of all eligible employees, scheduled annual savings increases through the Thaler and Benartzi SMarT program, and a selection of default investment choices that represent optimal portfolio choices, such as a series of age-based model portfolios.

In this way, the passive decision-maker may rely on system design to reach a near-optimal retirement outcome. Workers will still retain the right to opt out of this arrangement, allowing for freedom of choice, but the system design will direct workers toward desirable saving and investment behaviors.

Just as employees are easily influenced by their employers' plan-design decisions, so employers are influenced by implicit and explicit policymaker directions. Clear-cut regulatory guidance now exists only for automatic enrollment components; to generalize this success, some type of regulatory or statutory endorsement for automatic saving and age-based investment choices would be required. A further consideration, of course, is whether the auto-pilot 401(k) model would be an alternative to existing nondiscrimination testing requirements. From a policy perspective, nondiscrimination testing rules were introduced to ensure that low-paid workers take sufficient advantage of tax-deferred retirement savings plans and that the tax benefits of such plans did not accrue solely to the highly paid. An auto-pilot 401(k), perhaps with some standardized eligibility and matching contributions (as in today's safe-harbor design), might be the optimal plan design.

The Investment Menu Must Be Simplified

One of the more practical conclusions from behavioral finance is that investment menu design must be closely scrutinized. As an example, choice overload and complex investment menus may discourage plan participation. But it is also clear that even simple pension-design decisions, such as the composition of equity versus fixed-income funds, can also strongly influence participant investment behavior. We explore this further in the chapter on model portfolios.

Certainly, one implication from the research is that many participants lack the skills needed to make complex investment choices among many options. There is little evidence that participants are constructing the optimal portfolios that employers use to justify the inclusion of different investment classes, styles, and managers. Instead participants use informal shortcuts, especially recent past performance, to make choices.

As a result, the research suggests that the laundry-list approach to investment options—where workers are given fifty or one hundred choices of funds—will be confusing and overwhelming for many. Plan sponsors might experiment with tiered investment choices, where communication resources are devoted to educating participants about a limited menu of core options, and additional choices for sophisticated investors could be segregated from the core menu.

More broadly, both employers and policymakers need to rethink the trend toward expanding the myriad and complex active saving decisions presented to workers. Behavioral research suggests that there are natural, inevitable limits to a policy of ever-increasing choices and decisions. Because the evidence suggests that many workers already struggle with the basic decisions to save, invest, and spend during retirement, it seems likely that new and more complex options will further challenge already burdened decision-makers.

Company Stock Risk Management

Congress and employers have attempted to address the risks of holding excessive company stock through education and educational/disclosure activities, yet the behavioral evidence suggests that this strategy will have limited effect.

One problem is inertia; reducing concentrated stock positions requires taking a disciplined approach to selling stock holdings, but few participants tend to follow such a self-motivated, disciplined approach to managing their saving due to inertia and procrastination. Other problem is risk perception and the influence of past returns with company stock.

Employees significantly underestimate the risks of their own company's stock, and they are also unduly and erroneously influenced by past stock performance. The findings regarding overconfidence and aversion to realizing losses may also come into play with company stock. Many workers have too rosy a view of their company's future and have trouble selling their company stock at a loss. Thus it is unlikely that providing additional information will quickly alter these attitudes and produce changes in investment portfolios.

As in the auto-pilot 401(k) case, one policy option would be to provide employees with an optional statutory mechanism that automatically reduces their exposure to company stock to a given percentage that declines with age (e.g., 20% or 10% of assets by age sixty-five. For example, a plan might offer a provision that drew down the participant's position steadily each quarter over some prescribed period, say three or five years. In other words, participants may need a precommitment device that works automatically for them as they near retirement.

Help Must Continue at Retirement

Current policy has permitted the conversion of pensions from plans that pay life annuities into programs that give workers a choice to receive their lifelong savings in a lump sum at retirement. Behavioral research suggests that decisions about annuity versus lump sum payments at retirement could be better framed, taking into account participants' understanding of mortality and investment risks.

One question has to do with what should be the default choice. In defined benefit plans, the default has traditionally been an annuity, though more plans are now offering lump-sum options. In defined contribution plans, the default is generally a lump sum, with no annuity option.

An alternative approach might be to frame the default as some mixture of annuity and lump sum rather than as an either-or decision. Of course, it would be essential to ensure that the two options are compared on an apples-to-apples basis to avoid framing bias. To better preserve the longevity protection that pensions once offered, policymakers may find it sensible to make the holding of annuities the default and to make loans against the pension accruals more difficult to obtain. In other cases, the optimal solution may be a combination of both annuities for a portion of the account and a managed portfolio of the remaining assets.

For Further Reading

Agnew, J., Pierluigi B., and Sundén A. "Portfolio Choice and Trading in a Large 401(k) Plan." *American Economic Review* 93, no. 1, 193–215. (2003).

Aizcorbe, A., Kennickell, A, and Moore, K. "Recent Changes in U.S. Family Finances: Evidence from the 1998 and 2001 Survey of Consumer Finances." Federal Reserve Bulletin, 1–32, (January 2003).

Ameriks, J., Caplin, A., and Leahy, J. "Wealth Accumulation and the Propensity to Plan." *Quarterly Journal of Economics*, 1007–1047, (May 2002).

Arkes, H., Dawson, N., Speroff, T., Harrell, F, et al. "The Covariance Decomposition of the Probability Score and Its Use in Evaluating Prognostic Estimates." *Medical Decision Making* 15, no. 2, 120–131. (2003).

Baber, B. and Odean, T. "Trading Is Hazardous to Your Wealth: The Common Stock Investment Performance of Individual Investors." *Journal of Finance* 55, no. 2, 773–806, (2000).

Banks, B., and Tanner, S. "Is There a Retirement-Savings Puzzle?" *American Economic Review* 88, no. 4, 769–788, (1998).

Barber, B. and Odean, T. "Boys Will Be Boys: Overconfidence and Common Stock Investment." *Quarterly Journal of Economics* no. 4, 261–292. (February 2001).

Barberis, N. "Mental Accounting, Loss Aversion, and Individual Stock Returns." *Journal of Finance* 56, no. 4: 1247–1292.(1999).

Barberis, N., and Thaler, R. "A Survey of Behavioral Finance." NBER Working Paper, 9222, (2002).

Benartzi, S. "Excessive Extrapolation and the Allocation of 401(k) Accounts to Company Stock." *Journal of Finance* 56, no. 5, 1747–1764. (2002).

Benartzi, S., and Thaler, R. "Naive Diversification Strategies in Retirement Saving Plans." *American Economic Review* 91, no. 1, 79–98 (1997).

Benartzi, S., and Thaler, R. "How Much Is Investor Autonomy Worth?" *Journal of Finance* 57, no. 4, 1593–1616 (1999).

Benartzi, S., and Thaler, R. "Save More Tomorrow." *Journal of Political Economy* (2003).

Bernheim, B., Skinner, J., and Weinberg, S. "What Accounts for the Variation in Retirement Wealth among U.S. Households?" *American Economic Review* 91, no. 4, 832–857 (2001).

Bodie, Z. "On the Risk of Stocks in the Long Run." *Financial Analysts Journal* 51, no. 3, 18–22 (2000).

Bodie, Z., Hammond, B., and Mitchell, O. "A Framework for Analyzing and Managing Retirement Risks." In *Innovations in Financing Retirement*, edited by Zvi Bodie, Brett Hammond, Olivia S. Mitchell, and Stephen Zeldes, 3–19. Philadelphia: University of Pennsylvania Press, (2003).

Brown, J., Mitchell, O., and Poterba, J. "The Role of Real Annuities and Indexed Bonds in an Individual Accounts Retirement Program." In *Risk Aspects of Investment-Based Social Security Reform*, edited by John Y.

Campbell, and Martin Feldstein, 321-360. Chicago: University of Chicago Press, (2003).

Brown, J., Mitchell O., and Poterba, J. "Mortality Risk, Inflation Risk, and Annuity Products." In *Innovations in Financing Retirement*, 175-197.(2002).

Campbell, J. and Viceira, L. "Strategic Asset Allocation: Portfolio Choice for Long-term Investors." Oxford: Oxford University Press, (2002).

Choi, J., Laibson, D., Madrian, B., and Metric, A. "Defined Contribution Pensions: Plan Rules, Participant Decisions, and the Path of Least Resistance." NBER Working Paper 8655, (2001).

Choi, J., Laibson, D., Madrian, B., and Metrick, A. "For Better or for Worse: Default Effects and 401(k) Savings Behavior." NBER Working Paper 8651, (2001).

Choi, J., Laibson, D., Madrian, B., and Metrick, A. "Passive Decisions and Potent Defaults." NBER Working Paper 9917, (2003).

Frederick, S., Loewenstein, G., and O'Donoghue, T. "Time Discounting and Time Preference: A Critical Review." *Journal of Economic Literature* 40, no. 2, 351–401 (2002).

Goetzmann, W., and Kumar, A. "Equity Portfolio Diversification." NBER Working Paper 8686, (2001).

Laibson, D. "Golden Eggs and Hyperbolic Discounting." *Quarterly Journal of Economics* 112, no. 2, 443–478, (1997).

Laibson, D., Repetto, A., and Tobacman, J. "Self-Control and Saving for Retirement." Brookings Papers on Economic Activity I, 91–196, (1998).

Madrian, B., and Shea, F. "The Power of Suggestion: Inertia in 401(k) Participation and Savings Behavior." *Quarterly Journal of Economics* 116, no. 4, 1149–1187, (2001).

"The MetLife Retirement Income IQ Test: Findings from the 2003 National Survey of American Pre-Retirees." New York: Metlife Mature Market Institute, (2003).

Mitchell, O., and Utkus, S. "Lessons from Behavioral Finance for Retirement Plan Design." Pension Research Council Working Paper, Wharton School, (2003).

Mitchell, O., Poterba, J., Warshawsky, M., and Brown, J. "New Evidence on the Money's Worth of Individual Annuities." *American Economic Review* no. 3, 1299–1318, (2002).

Moore, J., and Muller, L. "An Analysis of Lump-Sum Pension Distribution Recipients." *Monthly Labor Review,* no.5, 29–46, (May 2002).

Shefrin, H., and Statman, M. "The Disposition to Sell Winners Too Early and Ride Losers Too Long: Theory and Evidence." *Journal of Finance* 40, no. 3, 777–790, (July 1985).

Thaler, R., and Benartzi, S. "Risk Aversion or Myopia? Choices in Repeated Gambles and Retirement Investments." *Management Science* 45, no. 3, 364–381, (1998).

Thaler, R., and Johnson, E. "Gambling with the House Money and Trying to Break Even: The Effects of Prior Outcomes on Risky Choices." *Management Science* 36, no. 6, 643–660, (1998).

Thaler, R. "The End of Behavioral Finance." Association for Investment Management and Research, 12–17, (November/December 1999).

Thaler, R. "An Economic Theory of Self-Control." *Journal of Political Economy* 89, 392–406, (2001).

Warner, J., and Pleeter, S. "The Personal Discount Rate: Evidence from Military Downsizing Programs." *American Economic Review* 91, no. 1, 33–53, (1994).

Worden, D., and Schooley, D. "Generation X: Understanding Their Risk Tolerance and Investment Behavior." *Journal of Financial Planning* 58–63, (September 2003).

"It Pays to Delay: The Longer You Wait to Buy an Annuity, the More You Get" *Wall Street Journal*, (September 3, 2003).

Chapter 5

Plan Design Methods That Increase Savings

Chapter Summary

The growth of 401(k)-type savings plans and the associated decline of defined benefit plans has generated new concerns about the adequacy of employee savings. An adequate savings rate plays a crucial role in retirement success. Unfortunately, published data are overwhelmingly clear that the average plan participant is failing to save enough money. Most published data reveal the importance of passive decision-making for most plan participants. For better or for worse, many households appear to passively accept the status quo.

Financial education programs can teach many employees that they must save more. But most educated employees fail to follow through with their needed plans of action on their own.

Most employers are unaware as to how much they can influence employees' outcomes through their plan designs and default pathways. The following programs take advantage of passive employee behavior and improve the savings rate by using default success pathways:

- Automatic enrollment
- Automatic annual deferral rate increases
- Automatic calculation of success probability and required saving rates
- Shorter eligibility periods
- Default investment selection

Increasing the Plan Saving Rate Is Necessary for Success

Adequate savings (see Chart 5-1 below) is one of the Three A's essential for a successful retirement. Earlier we described the actuarial and funding-assessment-specialist areas of expertise (see Chart 5-2 on the next page) that participants need to master in order to manage their personal retirement programs. An adequate saving rate plays a crucial role in retirement success. Unfortunately, the published data are overwhelmingly clear that the average plan participant is failing to save enough money. As an example, the Profit Sharing Council of America reported that in 2002, the average 401(k) plan participant (meaning those who actually signed up for the plan) deferred only 5.2% of pay and received a company contribution of 2.8%, for a total of 8.0%. Chart 5-3 demonstrates that even young (thirty-to-forty-year-old) employees need to be saving larger amounts. We will focus in this chapter on proven methods that increase savings, despite the participant behavior that normally diminishes success.

Chart 5-1: Adequate Savings Is One of the "Three A's" for Retirement Success

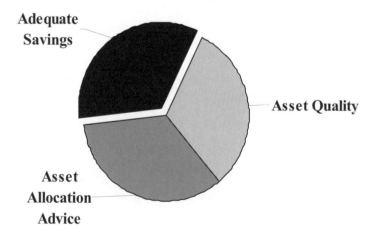

Chart 5-2: Areas of Expertise That Defined Contribution Plan Participants Must Master Include Savings Adequacy Assessment

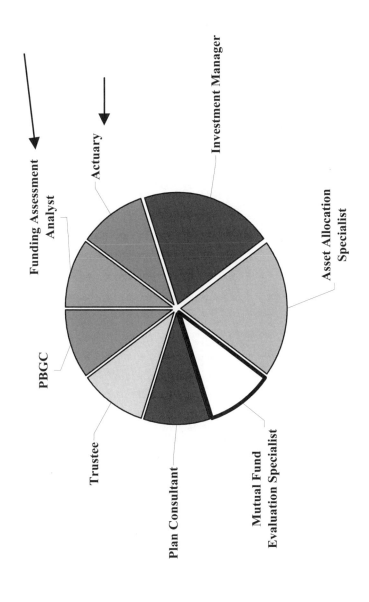

Chart 5-3: Comparison of Various Savings Rates Needed to Produce a 75% Probability of Success at Retirement Age for a 30- or 40-Year-Old Worker (3% Real Return)

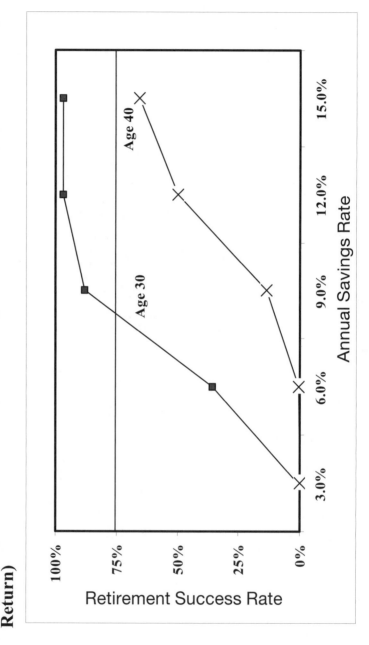

Financial planners usually suggest that households should aim to replace between 65% and 85% of preretirement income in retirement in order to maintain preretirement living standards. Some households can achieve replacement rates that are in the recommended range through Social Security and pension income alone. Others can reach these replacement rates with the addition of income from part-time work during retirement, housing equity, and inheritances. But most households are not saving enough of their personal (take-home) income for retirement and will need to increase their savings rates, especially inside their tax-deferred retirement plans.

The growth of 401(k)-type savings plans and the associated decline of defined benefit plans have generated new concerns about the adequacy of employee saving. Defined contribution pension plans place the burden of ensuring adequate retirement saving squarely on the backs of individual employees. However, employers make many decisions about the design of 401(k) plans that can greatly help or hurt their employees' retirement saving activity. Although the government places some limits on how companies can structure their 401(k) plans, employers nonetheless have broad discretion in the design of their 401(k) plans. Most employers are unaware as to how much they can influence employees' outcomes through their plan designs and default pathways.

Recent studies have demonstrated that more than two-thirds of employees believe that they are saving too little. In addition, nearly one-third of these self-reported low-savers intended to raise their savings rate in the two months following their counseling sessions. By matching survey responses to administrative records, researchers found that employees who reported that they save too little actually did have low 401(k) saving rates. In general, the employees were saving about half as much as they needed. However, almost none of the employees who reported their intention to raise their saving rate over the next two months had done so when their account was reviewed at a later date. Thus, employee awareness seldom is translated into appropriate action.

Employees Tend to Go with the Flow

Thus, plan participants overwhelmingly do not follow through on their good intentions. To summarize, out of every one hundred participants, sixty-eight report that their saving rates are too low, and half planned to increase their 401(k) contribution rates in the next few months, but only three did. Hence, even though most employees described themselves as undersavers and many reported that they planned to fix their situation in the next few months, few followed through on the plan. These data are consistent with the idea that employees have a hard time carrying out the actions that they themselves say they wish to take.

Behavioral finance studies have demonstrated that employees are likely to do whatever requires the least current effort: employees most often follow the path of least resistance. Almost always, the easiest thing to do is nothing (inertia), a phenomenon that researchers call a "passive decision." Passive decision-making means that employers have a great deal of influence over the savings outcomes of their employees. Careful consideration should be given to employer choices of default saving rates and default investment funds, because the defaults strongly influence employee saving levels. Even though employees have the opportunity to opt out of such defaults, few do so.

Passive decision-making partially explains the powerful influence of defaults, the anchoring effects of the match threshold, the remarkable success of automatic schedules of slowly increasing contribution rates, and the effects of mutual-fund menus on asset allocation decisions. Employers must implement most of these features for their 401(k) plans to produce a high probability of success for most participants. Employers and policy-makers need to recognize that there is no such thing as a neutral menu of options for a 401(k) plan. Framing effects will influence employee choices, and passive employee decision-making implies that the default options will usually be the outcome.

Automatic Enrollment

Employers and policy makers should be concerned about the low rate of retirement success for most participants. One area of preventable failure is the mistake of not signing up for the plan. The typical 401(k) plan requires an active election on the part of employees to initiate participation. A growing number of companies, however, have started automatically enrolling employees into 401(k) plans unless employees actively opt out of 401(k) participation. While automatic enrollment is still relatively uncommon, several recent surveys indicate that its adoption has increased to around 10–14% of companies, up from only 5–9% in 1999.

The original interest of many companies in automatic enrollment stemmed from their persistent failure to pass the IRS nondiscrimination rules that apply to pension plan provision. As a result of failing these tests, many companies have either had to make excess 401(k) contribution refunds to highly compensated employees or retroactive company contributions on behalf of employees who are not highly compensated to be in compliance. In addition, many companies have tried to reduce the possibility of nondiscrimination testing problems by limiting the contributions that highly compensated employees can make. The hope of many companies adopting automatic enrollment has been that participation among employees at the firm who are not highly compensated will increase sufficiently that nondiscrimination testing is no longer a concern.

A growing body of evidence suggests that automatic enrollment—a simple change from a default of nonparticipation to a default of participation—substantially increases 401(k) participation rates. Although some companies have been concerned about the potential legal repercussions of automatically enrolling employees in 401(k) plans, the U.S. Treasury Department has issued several opinions that support employer use of automatic enrollment.

In its first opinion on this subject (Revenue Ruling 98-30), issued in 1998, the Treasury Department sanctioned the use of automatic enrollment for newly hired employees. A second ruling, issued in 2000 (Revenue Ruling 2000-8), also approved the use of automatic enrollment for previously hired employees not yet participating in their employers' 401(k) plans. For a detailed review of these and other important rulings, please see the Appendix.

A growing body of published studies demonstrates that automatic enrollment substantially increases 401(k) participation rates. Listed below in Table 5-1 are the improvements in plan participation that have been reported by James Choi and David Laibson from employers who have adopted automatic enrollment programs.

Table 5-1: Plan Participation before and after Adoption of an Automatic Enrollment Program

Tenure	Before Auto Enroll	After Auto Enroll	Difference
6 Months	26.4%	93.4%	67.0%
12 Months	37.8%	95.7%	57.9%
18 Months	47.7%	97.0%	49.3%
24 Months	54.1%	97.6%	43.5%
30 Months	60.0%	97.7%	37.7%
36 Months	64.7%	98.8%	34.1%

These data demonstrate that 401(k) participation for employees hired before automatic enrollment starts out low and increases over time with greater tenure. At six months of tenure, 401(k) participation rates are 26%, and rates increase to 54% at twenty-four months of tenure. The employee participation in the 401(k) plan for those employees hired under automatic enrollment is quite different. For these employees, the 401(k) participation rate starts out high and remains high. At six months of tenure, 401(k) participation is 93%, an increase of 67% relative to 401(k) participation rates before automatic enrollment.

Most companies that implement automatic enrollment do so only for newly hired employees; however, some companies have applied automatic enrollment to previously hired employees who have not yet initiated participation in the 401(k) plan. Studies show that for previously hired employees, automatic enrollment also substantially increases the 401(k) participation rate, although the increase in participation is slightly less than that seen for newly hired employees. While automatic enrollment increases 401(k) participation for virtually all demographic groups, its effects are largest for those individuals least likely to participate in the first place: younger employees, lower-paid employees, and blacks and Hispanics.

Employers may conclude that because 401(k) participation under automatic enrollment is so much higher than when employees must choose to initiate plan participation, automatic enrollment "coerces" employees into participating in the 401(k) plan. Perhaps they fear a backlash from employees, even though the program is designed to benefit employees.

But, if this were the case, one would expect to see participation rates under automatic enrollment decline with tenure as employees vetoed their "coerced" participation and opted out. In other words, the employees would vote with their feet. But remarkably few 401(k) participants in these studies, whether hired before automatic enrollment or hired after, reversed their participation status and opted out of the plan.

The percentage of 401(k) participants hired before automatic enrollment who dropped out in a twelve-month period ranged from 1.9% to 2.6%, while the percentage of participants subject to automatic enrollment who dropped out was only 0.3% to 0.6% higher. This evidence suggests that most employees do not object to saving for retirement. In the absence of automatic enrollment, however, many employees tend to delay taking action. Thus, automatic enrollment appears to be an effective tool for helping employees start saving for retirement.

Interestingly, while automatic enrollment is effective in getting employees to participate in their company-sponsored 401(k) plans, it is less effective at motivating them to make well-planned decisions about how much to save for retirement or how to invest their retirement savings. Because companies cannot ensure that employees will choose a contribution rate or an asset allocation before the automatic enrollment deadline, the company must establish a default contribution rate and a default asset allocation. Most employees follow the path of least resistance and passively accept these defaults. Often the default rate is set at 3%, which is too low for most participants to develop a reasonable success probability.

Before automatic enrollment, roughly two-thirds of plan participants studied contributed at or above the match threshold. Only about one in ten voluntarily chose the contribution rate specified by their employers as the default under automatic enrollment. In contrast, about half of participants hired under automatic enrollment contributed at the default rate, while only one-quarter contributed at or above the match threshold. Thus many plan participants were now participating in the plan, but at a substantially lower deferral rate than they needed for success

Automatic enrollment has similar effects on the asset allocations of plan participants. In most companies, the default fund under automatic enrollment is a stable value fund or a money market fund. For the group of participants hired under automatic enrollment, nearly two-thirds of their assets were invested in stable value or money-market funds, and only one-third of assets were invested in the stock market. Overall, the fraction of assets allocated to the stock market fell by about half when compared with the other participants in the plan, while the fraction of assets allocated to stable value funds or the money market was much higher. Over time, employees move away from the automatic enrollment defaults. Nonetheless, after three years, almost half of participants were stuck at the default rate and investment. In general, however, when viewed in terms of promoting overall saving for retirement, automatic enrollment as structured by most employers has a limited impact. Clearly, automatic enrollment is effective at promoting one important aspect of saving behavior, 401(k) participation. This simple change in the default from nonparticipation to participation has a tremendous improvement in plan participation.

Most employers that have adopted automatic enrollment have chosen low default contribution rates and conservative default funds. These default choices are inconsistent with the retirement savings goals of most employees. This evidence does not argue against automatic enrollment as a tool for promoting retirement saving; rather, it argues against the specific automatic enrollment defaults chosen by employers.

Employers who seek to facilitate the retirement saving of their employees need to respond to the tendency of employees to stick with the default. Employers should choose defaults that foster successful retirement saving when the defaults are passively accepted in their entirety. Automatic enrollment coupled with higher default contribution rates and more aggressive default funds (i.e., model portfolios) greatly increases wealth accumulation for retirement.

The impact of automatic enrollment is not just an illustration of framing questions. It is also part of a broader behavioral phenomenon, namely, the power of the default option and its influence on decision-making. When confronted with difficult decisions, individuals tend to adopt shortcuts that simplify the complex problems they face. One simple shortcut is to accept the available default option with the implicit assumption that it must be "reasonable" or it wouldn't be the default and just go with the flow.

Automatic Annual Saving-Rate Escalators

As described above, merely adding automatic enrollment to the plan will not produce the saving rate needed for a high probability of success, because too many employees stay at the low (usually 3%) default deferral rate. One 401(k) plan feature designed to capitalize on this inertia is the Save More Tomorrow (SMarT^{TM}) plan developed by Shlomo Benartzi and Richard Thaler.

Under this plan, participants commit in advance to saving portions of future raises. For example, suppose that a worker commits to allocate one-half of future nominal pay raises to increases in his 401(k) contribution rate. If a worker receives 3% raises in each of the following three years, his contribution rate would rise by 1.5% per year over this period. This plan is carefully constructed to make use of several themes in behavioral economics. By requiring a present commitment for future actions, the SMarT^{TM} plan alleviates problems of self-control and procrastination. In addition, by taking the additional savings out of future salary raises, participants in the SMarT^{TM} plan are not hurt by loss aversion, because workers will never see a reduction in their nominal (noninflation-adjusted) take-home pay.

Benartzi and Thaler reported fantastic results from the first experiment with the SMarT^{TM} plan. This first experiment was conducted at a midsize manufacturing company. This company, which did not match employee contributions, was experiencing problems in getting low-salary workers to participate and to contribute at high levels to the 401(k) plan. To overcome these problems, the company hired an investment consultant to meet with employees and help them plan their retirement savings. After initial interviews with each employee, the consultant gauged the employees' willingness to increase their saving rates. Employees judged to have a high willingness to save more would receive an immediate recommendation for a large increase in their saving rate; seventy-nine workers fell into this group. Employees judged to be reluctant to save more would be offered the option of enrolling in the SMarT™ plan; 207 workers fell into this group. The version of the SMarT™ plan that was implemented set up a schedule of annual contribution rate increases of three percentage points. This is a relatively aggressive implementation, as the annual nominal salary increases at this company were only slightly higher than 3%.

The results of the experiment show that the SMarT™ plan can have an enormous impact on contribution rates. Of the 207 participants offered the SMarT™ plan option, 162 (78%) chose to enroll. Furthermore, 129 of these 162 (80%) stayed with the plan through three consecutive pay raises. At the beginning of the SMarT™ plan, these 162 workers had an average contribution rate of 3.5%; by the time of their third pay raise, these workers, along with those who dropped out, had an average contribution rate of 11.6%. Keep in mind that the national average deferral rate is 5.2%. The SMarT™ plan worker went from barely half of the national average to more than double in just three years. These data are illustrated in Chart 5-4 below.

Chart 5-4: Improvement in Annual Deferral Rate from Automatic Savings Escalator Program

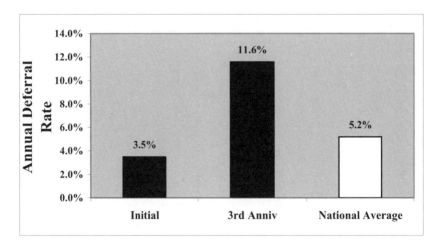

Despite the clear success of the SMarT™ plan in increasing deferral rates, there remain several important caveats. First, the Thaler SMarT™ plan was not guided by any well-specified model of what ideal savings should be. For this, we need to employ the SR-RR Index calculation we outlined in chapter 3. The reality is that to meet the long-term goal of participant success, there really are no "defined contribution" plans. Every 401(k) plan must be operated as a series of tiny defined benefit plans, one for each plan participant. This means that actuarial calculations, periodic review and assessment of adequate funding, ongoing mutual-fund evaluation, investment manager reviews, etc., must be provided to individual participants, as they cannot do it themselves.

Eliminate Automatic Cash-outs and Shorten Eligibility Periods

Shortening eligibility periods can make a modest improvement in saving rates. Many 401(k) plans have one-year eligibility waiting periods. The reasoning behind this rule is that short-term workers cannot sign up for the plan and hurt the discrimination testing. Automatic enrollment solves the problem of short-term workers who do not sign up for the plan, and a shorter eligibility period will bring employees into the plan faster.

Elimination of automatic cash-outs of amounts under $5,000 will also improve savings by keeping the money from being consumed by the employee. Of course, even in the case of an automatic cash distribution, the former employee has the option of rolling over the account balance into an IRA or the 401(k) plan of another employer, regardless of the size of the account balance. Research based upon national plan data suggests that the probability of receiving a cash distribution and rolling it over into an IRA or another 401(k) plan is low when the size of the distribution is small. Instead, these small distributions generally tend to be consumed. The terminated employee simply receives a check in the mail and spends it.

The Matching Contribution

A common feature of most 401(k) plans is some type of employer match. For each dollar contributed by the employee to the plan, the employer contributes a matching amount up to a certain threshold (e.g., 50% of the employee contribution up to 8% of compensation). Although the effects of employer matching on 401(k) participation and contribution rates have been widely studied, the conclusions from this research have been confusing.

The confusion stems in part from the inherent difficulties associated with identifying the effect of matching on 401(k) saving behavior. In theory, introducing an employer match should increase participation in the 401(k) plan. In practice, however, it is difficult to isolate this effect from the potential correlation between the saving preferences of employees and the employer match.

For example, companies that offer generous 401(k) matches may attract employees who like to save, biasing upward the estimated effect of an employer match on 401(k) participation. However, in general, most studies have reported a positive correlation between the availability of an employer match and increasing 401(k) participation. Studies report that increasing the match rate usually increases the deferral rate.

In general, most employees tend to cluster around the match rate when selecting their deferral rates. Interestingly, some studies have reported that too high of a match rate actually reduces employee deferrals. The explanation of this phenomenon is that employees see the company doing "most of the work" for them and feel little need to do anything extra. In most cases, the employees have not calculated what they need to save, so they are most likely wrong in their assessment of no further need for saving. An automatic savings-escalator program would probably solve this complacency problem.

Does Financial Education Really Help?

Recently there has been a move toward more education in the workplace. Recognizing that many employees are ill-equipped to make well-informed retirement saving decisions, particularly with respect to asset allocation, many employers have turned to providing various forms of financial education to help their employees meet the challenges of planning for an economically secure retirement.

These efforts, which vary widely across employers, include paycheck stuffers, newsletters, summary plan descriptions, seminars, and individual consultations with financial planners. Besides the colorful brochures and handouts, several groups now offer online financial education. In some cases, the education is supplemented with advice. For example, Unified Trust Company, N.A., offers saving rate calculations, outcome probability analysis, asset allocation models and investment advice through its online Unified Retirement Counselor[SM] system.

Numerous studies examining the effects of financial education on saving behavior have found that financial education positively affects what plan participants *say* they will do to improve their saving behavior. Unfortunately, a growing body of published data illustrate that despite the best intentions of employees, retirement saving is one area in which individuals excel at delay. Thus, such measures of intended behavior may dramatically overstate the actual effects of financial education, which is evident when the participant accounts are re-examined several months later.

Overall, financial education is important, but it does not appear to be a powerful mechanism for encouraging 401(k) retirement saving. Inertia and procrastination are just too powerful for most employees to overcome.

For Further Reading

Bayer, P., Bernheim, B., and Scholz, J. "The Effects of Financial Education in the Workplace: Evidence from a Survey of Employers," NBER Working Paper 5655, (1996).

Benartzi, S., and Thaler, R. "Naive Diversification Strategies in Retirement Saving Plans," *American Economic Review* 91, no. 1, 79–98. (2001).

Benartzi, S., and Thaler, R. "Save More Tomorrow." *Journal of Political Economy,* (2001).

Bernheim, B., Skinner, J., and Weinberg, S. "What Accounts for the Variation in Retirement Wealth among U.S. Households?" *American Economic Review* 91, no. 4, 832–857 (1997).

Bernheim, B. "Do Households Appreciate Their Financial Vulnerabilities? An Analysis of Actions, Perceptions, and Public Policy." In *Tax Policy for Economic Growth in the 1990s*, 1–30, Washington, D.C.: American Council for Capital Formation, (1995).

Bernheim, B. and Garret, D. "The Determinants and Consequences of Financial Education in the Workplace: Evidence from a Survey of Households," NBER Working Paper 5667, (1996).

Choi, J., Laibson, D., Madrian, B., and Metrick, A. "Defined Contribution Pensions: Plan Rules, Participant Decisions, and the Path of Least Resistance." NBER Working Paper 8655, (2001).

Choi, J., Laibson, D., Madrian, B., and Metrick, A. "For Better or for Worse: Default Effects and 401(k) Savings Behavior." NBER Working Paper 8651, (2001).

Laibson, D., Repetto, A., and Tobacman, J. "Self Control and Saving for Retirement." Brookings Papers on Economic Activity 1: 91–196, (1998).

Madrian, B., and Shea, D. "The Power of Suggestion: Inertia in 401(k) Participation and Savings Behavior." *Quarterly Journal of Economics* 116, no. 4: 1149–1187, (2001).

Mitchell, O., and Utkus, S. "Lessons from Behavioral Finance for Retirement Plan Design." Pension Research Council Working Paper, Wharton School, (2003).

Poterba, J., Venti, S. and Wise, D. "Lump Sum Distributions from Retirement Savings Plans: Receipt and Utilization." In *Inquiries in the Economics of Aging*, edited by David A. Wise, 85–105. University of Chicago Press, (1998).

Thaler, R. "The End of Behavioral Finance." Association for Investment Management and Research, pp 12–17, (November/December 1999).

Chapter 6

Risk Management from the Investor's Perspective

Chapter Summary

Investors worry about losses or failing to meet financial goals. They tend to think of risk in these concrete terms. They don't worry about expecting 7% and instead earning 14%. They worry that they may earn only 2% and fail to meet their goals. Traditionally, standard deviation was used to represent risk. It measures the variability of returns, not the possibility of a loss. Thus standard deviation measures uncertainty, not true risk. Recently, a new way to measure risk from the investor's perspective has been introduced. It is called downside risk, or by the name of its inventor, Frank Sortino of San Francisco's Pension Research Institute, the Sortino Ratio. Downside risk has the following advantages for the plan participant:

- Downside risk considers the investor's goal, while most traditional risk measures, such as beta, Sharpe Ratio or standard deviation, do not.

- Downside risk defines risk in accordance with an investor's perception of risk, i.e., failure to meet the goal. Standard deviation measures only the dispersion of returns around the average.

- Downside risk uses a statistical method of "bootstrapping" that gives the investor a view of many observations, rather than just a few, in order to understand what the true downside potential might be.

How Much Risk Do Plan Investments Really Entail?

Do you know how much risk your mutual fund really entails? Many plan sponsors and plan participants think they understand risk; however, risk can be a deceiving concept that varies from case to case. Differing risk-measurement techniques have confused most plan participants. To begin this discussion, we need to review some basic statistics and definitions.

Standard Deviation

The most widely accepted measure of investment risk is standard deviation. When used to gauge performance risk, it measures the degree to which returns have been spread out around their historical average. Most mutual fund reports carry some information about standard deviation, although most people reading it, and many writing about it, don't understand what it means.

Standard deviation is a statistical measurement of dispersion around an average, which, for an investment, depicts how widely the returns varied over a certain period.

Investors use the standard deviation of historical performance to try to predict the range of returns that is most likely for a given fund. When a fund has a high standard deviation, the predicted range of performance is wide, implying greater volatility.

For example, a portfolio return of 15% annually over ten years is generally good. But an investment style that returns 15% every year is more valuable than one that is up 100% one year and then down 75% another, even if it also averages 15% over a long period.

Most investors prefer a return that meets their financial goals and expectations with the least possible risk. They seek investments with the least variability of return, or annual difference from the expected return.

Investors look at returns to gauge the likelihood of future excess performance. Standard deviation measures how consistently that return was delivered. The more consistently a return occurred in the past, the more likely the investor will receive that return in the future.

The main problem with standard deviation is that it is not a measure of risk. Rather, it is a measure of uncertainty. As we will see a bit later in this chapter, investors think of risk and uncertainty differently. Any risk measure based upon standard deviation is flawed. Investors worry about not meeting their goals, not about higher-than-expected returns (uncertainty).

Normal Distribution

The normal distribution (the "bell-shaped curve," which is symmetrical about the mean) is a theoretical function commonly used in statistics as an approximation to sampling distributions. In general, the normal distribution provides a good model for a random variable when (1) there is a strong tendency for the variable to take a central value, (2) positive and negative deviations from this central value are equally likely, and (3) the frequency of deviations falls off rapidly as the deviations become larger.

For an example of a normal distribution, look at Chart 6-1. Assume that we have a mutual fund that has averaged 9% over its life span. This is the mean return. The standard deviation is 21%. One standard deviation on each side of the mean is roughly two-thirds of all returns. Two standard deviations on each side are about 95% of all returns, and three standard deviations on each side are more than 99% of all returns. The average value seldom occurs. What we can tell the investor is that returns will fall somewhere between various bands. Standard deviation describes the width of the bands.

Chart 6-1: Normal Distribution Curve

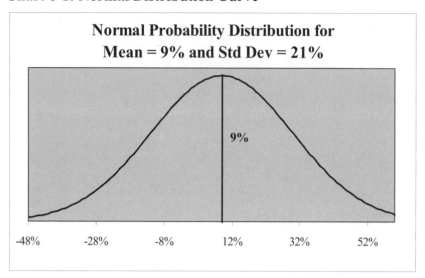

Much to the investor's surprise, the average value seldom occurs. As illustrated in Chart 6-2, what we can tell the investor is that 95% of all returns will be somewhere between –33% and +51%.

Chart 6-2: 95% of All Values

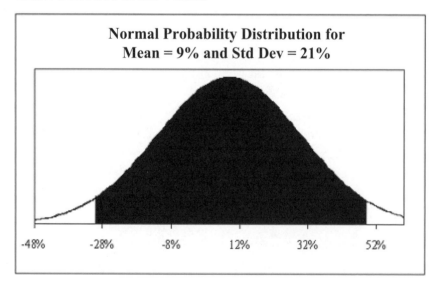

Unfortunately for investors, the normal distribution does not represent what stock and bond returns actually look like. In other words, stock and bond returns are skewed. Equally frustrating for our investor is that standard deviation does not describe risk the way the investor thinks about it.

Chart 6-3: Skewed Distribution

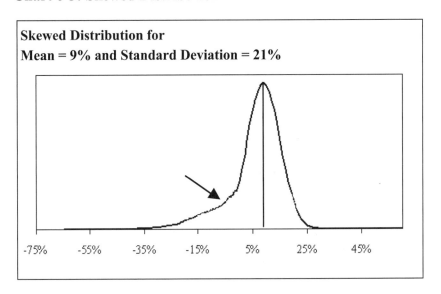

Skewed Distribution for
Mean = 9% and Standard Deviation = 21%

"Skewness" measures the asymmetry of a distribution. In other words, the historical pattern of returns does not resemble a normal (i.e., bell-curve) distribution. Negative skewness occurs when the values to the left of (less than) the mean are fewer but farther from the mean than the values to the right. For example: the return series of –30%, 5%, 10%, and 15% has a mean of 0%. There is only one return less than 0% and three higher; but the negative return is much further from zero than the positive ones.

Chart 6-3 shows a distribution that is negatively skewed (i.e., where there are more returns below the median than above it). Performance was achieved with more risk than standard deviation suggests. Stock returns tend to be negatively skewed.

Behavioral finance studies have found that, in general, investors prefer assets with positive skewness. This is evidenced by their willingness to accept low or even negative expected returns when an asset exhibits positive skewness.

A classic example is the lottery ticket, where the odds of winning the jackpot are extremely low, but the few times it does occur, the winnings are extremely high. At the same time, investors generally avoid assets with negative skewness. High-risk asset classes (such as junk bonds or emerging markets) typically exhibit negative skewness, as do some investment vehicles, such as hedge funds.

Beta

This is another commonly misunderstood risk measurement. Beta does not measure risk. Beta is a measure of a fund's sensitivity to market movements. The beta of the market is 1.00 by definition. Generally, a stock fund is correlated to the S&P 500. If a fund has a beta of 1.50, it tends to move 1.5 times as much in either direction as the S&P 500. For example, if the S&P 500 were up 10%, the fund would be expected to be up 15%. It is a correlation indicator, not a risk indicator.

It is important to note that a low beta for a fund does not necessarily imply that the fund has a low level of volatility. A low beta signifies only that the fund's market-related correlation is low. A specialty fund that invests primarily in gold, for example, will usually have a low beta, as its performance is tied more closely to the price of gold and gold-mining stocks than to the overall stock market. Thus, the specialty fund might fluctuate wildly because of rapid changes in gold prices, but its beta will remain low. The R^2 general correlation to the overall stock market would be lower than most funds, but the volatility would still be high.

Alpha

Alpha is a measure of the difference between a fund's actual returns and its expected performance, given its level of risk as measured by beta. A positive alpha figure indicates that the fund has performed better than its beta would predict. In contrast, a negative alpha indicates the fund's underperformance, given the expectations established by the fund's beta. Alpha is a measure of excess return, not risk.

> **Alpha = Excess Return - [Beta x (Benchmark - Treasury)]**
>
> **Where:**
>
> **Benchmark = the total return of the benchmark index**
>
> **Treasury = the return on risk-free treasuries**
>
> **Beta= the fund's beta**

Sharpe Ratio

The Sharpe Ratio is risk-adjusted measure developed by Nobel laureate William Sharpe. It is calculated by using standard deviation and excess return to determine reward per unit of risk. This idea is that the higher the Sharpe Ratio, the better the fund's historical risk-adjusted performance.

$$\text{Sharpe Ratio} = \frac{\text{Alpha}}{\text{Standard Deviation}}$$

Any measurement that uses the standard deviation in the equation, such as the Sharpe Ratio, is a flawed measure of risk. The standard deviation measures uncertainty, not risk the way an investor thinks of risk.

Describing Risk in a Way That Corresponds to Investors' Thinking

As mentioned above, there are drawbacks to using standard deviation as a measure of risk: it interprets any difference from the average, above or below, as bad, not how most investors feel about returns. Few investors fret about their portfolios doubling; most only worry about the downside—their returns being below average. Investors think of risk as downside risk only.

Downside risk, as the name implies, measures risk below a certain point. For example, if an investor is worried only about losing money, that point would be zero, and the possibility of negative returns would be viewed as risky. If an investor needs to earn a 7% annual return in order to meet goals, any return under 7% would be considered risky. This investment return floor, which serves as the dividing line between good and bad outcomes, is called the minimum acceptable return (MAR).

Unlike standard deviation, downside risk accommodates different views of risk. Institutional investors often view investment risk as the possibility of underperforming the benchmark, whereas retail investors tend to regard risk in absolute terms as the possibility of loss.

Investors can customize the downside risk calculation using their own MAR. The institutional investor typically uses the benchmark rate as the minimum acceptable return, while the retail investor often uses the risk-free rate. Because standard deviation can only measure how tightly distributed returns are situated around a mean, it cannot be customized for individual investors.

The amount of risk in a set of returns changes considerably when the MAR changes. For example, if Investor A needs an investment that returns no less than 4% annually, any amount less than this will result in the underfunding of A's pension plan. Investor B wants a good return but doesn't want to incur losses. By raising the MAR from zero to 4%, a larger amount of the return distribution violates the MAR. This additional area—the amount between zero and 4%—is considered risk for Investor A, but not for Investor B.

Chart 6-4: Minimum Acceptable Return
MAR of 4%
Mean = 9% and Standard Deviation = 21%

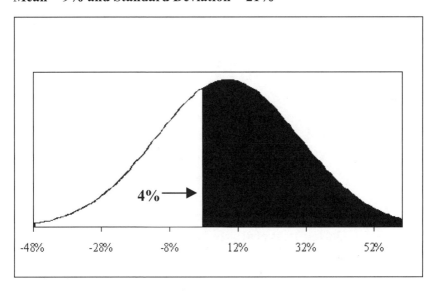

Risk is one of those subjects where there is widespread agreement on the surface but little agreement on the details. Many plan sponsors agree that they do not like risk, but they often disagree on just how much risk is involved in a particular investment.

Downside risk can accommodate this diversity in risk perception. Downside risk measures risk below some point. If an investor is worried only about losing money, the possibility of negative returns would be viewed as risky. If an investor needs to earn x% return to meet goal, any return under x% would be unacceptable (risky). This represents the MAR floor that is tolerable for this particular investor.

The key difference between standard deviation and MAR is as follows: Standard deviation interprets any difference from the average return, above or below, as bad. Most investors' views of risk are toward the downside only. That is, investors only worry about their returns being below some point. In addition to being a more intuitive definition of risk, the major advantage to downside risk over standard deviation is that it accommodates different views of risk.

The following example will illustrate the importance of this unique ability of downside risk to accommodate a wide range of risk perceptions. Chart 6-5 shows the range of returns of an investment from −48% to +52%. It illustrates how two investors might view the same asset quite differently in terms of risk, due to different goals that require different MARs. Investor A needs an investment that never returns less than 6% annually to maintain her standard of living as a retired participant, while B can not earn less than 3%. The additional area between lines A and B represents the additional risk perceived by investor A, as opposed to that perceived by Investor B.

Chart 6-5: Minimum Acceptable Return
MAR of 3% or 6%

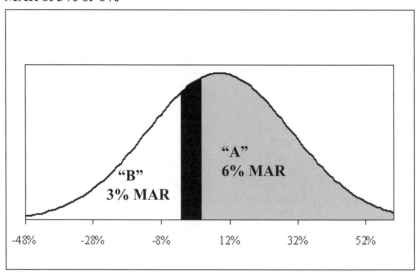

Institutional investors often view investment risk as the possibility of underperforming the benchmark. Pension plan participants usually view risk in absolute terms, as the risk of not accomplishing their goal. By using downside risk, each investor can customize the risk calculation using an individualized MAR. In the above examples the institutional investor would use the benchmark rate as the minimum acceptable return, while the plan participant would want to know the risk of falling below 7%. Standard deviation can only measure how tightly distributed returns are situated around a mean, so it cannot be customized for the individual investor.

Another limitation to standard deviation as a measurement of investment risk lies with the underlying data. Most investors will recall the "normal distribution" from their Introduction to Statistics course. This nicely proportioned bell-shaped curve is what underlies all the assumptions about standard deviation. If the underlying data is not normally distributed, the standard deviation is likely to give misleading results.

A number of studies have demonstrated that investment returns are not normally distributed. If the returns are not normally distributed, investors using standard deviation are likely to reach the wrong conclusions.

A further enhancement to the downside risk calculation is available in systems that use bootstrapping routines. Bootstrapping is a technique that tries to increase the explanatory power of a limited amount of data. Bootstrapping in this case selects twelve months at random and links them together to form a one-year return. This process is repeated thousands of times, resulting in a distribution with many observations instead of just a few.

An underlying assumption to bootstrapping is that the data is independent. That is, one period's return has no connection to another period's return. Most investors believe that the return from one period has something to do with that from another period, but the two values have little correlation. Studies suggest that sequential returns are not entirely independent, but the correlation between a return and that of a return two periods later is approximately zero.

One must weigh the additional explanatory power gained by the increased number of observations against the error introduced because returns are not entirely independent. In spite of its possible drawbacks, we prefer to bootstrap data, because we believe that it is able to capture returns that could have happened but never did happen, therefore providing a more complete picture of the nature of uncertainty.

A good example of the effectiveness of bootstrapping is the Japanese market during the 1980s. From 1980 to 1990, there were no years in which the market was down. Based just on this limited amount of data, it appears that the Japanese stock market had no risk during that period. However, bootstrapping the monthly data produced a distribution that clearly indicated the potential for negative annual returns. This riskiness showed itself in the 1990s as the Japanese equity market suffered marked declines. Looking at the bootstrapped data might have alerted an investor that a sharp correction was possible.

Downside Risk Statistics

Downside risk calculations provide the user with more information than just a downside deviation number. The additional statistics provide insight into the causes of the risk.

Downside frequency tells the user how often the returns violated the MAR. This is important, because in order to assess the likelihood of a bad outcome, it is necessary to know how often one occurred.

Average downside deviation indicates the average size of the unacceptable returns. This statistic helps an investor judge the severity of the average "bad" return. An investment that lost money twice as often as a second investment may still be preferable if it tended to lose far less than the second investment. Downside magnitude is the return at the ninety-ninth percentile on the downside. This is a worst-case scenario. An investment may lose money only occasionally, may average small losses when they do occur, and yet may prove unacceptable if the potential exists for huge losses.

All of these statistics are combined into the downside risk statistic. It includes the size and the frequency of unacceptable returns. Downside risk can be thought of as the equivalent to the standard deviation of just bad results. One method of ranking investments is by their risk-adjusted returns.

For downside risk, the accepted risk-adjusted return is the Active Sortino Ratio, which is the annualized return of the manager minus the MAR, divided by the downside risk. Similar to the Sharpe Ratio (which uses standard deviation), the Active Sortino Ratio measures how many units of excess return were received per unit of risk experienced. However, it defines risk in a way more like the average investor thinks of risk. A positive (> 0) Active Sortino Ratio is good and a negative (< 0) is bad.

Table 6-1 provides an example of some downside risk statistics calculated on a variety of market benchmark indexes. It is important to note that these statistics were calculated with an annual MAR of between 5% for Treasury bills to an annual MAR of 10% for stocks. Again, any return less than the MAR was seen as bad. For model portfolios (Figure 15-2 page 381) we use the following MAR values:

Ultra Conservative 100: Quarterly MAR = 1.50% (6.14% annualized)
Conservative 20 80: Quarterly MAR = 1.75% (7.19% annualized)
Balanced 40 60: Quarterly MAR = 2.00% (8.24% annualized)
Balanced 60 40: Quarterly MAR = 2.25% (9.31% annualized)
Aggressive 80 20: Quarterly MAR = 2.50% (10.38% annualized)
Ultra Aggressive 100: Quarterly MAR = 2.75% (11.46% annualized)

Table 6-1: Sortino Downside Risk Statistics 1984-2003

Analysis Based Upon Market Index Returns for Each Class

Portfolio Name	Portfolio Return	MAR Benchmark Return	Active Excess Return	Active Sortino Ratio	U-P Ratio	Upside Potential	Upside Probability	Downside Risk	Average Under Performance	Downside Probability	99th Percentile	Number of Bootstrapped Years
US Equity Indexes												
Wilshire Large Cap 750	12.99%	10.00%	2.99%	0.18	0.93	15.44%	62.00%	16.69%	-13.22%	38.00%	-37.37%	1000
Wilshire Mid Cap 500	14.39%	10.00%	4.39%	0.24	1.06	19.49%	59.60%	18.47%	-14.94%	40.40%	-38.74%	1000
Wilshire Small Cap 750	12.60%	10.00%	2.60%	0.13	1.00	20.53%	57.80%	20.53%	-16.51%	42.20%	-45.63%	1000
Wilshire Large Growth	12.22%	10.00%	2.22%	0.12	0.94	17.94%	57.80%	18.99%	-15.25%	42.20%	-42.18%	1000
Wilshire Large Value	13.05%	10.00%	3.05%	0.19	0.94	14.94%	60.90%	15.88%	-12.53%	39.10%	-35.80%	1000
Wilshire Mid Cap Growth	12.72%	10.00%	2.72%	0.13	1.07	22.49%	58.60%	21.04%	-16.83%	41.40%	-46.41%	1000
Wilshire Mid Cap Value	15.02%	10.00%	5.02%	0.29	1.03	17.88%	62.40%	17.31%	-13.56%	37.60%	-40.24%	1000
Wilshire Small Growth	10.52%	10.00%	0.52%	0.02	0.92	23.41%	52.30%	25.34%	-20.72%	47.70%	-54.60%	1000
Wilshire Small Value	14.06%	10.00%	4.06%	0.21	1.02	19.74%	62.50%	19.36%	-15.30%	37.50%	-40.52%	1000
Wilshire REIT	10.14%	8.00%	2.14%	0.18	1.00	12.29%	57.20%	12.24%	-9.56%	42.80%	-28.23%	1000
Foreign Stocks												
MSCI EAFE	9.52%	10.00%	-0.48%	-0.02	0.88	17.50%	49.20%	19.90%	-16.25%	50.80%	-43.25%	1000
US Fixed Income Indexes												
US Treasury Bills	4.98%	5.00%	-0.02%	-0.02	0.64	0.70%	47.90%	1.09%	-0.86%	52.10%	-2.66%	1000
Stable Value Fund Index	6.72%	5.00%	1.72%	5.85	5.56	1.63%	95.00%	0.29%	-0.22%	5.00%	-0.27%	1000
US Intermed Govt Bond	7.50%	6.00%	1.50%	0.29	1.23	6.27%	55.30%	5.09%	-4.00%	44.70%	-12.54%	1000
US Long Govt Bond	7.91%	6.00%	1.91%	0.20	1.06	10.10%	55.50%	9.56%	-7.50%	44.50%	-21.97%	1000
High Yield Bond Index	7.08%	6.00%	1.08%	0.11	0.83	8.04%	52.70%	9.68%	-7.68%	47.30%	-21.99%	1000

When discussing Sortino Downside Risk, some may question why it was not adopted earlier. Part of the reason may be the more complex calculation required. Today, computing power and memory are relatively cheap commodities. Desktop software that will calculate downside risk is readily available. We have found this methodology very useful in building asset allocation model portfolios with better risk/return characteristics.

If software is readily available and most investors agree that downside risk more closely parallels actual risk preferences, why don't more plan sponsors and plan participants use it on a regular basis? The likely answer is inertia. Investors do not accept new statistical methodologies rapidly. They tend to use what they are comfortable with. Investors have a healthy skepticism for new statistics.

For most investors, downside risk is a new concept. However, it is gaining acceptance among some in the financial community. We like the concept of defining risk as a return below some point, as this is consistent with most investors' views of risk.

In summary, we need downside risk measures like the Active Sortino Ratio to improve investment analysis. These measures cope with the complexity (and the reality) of the financial markets—particularly as viewed by plan participants. Downside risk measures are a closer match to how investors actually behave in investment situations. This is an improvement over the traditional capital asset pricing models used by many financial planners and plan participants.

For Further Reading

Balzer, L. "Measuring Investment Risk: A Review." *Journal of Investing* 3, no. 3 (1994).

Bear, L. and. Maldonado-Bear, R. *Free Markets, Finance, Ethics, and Law.* Englewood Cliffs, N.J.: Prentice Hall, (1994).

Benartzi, S., and Thaler, R. "Myopic Loss Aversion and the Equity Premium Puzzle." *Quarterly Journal of Economics* 110 no.4, (1995).

Fishburn, P. "Mean-Risk Analysis with Risk Associated with Below-Target Returns." *American Economic Review* 67, no. 2 (1977).

Merriken, H. "Analytical Approaches to Limit Downside Risk: Semivariance and the Need for Liquidity." *Journal of Investing* 3, no. 3 (1994).

Nelson, R., and Winter S. *An Evolutionary Theory of Economic Change.* Cambridge: Harvard University Press, (1982).

Peters, E.. *Chaos and Order in the Capital Markets.* New York: John Wiley and Sons, (1991).

Sortino, F., and Satchell, S. *Managing Downside Risk in Financial Markets: Theory, Practice and Implementation.* Oxford: Butterworth Heinemann, (2002).

Sortino, F, and van der Meer, R. "Downside Risk." *Journal of Portfolio Management* 17, no. 4, 27–32 (1991).

Chapter 7

Asset Allocation Optimization for Plan Participants

Chapter Summary

Asset allocation is a tool for reducing risk. In addition, it is also a key determinant of investment performance. Over time, asset allocation can explain 40– 90% of the participant's long-term investment return, so it should not be left to chance. Instead of simply using asset allocation software based upon standard deviation as a risk measure, we use the Sortino Downside Risk measurements to build asset allocation model portfolios that define risk as an investor thinks of risk.

However, many defined contribution plan participants do not understand or apply any type of effective asset-allocation policy. This is in stark contrast to defined benefit plans, where virtually every plan has a detailed asset-allocation investment policy managed by specialists hired by the plan sponsor. A professionally managed model portfolio solves this problem, especially when it is presented as part of an automatic, or default, pathway.

A model portfolio is a single selection of a prearranged series of mutual funds in a specific weighting designed for the plan participant's risk tolerance and needs. The plan trustee can automatically rebalance the participant's account in line with the model without any required action by the plan participant. Annual rebalancing is a simple and effective tool that can help plan participants improve their success rates. It is most effective if applied to the participant's account by way of a default pathway so that participant inertia and procrastination can be overcome.

The Importance of Asset Allocation

Designing an optimal portfolio for a total retirement plan, and now for each plan participant, has undergone dramatic changes over the last few decades. Not yet an exact science, portfolio construction has moved past the "art" phase of its development. Another term for portfolio construction is "asset allocation." Without proper asset allocation, there is little chance of a successful retirement because the real rate of investment return will be insufficient.

Chart 7-1: Asset Allocation Is Part of the Three A's Needed for Retirement Success

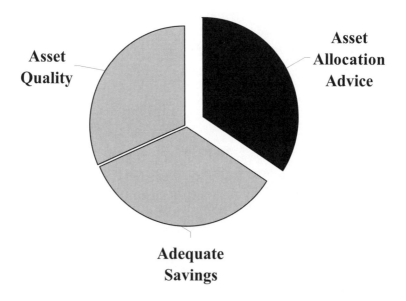

Anyone who has had even the slightest exposure to the teachings of investing has heard that determining one's asset allocation is the most important decision. Generally, the main asset classes under consideration are equities (stocks or stock mutual funds), fixed income (bonds or bond funds), and cash (money market securities).

According to the most often quoted study in this area, the allocation of one's investment dollars between stock, bond and cash asset classes determines 90% of the portfolio's performance over time. More recent studies report that asset allocation may only explain 40% of total return. But whether the figure is 90% or 40%, there is no doubt that asset allocation explains a substantial portion of return over time.

In a world of uncertainty, steps are often taken to offset or at least reduce the chance of loss or failure. Insurance policies, the military, and even seat belts are, for example, preventative measures used to offset the chance of loss. In investing, one of the preventative measures is asset allocation. All types of successful investors use asset allocation in their strategies.

However, many 401(k) plan participants do not understand or apply any type of effective asset-allocation policy. This is in stark contrast to defined benefit plans, where virtually every plan has a detailed asset-allocation investment policy. When used properly, asset allocation policy allows plan participants to grow their money, as well as protect it from the uncertainty that may result in loss.

Asset allocation can protect wealth from the dangers of a volatile market. From the Great Depression of the 1930s to the technology stock bust of the late 1990s, fluctuations in the stock market have plagued investors. Asset allocation allows investors to obtain growth while limiting the chances of huge loss.

In making retirement plan investment decisions, the initial challenge is to determine the amount of money required at retirement and next to calculate the rate of return need to compound the annual savings. The participant must balance risk and return and calculate how much to invest in the stock market and how much to invest in fixed income. The final step is to adjust their asset allocation to changing market conditions and in response to age, as retirement grows nearer.

Modern Portfolio Theory

In defining asset allocation, the terms "risk" and "volatility" are often used, and most plan participants assume that there should be less of it. What is risk, and what does it have to do with returns? In March 1952, Dr. Harry Markowitz published an article in the *Journal of Finance* that showed the tradeoff between risk and return. The higher the portfolio's return, the higher the risk—he used standard deviation as a measure of risk. This relationship is called modern portfolio theory.

Markowitz demonstrated the risk-reward relationship on a graph called the "efficient frontier," which plots "return" on the y-axis against "risk" (standard deviation) on the x-axis. Practically speaking, standard deviation measures uncertainty—either good or bad. (Note that in chapter 6, we defined risk as the possibility of a return below the minimum acceptable return, or MAR.) Markowitz further concluded that the most efficient portfolio was the one that gave the highest return for each level of portfolio risk. An inefficient portfolio exposed the investor to a higher level of risk without a corresponding higher level of return.

Chart 7-2: The Efficient Frontier

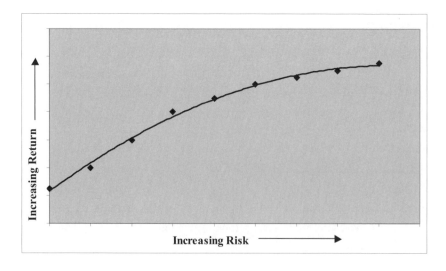

Capital Asset Pricing Model

Markowitz's work led to another concept of modern portfolio theory. This idea is the capital asset pricing model ("CAPM"). CAPM showed that there were two types of risk. One type of risk was systematic risk, or market risk (also known as beta), which was inherent in all stocks. This type of risk was affected by the volatility of the overall market and could not be diversified away. The other type of risk was unsystematic risk, or risk specific to a particular stock.

Unsystematic risk could be diversified away by adding stocks that could neutralize the risk of other stocks in the portfolio. Adding these stocks would balance the non-market risk in the portfolio to equal zero. The conclusion reached is that investors are rewarded for bearing market, or systematic risk, but not unsystematic risk, because unsystematic risk can be diversified away. For all investors as a total group the aggregate unsystematic risk is zero and does not contribute to their return. Many participants using self-directed brokerage accounts hold only a handful of stocks. Such accounts contain large amounts of unsystematic risk. The plan participant is not compensated for such a high risk portfolio. CAPM concludes that the market portfolio is the efficient portfolio, because no other portfolio with equal risk can offer a higher expected return. This is the true meaning of Markowitz's efficient frontier, which is a series of asset allocation risk-reward data points. Finding the proper asset allocation mix is the key to obtaining this efficient portfolio.

In modern portfolio theory, the CAPM and efficient market theory suggest that asset allocation is key to obtaining a market or efficient portfolio, which will yield the highest results with the least amount of risk. It is, however, difficult to quantifiably prove the importance of asset allocation in regards to long-term growth—studies conducted to quantify the importance of asset allocation are plagued by conflicts about realistic models, data, and even how the results are interpreted.

Because of these discrepancies among the studies, exact numbers to quantify the importance of asset allocation are not consistent. The only consistency in these studies has been that asset allocation does play a major role in long-term performance.

Because asset allocation plays a major role in long-term return, the concept of asset allocation should be more openly considered and integrated into all plan participant investment policies to raise the probability of obtaining better performance results. And because most plan participants are plagued with the inertia and procrastination behaviors, any system that applies the proper asset allocation for the participant as a default pathway is much more likely to succeed.

How Does Asset Allocation Reduce Risk over Time?

No doubt, some investors have heard the recommendation many times that in order to reduce risk you should diversify across asset classes—stocks, bonds, and cash investments—in proportions appropriate for your goals, time horizon, and risk tolerance.

Chart 7-3 demonstrates that how plan participants split their assets can make a big difference. The chart looks at five-year returns for six different asset allocations that were rebalanced annually for forty-three years. Depicted are the best and worst five-year annualized returns for each portfolio from 1960 to 2003. Not surprisingly, an all-stock portfolio had the highest highs and the lowest lows. But an all-bond portfolio also had five-year periods of negative returns. However, a portfolio roughly evenly balanced between stocks and bonds (60% stocks and 40% bonds, or 40% stocks and 60% bonds) had no negative returns for any five-year period. The future may be different, but it is comforting to know how various asset classes interacted with each other over the past forty-three years.

Chart 7-3: Worst and Best Five-Year Rolling Periods for Various Stock and Bond Mixes

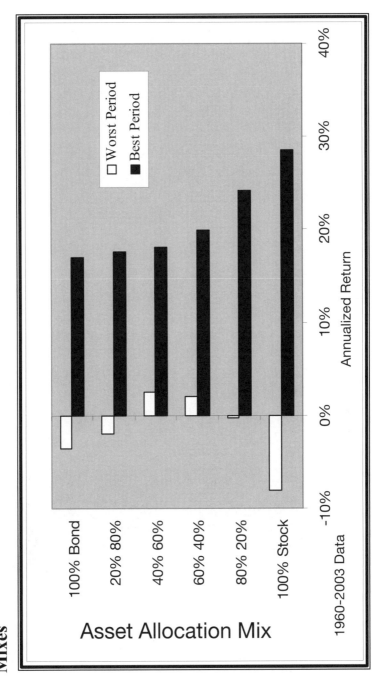

Diversification by Asset Class and Style

Stock funds can be segregated in many different ways. Useful subcategories include the size of the companies the funds invest in, such as large cap stocks (usually companies over $7 billion in market capitalization), mid cap stocks (between $1 billion and $7 billion) and small cap stocks (under $1 billion). Other useful subcategories include geographical location of the companies either inside the United States or outside, such as an international stock fund. Other subcategories include funds that hold real-estate trusts and funds that hold both stocks and bonds, namely balanced funds. Each of these subcategories has its own special features and risks. The goal is to combine a number of the different funds in a portfolio so that each fund moves somewhat differently from the others. The idea is that some of the risk of each individual fund is offset by the other funds. The risk cannot be eliminated this way, but it can be substantially reduced.

Chart 7-4: Asset Class Diversification by Fund Major Subcategory

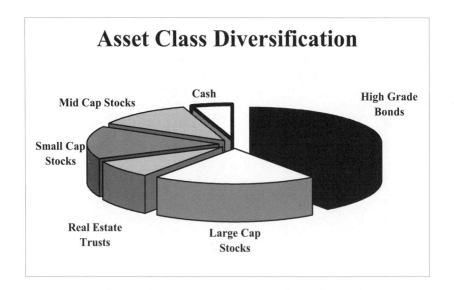

There are also many types of bond fund subcategories, including those issued by the U.S. government, state or local governments, and corporations. Bonds are issued for periods ranging from short-term bonds (such as U.S. Treasury bills) to long-term government or corporate bonds. The interest rate risk and credit risk vary, depending on the issuer, the bond, and the length of the term.

Finally, within subcategories of stock mutual funds, for example, there are investment styles, such as growth, value, or a blend of the two. Growth stocks tend to be more aggressive, and value stocks tend to be slightly more conservative. Thus, a fund could hold stocks in subgroups, such as large cap growth, large cap value, mid cap growth, small cap value, and so on. Evaluating and selecting the funds in each of these subgroups can be challenging. We define "asset quality" as selecting and maintaining better funds in each asset class. Asset quality is discussed in more detail in chapter 8.

Chart 7-5: Asset Class Diversification by Fund Subcategory Style

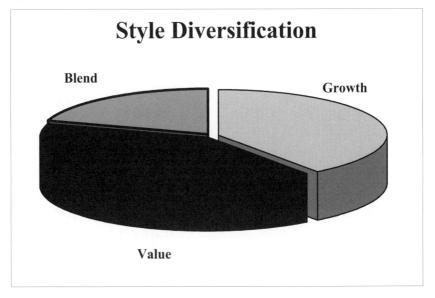

Why Model Portfolios Make Sense as Default Success Pathways

As said earlier, proper asset allocation explains 40% to 90% of the plan participant's long-term return. Because of inertia and procrastination, large-scale data show most plan participants make few changes to their accounts over time. Some plan sponsors have attempted to offer participants asset allocation choices with lifestyle funds. So far, lifestyle funds have produced little improvement in outcome success and haven't proved popular with employees, but that may be because they were not well explained. Data indicate that only one in three plan participants choose lifestyle funds when they are offered.

A professionally managed model portfolio can overcome many of these problems, especially when presented as part of an automatic, or default pathway. Some may assume that model portfolios and lifestyle funds are basically the same, but there are significant differences between the two. A properly constructed and managed model portfolio is superior to a lifestyle fund. Most participants that use lifestyle funds try to combine the lifestyle fund with other funds and defeat its purpose. In contrast, plan participants can invest in only one model in order to ensure they have proper asset allocation. The plan trustee can automatically rebalance model portfolios without any actions by plan participants.

Another advantage over lifestyle funds holding other funds is that with model portfolios, a potential second layer of mutual fund fees is avoided. More importantly, most lifestyle funds use mutual funds from the same mutual fund company—giving a proprietary taint to the objectivity of fund selection and replacement. A model portfolio is made up of mutual funds selected and monitored on a totally objective basis. Asset quality can be maintained within the model. In a lifestyle fund, the participant is stuck with the underlying proprietary holdings. See chapter 15 for a detailed discussion of lifestyle funds and model portfolios.

The Importance of Annual Rebalancing

Annual rebalancing is a simple and effective tool that can help plan participants improve their success rates. It is most effective if applied to plan participants' accounts by way of a default pathway so that the desired action does not depend upon participants' overcoming their inertia and procrastination behaviors.

The stock-bond mix in their accounts will naturally vary as the two asset classes perform differently from one another. The portfolio can be kept on track by rebalancing—periodically making adjustments to the investments to bring the mix of stocks, bonds, and cash back in line with the original asset allocation.

During bull markets for stocks, the proportion of participants' accounts in stocks will grow and can make the accounts more risky than intended. For example, an account that was 50% stocks and 50% bonds in 1995 would have grown to 71% stocks and just 29% bonds in 1999—just before the three-year bear market in stocks in 2000-2002.

Chart 7-6: Difference between 1999 Stock-Bond Mix and 50:50 Mix Just Four Years Earlier

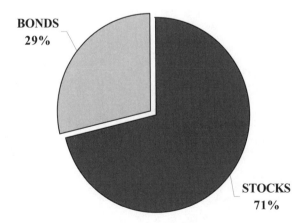

Allowing the account that was supposed to be 50% stocks and 50% bonds in 1999 to remain at 71% stocks and just 29% bonds would make a total performance difference over the next three years of -15.04% as compared to the rebalanced mix.

Chart 7-7: Comparison of Performance in 2000–2002 of 50:50 vs. 71:29 Stock-Bond Mix

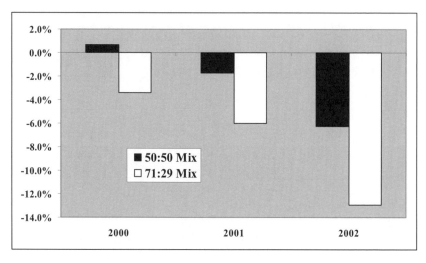

Chart 7-8: Annual Performance Improvement in 2000–2002 of 50:50 vs. 71:29 Stock-Bond Mix

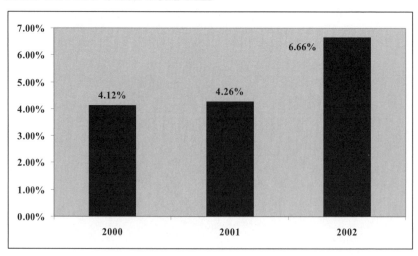

Likewise, during bear markets for stocks, the proportion of an account in stocks will decline and can make the account more conservative than was intended. Having a lower proportion of stocks than intended may limit returns when the stock market rebounds. For example, an account that was 50% stocks and 50% bonds in 1999 would have declined to 32% stocks and 68% bonds in late 2002.

Chart 7-9: Difference between 2002 Stock-Bond Mix and 50:50 Mix Just Three Years Earlier

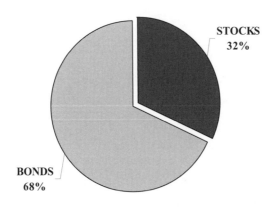

In 2003, the stock market rebounded, and the bond market was fairly flat. A portfolio made up of 50% stocks and 50% bonds outperformed a 32:68 portfolio by 3.47%. Over the full four years of 1999–2003, rebalancing the portfolio added a significant amount (18.51%) to the plan participant's return.

Because of the potential for such big changes in performance, most financial advisors say investors should rebalance their portfolios back to their target mix of asset classes every year or so. However, that isn't always an easy thing to do, because by definition, rebalancing requires the participant to sell the type of security that has been performing well—say stocks in late 1999—and pump money into what had performed terribly.

Do Participants Adjust Their Allocations?

As people get closer to retirement, most financial planners recommend adjusting their asset allocation. As they grow closer to retirement and the number of future time periods to earn labor income declines, their ability to tolerate financial asset risk generally declines. The best way for most people to stabilize the risk in their portfolio over time is to increase bond holdings as a share of their total portfolio. Many planners recommend a simple rule of thumb that investors hold a stock allocation equal to 100 minus their age.

So the question is what asset allocation actions do people actually undertake? The only way to see whether people actually reduce their equity holdings as they age is to follow a group of people over time. Researchers put together quarterly data from 1990 through 1999 for both the allocation of assets and the flow of contributions for about 4,000 TIAA-CREF participants.

This is a good sample for testing whether people reduce equity holdings as they age because for many participants TIAA-CREF is their only retirement plan and often represents most of their financial asset wealth. On the other hand, the sample is not representative of the general population, because TIAA-CREF participants are generally better educated than the population as a whole. Therefore, even if TIAA-CREF participants did a good job in reallocating, it does not mean that the whole population was adjusting their asset allocation to improve their success.

The TIAA-CREF data show that, over the study time period, equity holdings increased for almost all participants who were in the accumulation phase of life. Instead of declining about 9% because the population aged 9 years, the equity allocation actually increased 9.2%. The asset allocation for the participants was much more risky than expected.

The main reason for the 9.2% overall equity increase was the high return on equities during the 1990s. Consider this outcome in the context of the standard rule we mentioned earlier that equities as a percentage of total assets should equal one hundred minus one's age. This rule implies that individuals should reduce their equity share by 1% a year, or 9% over the nine-year period. But since the market increased the equity share by 9.2%, individuals should have reduced their equity share by 18.2%. The main conclusion is that people do not reduce their equity holdings as they age. Of course, this study was done in a high-return environment; people might be more likely to reallocate if equity returns were flat.

Now consider a participant with a $500,000 account balance in 1999. Over the declining stock market 2000-2002 time period, the additional 18.2% equity asset allocation imbalance cost this participant over $67,500 (-13.5%) in market value by the time the bear market ended.

Age is not the only reason that people should adjust their portfolios over time. The other reason is investment returns. People select a target allocation depending on returns among stocks, bonds, and money market instruments. Over time, their account balances reflect both their initial choices and returns on assets. If participants never change their investment allocation, even in normal times they will see the ratio of stocks to bonds increase since equities on average have a higher rate of return. This phenomenon was exacerbated during the 1990s, when stocks rose at more than 20% a year. Without some reallocation, the bull market would have greatly increased equity holdings as a share of most people's portfolio.

An important question is whether 401(k) participants rebalanced in the face of the unprecedented run-up in stock values. No study has addressed this question directly, but comparing the performance of defined contribution and defined benefit plans during the 1990s bull market provides some interesting insights. The data reveal significant differences in performance by defined benefit plans.

Every employee benefit plan must file a Form 5500 annually with the Internal Revenue Service, summarizing its results. Using a representative sampling of Form 5500 data tapes for the years 1990 through 1995, the consulting firm Watson Wyatt identified 503 employers that sponsored both a 401(k) plan and a defined benefit plan during all six years. Their study found that the average defined benefit plan earned an annual return 1.9% better than the 401(k) plan. For one quarter of all plan sponsors, their defined benefit plan return exceeded that of their 401(k) plan by 3.5% or more each year.

In the late 1980s and early 1990s, both types of retirement plans held roughly 40-45% percent of their total assets in equities, either directly or through mutual funds. As the market began its swift rise in the mid-1990s, the share of equities in defined contribution plans rose significantly more than those in defined benefit plans. The notion is that the professionals who manage defined benefit plans sought to maintain a balance between stocks and interest-earning assets, while individual 401(k) participants did little to rebalance their portfolios.

Thus the changes in the equity composition of retirement assets during the boom market appear consistent with the finding that individuals do little to rebalance their portfolios as they age. In both cases, individual investors demonstrate an enormous amount of inertia.

Plan participants seldom make changes to their asset allocations for any reason. Some recent studies document this inertia and procrastination in detail. In the TIAA-CREF study, 73% made no asset allocation changes over the nine-year period, and another 14% percent made only one change. Another study, which examined trading behavior in one large 401(k) plan during 1994-1998, found that trading was infrequent. Of all participants, 88% never changed allocations, and 6% made only one change. Thus defined contribution plan participants chronically display huge amounts of procrastination in regard to changing investments.

Chart 7-10: Equity Holdings in Defined Benefit Versus Defined Contribution Plans

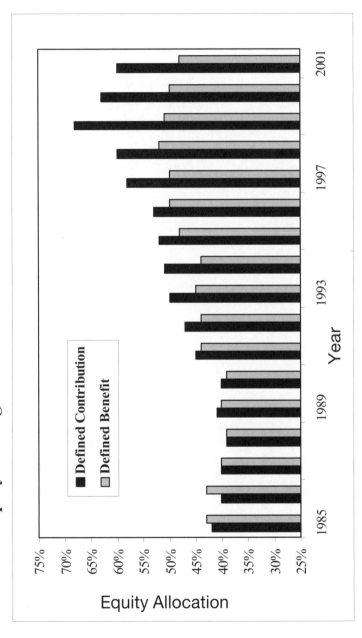

Building Asset Allocation Portfolios with Sortino Downside Risk Measurements

Traditional asset allocation software creates an efficient frontier of various asset allocation mixes by plotting portfolio return against risk, and relies upon standard deviation as risk. As we pointed out in chapter 6, standard deviation measures uncertainty, but not really measure risk the way an investor thinks of risk. A far better way to build asset allocation mixes is with the Sortino Downside Risk statistics as the risk measurement. Downside risk, as the name implies, measures risk below a certain point. If an investor needs to earn a 5% annual return in order to meet goals, any return under 5% would be considered risky. This investment return floor is called the minimum acceptable return (MAR). Chart 7-11 shows that adding increasing amounts of value to a growth equity portfolio progressively increases return and reduces downside risk, until the portfolio is 100% value.

Chart 7-11: Wilshire Value Index and Growth Index Asset Allocation Mix Returns vs Sortino Downside Risk 1984-2003

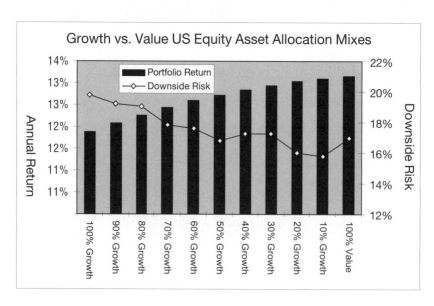

Many asset allocation optimizer software packages routinely recommend 10-20% of the equity portfolio be invested in international equities. Many financial planners then make a blanket recommendation that adding international equities "reduces risk and increases return", when in reality the chances of an investor earning a return below their MAR are actually greater when they add foreign stocks to their account.

When the analysis is done using the Sortino Downside Risk statistics, this long-standing recommendation is open to question. Chart 7-12 shows that adding increasing amounts of foreign stocks (Wilshire EAFE) to a domestic stock portfolio (Wilshire 5000) reduces return and increases the downside risk.

Chart 7-12: Wilshire 5000 Index Domestic Stock and Foreign Stock Asset Allocation Mix Returns vs Sortino Downside Risk 1984-2003

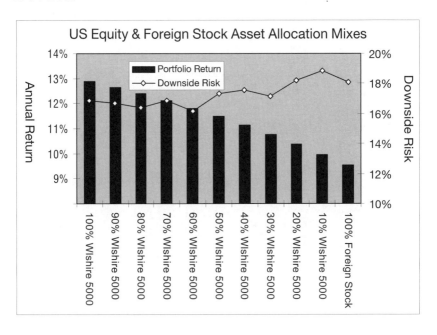

Using Sortino Downside Risk methodology, it is possible to show that adding 10-20% REITs to an all equity portfolio (Wilshire 5000) does reduce downside risk with minimal impact on long-term return. Adding a stable value fund to an intermediate government bond mix will also reduce downside risk without impacting return. In terms of large cap, mid cap and small cap equity mixes, the optimal mix must contain at least 40% to 60% small and mid cap to reduce downside risk and slightly boost return. It is not necessary to hold all nine equity styles. Virtually all the benefit of the equity asset classes can be obtained by holding only four equity classes, but two of them must be mid cap blend or mid cap value, and also small cap blend or small cap value. Many asset allocation optimizer software packages routinely recommend 10-20% of a fixed income portfolio be invested in high yield or "junk" bonds. Chart 7-13 demonstrates the chances of an investor earning a return below their MAR are actually greater when they add junk bonds to their account.

Chart 7-13: Adding High Yield Bonds to Intermediate Government Bonds vs Sortino Downside Risk 1984-2003

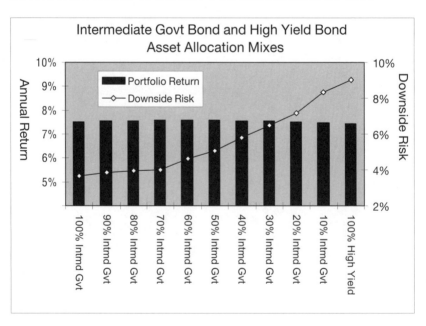

For Further Reading

Amerikus, J. and Zeldes, S. "How Do Household Portfolios Shares Vary with Age?" Working Paper 6-120101. New York: TIAA-CREF Research Institute. (2001)

Balzer, L. "Measuring Investment Risk: A Review." *Journal of Investing* 3, no. 3 (1994).

Brinson,G., Hood, R., and Beebower. G. "Determinants of Portfolio Performance." *Financial Analysts Journal* 42, no. 4, 39–48 (1986).

Gibson, R. *Asset Allocation: Balancing Financial Risk.* Chicago, IL: Irwin Professional Publishing, (1996).

Goetzmann, W., and Ibbotson, R. "Do Winners Repeat?" *Journal of Portfolio Management* 20, no. 2, 9–18 (1994).

Hensel, C., Ezra, D., and Ilkiw, J. "The Importance of the Asset Allocation Decision." *Financial Analysts Journal* 47, no. 4, 65–72. (1991).

Ibbotson, R., and Kaplan P. "Does Asset Allocation Policy Explain 40, 90, or 100 Percent of Performance?" *Financial Analysts Journal* 56, no.1, 26–32. (2000).

Stevens, D., Surz, R., and Wimer, M. "The Importance of Investment Policy." *Journal of Investing* 8, no. 4, 80–85 (1999).

"Investment Returns: Defined Benefit vs 401(k)". Watson Wyatt Insider (1996).

Chapter 8

Defining and Measuring Asset Quality

Chapter Summary

Ranking in importance just below asset allocation, asset quality is an important investment-performance factor. We define asset quality as a comprehensive process, based upon published large-scale data rather than anecdotal guesswork, that seeks to identify above-average to superior investment vehicles in every sector of the asset allocation mix.

Today there are more mutual funds than publicly traded stocks. The number of mutual funds has grown from 68 in 1940, to 363 in 1970 and more than 14,200 in 2003. Recent studies have pointed out the prediction difficulties inherent in using the popular systems for rating and evaluating mutual funds, namely Morningstar, Standard & Poors, and Value Line. Investors heavily rely upon the unpredictable star rating systems. Four- and five-star funds account for only 32% of all mutual funds but now gather virtually 100% of the net cash flow from investors.

This chapter reviews published studies that sought to explain portfolio performance and develop at least a modest predictive capability. Numerous primary factors, such as the funds' expense ratios, turnover rates, peer group relative rankings over various periods, as well as other important factors, are discussed. Secondary predictive factors, such as boards of directors committed to shareholder fairness, investment style (category) consistency, asset size, funds employing a multimanager approach, revenue sharing, and asset quality consistency over time, are also reviewed.

Using Asset Quality to Sort Mutual Funds

Throughout this book, we have focused on the Three A's that are essential for a successful retirement: Adequate Savings, Asset Allocation Advice and Asset Quality. In this chapter, we focus on asset quality. Without good asset quality, there is little chance of a sufficiently high real rate of investment return for successful retirement.

Chart 8-1: Asset Quality Is Needed for Retirement Success

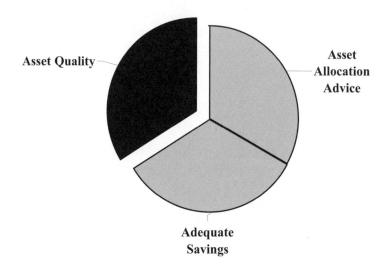

Next to asset allocation in overall importance, asset quality is an important factor in determining long-term investment return. We define "asset quality" as a comprehensive process, based upon published large-scale data rather than anecdotal guesswork, that seeks to identify above-average to superior investment vehicles in every sector of the asset allocation mix. In other words, if the asset allocation policy calls for 10% of the retirement account to be invested in large-cap value stocks, which large-cap value-stock investment vehicle should be picked? How should it be monitored? When should it be replaced? The process of maintaining high asset quality answers these important and difficult questions that face both plan sponsors and plan participants.

Understanding Mutual Funds

In this chapter, we will focus on defining asset quality for investment accounts. Over the past two decades, American investors have increasingly turned to mutual funds to save for retirement and other financial goals. Mutual funds can offer the advantages of diversification and professional management. But, as with other investment choices, investing in mutual funds involves both the financial risk of outright losses and the more subtle risk of failure to meet the retirement savings goals because the real rate of return was too low. It is vitally important to understand both the upsides and the downsides of mutual fund investing and how to choose products that match participants' goals and tolerances for risk.

A mutual fund is a type of investment that gathers assets from investors and collectively invests those assets in stocks, bonds, or money market instruments. Through the collective investments of the mutual fund, each investor shares in the returns from the fund's portfolio while benefiting from professional investment management, diversification, liquidity, and other benefits and services. Today more than 14,000 mutual funds are in existence—more than the number of publicly traded stocks!

How a Mutual Fund Is Organized

A mutual fund is organized as either a corporation or a business trust. Individuals and institutions invest in a mutual fund by purchasing shares issued by the fund. Through these sales of shares, the mutual fund raises the cash used to invest in its portfolio of stocks, bonds, and other securities. A mutual fund is typically externally managed: it is not an operating company with employees in the traditional sense. Instead, a fund relies upon third parties, either affiliated organizations or independent contractors, to carry out its business activities, such as investing in securities. Chart 8-2 on the next page illustrates a typical fund structure.

Chart 8-2: The Structure of a Mutual Fund

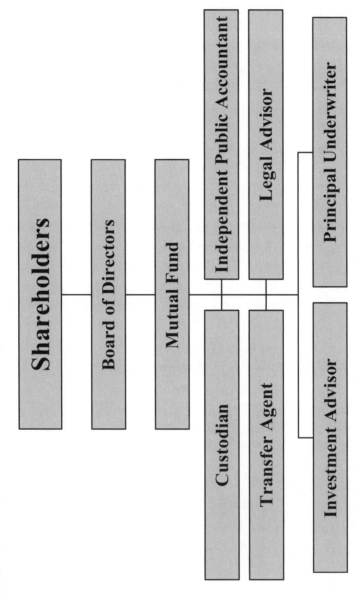

Shareholders

At the end of 2003, more than $2.4 trillion in mutual fund retirement assets were held by mutual fund shareholders, representing about one-third of all mutual fund assets. See chart 8-3 for the growth of mutual fund assets over the past 30 years. Mutual fund retirement assets consist primarily of two sources: Individual Retirement Accounts (IRAs) and employer-sponsored defined contribution plans, such as 401(k) plans.

The mutual fund shareholders own the underlying fund assets. Like shareholders of other companies, mutual fund shareholders have specific voting rights. These include the right to elect directors at meetings called for that purpose (subject to a limited exception for filling vacancies). Shareholders must also approve material changes in the terms of a fund's contract with its investment advisor, the entity that manages the fund's assets. Furthermore, funds seeking to change investment objectives or policies deemed fundamental must obtain the approval of the holders of a majority of the fund's outstanding voting securities.

Shareholders are provided comprehensive information about the fund to help them make informed investment decisions. A mutual fund's prospectus describes the fund's goals, fees and expenses, investment strategies, and risks, as well as information on how to buy and sell shares. The U.S. Securities and Exchange Commission (SEC) requires a fund to provide a full prospectus either before an investment or with the confirmation statement of an initial investment. In addition, the SEC requires periodic shareholder reports prepared at least every six months, discuss the fund's recent performance and include other important information, such as the fund's financial statements. In addition, some mutual funds also furnish investors with a "profile," which summarizes key information contained in the fund's prospectus, such as the fund's investment objectives, principal investment strategies, principal risks, performance, fees and expenses, identity of the fund's investment adviser, investment requirements, and other information.

Chart 8-3: Growth of Mutual Fund Assets 1970-2003

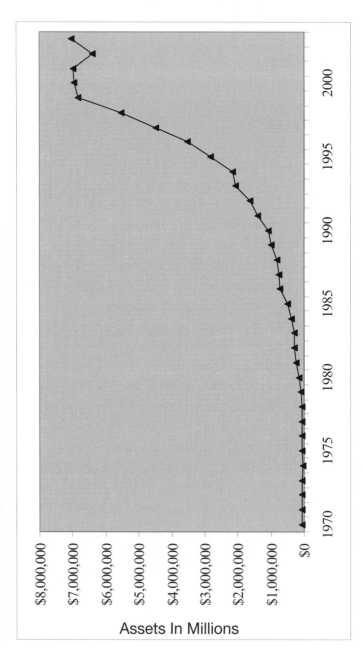

Directors

A board of directors, elected by the fund's shareholders to govern the fund, is responsible for overseeing the management of fund business affairs. Because mutual fund directors are looking out for shareholders' interests, the law holds them to a very high standard. Directors must exercise the care that a reasonably prudent person would take with his or her own business. They are expected to exercise sound business judgment, establish procedures, and undertake oversight and review of the performance of the investment adviser and others that perform services for the fund. The 2003 mutual fund trading scandal that erupted among numerous mutual fund firms brought into question just how effective the directors were in looking out for shareholder interests.

As part of this fiduciary duty, a director is expected to obtain adequate information about items that come before the board in order to exercise his or her "business judgment," a legal concept that involves a good-faith effort by the director. In addition, mutual funds are required by law to include independent directors, individuals that cannot have any significant relationship with the fund's adviser or underwriter so that they can provide an independent check on the fund's operations. Furthermore, SEC rule changes from January 2002 require, in most instances, that a majority of most funds' boards of directors be independent.

Independent directors are supposed to serve as watchdogs for the shareholders' interests and oversee a fund's investment adviser and others closely affiliated with the fund. As the 2003 systemic mutual fund trading scandals emerged, this system of overseeing the interests of mutual fund shareholders was brought into question. In November 2003, the U.S. House of Representatives, by a vote of 418-2 passed **The Mutual Funds Integrity and Fee Transparency Act**, (H.R. 2420) to reduce the industry problems and restore public confidence in mutual funds.

The Mutual Fund's Investment Advisor

An investment advisor manages the money accumulated in a mutual fund. The investment advisor invests the fund's assets on behalf of shareholders in accordance with a fund's objectives as described in a fund's prospectus. Fund managers invest in a variety of securities, providing fund shareholders with investment diversification. A diversified portfolio helps reduce risk by offsetting losses from some securities with gains in others. Mutual funds provide an economical way for the average investor to obtain professional money management and diversification of investments much like large institutions and wealthy investors receive. Some studies have shown that mutual fund advisory fees are modestly higher (10–30 basis points, or 0.10% to 0.30%) than those paid by large defined benefit plans using separate accounts. As we will see later, the performance superiority of defined benefit plans over participant-directed defined contribution plans is much larger than the fee differences.

Investment advisors who oversee "actively managed" fund portfolios base their investment decisions on extensive knowledge and research of market conditions and on the financial performance of individual companies and specific securities in the effort to meet or beat average market returns. As economic conditions change, the fund investment advisor may adjust the mix of investments to adopt a more aggressive or a more defensive posture in meeting the investment objectives. Investment managers who oversee "passively managed" funds typically try to track a market index—such as the S&P 500—by buying and holding all, or a large representative sample of, the securities in the index. A fund investment advisor is subject to numerous standards and legal restrictions, especially regarding transactions between the advisor and the fund being advised. A written contract between a mutual fund and its investment advisor specifies the services that the advisor performs. Most advisory contracts provide that the advisor receive an annual fee based on a percentage of the fund's average net assets.

Custodians

Mutual funds are required by law to protect their portfolio securities by placing them with a custodian. Nearly all mutual funds use qualified bank custodians. The SEC requires mutual fund custodians to segregate mutual fund portfolio securities from other bank assets.

Transfer Agents and Administrators

A transfer agent is employed by a mutual fund to maintain records of shareholder accounts, to calculate and disburse dividends, and to prepare and mail shareholder account statements, federal income tax information, and other shareholder notices. Some transfer agents prepare and mail statements confirming shareholder transactions and account balances and maintain customer service departments to respond to shareholder inquiries. In addition, administrative services may be provided to a fund by an affiliate of the fund, such as the investment advisor, or by an unaffiliated third party.

Administrative services include overseeing the performance of other companies that provide services to the fund and ensuring that the fund's operations comply with legal requirements. Typically, a fund administrator pays for office costs and personnel and provides general accounting services; a fund administrator may also prepare and file SEC, tax, shareholder, and other reports.

Principal Underwriters

Most mutual funds continuously offer new shares to the public at prices based on the current values of fund net assets plus any sales charges. Mutual funds usually distribute their shares through principal underwriters. Principal underwriters are regulated as broker-dealers and are subject to National Association of Security Dealers (NASD) rules governing mutual fund sales practices.

Mutual Fund Fees and Expenses

Mutual fund shareholders should receive full disclosure of mutual fund fees and expenses. A fund's fees and expenses are required by law to be clearly disclosed to investors in a standardized fee table at the front of the fund's prospectus. The fee table breaks out the fees and expenses that shareholders can expect to pay when purchasing fund shares and allows investors to compare the cost of investing in different funds.

Mutual fund fees are a hot topic. Over the years, many Wall Street brokerage houses have looked at all sorts of clever ways to extract as many fees as possible via elaborate schemes to boost their profit results by billions annually. Now, in the wake of the fund-trading scandal, these practices are getting more scrutiny. Many fees are hidden. Trading commissions, including soft-dollar transactions, aren't included in a fund's expense ratio, so investors can't really measure how efficiently a fund is managing its trading costs. Listed below are direct fees.

Direct Shareholder Fees

? **Sales Charge**. A sales charge may be attached to the purchase or sale of mutual fund shares. This fee compensates financial professionals for their services.

? **Redemption Fee**. This fee is paid to a fund to cover the costs, other than sales costs, involved with a redemption.

? **Exchange Fee**. This fee may be charged when an investor transfers money from one fund to another within the same fund family.

? **Annual Account Maintenance Fee**. This fee may be charged by some funds, for example, to cover the costs of providing service to low-balance accounts.

Defining Asset Quality in Mutual Funds

Investors need both proper asset allocation and high asset quality in each sector of their asset allocations. When trying to select investments, every investor has been warned: "Past performance does not predict future performance." Today, with more than 14,000 mutual funds for retirement plan and individual investors to consider, which asset quality criteria are useful if raw past performance is not predictive?

A recent article in the *Wall Street Journal* pointed out the prediction difficulties inherent in popular mutual-fund rating and evaluation systems, namely Morningstar™, Standard & Poors™ and Lipper™. These evaluation systems are good for identifying mutual funds that performed well historically but have been mostly unreliable when used in an attempt to predict the performance outcome of mutual funds in future time periods.

However, as Table 8-1 below shows, investors continue to send their cash to funds that are highly rated by these mostly unreliable systems. Four- and five-star funds account for only 32% of all mutual funds, but they gather virtually 100% of the net cash flow.

Table 8-1: Star Rating Determines Cash Flow

MORNINGSTAR STAR RATING ATTRACTS CASH FLOW

Investor cash flows to highly rated funds (Four or Five Star) dwarfed those of funds with weak ratings. Figures in billions of dollars.

Fund Categories	Four- and Five-Stars	One-, Two-, Three-Stars
Equity	$79.6	-$108.2
Fixed Income	$64.6	$28.8
Total	$144.2	-$79.4

Source: Financial Research Corp. 2002 mutual fund data.

For any mutual-fund evaluation program to be useful, its outcome analysis must be based upon prospective results—meaning what happens to the funds after they are rated. Most investors and retirement plan sponsors need help. Since 1994, the Boston fund consulting firm Dalbar has released an annual study that blends sales figures with fund returns to measure the average mutual fund investor's actual performance.

Table 8-2: Fund Investors Lag the Average Fund and Market Benchmarks

Investment Entity	1984 to 2000	2000 to Dec. 2002	1984 to Dec. 2002
S&P 500	16.3%	-14.3%	12.2%
Average Fund	13.1%	-14.6%	9.3%
Average Investor	5.3%	-16.9%	2.7%
Inflation	4.2%	2.5%	4.1%
Average Investor (net)	1.1%	-19.4%	-1.4%

Source: Dalbar and Bogle Financial Markets Research Center
Ibbotson Inflation Data

The 2002 edition found that the average stock-fund investor eked out a paltry 2.7% pre-inflation annual gain from 1984 through 2002, compared with 12.2% for the S&P 500 stock index. The real rate of return (after inflation) was –1.4%. Interestingly, the study also revealed that investors, having missed out on much of the bull market, lost more money than the average fund and the overall market in the bear market of 2000–2002.

Indexing proponents will note that the average equity fund lagged the S&P 500 by a significant margin (9.3% vs. 12.2%). However, indexing does not explain the much greater shortfall that the average investor experienced (2.7% vs. either 9.3% or 12.2%) to both the market benchmark and the average fund. The -9.5% shortfall (12.2%-2.7%) has more to do with poor asset allocation, adverse market timing, and mediocre fund selections (asset quality) by the participant.

Do Financial Service Company 401(k) Retirement Plans Perform Any Better?

In 1998 Moringstar.net published an article: "Telescoping in on Morningstar's 401(k)." The article took a candid look at some strategic decisions, results and dilemmas experienced by Morningstar plan participants after a wild 1997. A fair and careful reading clearly shows that even Morningstar employees were subject to some of the same errors we see in other plans: among them, performance chasing and letting allocations grow disproportionately out of alignment. Some 20% of Morningstar employee dollars were allocated to three international funds, which all managed to lose substantial amounts of money in 1997.

Another study looked at the 401(k) plans of several well-known investment firms and found the same bad results as the general public. While not all employees of these firms are financially savvy, it is reasonable to expect that they would have a higher level of interest, concern and knowledge than employees at non-financial services firms. The results show that the firms together lagged a 60% stock 40% bond mix by –8.9%, about like the –9.5% average investor from 1984-2002.

Table 8-3: Financial Service Firms' 401(k) Performance

Investment Firm	1995	1996	1997	1998	All 4 Years
Merrill Lynch	21.2%	12.5%	13.4%	0.2%	11.8%
Prudential	11.3%	11.1%	13.4%	6.9%	10.7%
Hewitt Consulting	17.6%	11.6%	22.6%	-1.6%	12.6%
CitiGroup	29.2%	21.2%	10.3%	13.3%	18.5%
Morningstar	21.0%	15.2%	11.2%	6.8%	13.6%
Average of All Groups	20.1%	14.3%	14.2%	5.1%	13.4%
60/40 Stock/Bond Mix	32.3%	12.0%	24.3%	20.8%	22.4%
Group Perf. to Benchmark	-12.2%	2.3%	-10.1%	-15.7%	-8.9%

Source: Hamilton, B. and Burns, S. "Reinventing Income in America"
National Center for Policy Analysis (2001)

Equity Fund Redemptions and Shareholder Turnover

The redemption rate for all equity funds, measured as redemptions and redemption exchanges divided by average assets, rose to 41% in 2003, up from just 6% in 1970. U.S. stock prices declined for the third consecutive year in 2002, marking the first three-year run of losses since 1941. Stock market indexes for large corporations fell by more than 20%, bringing the cumulative drop for the three years ending in 2002 to 45%, the largest since 1930–1932. The response of equity fund shareholders to the unusual financial conditions and slow economic growth was consistent with the well-established pattern of selling during periods of low stock-market returns. Equity fund investors sold their equity fund holdings amidst the stock market downturn. The outflows generally conformed to investor behavior during the brief market downturns that occurred during the 1990s. Cash outflows occurred to a greater extent during the bear markets of the 1970s and after the 1987 stock market crash. In other words, investors buy at the top and sell at the bottom.

Chart 8-4: Growth in Shareholder Selling (Redemptions) in Mutual Funds, 1970–2003

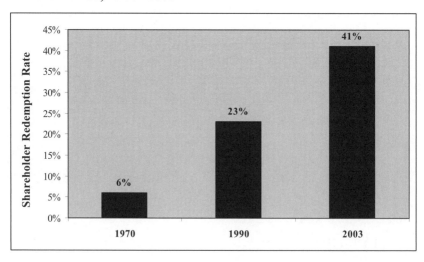

Investor Dollars Chase Past Performance

In a July 2003 editorial in the *Wall Street Journal*, John Bogle, the former chairman of Vanguard, said, "The bewildering array of choices among nearly 5,000 equity funds has ill served investors. The returns incurred by the average equity fund investor since 1984 have averaged just 2.7% per year, a shocking shortfall to the 9.3% return earned by the average fund. The result is that the average fund investor has earned less than one-quarter of the stock market's annual return."

The dollar return investors earn is less dependent on the long-term average return of the fund than on when they placed their dollars in the fund. We conducted studies to analyze the fund selection and timing effectiveness of investors by analyzing the annual return of the Vanguard Index 500 from 1991 to 2002. We looked at total cash flow in and out of the fund to see the returns actually earned on the dollars that went into the fund. We found that most investors fared poorly and that they would have been better off in cash for the past decade.

We selected the Vanguard Index 500 fund because at one point in late 1999, nearly $100 billion was invested in the fund, making it the largest mutual fund in the world. Theoretically, 1991–2002 should have been a good period for investors, with the S&P 500 up nearly 12% annually on average.

The actual annual return on each dollar invested was about 1.7%. We found that the total dollars earned in the Vanguard Index 500 were much less than would have been earned from a fixed investment paying 5%. The $50.4 billion invested in the Index 500 earned a cumulative $10.7 billion over the twelve years. Had the exact same cash flow been invested in a fixed income fund paying 5%, investors would have earned $24.6 billion.

Chart 8-6: Cash Flow Chases Performance to Detriment of Investors

Vanguard Index 500 Asset Flow Study

All dollars in millions.

	1991	1992	1993	1994	1995	1996	1997	1998	1999	2000	2001	2002	Totals
Net Cash Flow	$715	$1,880	$1,083	$993	$4,516	$8,999	$8,956	$10,755	$14,836	$1,244	$2,113	-$5,721	
Fund Return	30.2%	7.4%	9.8%	1.1%	37.4%	22.8%	33.2%	28.6%	21.0%	-9.0%	-12.0%	-20.0%	150.5%
Net Cash Flow	$715	$1,880	$1,083	$993	$4,516	$8,999	$8,956	$10,755	$14,836	$1,244	$2,113	-$5,721	$50,370
Net Dollars Earned	$842	$322	$642	$91	$3,499	$3,961	$10,070	$14,116	$15,588	-$9,419	-$11,577	-$17,403	$10,731

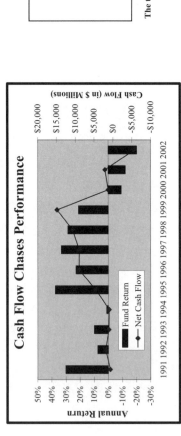

Cash Flow Chases Performance

1991 1992 1993 1994 1995 1996 1997 1998 1999 2000 2001 2002

Legend: Fund Return / Net Cash Flow

Annual Return axis: 50%, 40%, 30%, 20%, 10%, 0%, -10%, -20%, -30%

Cash Flow (in $ Millions) axis: $20,000, $15,000, $10,000, $5,000, $0, -$5,000, -$10,000

Vanguard Index 500
Twelve Year
Total Dollar Weighted Returns

$$\frac{\$10,731}{\$50,370} = 21.3\% = 1.7\% \text{ per year}$$

The time weighted arithmetic average return was +12.4%.

Survivorship Bias

When conducting historical mutual-fund performance studies, it is important to understand the concept of survivorship bias. In the context of mutual funds, survivorship bias is the tendency for poor performers to drop out over time while strong performers continue to exist, resulting in an overestimation of past returns for the surviving group as compared with the entire beginning group. The reported returns of the now merged funds will only contain the live (better) returns of the surviving fund. Of course, the poor returns that investors received from the defunct fund did not disappear; they were just unreported, as if they were never experienced.

For example, a mutual fund company's selection of funds today will include only those that have previously been successful. Many losing funds are closed and merged into other funds to eliminate poor performance. In the most comprehensive study ever done on mutual funds, covering the period 1962–1993, the authors found that by 1993, fully one-third of all funds in the sample had disappeared. This is important to take into account when analyzing past performance.

The survivorship-bias problem has increased in recent years as mutual fund families have tried to bury poor performance. In 1998 alone, 387 stock and bond funds were merged out of existence, an increase of 43% over the previous year. A further 250 funds were liquidated due to investor redemptions. The trend managed to accelerate even further in 2000 as 451 funds were shut down or merged out of existence. We have found that survivorship bias in average performance typically increases with the sample length. This is relevant, because evidence suggests a multiyear survival rule for U.S. mutual funds. In the published data, we find that the annual bias increases from 0.1% for one-year samples to 1.0% for samples longer than fifteen years. We believe that survivor conditioning must be taken into account when examining data.

The Importance of Measuring a Fund against Its Peers

Everyone would intuitively agree that it makes no sense to compare a stock fund to a money market fund, because the underlying investment portfolios are so different in terms of risk and return. Once you get past the clear-cut examples, the classification of funds becomes far more difficult.

Each fund's prospectus should outline the general objectives and the fund's investment goals. This is a starting point for fund classification for peer-group comparison purposes. Unfortunately, some 10% to 25% of funds have a significantly different portfolio from their prospectus objective. This makes classifying a fund based merely on its prospectus objective unreliable.

In classifying funds, we observe fund behavior instead of relying exclusively on stated investment objectives or outdated portfolio holdings. After all, from an asset allocation perspective, what a fund claims to be isn't nearly as important as how it performs and moves relative to other asset classes. ABC Growth Fund, for example, may purport to be a plain-vanilla domestic equity fund, yet it could behave similarly to a small-cap fund. Alternatively, if it invests in domestic companies that rely heavily on overseas customers for revenues, its behavior may closely resemble that of an international fund.

In an effort to distinguish funds by what they own, as well as by their prospectus objectives and styles, we developed a method to identify funds based on their actual investment styles as measured by their underlying portfolio holdings (portfolio statistics and compositions over various periods). When necessary, we may change a category assignment based on current information. There is no perfect system, and some overlap may occur, but simply relying upon the prospectus objective is not accurate and results in significant errors.

Results of Major Studies That Examined Mutual Fund Performance

Carlson Study: Conducted in 1970, this study examined all equity funds from 1948 to 1967. The author found that a partial performance persistence for funds correlated most strongly to five-year past-performance periods.

Grinblatt and Titman Study: Conducted in 1989, this study examined all equity funds from 1974 to 1989. The authors found a partial performance persistence for funds by examining five-year past-performance periods. The strongest correlation was with the fund's expense ratio.

Grinblatt and Titman Study (II): Conducted in 1992, this study examined 279 equity funds from 1974 to 1989. The authors found that a partial performance persistence for funds was weakly correlated to the five-year past-performance periods.

Brown, Goeztmann, Ibbotson, and Ross Study: Conducted in 1992, this study examined all equity funds from 1976 to 1987. The authors found a partial performance persistence for funds by examining three-year relative (peer group) past-performance periods.

Hendricks, Patel and Zeckhauser Study: Conducted in 1993, this study examined all equity funds from 1974 to 1988. The authors found a partial performance persistence for funds by examining quarterly past-performance periods. They found that the performance persistence continued for two to eight quarters in the future.

Grinblatt and Titman Study (III): Conducted in 1995, this study examined 209 equity funds from 1975 to 1994. The authors found a partial performance persistence for these funds by examining turnover rate, expense ratio, and past relative return factors.

Elton, Gruber, and Blake Study: Conducted in 1996, this study examined 188 equity funds from 1977 to 1993. The authors found partial performance persistence for these funds by examining expense ratio and past one- and three-year relative return factors.

Carhart Study: Conducted in 1997, this study examined all equity funds from 1962 to 1993. The author found a partial performance persistence for these funds by examining turnover rate, expense ratio, and past relative return factors. The author found that poorly performing funds tended to continue to be strongly poorly performing funds. In other words, "negative persistence" was a greater predictor than "positive persistence."

Jain and Wu Study: Conducted in 2000, this study examined 294 advertised equity funds from 1994 to 1996. The authors found that once performance was advertised, the fund's performance deteriorated.

Wermers Study: Conducted in 2001, this study examined all equity funds from 1974 to 1994. The authors found partial performance persistence for these funds by examining expense ratios and past one- and three-year relative return factors. They related one-year to fund momentum and three-year to overall manager skill.

Bollen and Busse Study: Conducted in 2002, this study examined 230 equity funds from 1985 to 1995. The authors found a partial performance persistence for these funds by examining expense ratio and past-quarter and one-year relative return factors.

Ibbottson and Patel Study: Conducted in 2002, this study examined all equity funds from 1978 to 1999. The authors found a partial performance persistence for these funds by examining expense ratio and past-quarter and one-year relative return factors. They saw persistence after adjusting for the fund's style. Top group funds tended to repeat.

Table 8-3: Important Mutual Fund Evaluation Factors

- Each fund must be compared to its peer group
- Survivorship bias skews the results and must be taken into account when examining the data
- The expense ratio is important
- The turnover rate is important
- The fund's relative ranking among its peers over varying time periods is important
- Poor performing funds (when compared to peers) typically tend to remain poor performers
- There can be significant amounts of random variation between funds

Mutual Fund Size Does Matter

Investment research has confirmed an inverse relationship between the size of assets under management and investment performance — that is to say, the larger a stock portfolio's asset base, the more deleterious the effect on performance. The key questions are at what level of assets does the performance change? What is the largest amount of assets that a fund manager can accept and still efficiently execute their investment strategies and retain their potential to outperform?

Assume two portfolio managers with similar investment styles each own 100 stocks in their portfolio. Each attempts to buy a 1% portfolio position in the same stock that was selling at a price of $20 per share when the issuing company announced positive news. Assume that the price rises over the next six days following the announcement. Most importantly, assume that one fund manager's portfolio has $100 million in assets, and the other manager's portfolio has $1 billion.

The manager with the $100 million portfolio is able to build a 1% position in one day. He purchased 45,000 shares (representing 10% of the stock's average daily trading volume) at an average price of $22.22. Conversely, the manager with the $1 billion portfolio was compelled to buy the stock over five days to achieve a 1% position. That manager bought 408,000 shares at an average price of $24.50 (representing 18% of the stock's average daily volume). Due to his superior trading efficiency, the first manager is able to gain 0.10% of out-performance in this stock relative to the second manager.

If both managers average about 100% turnover in holdings annually and if the first manager continues to execute most trades in one day, he may outperform the manager with the larger portfolio by 10% in the course of a year. As this example shows, the time needed to build (or eliminate) positions in a portfolio directly affects a mutual fund's results.

We define maximum asset capacity as the largest amount of assets in a stock portfolio that permits the manager to execute the investment strategy efficiently and reasonably quickly. We measure capacity in millions or billions of dollars for each portfolio according to the following formula:

Portfolio Capacity = (#S * $DV * #D * %V)/(1 - %C)

Here are the individual formula components:

#S - the average number of securities held in the portfolio;

$DV - the weighted average daily dollar volume of all stocks traded in the applicable universe;

#D - the maximum number of days required to build and eliminate positions without compromising the investment strategy's potential alpha;

%V - the maximum percentage of the average daily volume that can be traded without materially affecting the stock price;

%C - the percentage of the portfolio typically held in cash.

Based upon this analysis some useful guidelines can be established. In general, the asset limit is $9 billion to $11 billion for core growth, blend and value funds, $6 to $8 billion for mid cap growth, value and blend funds, $700 million to $1.5 billion for small growth and blend funds, $1.1 billion to $1.7 billion for small cap value funds and $400 million to $750 million for micro cap growth and value funds. In general, ultra large cap funds (such as S&P 500 index or large cap blend funds) can reach asset levels of at least $20 billion to $35 billion due to the extreme liquidity of the stocks they typically trade.

Secondary Factors Related to Mutual Fund Performance, Selection, and Retention

At Unified Trust Company, we focus on factors that are useful in identifying and maintaining high asset quality for each asset allocation subgroup. Our fund evaluation process is designed to objectively measure asset quality. It is designed to improve outcomes. It does not affect asset allocation per se.

In order to understand which mutual-fund measurement criteria may have a predictive outcome, we have reviewed all major academic finance publications. We have compiled these predictive criteria into a single mathematical formula to create the Unified Fiduciary Monitoring Index®.

The Unified Fiduciary Monitoring Index® (described in detail in chapter 12) is a composite percentile ranking of more than 14,000 mutual funds as compared with their peer groups (investment categories). The mathematical calculation does not look at raw investment performance; instead, it incorporates several factors described previously in this chapter shown to be at least partially predictive in academic studies.

The finalist funds undergo additional fund-selection criteria. These supplemental criteria include but are not limited to fund asset size, investment style (peer group category) consistency, Unified Fiduciary Monitoring Index® score consistency, manager tenure, revenue sharing back to the plan sponsor, and funds employing a multi-manager approach.

Some may wonder why risk is not included in the asset quality equation. For a detailed discussion of risk, especially risk the way an investor thinks about risk, see chapter 6.

The Market Timing and Late-Day Mutual Fund Trading Scandals

"It's bad stuff — and it's bad that it seems to be pervasive," said John Bogle, founder of the Vanguard family of mutual funds and one of the few outspoken critics inside the industry. Unified Trust Company, N.A., did not engage in late-day trading or market timing, the two abuses of the mutual fund scandal. But apparently, many other groups saw this as an easy way to make a quick buck off the back of the mutual fund shareholder.

In 2003, numerous mutual fund companies were implicated in a broad-reaching trading scandal that clearly showed that they put the fund companies' interests ahead of those of the shareholders. By the end of 2003, the fund companies cited included some of the most popular with investors: Janus, Putnam, Bank of America's Nations Funds, Pilgrim-Baxter, Strong, American Express, Bank One, U.S. Trust, Federated Investors, and Loomis Sayles. Regulators were also probing brokerage firms that allegedly aided or engaged in the trading schemes, including Morgan Stanley, Charles Schwab, and Prudential Securities. The questions the scandal raised were as troubling as they were complicated and affect an industry entrusted with a huge portion of the nation's savings, much of it in 401(k) retirement accounts.

Market Timing

What is market timing? This is a practice of rapidly buying and selling fund shares to take advantage of "stale prices" of foreign shares. Mutual funds that buy foreign shares are priced at the end of New York trading, many hours after foreign markets close. If U.S. markets rally, it's a safe bet that foreign stocks will rise tomorrow.

Market timers buy today, knowing that the funds are undervalued, and then sell them the next day when they rise. These profits come at the expense of other investors in the fund, who are essentially selling shares to market timers at the low price and buying shares at a higher price the next day. The SEC recently said that about half of mutual fund companies and nearly 30% of broker-dealers engage in market timing. Another 40%, the SEC said, know about market timing and may let customers engage in it, even if they don't do it themselves. Other estimates are higher. One academic study estimated that 90% of the international mutual funds in its sample engaged in market timing.

Who benefits? Regulators alleged that one of the biggest market timers was Canary Capital Partners, a New Jersey hedge fund. Hedge funds are lightly regulated and often attract money from rich folks who can afford to take a little more risk. Security Trust Company in Phoenix, Arizona, facilitated the trading for Canary Capital Partners in return for a share of the profits. But market timing was also carried out for other big institutions, which typically ask for the favor in exchange for putting a chunk of investment money with the fund company for a longer period.

In many cases, regulators alleged, fund managers, brokers, and fund-company executives engaged in market timing for their own personal accounts, violating the trust placed in them as stewards of those investments. The chairman of Strong funds resigned after his personal trading abuses were brought to light.

Is this legal? This quick in-and-out trading to capture small gains is called arbitrage. Though legal and widely practiced in the world of stocks, it is considered improper for most mutual funds, because it harms other investors. Documents released by New York Attorney General Eliot Spitzer, who helped launch the probe of fund scandals in September, show how casually officials at Bank of America, Janus, Putnam Investments, and others handled market timing. None of the funds that had special market-timing arrangements disclosed the existence of the arrangements to investors.

Late-Day Trading

What is late-day trading? The original intent of late-day trading was for 401(k) investors to be able to sell and buy funds ("exchange") from two different fund families on the same trade day. To finish the second part of the transaction, the trading institution had to know exactly how many dollars were obtained from the original sell. After that, they could enter the buy side of the transaction. Some mutual fund groups allowed trades to be placed as late as 9:00 P.M. to finish the transaction.

Late-day trading abuses occur when privileged non-401(k) investors are "hidden" in the bunched 401(k) trade orders. They then buy or sell mutual fund shares after the fund has closed for the day. In essence, they go back in time and buy before a market-moving piece of news. In one form of this trade, investors submit buy and sell orders for the same number of mutual fund shares before the markets close on a day when market-moving news is expected after the fund closes. When the news comes out, they cancel one of the orders and keep the profitable one.

Who benefits? Again, hedge funds or other large investors are granted the privilege, often in exchange for putting some money with the fund company or broker. In some cases, brokers and fund managers also may have engaged in late trading.

The practice costs other investors in the mutual fund, because they are, in essence, selling to the late traders at an unfairly low price or buying at an unfairly high price. Some experts believe that this costs fund investors $1 billion a year. Is this legal? No, it's illegal. But until the scandal broke, regulators had not banned manipulative double-order cancellations. Before the scandal occurred, they had made late trading even easier by allowing fund companies and brokerages to process orders for many hours after the official close. The lengthy process created plenty of opportunities for some people along the processing trail to game the system.

Predictability of Mutual Fund Performance

Historically, the performance predictability of mutual funds has been variable. The same confidence range issues we discussed earlier apply to mutual fund performance. However, several factors favor mutual fund performance predictability over individual managers.

AIMR Compliance Enhances Due Diligence

Mutual funds, by definition, are required to report their performance in a standardized fashion, and each mutual fund calculates a net asset value (NAV) each day. There are large standardized raw performance databases for almost every mutual fund. In contrast, there are many formats by which a separate account manager may report its performance, and most separate account managers do not claim Association for Investment Management and Research ("AIMR") compliance.

AIMR compliance is a specific way to report performance that allows the results to be fairly compared with another manager or benchmark. Without performance standardization, it is difficult to study all separate accounts as a level playing field. We believe that the data are much more accurate and reliable in mutual funds.

Security Holdings Diversification

A concentrated portfolio that holds fewer securities can be a hit-or-miss phenomenon. The average separate account holds thirty-four stocks; the average mutual fund holds sixty-five stocks. A concentrated portfolio is more likely to have returns that vary from the group average. As long as the variation is positive, the investor will not complain. But sooner or later, the investor will learn that variation is random, and it is just as likely that the variation will be negative.

Multi-Manager Diversification

Within the same investment style, many mutual funds use a multi-manager approach, selecting and monitoring many of the most talented money managers in the world. The idea is that this blending of managers can help provide more consistent returns through all kinds of market environments. Assets of each fund are divided into smaller, more manageable portions. Portions are managed by portfolio managers who operate autonomously, investing their portions as though they were an entire fund—subject to fund objectives and overall guidelines.

Because each investment professional offers unique expertise and has different convictions, this approach magnifies the benefits of diversification inherent in mutual fund investing. Over time, having more than one person managing assets has tended to smooth out the peaks and valleys of investing. Finally, continuity is an issue. When one portfolio manager retires or changes responsibilities, only a portion of portfolio control changes hands under this approach. Smooth, gradual transitions help the fund's investment approach remain consistent.

Subsequent Poor Performance Is the Big Problem

Many groups, such as bank trust departments, Frank Russell and Company, SEI Investments, Lockwood, Solomon Smith Barney, Merrill Lynch, and others, have managed account programs or their own proprietary mutual funds. A typical example of due diligence can be found by studying Frank Russell. Each year, through an integrated worldwide network of more than fifty analysts, Frank Russell and Company evaluates more than 1,700 investment managers and more than six thousand investment products. Russell's fifty analysts hold more than two thousand research meetings annually to study each manager's quantitative and qualitative approaches. They use extensive qualitative and quantitative research to find roughly three hundred managers, who are then subject to further scrutiny.

Russell Company found that picking today's hot manager wasn't the solution for long-term success. To be on top one year, a manager has to take risk—risk that is just as likely to land them on the bottom in the following years. For example, in 1996, of Russell's total of 293 U.S. equity managers, 75 managers composed the top quartile, or the top 25% of U.S. equity managers. Out of those seventy-five, seventeen remained in the top quartile the next year. Exodus from the top quartile was swift, and no manager was still there in either 2000 or 2001. Most dropped out in the first two years. These results are shown in Chart 8-7.

Why do so many managers drop out? The major factor is the fact that a manager's future performance is hugely unpredictable. On a statistical basis, it could not be otherwise. In other cases, managers lose key research or investment personnel, and their ongoing operations suffer.

Chart 8-7: Top-Tier Managers Seldom Remain There

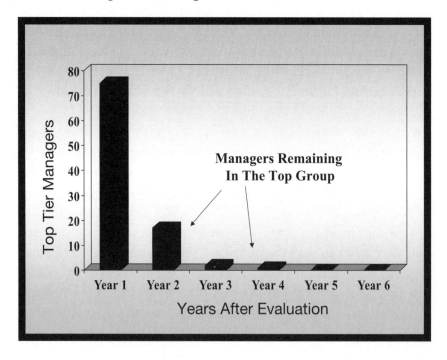

To understand how a single manager of a proprietary mutual fund or managed account program can fail so miserably after being hired, we must understand the basic probability statistics of money management. Investing and money management are a series of probability outcomes. Over short periods, results may differ from their long-term probabilities, but as time elapses and more observations are noted, the results move toward the "law of large numbers."

The law of large numbers simply states that over time and with enough observations, results are exactly as the large pool of data indicates. For example, assume that we have 100 million registered voters in the United States and that 51.31% are registered Democrats. If we ask two people how they vote, we might get two Democrats (100%) and zero Republicans (0%). We haven't collected enough observations for our small sample to look like the large pool. As we question more and more people, our results begin to look more like the overall results. If we question ten people, we might find 70% Democrats and 30% Republicans. If we question 100 people, we might find 55% Democrats and 45% Republicans. If we question 10,000 people, we might find 52% Democrats and 48% Republicans. Finally, if we question 10 million people, we might find 51.29% Democrats.

Because our small sample of money manager observations is always smaller than the universe, we need to know how likely it is that our small sample looks like the big group. Is it 10% likely to look like the big group or 95% likely? There is a big difference in confidence between the two. Statistics allow us to create a probability diagram to tell how close we are getting with our small sample to the overall picture.

We need to understand one more term: standard deviation. Standard deviation tells us how much a sample varies around its mean or average value. Approximately 65% of all values fall within one standard deviation on each side of the mean, and 95% fall between two standard deviations. If the mean value is 5 and the standard deviation is 6, 65% of all values are between -1 and 11, and 95% are between –7 and 17. Illustrated below is a simplified case:

Investment Style:	**Large Cap Value Equity**
Overall Total Group Size:	**500 Managers**
Average 3 Yr. Return Total Group	**+8.54%**
Average 3 Yr. Return of Top 25% Group	**+11.33%**
Average 3 Yr. Return of Bottom 25% Group	**+5.75%**
Advantage Of Top 25% Versus Total Group	**+2.79%**
Standard Deviation of Total Group	**8.66%**

We are hiring this manager because we want to beat the average manager. What is the probability that the manager we just hired is representative of the entire top 25% group, who, as a group, beat the average manager? The top 25% group has 125 managers (one-fourth of 500). If we hired all 125 managers, we could be sure they would look like the top 25% group, as they are one and the same. But what if we hire just one manager out of this group? We cannot be sure that this manager looks like the larger group.

Based upon the following variables, we can draw a confidence graph that helps us determine how many managers we would need to hire to have a certain level of confidence that our small group looks like the large group. The confidence graph shows us how much a small group might vary from the larger group results to which they belong. The larger the standard deviation, the more observations we need to be sure our small group looks like the larger group.

Overall Top 25% Group Size:	**125 Managers**
Average Three-Year Return of Top 25% Group	**+11.33%**
Standard Deviation of Total Group	**8.66%**

If we hire one manager, the 70% confidence range is 8.98%. What does this mean? It means that we can say with 70% confidence that any individual out of the "select group" of managers was plus or minus 8.98% of the entire select group result. Our manager has to beat the average return of 8.54%. In our example, the select group return was 11.33%, so plus or minus 8.98% gives us a possible range of 20.31% to 2.35%. If the result was 20.31%, the client would be happy; but the client would not be happy at the low end of the range, as 2.35% does not beat 8.54%. With just one "successful" manager, we cannot be 70% confident that the manager can beat the group average.

So, how many managers do we need to hire in order to be 70% confident that the worst range of their returns will still beat the entire group average? The answer is that we need to hire at least <u>eleven managers</u> to be 70% confident that they, as a group, will have a range of returns similar enough to beat the average manager, even if we get the low end of their return ranges.

Chart 8-8: 70% Confidence Level Range Variation

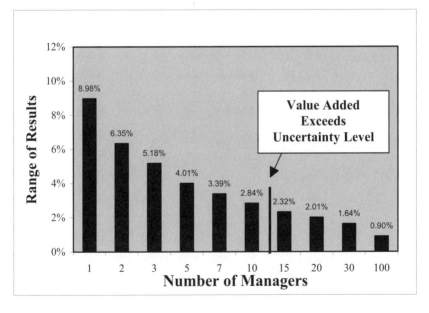

For Further Reading

Bollen, P., and Busse, J. "On the Timing Ability of Mutual Fund Managers." *Journal of Finance* 56, 1075–1094 (2001).

Brown, K., and Harlow, W. *Staying the Course: The Impact of Investment Style Consistency on Mutual Fund Performance*. Dallas, University of Texas Press, (2002).

Brown, S., Goetzmann, W., Ibbotson, R., and Ross, S. "Survivorship Bias in Performance Studies." *Review of Financial Studies* 5, 553–580. (1992).

Brown, S., and Goetzmann, W. "Performance Persistence." *Journal of Finance* 50, 679–698 (1995).

Busse, J., and Irvine, P. "Bayesian Alphas and Mutual Fund Persistence." Working paper. Atlanta, Ga.: Emory University, (2002).

Carhart, M. "On Persistence in Mutual Fund Performance." *Journal of Finance* 52, 57–82 (1997).

Carlson, R. "Aggregate Performance of Mutual Funds, 1948–1967." *Journal of Financial and Quantitative Analysis* 5, 1–32 (1970).

Elton, E., Gruber, M., and Blake, C. "The Persistence of Risk-Adjusted Mutual Fund Performance." *Journal of Business* 69, 133–157 (1996).

Goetzmann, W., and Ibbotson, R. "Do Winners Repeat? Patterns in Mutual Fund Performance." *Journal of Portfolio Management* 20, 9–18 (1994).

Grinblatt, M., and Titman, S. "Mutual Fund Performance: An Analysis of Quarterly Portfolio Holdings." *Journal of Business* 62, 393–416 (1989).

Grinblatt, M., and Titman, S. "The Persistence of Mutual Fund Performance." *Journal of Finance* 47, 1977–1984 (1992).

Grinblatt, M., and Titman, S. "Performance Measurement without Benchmarks: An Examination of Mutual Fund Returns." *Journal of Business* 66, 47–68 (1993).

Grinblatt, M., and Titman, S., and Wermers, R. "Momentum Investment Strategies, Portfolio Performance, and Herding: A Study of Mutual Fund Behavior." *American Economic Review* 85, no. 5, 1088–1105 (1995).

Gruber, M. "Another Puzzle: The Growth in Actively Managed Mutual Funds." *Journal of Finance* 51 (1996).

Hendricks, D. "Hot Hands in Mutual Funds: Short-Run Persistence of Performance, 1974–88." *Journal of Finance* 48, 93–130 (1993).

Ibbotson, R., and Patel, A. "Do Winners Repeat with Style? Summary of Findings." Ibbotson Associates.
http://www.ibbotson.com/Research/papers/toc.asp (2002).

Jain, P., and Shuang Wu, J. "Truth in Mutual Fund Advertising: Evidence on Future Performance and Fund Flows." *Journal of Finance* 55, 937–958 (2000).

Kahn, R, and Rudd, A. "Does Historical Performance Predict Future Performance?" *Barra Newsletter*, (Spring 1995).

Burton M. "Returns from Investing in Equity Mutual Funds, 1971–1991." *Journal of Finance* 50, 549–572 (1995).

Phelps, S., and Detzel, L. "The Non-Persistence of Mutual Fund Performance." *Quarterly Journal of Business and Economics* 36, 55–69 (1997).

Predicting Mutual Fund Performance II: After the Bear. Financial Research Corporation, Boston, (2003).

Sauer, D. "Information Content of Prior Period Mutual Fund Performance Rankings." *Journal of Economics and Business*, 549–567, (1997).

Shukla, R. "The Value of Active Portfolio Management." Working paper. Syracuse, N.Y.: Syracuse University, (1999).

Shukla, R. "Identifying Superior Performing Equity Mutual Funds." Working paper. Syracuse, N.Y.: Syracuse University, (2000).

Wermers, R. "Momentum Investment Strategies of Mutual Funds, Performance Persistence, and Survivorship Bias." Working paper. Boulder: University of Colorado at Boulder, (1997).

Wermers, R. "Mutual Fund Performance: An Empirical Decomposition into Stock-picking Talent, Style, Transaction Costs, and Expenses." *Journal of Finance* 55, 1655–1695 (2000).

Wermers, R. "Predicting Mutual Fund Returns." Working paper. University of Maryland, (2001).

"Morningstar Study Debunks Fund World's Oldest Myth." *Wall Street Journal*, (2003).

"The Stars in the Sky Flicker, and Fund Stars Do the Same." *Wall Street Journal*, (2003).

"The Emperor's New Mutual Funds." *Wall Street Journal*, (2003).

"Who's Fiddling with Your Funds?" *Wall Street Journal*, (2003).

"House Passes Bill to Curb Mutual-Fund Corruption." *Wall Street Journal*, (2003).

"Merck Becomes Latest to Drop Putnam from Its 401(k) Plan." *Wall Street Journal*, (2003).

Chapter 9

ERISA Fiduciary Issues Plan Sponsors Must Understand

Chapter Summary

The Employee Retirement Income Security Act of 1974 (ERISA) regulates all Internal Revenue Service (IRS)–qualified retirement and other benefit plans. This law and subsequent amendments impose significant fiduciary responsibilities and liabilities on plan sponsors and plan managers. The plan sponsor is held to the "prudent expert" standard of conduct. Fiduciaries are subject to four specific standards in regard to their involvement with the plan. The four standards are: (1) the duty of loyalty; (2) the duty of prudence; (3) the duty to diversify investments; and (4) the duty to follow plan documents. The plan sponsor is always required to act in the best interests of participants and beneficiaries.

Although financial risks of fiduciary status are huge, most plan sponsors carry no fiduciary liability insurance. The fiduciary is personally liable for breaches of fiduciary duty. Merely offering plan participants the ability to direct their own investments under ERISA Section 404(c) through a variety of investment choices does not relieve the plan sponsor of fiduciary responsibility and liability.

Fiduciaries are not required to always be right, but they must have a process, and that process must be prudent. The current complex regulatory and investment environment makes satisfying the fiduciary responsibility provisions of ERISA more difficult than ever for most plan sponsors and requires a careful and well-documented process.

"Fiduciary" Defined

A fiduciary is an individual, company, or association that is responsible for managing another's assets. Fiduciaries include executors of wills and estates, trustees, and those responsible for managing the finances of a minor. *Black's Law Dictionary* describes a fiduciary relationship as "one founded on trust or confidence reposed by one person in the integrity and fidelity of another." A fiduciary has a duty to act primarily for the beneficiary's benefit in matters connected with the undertaking and not for the fiduciary's own personal interest. Scrupulous good faith and candor are required. Fiduciaries must always act in complete fairness and may not exert influence or pressure, take selfish advantage, or deal with beneficiaries in such a way that it benefits themselves or prejudices beneficiaries. Business shrewdness, hard bargaining, misrepresentation, and taking advantage of the forgetfulness or negligence of beneficiaries by a fiduciary are prohibited.

A fiduciary has rights and powers that would normally belong to another person. The fiduciary holds those rights and exercises them to the benefit of the beneficiary. Fiduciaries must not allow any conflict of interest to infect their duties toward their beneficiaries and must exercise a high standard of care in protecting or promoting the interests of beneficiaries.

Whereas financial services salespeople may have their own motives and interests at heart and offer goods and services for a high or low price, a fiduciary must serve the beneficiary, if necessary at the cost of the fiduciary's own interests. It is generally believed that fiduciaries perform their trades for reasons other than money alone and feel a sense of responsibility that goes beyond simply making a living. To paraphrase Supreme Court Justice Louis D. Brandeis: "It is an occupation that is pursued largely for others and not merely for oneself. It is an occupation in which the amount of financial return is not the accepted measure of success."

Why Congress Created ERISA

Before a major pension law was enacted a little more than a quarter of a century ago, the regulation of pension plans was modest in scope. By today's standards, the rules applied to pension plans were minimal, and they originated almost exclusively in the Internal Revenue Code. The central requirement a pension plan had to meet was that it was "qualified" — that is, it satisfied IRS rules for special tax treatment. A few sections of the Internal Revenue Code contained most of the relevant rules governing contributions, and those rules were largely intended to make at least some of those special tax benefits flow to the rank-and-file workers.

In 1963, more than four thousand workers with vested pension rights lost most of their pensions when the Studebaker Car Company stopped producing automobiles and closed its plants. You may not remember the Studebaker Car Company. The company had a good pension plan for its employees. But fate was not kind to Studebaker or to its employees. When the employees tried to draw their pensions, they were horrified to discover that there was nothing left for them.

But Studebaker was not to blame. The company and its executives had not broken any laws. Unfortunately for the employees, there were no laws were to protect them. People were shocked to hear about one employee at Studebaker who had worked for ten straight years. After a short break in service, he worked another ten years. But his tenure did not satisfy the company's twenty-year service requirement, because the years of service had to be consecutive. So this employee got nothing. In fact, Studebaker could lay off an employee with nineteen years of service for a few weeks and then call the worker back to work. The worker would then need to start the twenty-year cycle all over again! It was possible for workers to spend most of their adult life at the same company and never receive a dime of promised pension benefits. Many stories like this forced Congress to act.

This experience and similar stories of losses in the private pension system became the major impetus for pension reform through the enactment, on Labor Day 1974, of ERISA. ERISA imposed funding rules and vesting requirements on pension plans so that retired workers would get the benefits they had earned.

ERISA regulates all IRS-qualified retirement and other benefit plans. The overwhelming purpose of the ERISA statute as enacted in 1974 was not to create free markets in employment fringe benefits, but rather to regulate the fringe-benefit market in order to respond to two types of massive market failure.

The first was the frequent refusal of management and labor to set aside actuarially adequate assets to fund collectively bargained pensions. In other words, promised benefits were never funded. When companies and whole industries went into economic decline in the 1960s, they were able to pay only a small fraction or none of the pensions they had promised to long-term employees. (Note how the move to defined contribution plans has caused most workers to underfund their accounts, because they do not function well as their own actuaries.)

Second, pre-ERISA state and federal law did not provide adequate remedies for malfeasance by the trustees or plan sponsor of fringe benefit funds. The congressional hearings leading up to ERISA were filled with accounts of trustees engaged in self-dealing and otherwise diverting funds from the intended beneficiaries. Sometime the funds were stolen outright; in many cases, employers simply failed to segregate the employees' contributions from general corporate assets and used the money as short-term interest-free loans from the pension plan. ERISA attempted to clean up such activity by regulating and insuring pension plan assets, and by imposing federal fiduciary duties and legal remedies on benefit plan decision-makers.

ERISA Preempts Most State Laws

The U.S. Supreme Court has ruled that ERISA preempts most state laws that apply to all ERISA-covered plans, such as life insurance, retirement, and most types of executive deferred-compensation plans. Although Congress had exhaustively considered the bills leading up to ERISA for many years, the law's final version included a preemption of state laws that was the product of last-minute changes in the conference committee. Prior to the conference committee, both houses of Congress had passed bills that, in the usual way of federal statutes, preempted only state law regarding "subject matters regulated by this Act." However, just before the final vote, the House-Senate conference committee added a preemption provision to cover "any and all State laws insofar as they may now or hereafter relate to any employee benefit plan." In addition, language was added stating that "no employer benefit plan shall be deemed an insurance company" for purposes of state insurance law.

Two researchers, Daniel Fox and Daniel Schaffer, have studied ERISA's legislative history. Their work reveals that the broad preemption provisions were the product of powerful but narrowly focused interest groups. Although there is no reference to these events in the legislative history, based on interviews in the mid-1980s with key participants in the 1974 events, Fox and Schaffer conclude that the motivation behind the last-minute expansion of ERISA preemption was the desire of certain large corporations and unions who operated multistate, joint management-labor self-insured health and pension plans to avoid state regulation and taxation of their funds as "insurance" and to increase their freedom to bargaining collectively. The text of the ERISA preemption provision was not limited to state insurance taxes, collectively bargained national contracts, multistate corporations, or even collective bargaining. Rather, it came to be interpreted as displacing virtually all state laws regarding any employment-based ERISA-covered plan, including life insurance, retirement, health, and most types of executive deferred-compensation plans.

Who Is a Fiduciary under ERISA?

ERISA specifies that a person is a fiduciary with respect to an employee benefit plan to the extent that such a person does any of the following:

1. Exercises any discretionary authority or control over the management of a plan or over the management or disposition of plan assets

2. Renders investment advice for a fee or other compensation, direct or indirect, over the disposition of plan assets, or has any authority or responsibility to do so

3. Has any discretionary authority or discretionary responsibility in the administration of such plan

Before the enactment of ERISA, under traditional trust law, only plan trustees had fiduciary obligations. When Congress enacted ERISA in 1974, it expanded the universe of persons subject to fiduciary duties. Courts apply a so-called functional test when trying to determine if a person is a fiduciary under ERISA. In applying the functional test, the focus is on whether a person has performed any of the functions described in ERISA Section 3(21)(A), not on the person's title. Therefore, the term "fiduciary" is broadly construed. A person can be a fiduciary even if that person has acted on behalf of the plan without proper authority, if the person performed any of the fiduciary activities. Whether a person believes that the fiduciary title applies does not matter. A person's fiduciary status is determined by an objective evaluation of whether the person performed any of the functions described above. In addition, a person need not have exclusive, complete, or final decision-making authority to be a fiduciary within the meaning of ERISA. Anyone with discretionary authority or responsibility over the discretionary administration of the plan is a fiduciary.

In general, under ERISA, a person can only be a fiduciary if that person has the power to make decisions for the plan. A person who performs purely ministerial duties without decision-making power or discretionary power is generally not a fiduciary. Most discretionary activities are fiduciary in nature. Discretionary or decision-making activities that have been found by various courts, including the U.S. Supreme Court, to give rise to fiduciary status include the following:

1. Appointing other plan fiduciaries

2. Delegating responsibility to or allocating duties among other plan fiduciaries

3. Selecting and monitoring plan investment vehicles

4. Giving investment advice to the plan for a fee

5. Selecting and monitoring third-party service providers

6. Negotiating the compensation of third-party service providers

7. Interpreting plan provisions

8. Denying or approving benefit claims

ERISA precludes certain persons from serving in a fiduciary role. Persons convicted of various crimes, including fraud, grand larceny, robbery, murder, perjury, certain violations of the Investment Company Act of 1940, violation of the anti-kickback provisions of the Labor-Management Relations Acts, the Racketeer Influenced and Corrupt Organizations Act, conspiracy, mail fraud, wire fraud, and certain violations of ERISA Section 411. In addition, a court can temporarily or permanently bar a person from serving as a fiduciary if that person has been found to have breached a fiduciary obligation to a plan.

There are some limitations on a person's fiduciary scope. Accordingly, a person is a fiduciary only to the extent that the person performs any of the activities described. However, fiduciary status is not an all-or-nothing concept. It is possible for a person to be a fiduciary for one purpose but not for another. For example, a bank that meets the definition of a fiduciary within the meaning of ERISA because it provides investment advice to a plan for a fee would not be acting in a fiduciary capacity for honoring a forged signature on a check drawn from the plan account held by the bank.

Similarly, a service provider to a plan who had no power to select itself would not be a fiduciary with respect to the selection process but would be a fiduciary if it controlled its own compensation. In the single-employer context, the employer usually is the plan administrator or named fiduciary. Employers, however, will assume fiduciary status to the extent that they function in their capacity as plan administrators but not when they conduct business that is not regulated by ERISA. Thus, ERISA allows employers to wear two hats.

Some functions that affect employee benefit plans are not considered fiduciary functions. This is true even when the person who performs the function is a plan fiduciary, such as the plan sponsor serving as the named plan administrator. Activities that are not usually considered fiduciary functions involve establishing, terminating, and amending plans.

ERISA's primary concern is to protect plan assets from abuse once a plan is established and to ensure that promised benefits are paid. Accordingly, the decision to establish, terminate, or amend a plan is generally construed to be a settlor function. However, in the context of Taft-Hartley or union-sponsored plans, the majority view is that the trustees act in a fiduciary capacity when they amend or design the plan.

Named Fiduciaries and Cofiduciary Status

In addition to those people who are fiduciaries as a result of their conduct or authority over the plan, ERISA Section 402(a)(1) also requires that every plan provide for at least one named fiduciary, who will have authority to control and manage the plan. The term "named fiduciary" is frequently confused with those who are fiduciaries as a result of their conduct or authority but who are not named in the plan instrument.

A named fiduciary is someone designated in the plan instrument by name or by title to enable employees or other interested parties to ascertain the person responsible for plan operations. Any plan that designates a corporation as a named fiduciary should provide for designation by the corporation of specified individuals or other persons to carry out specified fiduciary functions under the plan.

In addition, ERISA also permits the appointment of the plan committee as the named fiduciary, as long as the plan states explicitly that the committee's functions include the authority to control and manage the operation and administration of the plan and as long as the plan specifies, by name and position, who shall constitute that committee.

In some cases, a fiduciary is responsible for the acts of another fiduciary. A fiduciary is liable for a cofiduciary's breach of its duties if the fiduciary knowingly participates in, conceals, or enables the cofiduciary's breach. A fiduciary also has cofiduciary liability if the fiduciary has knowledge of a cofiduciary's breach of duty, and the fiduciary fails to make reasonable efforts to remedy the breach.

A fiduciary must use reasonable care to prevent a cotrustee from committing a breach of trust or to compel a cotrustee to redress a breach of trust. A fiduciary's inaction or failure to act promptly to halt another fiduciary's breach can give rise to cofiduciary liability.

Fiduciary Risk Follows Discretion:
Cofiduciaries Not Always Discretionary Fiduciaries

The Department of Labor (DOL) Regulation Section 2510.3-21(c)(1) provides that a person will be considered to be rendering investment advice only if the person renders advice to a plan as to the value of securities or makes recommendations as to the advisability of investing in, purchasing, or selling securities or other property. In addition, the person, either directly or indirectly, must have discretionary authority or control, whether or not pursuant to agreement, arrangement, or understanding, with respect to purchasing or selling securities or other property for a plan. The person must render any advice with respect to the value of a security on a regular basis such that these services will serve as the primary basis for investment decisions, on an individualized basis depending on the particular needs of the plan, and for a fee or other compensation, direct or indirect.

The buck stops with whoever makes the final decision.

Some financial intermediaries now function as cofiduciaries to help plan sponsors select, monitor, review, and recommend fund changes as necessary. In many cases, plan sponsors have not objectively determined if the cofiduciary's monitoring system makes any positive difference in outcomes. Even if the monitoring system adds value, however, the plan sponsor must make the final decision. The cofiduciary does not have the final discretion. In such cases, the financial advisor functions in a carefully crafted, limited cofiduciary capacity. The financial advisor provides nondiscretionary investment recommendations and ongoing data in a cofiduciary role. In such limited-capacity cofiduciary cases, the final discretionary authority and ultimate fiduciary risk belongs to the plan sponsor. Unless the cofiduciary has discretion over the selection and replacement of plan investments, the fiduciary risk belongs to the plan sponsor, who must make the final decisions.

Figure 9-1: Discretion: The ERISA Risk Pathway

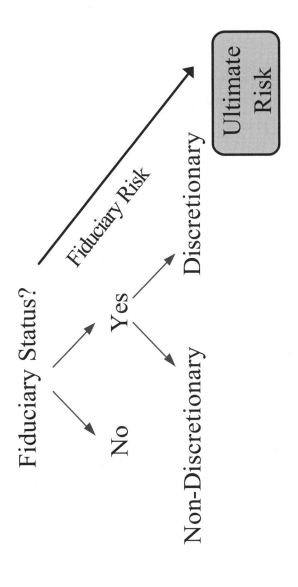

The Basics of Fiduciary Responsibility

All qualified plans, including 401(k) plans, are subject to the extensive fiduciary responsibility provisions that apply to qualified plans generally. However, because of the presence of employee contributions and the likelihood that participants will have some say in the investment decisions respecting the management of their individual accounts, 401(k) plans are generally fraught with potential for fiduciary pitfalls. As a result, people associated with management of 401(k) plans need to be aware of the overall responsibilities related to the plans, as well as some sensible ways to manage them.

In its most basic terms, ERISA section 404(a) directs fiduciaries of all plans to act solely in the interest of the plan's participants and beneficiaries and for the exclusive purpose of providing benefits for these people. Further, fiduciaries must act prudently, diversify the investment of plan assets, and generally act in a manner consistent with plan documents. In addition to this general requirement, plan fiduciaries are subject to the "prudent man" standard of care. This standard requires a fiduciary to act "with the care, skill, prudence, and diligence under the circumstances then prevailing that a prudent man acting in a like capacity and familiar with such matters would use."

With these standards, it is little mystery why plan fiduciaries can become confused about the scope of their responsibilities under ERISA. This nebulous standard forms the foundation of ERISA's fiduciary responsibility provisions, and it is from this language, as well as the legislative history of ERISA, that the DOL and the courts have fashioned a body of law that governs the conduct of plan fiduciaries. In view of the fact that this language is so open-ended, it is fairly easy to see how plan fiduciaries might be nervous about how their investment decisions might be interpreted after the fact.

The legislative history of ERISA shows that Congress intended to incorporate the core principles of fiduciary responsibility as they developed in the common law of trusts. These common law rules date back hundreds of years and basically govern the relationship that a common law trustee has to the beneficiary of the trust. It was on these principles that U.S. Judge Samuel Putnam formulated the Prudent Man Rule in 1830. In enacting ERISA, Congress borrowed the Prudent Man Rule. Thus, courts interpreting ERISA have found it useful and practical to draw on these common law principles in deciding fiduciary questions under ERISA.

Interestingly, however, Congress specifically noted that the common-law fiduciary standards were not to be applied automatically to employee benefit plans; rather, they were to be applied "bearing in mind the specific nature and purpose of employee benefit plans." Thus, the rigid rules of the common law are generally not to be incorporated reflexively under ERISA; rather, they are to be drawn on by courts in fashioning analogous principles.

From these rigorous principles, developed over hundreds of years in the common law, has evolved the fiduciary-responsibility body of law under ERISA. This body of law is still in its evolutionary stages, which suggests why it is so difficult for plan fiduciaries to properly gauge whether their conduct is permissible under the statute. Fiduciaries today should at least know that there is no bright-line test for determining whether a given action is permissible; any decision can be reviewed and second-guessed.

Nowhere is the fiduciary body of law less developed than in the area of participant-directed 401(k) plans. This area is still so new that no courts have addressed the unique issues relating to these plans. As a result, plan fiduciaries are left with little guidance about how to manage their fiduciary responsibility in these plans, where employee dissatisfaction runs higher than in any other type of plan.

The Exclusive Purpose Rule

Under section 404(a)(1)(A) of ERISA, a fiduciary of a plan must discharge investment duties for the exclusive purpose of providing benefits to participants and beneficiaries. Courts have taken a narrow view of this provision, requiring that any action with respect to the investment or expenditure of plan assets be made with the sole purpose of benefiting participants and beneficiaries. At the heart of the fiduciary relationship is the duty of complete and undivided loyalty to the beneficiaries of the trust.

The duty of loyalty does not allow fiduciaries to use the assets of the plan for their personal accounts or personal interests and forbids favoring a third party over the interests of a plan participant. As an example, in the case of 401(k) plans, one of the more apparent risks of violating this provision would be in decisions that are made because of business objectives or priorities. For instance, the decision to hire a commercial bank as the investment advisor to the plan in exchange for a favorable interest rate on business loans or more favorable terms for a line of credit would violate ERISA's exclusive-purpose rule.

ERISA does allow a person to function as both the plan sponsor and the plan administrator. When a fiduciary is acting in these two divergent capacities, the potential for conflicts of interest exists. In some instances, it may be impossible for a fiduciary to act solely in the interest of the participants.

Circumstances that give rise to a conflict of interest that is nearly impossible for a fiduciary to overcome generally involve cases in which a plan sponsor is confronted with difficult "life and death" business situations or conditions, such as fighting a hostile tender offer or bankruptcy. In such situations, a fiduciary may be under a duty to seek the advice of independent counsel or take other reasonable measures to ensure that the decision is solely in the interest of plan participants.

The Prudent Expert Rule

"A pure heart with an empty head is no defense."

Under Section 404(a)(1)(B) of ERISA, fiduciaries must discharge their investment duties "with the care, skill, prudence, and diligence under the circumstances then prevailing that a prudent man acting in a like capacity and familiar with such matters would use in the conduct of an enterprise of a like character and with like aims."

This rule is often referred to under the common law as the Prudent Man Rule. Within the context of ERISA, this rule is commonly known in the industry as the "prudent expert rule." The reason for this is because courts and the DOL have interpreted fiduciaries' actions by incorporating a standard of what an investment expert would do in similar circumstances. In attempting to fulfill these responsibilities, fiduciaries should bear in mind certain principles that have been set forth by courts applying these fiduciary rules in real-world situations.

1. A fiduciary's lack of familiarity with investments is no excuse; under an objective standard, fiduciaries are to be judged according to others acting in like capacity and familiar with such matters. This means that plan fiduciaries are held to a standard of a prudent fiduciary with experience. Plan fiduciaries may not blindly make investment decisions or blindly rely on others; they must make decisions within a meticulous framework.

2. The standard is not that of a prudent layperson, but that of a prudent fiduciary who has experience dealing with similar situations. It is not sufficient that plan fiduciaries act prudently in their own minds. Instead, they must act prudently by comparison with a standard based on an experienced professional fiduciary. Thus, where the fiduciary lacks this experience, there is an affirmative obligation to seek independent advice.

3. The test of prudence focuses on the fiduciary's conduct in investigating, evaluating, and making the investment. In other words, the fiduciary's independent investigation of the merits of a particular investment is at the heart of the prudent-expert standard. It is the process in which a fiduciary engages that determines the fulfillment of ERISA's fiduciary responsibility provisions.

4. Fiduciaries have an affirmative obligation to seek independent advice when they lack the requisite education, experience, and skill, and must go to great lengths to establish a record for their actions. When selecting a professional investment manager to manage all or a piece of a plan's portfolio, a fiduciary has an obligation to seek the advice of independent consultants. The failure to make an independent investigation and evaluation of a potential plan investment is in and of itself a breach of fiduciary obligations.

5. The plan fiduciary maintains the fiduciary obligation to monitor the performance of that manager and to take corrective action if necessary. Even after the selection of the investment advisor, the plan fiduciary must monitor the performance of that advisor. The plan fiduciary is not permitted to ignore the plan after the delegation has been made; rather, the plan fiduciary should be monitoring the investments on an ongoing basis by reference to an objective and relevant series of indexes.

ERISA Section 402(c)(2) permits either a named fiduciary or a fiduciary designated by a named fiduciary to employ others for the purpose of rendering advice regarding any responsibility the fiduciary has under the plan. Section 402(c)(3) further permits the named fiduciary to appoint an investment manager or managers to manage the assets of the plan. When this appointment is properly made, the plan fiduciaries are not liable for the acts and omissions of the investment manager. It has been well established that the decision to hire an investment manager to manage assets of a plan is a fiduciary decision in and of itself that requires the application of ERISA's prudence requirements.

All plan sponsors that seek to delegate investment responsibilities to an independent investment advisor should follow a careful process to ensure that their decisions to hire and continue with such a manager are prudent from the standpoint of ERISA. In other words, it is not enough to blindly hire an asset manager to manage all or a portion of the assets in the plan; rather, the plan fiduciary must undergo a fairly rigorous process in order to justify that the decision to hire any given manager was prudent in light of the circumstances surrounding that decision.

The DOL has suggested certain guidelines that may be followed in a prudent selection of a person or entity to invest ERISA plan assets. These guidelines, also examples of common sense, would require a plan fiduciary to evaluate the person's or organization's qualifications, including:

1. Expertise in the particular area of investments under consideration and with other ERISA plans

2. Educational credentials

3. Whether the person or entity is registered with the Securities and Exchange Commission under the Investment Advisors Act of 1940

4. Qualifications by means of widely enjoyed reputation in the business of investments, client references, or the advice of a professional third-party consultant

5. Record of past performance with investments of the type contemplated

6. Reasonableness of fees

7. Documents reflecting the relationship to be established

8. Adequate periodic accountings and monitoring

Prohibited Transactions under ERISA

Under ERISA and the Internal Revenue Code, certain classes of transactions are prohibited between a plan and parties-in-interest. The group of people falling under "party-in-interest" definition is much broader than those falling under the fiduciary definition. These transactions are prohibited regardless of the terms of the transaction and whether it provides economic or other benefit to the plan.

In addition to these technically prohibited transactions, plan fiduciaries are prohibited under ERISA from engaging in any transaction or conduct that would jeopardize their duty of loyalty to the plan. Plan fiduciaries and their advisors must be aware of these particular restrictions, because even an inadvertent violation can subject the party-in-interest and the fiduciary to severe penalties.

Specifically, under ERISA Section 406, a prohibited transaction occurs if a plan fiduciary causes the plan to enter into any of the following transactions with a party-in-interest:

1. Sale, exchange, or lease of property

2. Loan or extension of credit

3. Provision of goods, services, or facilities

4. Transfer of plan assets or use of plan assets

5. Acquisition of employer securities or employer real property in excess of certain limits

Unfortunately, prohibited transactions are not always immediately recognizable. ERISA dictates that a pension plan that owns an office, industrial, apartment, or retail property cannot lease to anyone affiliated directly or indirectly to the pension plan. Thus, entering into a lease for building space with a tenant who happens to be a family member of someone providing services to the pension plan or who falls within the broad party-in-interest definition in ERISA, may be a prohibited transaction.

In addition to the above prohibitions, ERISA prohibits a plan fiduciary from doing any of the following:

1. Dealing with plan assets in the fiduciary's own interest

2. Representing adverse interests in any transaction with the plan

3. Receiving remuneration in any form from a party dealing with the plan in connection with a transaction involving plan assets

The penalties for violating these prohibited transaction provisions can be steep. Under the Internal Revenue Code, the IRS can impose a penalty tax on the party-in-interest to the transaction equal to 5% of the amount involved in the transaction for each year the transaction remains uncorrected. An additional tax of 100% can be imposed if the transaction is not corrected in a timely manner.

Section 408 of ERISA provides for certain statutory and administrative exemptions to the prohibited-transaction provisions. The statutory exemptions are narrowly drafted and provide little protection for the typical party-in-interest transactions that arise. However, ERISA gives the Secretary of Labor the power to grant administrative exemptions from prohibited transactions, provided that the exemption is administratively feasible; in the interest of the plan, its participants, and beneficiaries; and protective of the rights of the participants and beneficiaries of the plan.

Who Is a Party-in-interest under ERISA?

A party-in-interest is defined more broadly than a fiduciary. The term "party-in-interest" with respect to a plan is one of the following:

1. Any fiduciary (including but not limited to any administrator, officer, trustee, or custodian), counsel, or employee of such employee benefit plan

2. A person providing services to such plan

3. An employer, any of whose employees are covered by the plan

4. An employee organization, any of whose members are covered by the plan

5. An owner, direct or indirect, of 50% or more interest in any of the following:
5a. The combined voting power of all classes of stock entitled to vote or the total value of shares of all classes of stock of a corporation
5b. The capital interest or the profits interest of a partnership
5c. The beneficial interest of a trust or unincorporated enterprise, which is an employer or an employee organization as described in items (3) and (4) above

6. A relative (i.e., a spouse, ancestor, lineal descendant, or spouse of a lineal descendant) of any of the individuals in items (1), (2), (3), (4), or (5) above. (Note that the definition of a relative excludes siblings.)

7. A corporation, partnership, trust, or estate of which (or in which) 50% or more of:
7a. The combined voting power of all classes of stock entitled to vote or the total value of shares of all classes of stock of a corporation;
7b. The capital interest or the profits interest of a partnership; or

7c. The beneficial interest of such trust or estate is owned, directly or indirectly, or held by persons described in items (1), (2), (3), (4), or (5) above

8. An employee, officer, director (or an individual having power similar to an officer or director), or a 10% or more shareholder, directly or indirectly, of a person described in items (2), (3), (4), (5), or (7) above or of the employee benefit plan

9. A joint venture or partner owning at least a 10% interest in any of the entities described in items (2), (3), (4), (5), or (7) above

The list of enumerated persons who can be parties-in-interest with respect to a plan is generally strictly construed by courts under the theory that the list is so comprehensive that courts assume that Congress intended the list to be exhaustive.

The purpose of the prohibited-transaction rules is to prevent so-called insiders from using their influence over the plan to cause the plan to engage in a transaction under which they can personally benefit at the expense of the plan. Because of the relationships these persons have to the plan, the opportunity for abuse is too great to allow any transactions with the plan, except under certain narrow circumstances.

Finally, ERISA's party-in-interest provision is nearly identical to the definition of disqualified person under Code Section 49 75 (e) (2). The code, like Title I of ERISA, sets forth a series of transactions that are prohibited between a plan and a disqualified person. Although there are some differences between the code and ERISA Section 406 with respect to what constitutes a prohibited transaction, the two provisions, for the most part, overlap.

The Investment Policy Statement

Only about half of all sponsors of defined contribution plans have a written investment policy statement (IPS), according to published studies. It is nearly impossible for a plan sponsor to select and monitor investment options or ensure procedural prudence without having an IPS. There is some confusion about whether ERISA requires plans to have a written IPS and, if it is not clearly required, whether a fiduciary should nonetheless develop and document one.

Although it is clearly an investment "best practice" to have an IPS, ERISA does not specifically require that a written IPS be drafted. However, Section 402(b)(1) does state: "Every employee benefit plan shall provide a procedure for establishing and carrying out a funding policy and method consistent with the objectives of the plan and requirements of this title." Thus, ERISA is not clear whether the procedure must be in writing, or more importantly, what the procedure should encompass. Strictly speaking, a funding policy is not the same as an investment policy (although an IPS could address the investment needs of a plan relative to issues such as the anticipated timing of the distribution of benefits, that is, the need for cash for benefit payments in a pooled investment trust), and none of these provisions specifically require that plan sponsors have a written policy describing the guidelines for investment decisions.

We believe that a written investment policy allows plan fiduciaries to clearly establish the prudence and diversification standards that they want the investment process to maintain. Plan sponsors must develop written policies, whether or not they take an active role in the investment of retirement plan assets or delegate the task to outside investment managers or provide the participants with the right to direct their own accounts. The net effect of the written policy is to increase the likelihood that the plan will be able to meet the financial needs of the plan participants

A word of caution, however: at least one court has found that a fiduciary breached his ERISA duties under the general fiduciary requirements by not establishing an IPS for the plan. In addition, it is basically impossible to prudently select and monitor investments for a plan without an investment policy. But the question is whether an investment policy needs to be reduced to a written IPS.

As we discussed earlier, the legal responsibility for the investments in a qualified plan rests with the corporate officers who oversee the management of the plan's assets. Although those duties may be delegated to investment managers, most of the time the responsibility for selecting the investment options rests with key corporate officers. To the extent that they are responsible for selecting those funds, the officers are ERISA fiduciaries, either because they are appointed to the task (as plan committee members) or because they take on the responsibility. ERISA requires that fiduciaries generally act "with the care, skill, prudence, and diligence under the circumstances then prevailing that a prudent man acting in a like capacity and familiar with such matters would use in the conduct of an enterprise of a like character and with like aims."

The DOL has offered the following definition of an IPS: "The term 'statement of investment policy' means a written statement that provides the fiduciaries who are responsible for plan investments with guidelines or general instructions concerning various types or categories of investment management decisions."

A remaining question is whether the law requires a plan to have an investment policy, written or otherwise. Although ERISA does not explicitly require an investment policy, ERISA has indirectly imposed such a requirement by mandating that investment fiduciaries prudently select plan investments and monitor their performance. In the preamble to the final ERISA Section 404(c) regulations, the DOL explained: "In the case of look-through investment vehicles (mutual funds), the plan fiduciary has a fiduciary obligation to prudently select such vehicles, has a residual obligation to periodically evaluate the performance of such vehicles to determine, based on that evaluation, whether the vehicles should continue to be available as participant investment options."

The key points covered by an IPS for a qualified plan, or more specifically, a 401(k) plan, include permitted investments (core and noncore funds), self-directed brokerage accounts, and employer stock; as well as criteria and procedures for the selection, monitoring, removal, and replacement of each part of the investment structure, including standards for evaluating the designated core and noncore funds. It should also cover services such as investment education and investment advice to the plan fiduciaries and the participants

With regards to monitoring standards, one court has said: "Once the investment is made, a fiduciary has an ongoing duty to monitor investments with reasonable diligence and remove plan assets from an investment that is improper." For a fiduciary to prudently perform its selection and monitoring duties, it must select the appropriate benchmarks for each investment, compare the investment performance and expenses to those benchmarks, and analyze any difference.

It is highly likely that the courts will decide the determination of investment prudence after receiving testimony from investment experts, most likely consultants and academics. Those experts will say that 401(k) fiduciaries should, among other things, compare performance, expenses, and volatility to appropriate peer-group and index benchmarks.

In performing those duties, the fiduciaries should document the selection of the peer groups and benchmarks, the information gathered for comparison, the application of the benchmarks to the plan's investment options, and the conclusions reached. They must also preserve all their minutes, notes, and work papers. All reports given to the corporate board of directors should be preserved and included in the corporate minutes.

The DOL has opined that compliance with the duty to monitor necessitates proper documentation of the activities that are subject to monitoring. In other words, ERISA's general fiduciary rules require that the fiduciaries determine the key elements of an investment policy, even if those elements are not documented in writing. If a fiduciary does not prudently select and monitor a plan's investment options, however, a court may find that the failure to document the selection and monitoring criteria in an IPS is a breach of ERISA's fiduciary requirements. That is, one possible outcome is that if a fiduciary prudently performs its duties (e.g., the selection and monitoring of 401(k) investment options), a court may find that it was not a breach to fail to document an IPS. However, if the fiduciary fails to perform the duties typically described in an IPS, then a court may hold that the fiduciary breached its ERISA duties by failing to establish an IPS.

Some may question that because ERISA does not explicitly require that a 401(k) plan have an IPS, should a plan have a policy? ERISA and the court cases and DOL guidance that interpret it impose a duty on fiduciaries to prudently select and to periodically monitor their plan investments and their investment courses of action. There are few hard and fast rules for determining whether a fiduciary has succeeded or failed in that duty. Instead, ERISA defines fiduciary compliance in terms of procedural prudence. That is, in determining whether an investment fiduciary has fulfilled its duty, an investment option's performance is not as important as the procedure that the fiduciary employed in selecting and monitoring the investment options. ERISA's test of prudence is a test of conduct. The focus of the inquiry is how the fiduciary acted in the selection of the investment, not whether the investments succeeded or failed.

The first step in employing a prudent procedure is having a procedure. Although it may be possible for investment fiduciaries to follow procedures that they keep in their heads, that approach has its downfalls. First, any procedure or policy that isn't in writing is going to be difficult to articulate if it comes into question. If one fiduciary's conduct comes into question, it will be unlikely that all of the plan fiduciaries (assuming the plan has more than one) will have consistent understandings of what that unwritten policy is. Second, it will be difficult to document compliance with a policy that hasn't been documented itself. In short, if investment fiduciaries are procedurally prudent in the selection and monitoring of plan investments, a logical and prudent place to start is with a written IPS.

Others may argue that there is a reason for a 401(k) plan not to have a written IPS. Specifically, they point out that if the investment fiduciaries fail to comply with their own written policies, it makes them an easy target for complaining participants and the DOL. Others argue that, in the real world of 401(k) plan investing, the plan's investment fiduciaries abdicate their roles to brokers, insurance companies, and investment consultants and should not set themselves up for failure by implementing a policy that they have no intention of following.

Such theories are not valid reasons for avoiding a written investment policy. With or without a written IPS, plan fiduciaries are subject to requirements of procedural prudence. If fiduciaries are unable to consistently articulate the standards by which they judge the investments they make available to 401(k) plan participants, they are off to a bad start in satisfying the procedural prudence standard. By adopting and following an IPS, plan fiduciaries will be in a better position to establish that they did what the law requires. Of course, the IPS should be drafted in a way that does not increase the risk of failure by the investment fiduciaries. Like any other legal document, an IPS should be carefully drafted, typically by an attorney familiar with employee benefits issues and working in concert with the fiduciaries and their investment consultants. A well-crafted IPS should provide guidelines for the investment fiduciaries but should leave the decisions to their judgment. This flexibility will minimize the risk of a breach of fiduciary duty for a failure to follow the terms of the IPS.

Investment Managers

Investment management is the fiduciary activity required to allocate pension fund assets among suitable investment vehicles in order to meet the investment performance objectives set by the plan sponsor. The plan sponsor may decide it is in the best interests of the plan participant to hire an investment manager to manage part or all of the plan assets. The selection of an investment manager is a fiduciary act by the plan sponsor and must be handled by a detailed and well-documented process.

In the context of a participant-directed plan, investment management generally refers to buying and selling of securities and to maintaining a portfolio. Investment advice involves selecting investment options that will be offered to plan participants. Plan sponsors can select their own funds or hire an outside firm or individual to help select and monitor investment options. Investment advice also refers to information given to participants on investment selection and asset allocation. In many cases, an investment advisor will provide investment advice on both the plan and participant levels, if so desired.

ERISA does not offer specific guidance as to the manner and approach that a fiduciary should take in negotiating the investment management agreement between the fiduciary and the investment manager. The plan fiduciary (such as a retirement committee of a plan, trustee, or other named fiduciary) should consider the following steps for negotiating the investment management agreement:

1. Hire legal counsel to review the documents. Plan fiduciaries should have legal counsel analyze the investment management agreement, offering memoranda, subscription agreements, or other documents that set forth the terms of the relationship between the plan and the investment manager.

2. Maintain flexible termination provisions. The agreement should generally be terminable by the plan fiduciaries on little or no advance notice, generally no more than thirty days' notice, and any fees paid in advance to the manager prorated to the date of termination.

3. Obtain adequate representations and warranties. Unless the manager is a national bank or trust company, the agreement should also provide that the manager is an investment advisor registered with the SEC under the Investment Advisors Act of 1940 and acknowledges in writing being a fiduciary within the meaning of ERISA with respect to the plan's assets under investment.

4. Ensure that the manager has obtained a fidelity bond in accordance with ERISA, if necessary, under Section 412 bonding requirements.

5. Ensure that the manager maintains fiduciary liability insurance in an amount determined by the plan fiduciaries to be sufficient under the circumstances. Keep in mind that even though the manager is a fiduciary, the capability of the manager to pay a claim is relevant. The amount of liability insurance depends in part on the manager's size, financial condition, stature, background, and experience. ERISA does not mandate that fiduciaries obtain liability insurance, but it is highly recommended.

6. Ensure that the manager has made all necessary filings with appropriate government agencies. In addition, the manager must promptly notify the plan sponsor of any pending regulatory problems, examinations, or enforcement proceedings against the manager or its employees.

7. Ensure that the manager agrees to indemnify the plan fiduciaries for any damages arising out of a fiduciary breach by the manager of its agreement or its investment management duties.

Third-Party Plan Administrators, Stockbrokers, Insurance Agents, and Financial Planners Are Generally Not Discretionary Fiduciaries

The third-party administrator is responsible for overall administration of the plan. Most administrative duties are nondiscretionary in nature (ministerial tasks), so the administrator is generally not a fiduciary. This does not mean that administration is devoid of risk; on the contrary, errors are a constant source of exposure for any plan sponsor, but administrative error generally involves error in the conduct of ministerial, not fiduciary, tasks.

An insurance company, an insurance agent, a stockbroker, or a brokerage company will not be considered a fiduciary for selling its products to an employee benefit plan. If, however, they should provide investment advice for a fee to employee benefit plans, they will be deemed to be fiduciaries as set forth in DOL Regulation Section 2510.3-21(c)(1).

This DOL regulation provides that a person will be considered as rendering investment advice only if such person renders advice to a plan as to the value of securities or other property or makes recommendations as to the advisability of investing in, purchasing, or selling securities or other property. In addition, the person either directly or indirectly has discretionary authority or control, whether or not pursuant to agreement, arrangement, or understanding, with respect to purchasing or selling securities or other property for a plan.

The person must render any advice with respect to the value of a security on a regular basis such that these services will serve as the primary basis for investment decisions, on an individualized basis depending on the particular needs of the plan, and for a fee or other compensation, direct or indirect. In such circumstance, the broker could be a fiduciary because of such conduct, even if there is no written agreement stating that the broker is a fiduciary.

A Case in Point

This case is about a brokerage firm that made presentations to plan trustees recapping performance of investments, advising the trustees which investments to hold and which to sell, and offering the trustees a choice of recommended investments. The plan lost 30% of its funds invested in securities recommended by the brokerage firm (about a $300,000 loss). The plan pursued ERISA fiduciary action against the brokerage firm to recover losses: Farm King Supply Inc. Integrated Profit Sharing Plan and Trust vs. Edward D. Jones and Company, 884 F.2d 288 (7th Cir. 1989).

The plan sponsor had a relationship with one broker who was the sales representative for Edward D. Jones and sold investments to the trustees of a profit-sharing plan. The broker regularly met with the trustees and presented a choice among a few securities recommended by him specifically for the plan. The trustees would confer privately and then advise whether they had decided to buy any of the recommended securities. No evidence was presented at trial that the trustees had developed any type of prudent process to monitor the investments. When the original broker was transferred to another office, another broker took over the account, and the trustees increased the share of the plan's investments purchased at Edward D. Jones from 50% percent to 99%.

The new broker provided the trustees with portfolio summaries for the investments purchased through Edward D. Jones but not for investments purchased elsewhere, even after the trustees lost confidence and ceased buying. The court ruled that even though the plan lost money on some of the investments recommended by the Edward D. Jones brokers, neither brokers nor the brokerage company was a fiduciary. Both the broker-dealer and the brokers had no discretion with respect to the disposition of assets, and there was no understanding that brokers' sales pitches would be the primary basis for plan investments.

Fiduciary Aspects of Trustee-Directed Plans

Trustee-directed plans (also known as employer-directed plans) differ from participant-directed plans insofar as the investment decisions are made uniformly for all participants by either a plan fiduciary or an investment committee.

The assets are managed in a combined pooled account for all participants in the plan. No participant has an investment portfolio different from any other participant, and all experience the same rate of return. The plan administration may be under a daily valuation format, or it could be traditional balance forward accounting.

Today, although most 401(k) plans attempt to be self-directed, the majority of other, non-401(k) defined contribution plans are employer-directed (even though they are permitted to be participant-directed). Obviously, there is a greater measure of predictability in employer-directed plans about what the fiduciaries' responsibilities are with respect to the management of plan assets and their obligation to communicate to employees.

Besides the normal fiduciary obligations, the practical risk to plan fiduciaries in maintaining employer-directed plans is that participants will second-guess the fiduciaries' investment judgment, either that it was too conservative or too aggressive to be prudent under ERISA.

Plan fiduciaries who are well-informed about their responsibilities should be able to live with this risk. Prudent management and common sense, combined with an understanding of the landscape in which trustees operate, offer the best protections. Clearly, such plans must utilize a well-formulated IPS.

Fiduciary Aspects of Multi-Employer Plans

A single-employer plan is a plan established by a company exclusively for the benefit of the company's employees. The plan sponsor is the company or the employer. The plan may or may not be collectively bargained. A multi-employer plan (also known as a Taft-Hartley or union-sponsored plan) is established pursuant to collective bargaining agreements that are negotiated between a union on behalf of employees and two or more employers that are generally involved in the same trade.

Usually, a single-employer plan has one trustee, which may be a bank or an officer of the company. Sometimes, the board of directors, acting on the company's behalf, will appoint a committee and delegate fiduciary responsibilities to it. A joint board of trustees comprising an equal number of union representatives and management representatives runs a multi-employer plan. ERISA sets forth provisions relating to the administration, reporting, fiduciary responsibility, enforcement, participation, vesting, funding, and termination insurance for pensions plans. Many of ERISA's general provisions apply equally to multi-employer and single-employer plans.

The trustee of a multi-employer plan owes undivided duty of loyalty to the plan participants, not to the employer or the union that appointed him as trustee. This duty of loyalty can result in situations where the interests of the fund trustee conflict with the interests of the union or some of the contributing employers. As an example, the U.S. Supreme Court has held that a trust fund can sue an employer for back contributions owed to the trust fund without first arbitrating the underlying dispute over the terms of the applicable collective-bargaining agreement.

The Multi-employer Pension Plan Amendment Act (MPPAA) amended ERISA in 1980 and provides special rules and addresses special problems of multi-employer pension plans. MPPAA was enacted to protect participants against plan losses. The MPPAA sets forth specific requirements for participation, vesting, funding, and accrual of benefits for multi-employer pension plans.

The MPPAA made changes in the termination insurance provisions of ERISA that apply to multi-employer pension plans. Under the changes instituted by the MPPAA, employers of multi-employer pension plans are now required to pay their share of the plan's unfunded liabilities, whether they stay with the plan or not. Because employers who leave the plan incur withdrawal liability, employers no longer have an incentive to withdraw in order to avoid paying their share, and remaining employers no longer need to worry about being responsible for an increasing share of the plan's liabilities.

MPPAA added provisions governing mergers and transfers between multi-employer pension plans and multi-employer and single-employer pension plans. Certain requirements must be satisfied before a multi-employer pension plan can merge with or transfer assets or liabilities to another multi-employer pension plan or single-employee pension plan.

The MPPAA also made important changes regarding the termination of multi-employer pension plans. The MPPAA amended the definition of termination and modified the consequences resulting from termination. MPPAA also made changes to the PBGC, which manages the pension-plan termination insurance program.

Under ERISA's pension-plan termination insurance program, the PBGC guarantees a portion of the pension benefit of participants in defined-benefit multi-employer pension plans, even if the plan terminates with insufficient funds to make payments. In order to provide these payments, PBGC collects annual premiums from each multi-employer pension plan on behalf of each individual participating in the plan that year.

Indemnification Agreements

"Indemnification" is a promise to reimburse or hold a person harmless for acting in good faith. It can be important, because fiduciary liability can attach to a fiduciary that acted on behalf of a plan in good faith. A plan fiduciary may wish to consider obtaining an indemnity from the plan sponsor in lieu of or in addition to fiduciary liability insurance. Of course, indemnification is only as good as the financial viability of the company providing the indemnity.

ERISA Section 410 provides, generally, that any agreement that purports to relieve a fiduciary of liability or responsibility under ERISA shall be void as against public policy. However, the DOL has opined that indemnification agreements that leave a fiduciary fully responsible but that merely permit another party to satisfy any liability incurred by the fiduciary in the same manner as insurance would not be void under ERISA Section 410.

ERISA permits the indemnification of a fiduciary by an employer who sponsors a plan or by an employee organization whose members are covered by a plan. The indemnification does not relieve the fiduciary of responsibility or liability for fiduciary breaches. Rather, it leaves the fiduciary fully responsible and liable, but permits another party to satisfy any liability incurred by the fiduciary.

Although the plan sponsor may indemnify the fiduciary, the plan itself may not. ERISA expressly prohibits the indemnification and exculpation of a fiduciary by a plan. Therefore, the plan may not agree to excuse the fiduciary from responsibility for fiduciary breaches. Similarly, plan assets may not be used to reimburse a fiduciary for liability that it is found to have for its actions. A plan may, however, provide for indemnification of expenses of a fiduciary who successfully defends against a claim of breach of fiduciary duty.

Fiduciary Liability Insurance

Fiduciary liability insurance is designed to protect plan fiduciaries who, acting in good faith, violate the complex fiduciary rules as expressed in federal rules, regulations, and court rulings. Fiduciaries also need additional protection from liability for acts of cofiduciaries, especially where a fiduciary should have known of the breach by a cofiduciary and failed to remedy the breach.

Under ERISA, fiduciaries may be held personally liable for breach of their responsibilities in the administration or handling of employee benefit plans. Fiduciary liability insurance is not required by ERISA. However, it is strongly recommended if you are a fiduciary of a welfare or pension plan, because your personal assets are at stake. Many fiduciaries incorrectly believe that their ERISA fidelity bond protects their personal assets. Furthermore, many think that this type of coverage is included in their directors and officers (D&O) policy. Most D&O policies exclude fiduciary liability exposures under ERISA.

Plan sponsors should consider engaging an insurance agent with experience in writing such type of coverage and should also have the policies reviewed by their ERISA counsel. State insurance laws require many specific policy provisions, but there is significant opportunity to negotiate optional terms of coverage. Care should be taken to ensure that a policy covers the activities in which the plan and its fiduciaries intend to engage.

Fiduciary liability insurance pays, on behalf of the insured, legal liability arising from claims for alleged failure to prudently act within the meaning of ERISA. "Insured" is variously defined as a trust or employee benefit plan, any trustee, officer, or employee of the trust or employee benefit plan, an employer who is sole sponsor of a plan, and any other individual or organization designated as a fiduciary.

It should be noted that fiduciary liability insurance is different from the fidelity bond most plans are required to hold. Fidelity bonds are required by law (ERISA bonding). This form of bonding covers only dishonesty situations. When dishonest administrators or trustees have harmed an employee benefit plan, these bonds may be used, but only for the benefit of the plan and the plan's beneficiaries. This bonding will not protect the trustees themselves from liability claims and is distinct from fiduciary liability insurance.

In some cases the retirement plan itself can purchase a fiduciary liability policy. ERISA Section 410(b) requires that the insurance contract must, however, permit recourse by the insurer against the fiduciary for any loss resulting from a breach of a fiduciary obligation by such fiduciary. State law determines whether or not the fiduciary liability insurance may cover the fiduciary for the additional 20% excise tax for fiduciary breaches under ERISA. Some policies allow the fiduciary to purchase a nonrecourse rider to the policy. The nonrecourse rider provides that the insurance company waives its rights to proceed against the fiduciary. The fiduciary should make sure that plan funds are not used to purchase the rider.

Keep in mind that fiduciaries must act prudently and solely in the interest of plan participants and beneficiaries (duty of loyalty) when they undertake to recommend or choose fiduciary-liability insurance protection for the plan. Fiduciaries involved in purchasing insurance against fiduciary breaches for the plan must therefore do their best to secure the most suitable coverage for the plan at no greater expenditure of plan assets than is necessary.

In order to satisfy ERISA's prudence requirements, fiduciaries should ascertain that the insurance company from which they wish to purchase the policy has a satisfactory rating from a reputable rating agency.

The ERISA Fidelity Bond

ERISA requires pension plans to obtain a fidelity bond to protect the plan against theft of plan assets by fiduciaries and other "plan officials." Keep in mind that the fidelity bond covers only dishonesty and does not cover fiduciary breaches. The amount of the fidelity bond should be fixed at the beginning of each fiscal year of the plan. The bond should not be less than 10% of the amount of the plan assets, and the bond need not exceed $500,000.

ERISA requires that all plan fiduciaries that "handle" plan assets or that oversee the handling of plan assets must be covered. This includes not only the plan trustee but also the company's officers, employees, and third parties who handle plan funds or who oversee that process. Paying a third party to act as plan trustee doesn't alleviate bonding requirements. Persons who provide the corporate trustee with investment and benefit-payment instructions are considered handlers of plan funds and must also be bonded.

Many plan sponsors seek to comply with this requirement by obtaining riders to their corporate fidelity bonds or separate bonds through their casualty brokers. Unfortunately, many such bonds are inadequate and may not comply with the ERISA requirements. It is the plan sponsor's ERISA fiduciary duty to make sure that the plan is properly bonded.

The plan sponsor's ERISA legal counsel must examine the bond to make sure that all requirements have been met. For example, cases have been reported where the plan's fidelity bond covered only the named trustees of the plan. Following the theft of plan assets by a stockbroker, the bonding company was able to avoid paying the claim because, even though the bond said it was intended to comply with ERISA, it only covered employees under its terms. Cases like this highlight the importance of obtaining the proper fidelity-bond coverage.

ERISA Fiduciary Lawsuits Are Increasing

ERISA permits a civil action to be brought by a participant, beneficiary, or other fiduciary against a fiduciary for a breach of duty. The fiduciary is personally liable for any losses to the plan resulting from the breach of duty, and any profits obtained by the fiduciary through the use of plan assets must be turned over to the plan. The court may require other appropriate relief, including removal of the fiduciary. Even if fiduciaries are unaware that they are violating ERISA's fiduciary duties, they can be liable for the violation. The ERISA standard of conduct is an objective one: good faith is not sufficient. Similarly, fiduciaries will be liable under ERISA for engaging in a prohibited transaction if they knew or should have known that the transaction was prohibited. Under the Internal Revenue Code, excise taxes will be imposed on fiduciaries for engaging in certain transactions as disqualified persons, even if they do not satisfy the "knows or should have known" standard.

Chart 9-1: Increase in Number of ERISA Civil Cases

Year	Number Of New Cases	Year Over Year % Increase
2000	9,124	n/a
2001	10,292	12.8%
2002	11,128	8.1%
2003 (est)	12,500	12.3%

Source: Administrative Office of U.S. Courts

The U.S. Supreme Court has held that punitive damages are not available to a beneficiary in an action against the plan fiduciary for an alleged breach of fiduciary duty. However, ERISA does allow a court, in its discretion, to award reasonable attorneys' fees and costs to either party in an action by a participant, beneficiary, or fiduciary. The award of attorneys' fees is the exception rather than the rule.

Plan sponsors face financial risk in addition to participant litigation. Through its enforcement of ERISA, the DOL's Employee Benefits Security Administration (EBSA) can also get involved to ensure the integrity of the private employee-benefit-plan system. For the first time ever, total monetary results through the DOL activity were more than one billion dollars. In 2003, the figure was more than $1.4 billion, an increase of nearly 60% over 2002 monetary results of $881 million.

In 2003, EBSA closed 4,253 civil investigations, with 2,939 (69.1%) resulting in monetary results for plans or other corrective action. Although the number of cases actually dropped because of improved targeting and more resource-intensive investigations, the proportion of investigations closed "with results" increased by 18% over 2002.

EBSA often pursues voluntary compliance as a means to correct violations and restore losses to employee benefit plans. However, in cases where voluntary compliance efforts have failed or in cases that involve issues for which voluntary compliance is not appropriate, EBSA forwards a recommendation that litigation be instituted.

In addition, the DOL can impose additional penalties for breaches of fiduciary duty. There is a 20% civil penalty for breaches of fiduciary duties (or knowing participation in a breach). The DOL must levy a penalty of 20% of the amount recovered through a court order or settlement agreement with it. The DOL has a limited ability to waive or reduce the penalty if the fiduciary or other person acted responsibly and in good faith or will not otherwise be able to restore all plan losses without severe financial hardship.

For Further Reading

Coleman, B. *Primer on ERISA*. 4th ed.: BNA Books, (1993).

Fox, D., and Schaffer, D.. "Policy and ERISA: Interest Groups and Semi-Preemption." *Health Policy and Law* 239; 242, no.13; 243 (1989).

Freedman, B., and Schneider, L. *ERISA 2002: A Comprehensive Guide*. 2nd ed. Wiley Law, (2002).

Knickerbocker, D. *Fiduciary Responsibility under ERISA*. Candee Michie Publishing, (1994).

Levin, D., and Ferrera, T. *ERISA Fiduciary Answer Book*. 4th ed. New York: Aspen Publishers, (2003).

Marcus, B. *The Prudent Man: Making Decisions under ERISA*. ESP Corporation via Pensions & Investments (1978).

Reish, F. and Faucher, J. *Enron, 404(c), and the Personal Liability of Corporate Officers*. Reish, Luftman, Reicher, and Cohen, (2003).

Reish, F., and Faucher, J. *Who Are the Investment Fiduciaries for a 401(k) Plan?* Parts 1–5. Reish, Luftman, Reicher, and Cohen, (2003).

Reish, F., and Faucher, J. "What's in a Name? Director and Officer Liability under ERISA. Reish, Luftman, Reicher, and Cohen, (1998).

Song, J., and Michael K.. *ERISA Regulations: Current through June 30, 2001*. BNA Books, (2002).

Chapter 10

Fiduciary Issues of Participant-Directed Plans

Chapter Summary

Over the last decade, the term "401(k)" has become almost synonymous with the private pension system. In 401(k)-type plans, participants decide how much to save for retirement and how to manage their own investments. In an effort to reduce their fiduciary exposure, tens of thousands of plan sponsors have used ERISA Section 404(c) to transfer investment responsibility to participants.

Merely offering plan participants the ability to direct their own investments under ERISA Section 404(c) through a variety of investment choices does not relieve the plan sponsor of fiduciary responsibility and liability. Clearly, ERISA Section 404(c) does not relieve fiduciaries of all liability for plan investments. Although minimizing liability is a worthwhile goal, we believe that approaching fiduciary compliance by trying to minimize the plan sponsor's role in decision-making is counterproductive. By offering a 401(k) plan to its employees, a plan sponsor is necessarily signing on to be a fiduciary. The most effective way to manage this liability is to commit to an active approach that embraces the role of fiduciary and seeks to balance the responsibility with potential liabilities. An active approach has a number of advantages that can lead to better results. These include developing and following procedures for the fiduciary decision process and sponsoring a plan that enhances the retirement success probability of participants.

Introduction

Over the last decade, the term "401(k)" has become the popular symbol of the private pension system. In 401(k)-type plans, participants decide how much to save for retirement every year. These plans have increased in popularity; they seem to be the most revolutionary change in the private pension system. As we pointed out earlier, few participants are saving enough money or earning a high enough investment yield for a successful retirement. What are the risks to the plan sponsor when millions of employees find out that they cannot retire?

Employers have sought to reduce their legal as well as financial liabilities through pension simplification strategies. Forgetting the savings rate shortfall for the most part, plan sponsors instead focused on how to reduce their liability for participants' investment performances. So they were taught to focus not on 401(k), but rather on 404(c). For the first decade, the natural experiment that occurred in the private pension system seemed to work. In the early days (1991–1999), this development coincided with a bountiful stock market, and its risky significance was not well understood.

In an effort to reduce their fiduciary exposure, tens of thousands of plan sponsors have used ERISA Section 404(c) to transfer investment responsibility to participants. The trend to 404(c) plans raises some serious issues for ERISA in and of itself. What is the proper role of the employer in the modern defined-contribution plan? Should employees alone bear the risk of poor investment performance and failed retirement? Should investment and other service providers assume some liability under ERISA? Millions of plan participants, often without the benefit of unbiased investment advice or education, feebly attempt to manage their own retirement assets. But now, account shortfalls and lawsuits are here. They promise to transform an obscure section of ERISA into that phrase so familiar to lawyers: "a trap for the unwary."

The History of Participant-Directed Plans

Fiduciary responsibility rules take on special application in 401(k) plans and other defined contribution plans that allow for participant-directed investments. These provisions are generally covered under ERISA Section 404(c). In those instances, plan fiduciaries are trying to transfer the investment allocation responsibility to employees and may receive in exchange a reduction in their own level of personal liability.

Therefore, participant direction is often offered as an option because of the protection from fiduciary liability that is available in participant-directed plans. On October 13, 1992, the DOL issued final regulations on how participant-directed plans must be designed and operated in order to take advantage of this fiduciary relief.

Without the protection provided by ERISA Section 404(c), fiduciaries would be in the awkward position of having to follow the participants' directions while remaining responsible for the prudence of the instructions. This would have created the worst of all worlds for plan sponsors. In effect, it would be "Heads, I win; tails, you lose" from the plan participant's perspective. However, an inadvertent noncomplying participant-directed plan cannot rely on ERISA Section 404(c) as a defense in the event of an investment loss.

In other words, plan fiduciaries cannot argue that they are not responsible for an investment loss because a participant made the investment decisions. The DOL regulation is not a safe harbor. An employer cannot have a plan that almost satisfies the DOL regulation and raise ERISA Section 404(c) as a defense.

If the plan is not in full compliance with the minimum standards in the DOL regulation, plan fiduciaries will be judged according to the general ERISA fiduciary rules without any consideration of the impact of ERISA Section 404(c).

For several years, the DOL had struggled to finalize the Section 404(c) regulations that govern the transfer of investment control to participants. In essence, Section 404(c) of ERISA relieves plan fiduciaries of liability for investment losses if the plan permits its participants to exercise control over the investments and the losses resulted from the participant's exercise of control. This section of ERISA offers a theoretically compelling story to plan sponsors, and this idea has largely fueled the movement toward participant-directed plans.

Compliance with the requirements of Section 404(c) is optional. Plans that elect not to comply with the requirements do not violate ERISA solely by reason of that election. Yet, an election not to be treated as a Section 404(c) plan means that the plan fiduciaries may continue to be held completely responsible under ERISA for the results of participants' investments. For this reason, compliance with the regulation is generally advised by most experts, even though the fiduciary retains some liability. Finally, it should be recognized that plan fiduciaries that seek the protections of Section 404 (c) would have the burden of proof in litigation that they fully complied with the regulation.

Interestingly, the immense fiduciary duties imposed by ERISA did not immediately become problematic for employers. Litigation in the 1974–1990 period focused largely on the performance of the professional advisors typically hired to manage the large pools of assets found in defined benefit plans.

The DOL frequently exercised its new authority to pursue breaches of fiduciary duty by trustees and investment managers usually involving violations of the prohibited transaction rules. The standards incorporated into ERISA required fiduciaries to act prudently as investors from both procedural and substantive points of view. Fiduciaries were judged not so much on the outcomes of particular investment decisions but on whether they initially used appropriate methods to evaluate their merits and then monitored the results with appropriate documentation.

Little case law developed applying the new fiduciary rules to defined contribution plans. Not even the stock market crash in 1987 resulted in many lawsuits by the DOL or plan participants. There is no single explanation for the relative absence of defined-contribution-plan litigation. Unlike today, relatively few plans were self-directed. Those that were self-directed offered few investment options and permitted investment changes sometimes only once per year.

In the earlier period, plan participants had far less information about their investments. Many employers hired investment advisors to create unique investment pools for their plans. These options, unlike mutual funds, don't routinely provide information about their assets or value, so participants could not track investment performance easily or compare them with alternatives. Participants also received account statements infrequently. In short, it was a different investment environment: no daily pricing, no daily transfers, and little information available to participants. In those years, participants knew less about their investments and perhaps cared less as well.

As a result, few plan participants exercised their newly granted rights to challenge how their plans were being managed. This was a predictable result. ERISA gave participants the right to sue, but it included some features that almost guaranteed litigation to be a last resort. For example, the typical ERISA claim, a claim for individual benefits involving only a small amount of money, is not attractive to most litigators.

Participants can generally win, at most, the benefits to which they are entitled. ERISA does not permit punitive damages or damages for pain and suffering and effectively preempts state laws that do. Attorneys' fees are rarely awarded, so participants pay for litigation out of pocket or through any recovery. ERISA did not lead to a big increase in fiduciary litigation by plan participants. Thus, there was no significant plaintiffs' bar in the earlier days dedicated to pursuing ERISA claims for plan participants.

The evolution of the defined contribution plan in the last fifteen years has changed this. Today, these plans, not defined benefit plans, increasingly dominate the private pension system. Participants are much more knowledgeable about their benefits. They understand the significance of investment performance for their incomes in retirement and are more knowledgeable about investing. Employees have also come to assume a much higher share of the responsibility for funding their own pensions through 401(k)-type plans. In fact, today more money flows into 401(k) plans from the employee than from the employer.

Participants, especially those with more than modest means, have increasingly responded to the opportunity presented by 401(k) plans to make their own decisions about retirement savings, even though they receive fewer tax advantages for their contributions than their employers. In addition, participants have assumed responsibility for their investment performance. This last change is directly attributable to the 1992 issuance of final regulations under ERISA Section 404(c).

A participant-directed plan is one in which the participants choose how to invest the assets held in their accounts. Some of such plans are completely self-directed or open-ended (i.e., no limits are placed on what a participant can invest in). That type of participant-directed plan is increasing in number, but it is still somewhat uncommon, because it is usually expensive and difficult to administer, and because it requires a fairly high degree of investment knowledge on the part of plan participants.

In chapter 14 on self-directed brokerage accounts, we make a strong case against the open-ended account, because the participant investment outcomes are generally poor. Most participant-directed plans offer participants a choice of a limited group of funds designated by the employer or the investment fiduciary. That type of arrangement, quite common in most 401(k) plans, is the type of plan design on which the 1992 DOL regulation primarily focuses.

Setting Up a "Quick" ERISA Section 404(c)

Stockbrokers and other nonfiduciaries have told many plan sponsors (the real fiduciary) that setting up a participant-directed plan that "removes the liability from the plan sponsor" is easy. Typically, they are told that only a few requirements need be met as indicated in Chart 10-1 below.

Chart 10-1: The "Easy" 404(c) Plan Setup

Easy ERISA 404(c) Plan

- **Plan Must Offer at Least Three Different Investment Choices**
- **Participants Must Be Able to Switch Investments at Least Quarterly**
- **Participants Must Be Given Some Type of General Investment Education**
- **Employer Generally Not Liable for the Participant's Investment Results**

As we will shortly see, there is far more compliance required than the plan sponsor is typically told. Even with full compliance, ERISA Section 404(c) does not, as some may believe, relieve fiduciaries of all liability for plan investments.

If a plan complies with ERISA Section 404(c), the fiduciaries remain responsible for developing the plan's investment policy, selecting the investment options, and monitoring those options. These duties cannot be transferred to the participants.

ERISA Section 404(c) Compliance

For investment fiduciaries to have its protection, ERISA Section 404(c) requires that participants be permitted to control their accounts. However, the statute does not explain what is needed to satisfy that requirement. To fill that void, the DOL issued regulations under ERISA Section 404(c) that define the conditions for 404(c) protection. (See in the Appendix C.F.R. Section 2550.404c-1.)

There are more than twenty-five actual requirements in the Section 404(c) regulations. Under the regulations, participants are given the opportunity to control their accounts only if those requirements are satisfied. Three categories of information must be given to all participants: General Information, Specific Information, and Information Provided upon Request.

Participants must generally be given sufficient general information about their investment alternatives to make meaningful investment choices. Although some of the requirements are automatically handled by a plan's investment provider (a mutual fund company or an insurance company), most plan sponsors fail to satisfy the remaining requirements. As a result, their fiduciaries lose the "insurance" of Section 404(c) protection.

If a participant-directed 401(k) plan does not comply with 404(c), the plan fiduciaries are responsible for the prudence of the participant investment decisions. The most common failures include the failure to provide a prospectus immediately preceding or following initial investment, to identify the 404(c) fiduciary, to give notice of five categories of information available on request, and to notify that fiduciaries may be relieved of liability.

Specific Information That Must Be Provided

In addition to satisfying the general standard for providing investment information as outlined above, participants must automatically be given the following specific information:

1. An explanation stating that the plan is designed to be an ERISA Section 404(c) plan and that plan fiduciaries may be relieved of liability for any losses that are the direct and necessary result of a participant's investment instructions.

2. A description of the available investment alternatives. If the plan has a self-directed brokerage account, the disclosure can merely state that participants may invest in any administratively feasible option. Even in a self-directed or open-ended plan, however, plan fiduciaries must pass on copies of any prospectuses, financial reports, or similar materials that are furnished to the plan.

If the plan uses designated fund options, the disclosure must include a general description of each alternative. That description must address the investment objectives, risk and return characteristics, and type and diversification of assets that make up the portfolio.

The DOL recently issued Advisory Opinion 2003-11A under ERISA. This advisory opinion addressed the prospectus delivery requirement for participant-directed retirement plans, including so-called 401(k) plans, that are intended to comply with Section 404(c) of ERISA.

Under the securities laws, the prospectus delivery requirement may be satisfied by delivering a summary prospectus, or profile, instead of the entire Section 10(a) prospectus. In this advisory opinion, the DOL confirmed that, as a general matter, the prospectus delivery requirement under Section 404(c) may be satisfied by delivering a summary prospectus, or profile, for the mutual fund.

3. The procedures for giving investment instructions, including any limitations on transfers or any restrictions on the exercise of voting, tender, or similar rights.

4. If a designated investment manager is used, the identity of the manager. It is often helpful to include the manager's Form ADV Part II as required for SEC registered investment advisors.

5. A description of any transaction fees (e.g., commissions, sales loads, deferred sales charges) that will be directly assessed against a participant's account. Usually this information will be contained in the fund's prospectus or similar type document.

6. The name, address, and telephone number of the plan fiduciary responsible for providing information to participants upon request. The fiduciary may be identified by position (e.g., plan administrator, trustee) rather than by name.

7. If an investment alternative is subject to the Securities Act of 1933, a copy of the most recent prospectus on the security either immediately before or immediately following a participant's initial investment in that alternative.

8. To the extent that voting, tender, or other similar rights are passed through to participants, all materials relating to the exercise of those rights.

9. If the plan permits investment in employer securities, a description of the procedures for maintaining confidentiality of transactions as well as the name or title, address, and telephone number of the plan fiduciary responsible for monitoring compliance with the procedures. It is usually advisable to include information as to how the fair market value of the employer security is calculated if the security is not publicly traded.

Information That Must Be Provided upon Request

In addition to the automatic disclosure rules, plan fiduciaries must also respond to participants' requests for the following information on a timely basis. Each plan may establish reasonable procedures to limit the frequency of these requests.

1. A description of the annual operating expenses of each designated alternative. This includes any investment management fees, administrative fees, transaction costs, or any other type of fee that would reduce the rate of return to the participant. The disclosure should also include the aggregate amount of such expenses, addressed as a percentage of average net assets.

2. Copies of any prospectuses, financial statements, reports, or other materials related to an alternative that is provided to the plan.

3. If a designated investment alternative consists of assets that are plan assets (e.g., a fund managed by the employer):

3a. a list of such assets and the value of each such asset or its proportionate value of the investment alternative, and

3b. the name of the issuer of the contract, the term of the contract, and the rate of return for the contract, if the asset is a fixed-rate investment contract (e.g., a GIC,).

4. The value of shares or units in any designated investment alternative, as well as past and current investment performance of the alternative, determined on a reasonably consistent basis.

5. The value of shares or units in designated investment alternatives held in the account of a participant

Common Investment Activities That Are Usually Fiduciary Acts

The following activities, particularly when combined with the "final decision," "signing the agreement form," or other discretionary activity, tend to be fiduciary activities:

1. Determination of search criteria used to hire the investment manager, select the provider, or select the investments.

2. Decision on final investment package to be offered. Often the broker will prepare a package for the plan sponsor to "just sign off on." Under such conditions, the signing-off decision-making moves the liability back to the plan sponsor.

3. Preparation of investment policy statement.

4. Selection of asset classes.

5. Determination of criteria for investment choice selection and monitoring.

6. Selection of final list of investment options. Again, often the broker will prepare a package for the plan sponsor to just sign off on. Under such conditions, the signing-off decision-making moves the liability back to the plan sponsor.

7. Choosing the investment options for mapping.

8. Monitoring of investment options, including final authority to recommend fund replacements.

9. Investment advice to participants.

Investment Providers as Cofiduciaries

Usually, financial intermediaries will not be considered fiduciaries for selling their products to employee benefit plans. Today, under certain circumstances, they may be fiduciaries (nondiscretionary) to plans. "Cofiduciary" has become a marketing term that refers to an investment provider that assumes some subordinate role for prudently selecting and monitoring the 401(k) investment options. In such cases, the final decision-making authority (and risk) continues to reside with the plan sponsor.

In addition, because of concern about the investment abilities of participants, more employers are asking providers to provide participant-level advice. As with plan-level advice, providing participant-level advice is a fiduciary activity. The financial advisor must be prudently selected and monitored by the primary plan fiduciaries. The person or entity that provides investment advice to participants must act according to the fiduciary standards of ERISA Section 404(a) and avoid the fiduciary prohibited transactions of ERISA Section 406(b). Due to the provisions of Section 406(b), the advice is typically provided through an independent advisor, which is defined in the DOL's SunAmerica advisory opinion. (See the Appendix for this ruling).

Under ERISA, a financial consultant is a party-in-interest, because the broker provides services to an ERISA plan. As such, brokers can be nonfiduciaries or fiduciaries. In a fiduciary role, they can be discretionary or nondiscretionary. ERISA has a functional definition of fiduciary; it says that a person who behaves like a fiduciary is a fiduciary. Thus, a broker may render fiduciary investment advice as defined under ERISA, but the broker is a nondiscretionary fiduciary, as the plan sponsor must make the final decision. In such cases, the plan sponsor is still on the hook if things turn out bad.

Chart 10-2: Discretion Determines Fiducairy Liability

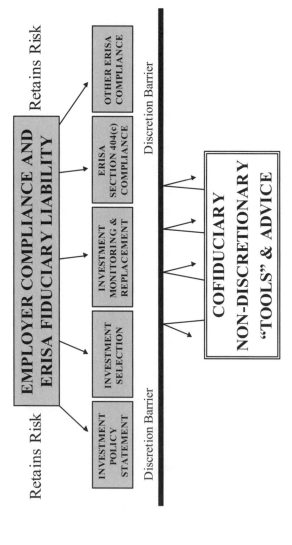

EMPLOYER LIABILITY
NON-DISCRETIONARY COFIDUCIARY

Retains Risk

Retains Risk

EMPLOYER COMPLIANCE AND ERISA FIDUCIARY LIABILITY

| INVESTMENT POLICY STATEMENT | INVESTMENT SELECTION | INVESTMENT MONITORING & REPLACEMENT | ERISA SECTION 404(c) COMPLIANCE | OTHER ERISA COMPLIANCE |

Discretion Barrier

Discretion Barrier

COFIDUCIARY NON-DISCRETIONARY "TOOLS" & ADVICE

-258-

Brokers or financial advisors who become fiduciaries are subject to the same standards as other fiduciaries, meaning that they must follow the exclusive-purpose, prudent-expert, and prohibited-transaction rules. The arrangement is under a specific written agreement between the plan sponsor and the investment provider. The plan sponsor's ERISA legal counsel should always review such an agreement. The primary plan fiduciaries (e.g., plan sponsor, officers, or retirement committee members) have a duty to prudently select and monitor the cofiduciary. The investment provider may assume the ERISA fiduciary duty to prudently do the following:

1. Select and monitor all investment options or just some of them

2. Provide advice concerning the general suitability of the options for retirement purposes

3. Provide advice concerning specific suitability for the demographics of the workforce

Upon becoming fiduciaries, investment providers must perform at the prudent-man level of ERISA's fiduciary standards under ERISA Section 404(a) and avoid the fiduciary prohibited transaction rules of ERISA Section 406(b). To avoid fiduciary status, the financial consultant may, as a practical matter, help the plan sponsor make decisions without offering ERISA fiduciary investment advice. In some cases, the provider may offer "near advice," or "investment guidance," which is designed to not be a fiduciary activity so that the provider can avoid sharing the fiduciary liability with the plan sponsor. "Investment guidance" is not defined, individualized, or based on the particular needs of the plan. It is based on general investment standards and common experiences of 401(k) plans. It may be provided by way of brochures, handouts, online services (tools), and information offered by investment providers. In such cases, the plan sponsor retains the liability for the investment process.

Employer Stock Issues in Participant-Directed Plans

About forty-five million workers now participate in 401(k)-type plans, and aggregate assets of these plans totaled $2 trillion in 2003. In addition to traditional investment choices, employees are often given the option to invest their 401(k) contributions in company stock. Company stock is offered as an investment option in 72% of retirement plans with more than five thousand participants.

No company illustrates the promise—and the pitfall—of the 401(k) more than Enron, the high-flying Houston energy firm that filed for bankruptcy in December 2001. Some eleven thousand Enron workers participated in the 401(k), and they received fifty cents' worth of Enron shares for each dollar they contributed up to 6% of their salaries. In late 2000, some 62% of the plan was held in Enron stock. But during 2001, the troubled energy company's stock plummeted, from around $85 a share to less than sixty-nine cents, wiping out about $1 billion in retirement savings.

In the Enron case, part of the high concentration reflected the company's match in Enron shares, but Enron employees also were allocating large fractions of their discretionary contributions to company stock. Such a high concentration of retirement assets in company stock is not unique to Enron. Many workers do not have well-diversified retirement plan portfolios. For example, at General Electric, Home Depot, and Pfizer, more than seventy-five cents of every dollar in defined-contribution-plan assets is held in company stock.

Including company stock in the plan's investment lineup is, in large measure, a plan design decision. When company stock is offered, the plan usually specifies it as an investment option. The law requires that employee stock ownership plans—whether as stand-alones or as part of other plans—be invested primarily in company stock. Most plan sponsors offer company stock to motivate employees by aligning their financial interests with those of the company. Though a valid business reason, this is not a fiduciary consideration for offering company stock in the plan.

If a design decision has been made to offer company stock, the plan sponsor must be able to conclude, as a fiduciary matter, that company stock is a prudent investment for the plan. If not, then fiduciary responsibility must override the plan design decision.

Many 401(k) critics claim that employers should have better educated their employees about diversifying their portfolios before the 2000–2002 economic downturn, especially because 401(k) plans had become the main source of retirement for many people. Many employers claim that 401(k) plans invested in company stock can boost morale and productivity, but investors claim that too much will hurt not just the employee, but the company as well. Over-concentration raises the absolute dollar exposure to liability and undercuts participants' chances for success through diverse asset-allocation strategies. However, high company stock balances are not automatically bad. At the plan level, this might be appropriate if the plan sponsor also offers a pension plan. At the participant level, it might be suitable for someone who has other savings, where the plan is just part of a diversified portfolio.

Exactly when company stock is or becomes an imprudent investment is being considered in the courts. This makes guidance in this area particularly difficult. The greatest fiduciary exposure does not necessarily come from making company stock a required, rather than an optional, investment; rather, it comes from over concentration in company stock. After all, if it is not a prudent investment, Section 404(c) does not offer protection anyway. In general, employees must be constantly reminded that if they have the option of investing in a company stock fund in their 401(k), they should remember that the investment is not diversified like a typical mutual fund, which invests in a number of different companies. It is a large bet on a single entity.

The Enron 401(k) Employer Stock Scandal

In December 2001, the Enron Corporation filed for bankruptcy. Its stock, which had been trading at a high of $90 per share a year earlier, plummeted and eventually became worthless. Those employees who had invested heavily in Enron stock through their participation in the company's 401(k) plan saw most of their retirement savings vanish. The employees filed a class-action suit claiming, among other things, that those acting as plan fiduciaries had breached their fiduciary duties under ERISA by failing to protect the plan participants' accounts. The plan participants were unable to sell their Enron stock during the worst part of freefall. This was because the plan's service provider was being changed to Northern Trust and the plan was in a nontrading blackout period to allow for records to be updated.

According to the complaint, participants were encouraged to continue investing in Enron stock, despite the fact that the company was heading toward bankruptcy. The suit was filed against the former Enron officers, outside directors, plan administrator, and others (e.g., Arthur Andersen, Northern Trust). The court found that the claims of fiduciary breaches and nondisclosure of material financial information had merit and that these claims could proceed to trial. This case has direct implications for employers that sponsor plans permitting investment in the employers' securities, as well as broad fiduciary responsibility implications for all ERISA plans. The court ruled that when fiduciaries have dual functions, they may wear only one hat at a time. Thus, in their role as ERISA plan fiduciaries, they must act in the best interests of plan participants and beneficiaries (e.g., discontinue buying Enron stock), even if this is contrary to corporate goals. Further, the court found that corporate officers may be held liable either as cofiduciaries or direct fiduciaries when they withhold material investment information from the administrative committee and do not stop the committee from making imprudent investments.

Does Section 404(c) Protect Plan Sponsors?

Before ERISA Section 404(c) can come into play, fiduciary protection comes through compliance with ERISA Section 404(a). The DOL emphasizes that the act of designating investment alternatives in Section 404(c) plans is a fiduciary function to which the limitation on liability provided by ERISA Section 404(c) does not apply. The fiduciary provisions of ERISA remain applicable to the initial designation of investment alternatives and investment managers (if any) and to the ongoing determination that such alternatives and managers (if any) remain suitable and prudent for the plan. Therefore, among other things, in connection with maintaining a plan that permits participants to self-direct investments, ERISA Section 404(a) requires the following:

- Procedural prudence in selecting the investment offerings from which the participants make their choice of investment.

- Monitoring the investment selections offered to the participants.

- Exercising the right (and duty) to change investment offerings where appropriate.

Thus, ERISA section 404(c) does not relieve plan fiduciaries from all of their fiduciary obligations under the plan. As noted earlier, plan fiduciaries are still required to perform all of their obligatory fiduciary duties under the plan, including prudent selection, ongoing monitoring, and due diligence. These obligations are identical to the general obligations imposed on a fiduciary in an employer-directed plan. This raises the question of whether maintaining a participant-directed plan offers any real advantage to plan fiduciaries in terms of reducing their potential exposure.

Compliance with Section 404(c) is unlikely to significantly decrease the incidence of lawsuits alleging fiduciary misconduct when a participant-directed investment goes sour. The DOL's regulatory requirement that Section 404(c) relief will be unavailable if the fiduciary has not disseminated sufficient information to participants to allow them to render prudent investment decisions affords participants and the DOL an effective enforcement tool by which to continue to impose liability on plan fiduciaries for imprudent investments. Rather than assert that a fiduciary has authorized a substantively imprudent investment, participants will simply argue that they did not receive enough information to render a prudent investment decision

Given the scope of disclosures required under the regulation and the fact that plan fiduciaries retain all of their prior responsibilities under ERISA, it appears unlikely that merely maintaining a participant-directed plan reduces a plan fiduciary's potential liability. Nevertheless, to the extent that a plan allows participants to direct their own investments, the prudent-plan fiduciaries should continue to perform all their basic responsibilities, comply with all the regulations, and make every attempt to communicate well with plan participants.

Clearly, ERISA Section 404(c) does not, as some may believe, relieve fiduciaries of all liability for plan investments. Although minimizing liability is a worthwhile goal, approaching fiduciary compliance by trying to minimize the plan sponsor's role in decision-making is counterproductive. By offering a 401(k) plan to its employees, a plan sponsor is necessarily signing on to be a fiduciary.

The most effective way to manage this liability is to commit to an active approach that embraces the role of fiduciary and that seeks to balance the responsibility with potential liabilities. An active approach has a number of advantages that can lead to better results. These include developing and following procedures for the fiduciary decision process and sponsoring a plan that enhances the retirement success probability of participants.

What Happens if the Plan Fails Section 404(c)?

Recently the Department of Labor (DOL) filed an amicus brief in the ongoing Enron 401(k) Plan litigation. {Tittle v. Enron Corp., S.D. Tex., Civil Action No. H-01-39131} This brief shed new light on the responsibilities of plan sponsors in the post-Enron world. In that brief, the DOL asserted that unless the plan complies with all of the requirements set forth in the DOL's regulation interpreting Section 404(c) of ERISA, the plan fiduciaries are responsible for all of the plan's investments, including investment choices made by participants. The DOL brief is not the law, and the DOL brief is not binding on any person. However, it is likely that the court will give the DOL's brief significant weight and, it could affect the outcome of the litigation.

In this case, the DOL filed the brief as a friend of the court in support of the plaintiffs' positions on several legal issues. The positions supported by the DOL include the potential liability of Enron, former CEO Kenneth Lay, the Plan Administrative Committee members, and the members of the board's Compensation Committee (the Enron Plan Fiduciaries) for losses sustained by the 401(k) participants in the wake of Enron's accounting scandals and bankruptcy. The DOL's amicus brief is not very friendly to 401(k) sponsors and fiduciaries.

The plan's investment fiduciaries can be held liable for participant investment choices if the plan does not comply with 404(c). Section 404(c) provides conditional, limited relief from ERISA's fiduciary responsibility provisions, and fiduciaries are relieved from liability for losses that resulted from the participant's exercise of control. If 404(c) does not apply, fiduciaries retain liability for the participant's investment directions. Thus, the DOL stated in its amicus brief: "absent a showing that the plan qualifies as a 404(c) plan, the fiduciaries retained full fiduciary responsibility for all of the plan's investments, including the Enron stock that the participants directed the directed trustee to purchase with their employee contributions."

The DOL's position—if accepted by the court—means that, in a case where a 401(k) plan does not comply with 404(c), plan fiduciaries are responsible for all participant investment decisions to the same extent they are responsible for plan investments in any retirement plan in which participants do not direct investment of the assets in their own accounts.

The general duties of plan fiduciaries in non 404(c) plans with respect to plan investments are set forth in ERISA 404(a). First, a plan fiduciary is obligated to discharge his duties with respect to a plan solely in the interest of the participants and beneficiaries and with the care, skill, prudence, and diligence under the circumstances then prevailing that a prudent man acting in a like capacity and familiar with such matters would use. This is otherwise referred to as the "prudent expert rule," since it requires fiduciaries to act with the skill required of "a prudent man" who is "familiar with such matters." Second, they are obligated to diversify the investments of the plan, and to minimize the risk of large losses, "unless under the circumstances it is clearly prudent not to do so."

In order to carry out these duties, the conduct of plan fiduciaries is typically measured by a standard of "procedural prudence." Courts have stated this standard as "whether the fiduciaries, at the time they engaged in the disputed transactions, utilized appropriate methods to investigate the merits of the investment and to monitor the investment.

Based on ERISA Section 404(a), a court could conclude that, in order for a fiduciary to establish "procedural prudence" in this context, the fiduciary would be required to (1) establish some benchmarks for use in determining whether the participants' accounts are prudently invested, including adequately diversified and protected against the risk of large losses, (2) evaluate each participant's account to determine whether the participants' investment allocations are in line with these benchmarks, and (3) establish a system for contacting participants whose accounts deviate from the benchmarks. This last point might require that the fiduciaries take control of the investments in the participant's account.

The First Union Bank Court Case

The First Union court case was a class-action suit against First Union Bank on behalf of its current and former employees. The action sought more than $300 million in damages, equitable relief, and permanent removal of current fiduciaries from the First Union 401(k) plan in favor of an independent, disinterested fiduciary. It alleged violations of ERISA's fiduciary provisions as well as other federal statutes. The claims centered on breaches of fiduciary duty under ERISA's prudence and exclusive-benefit standards, as well as violations of the Section 404(c) regulations.

The First Union case dramatically demonstrates that plan sponsors and fiduciaries have liability in connection with selecting and monitoring investment options in 401(k) plans. The lawsuit also illustrates that potential liability for breach of fiduciary duty exists even in rising markets. Keep in mind that the plan participant had fifteen investment choices.

The plaintiffs also alleged that the defendants named to the plan administrative committee a human resources executive who had no investment background and who was incapable of independently evaluating actions taken on behalf of the plan. To demonstrate his lack of sophistication, plaintiffs alleged in their complaint that while testifying in a deposition in a related case, he "did not even know the difference between the S&P 500 and the Fortune 500 and had no idea which one the plan's index fund tracked."

Because of the committee member's apparent inability to act independently and his lack of knowledge regarding the investments, the First Union Board of Directors and each of its members can be held liable for breach of fiduciary duty under ERISA and personally liable for any damage that results from a failure to prudently appoint the committee members or from the failure to monitor their performance.

The case was settled for $26 million. Interestingly, the legal counsel for the employees will receive approximately $8 million in fees and costs, with most of that sum allocated to payment of fees. That sum provides an incentive to opportunistic plaintiffs' attorneys to pursue other plan sponsors who may be perceived as having been less than diligent in selecting and monitoring their 401(k) plan investment options. Such litigation will likely involve claims that plan fiduciaries failed in their duties to prudently investigate, select, monitor, remove, and replace plan investment options.

As part of the settlement, First Union also agreed to hire an independent financial advisor from one of three large consulting firms to review the plan's investment options and advise the plan committee whether the addition of investment options other than First Union proprietary funds is appropriate. If the plan committee decides not to follow the advice of the independent advisor, First Union and the other defendants must give the employees' attorneys a copy of the advisor's recommendation and explain in writing why they decided not to follow the recommendation.

Although $26 million is less than what the $300 million employees sought in damages, it is a significant amount of money. The amount of the settlement should make plan sponsors take notice, and it signaled the importance of ERISA litigation to 401(k) plan sponsors. Even if the defendants felt that they had viable defenses to the claims, the amount is much higher than the cost of defending the case.

Industry observers conclude that First Union must have thought that there would have been significant exposure to much higher damages if the case went to trial. In the settlement, First Union and the plan administrative committee members denied any wrongdoing. The parties agreed that payments were made for alleged lost earnings on assets, because employees asserted that returns on investments were less than they should have been and fees associated with plan investments were higher than they should have been.

The Unisys Court Case

Unisys Corporation sponsored a retirement plan that allowed participants to direct investments. The plan was an individual account plan in which participants maintained their account balances. The plan was intended to comply with Section 404(c) of ERISA. The Unisys Savings Plan, made up of the Sperry Plan and the Burroughs Employees Savings Plan when the two companies merged, offered six choices to participants for the investment of pretax contributions.

One of the choices was an interest-bearing insurance contract fund that purchased three guaranteed investment contracts (GICs) from Executive Life insurance, totaling about 20% of the value of the fund. Unisys plan participants filed the class-action lawsuit after Executive Life was placed in receivership and Unisys froze the balances in participant accounts. The participants contended that Unisys made junk bonds available through the fund as a participant-directed investment.

The district court subsequently dismissed the lawsuits by ruling in favor of the defendants. However, the court of appeals remanded the decision back to the district court for further factual determinations. In addition, after the district court decision, the DOL filed a friend-of-the-court brief. The DOL sought to overturn the lower-court ruling, saying that it could result in retirement losses for the participants in the Unisys pension plan. In its brief, the DOL asked the appeals court to overturn the district-court decision by remanding the case back to the district court for trial.

The DOL contended that the court erred in its conclusions and that it failed to consider all the evidence in the case. The DOL claimed that the court also failed to consider whether participants had received sufficient information to exercise control over their pension accounts and whether the defendants had acted prudently in investing such a significant amount of money in Executive Life contracts.

After a checkered course through the legal system that ran close to a decade, a court-of-appeals decision in favor of Unisys was petitioned to the U.S. Supreme Court, which declined review. After many hundreds of thousands of dollars of legal expenses, Unisys was vindicated. As an employer and a fiduciary, Unisys was held not liable to participants for the purchase of Executive Life investment fund contracts.

Unisys was able to prove that the investment selections provided were what any prudent expert would have concluded was sound and appropriate. When they purchased the Executive Life GICs, the company had the highest ratings accorded by A.M. Best and Standard & Poor's. Unisys was able to show documentation from an outside consultant who, at the time, was considered the grandfather of GICs—Murray Becker of Johnson and Higgins. In short, Unisys was able to show prudence by having exercised an expert standard of care in selecting credible investment options. Although Executive Life ran into trouble, the law is not designed to prevent the vicissitudes of the marketplace.

To a certain extent, the Unisys case is an example of how to do things right. The company could prove that it had a philosophy for investing and a process for implementing and reviewing those investments and that it had retained outside counsel to provide guidance. Most important, the company had documented all of the above. The Unisys message is loud and clear: the plan sponsor must follow and document a detailed fiduciary oversight process.

The fiduciaries must independently examine the merits and intrinsic value of all options. They must adopt written investment guidelines and follow them. If plan fiduciaries lack sufficient investment expertise and knowledge, they should consider retaining a qualified investment advisor to help them select and regularly monitor the plan's investment options. Underperforming investments should be placed on special watch lists and removed as options when appropriate.

Market Timing and Late-Day Mutual-Fund Trading Litigation

In 2003, numerous mutual fund companies were implicated in a broad-reaching trading scandal that clearly showed that they had put the fund companies' interests ahead of those of the retirement plan participants. By the end of 2003, the fund companies cited included some of the most popular with investors: Janus, Putnam, Bank of America's Nations Funds, Pilgrim-Baxter, Strong, American Express, Bank One, U.S. Trust, Federated Investors, and Loomis Sayles. In addition, New York state and federal regulators filed civil and criminal charges against three former executives of Phoenix-based Security Trust Company for improper mutual-fund trading. In addition, federal officials will begin shutting down the company, authorities said.

New York Attorney General Eliot Spitzer filed felony charges, including six counts of grand larceny, against the former Security Trust Company chief executive officer, president, and senior vice president of corporate services. The criminal charges by Spitzer and the civil charges by the SEC accused the company of facilitating abusive trading by seeking hedge funds to make money in mutual funds and for illegally accepting fund trades after the 4 P.M. Eastern Standard Time cutoff.

According to SEC officials, Security Trust "facilitated hundreds of late trades in nearly four hundred different mutual funds" by bunching the trades together with 401(k) client trades over a period in excess of three years. The company received $5.8 million in direct compensation from the hedge funds, according to the SEC complaint. Spitzer said the actions of the accused resulted in the larceny of more than $1 million. The company was forced out of business by its chief regulator, the federal Office of the Comptroller of the Currency (OCC). The OCC announced that Security Trust Company will begin a process "that will result in an orderly dissolution of the bank by March 31, 2004."

DOL Urges Review of Mutual Funds Named in Probe

Retirement plan sponsors and fiduciaries must rethink the use of funds from firms named in Spitzer's complaint. So said the DOL's Ann Combs, who oversees all defined-contribution retirement plans in her role as the EBSA's assistant secretary.

In a speech before the National Defined Contribution Council in late 2003, Combs urged plan fiduciaries to look at their retirement offerings and ask the firms named in the complaint for additional information. She also said that the plans will have to decide whether they want to participate in class-action lawsuits against the firms. "Allegations of improper mutual fund practices where a plan is invested must be factored into the fiduciary's determination of the continuing appropriateness of that investment," said Combs. "The plan fiduciary may need to contact the mutual fund's management for information regarding the trading practices and take appropriate action," she said.

Those overseeing retirement plans have a legal obligation to act in the best interest of participants. But it is unclear whether that duty requires them to drop mutual funds that allow market timing, the practice at the center of the current scandals. However, if a plan sponsor has funds that have been named in market timing or late-day trading, they have a duty to investigate and document their actions.

As fiduciaries, the plan sponsors must keep a close eye on what their firms are doing to handle the situation and their funds. Plan fiduciaries must weigh the cost of participating in a lawsuit against the likelihood and the amount of the potential recovery. If the chances of recovery are high, plan sponsors may have an obligation to join the class action on behalf of plan participants. Plan sponsors must keep an eye on the restitution proceedings and make sure that their participants get their fair share.

Administrators Must Give Notice of ERISA Blackout Periods

Shortly after the Enron debacle, the DOL's Pension and Welfare Benefits Administration published interim final rules implementing a new federal law. The law required 401(k)-type plans to give participants thirty days' notice of blackout periods that would affect their rights to direct investments, take loans, or obtain distributions. The interim final rules contained model notice language to assist plan sponsors in carrying out this new obligation. The new rules went into effect January 26, 2003.

Blackout periods typically occur when plans change record keepers or investment options or when they add participants due to a corporate merger or acquisition.

Now, at least thirty days before the beginning of an ERISA blackout period, plan administrators must notify the affected participants and beneficiaries. The notice must include (1) the reasons for the blackout period, (2) identification of the investments and other rights that are affected, (3) the expected beginning date and length of the blackout period, and (4) a statement that individuals should evaluate the appropriateness of their current investment decisions in light of their inability to direct or diversify assets credited to their accounts.

The notice must be in writing; however, the requirement may be satisfied by electronic means, so long as the notice is "reasonably accessible" to the recipient. The plan administrator who fails to provide a required blackout notice may be fined up to $100 per day per affected participant or beneficiary. Thus, a plan with one thousand participants that fails to give the notice for the full thirty days would pay $100 x 1,000 x 30 = $3 million. If the blackout period involves employer securities, the plan administrator is required to also provide notice to the issuer of the employer securities.

For Further Reading

Brennan, M. "Relief at Last?: DOL's Final Regulation on Participant-Directed Individual Account Plans" 19, no. 1, 50–68 (1996).

"Investment Advice Survey 2002." From the *Forty-Sixth Annual Survey of Profit Sharing and 401k Plans*, Profit Sharing/401k Council of America, (September 2003).

Pension and Employee Benefits: Code, ERISA, and Regulations as of January 1, 2003. Commerce Clearing House, Chicago, (2003).

Perum, P., and Steuerle, E. *From Fiduciary to Facilitator: Rethinking the Role of Employers in Defined Contribution Plans.* Urban Institute, (2000).

Reish, R., and Faucher, J. *Department of Labor Sues Enron.* Reish, Luftman, Reicher, and Cohen, LLC, Los Angles, (July 2003).

Reish, R., and Faucher, J. *The Settlement of the First Union Cases.* Reish, Luftman, Reicher and Cohen, LLC, (April 2002).

Reish, R., and Faucher, J. *The DOL's Enron Brief: What It Means for 401(k) Investments.* Reish, Luftman, Reicher, and Cohen, LLC, (April 2003).

Sacher, S., and Miller, E. "Win, Lose, or Draw? An Analysis of the Proposed 404(c) Regulations." *Journal of Pension Planning and Compliance* 17, no. 3, 19–36 (1995).

Study of 401(k) Plan Fees and Expenses. Contract No. J-P-7-0046, U.S. Department of Labor Pension and Welfare Benefits Administration (1998).

"The Emperor's New Mutual Funds." *Wall Street Journal*, (July, 2003).

Chapter 11

Trustee Services

Chapter Summary

There are three types of plan trustee relationships: self-trustee, directed corporate trustee, and discretionary corporate trustee. Under the self-trustee approach, one or more individuals serve as plan trustee and are held to the prudent-expert standard of conduct. Unless these individuals are true experts, such a situation should be avoided. There are numerous advantages to the plan sponsor and plan participants in hiring a discretionary corporate trustee. The most important one is that a discretionary trustee has the final authority, or discretion, to make investment selections and replace investments if necessary. The discretionary trustee must always follow the ERISA prudent-expert rules and must maintain well-documented records of its actions. The decision to hire a discretionary trustee is a fiduciary decision on the part of the plan sponsor, and the plan sponsor must do so prudently.

Unlike discretionary trustees, directed corporate trustees serve in a limited cofiduciary role. They provide a custodial function to hold plan assets. They do not make discretionary investment decisions for the plan. In some cases, directed trustees may function in a carefully crafted limited cofiduciary capacity. They may provide nondiscretionary investment recommendations and ongoing data to the plan sponsor in a cofiduciary role. However, in such limited-capacity cofiduciary cases, the final discretionary authority and ultimate fiduciary risk belong to the plan sponsor. Unless the cofiduciary has discretion over the selection and replacement of plan investments, the fiduciary risk belongs to the plan sponsor, who must make the final decisions. The discretionary final decision-maker is where the buck stops.

Trustee Responsibilities

When ERISA was passed, Congress intended to ensure that a qualified retirement plan's assets would be used only to pay benefits to participants and beneficiaries and for reasonable plan operating expenses. Therefore, ERISA required that all qualified retirement-plan assets be held in a trust and managed by trustees. Trustees have complete control over plan assets held in the trust, although trust investment decisions may be made by the plan's administrative committee or by designated investment managers. To the extent that investments are directed, trustees may not be liable for investment decisions if they select the investment options in a prudent manner. When trustees choose investments, they are held to the same standards as any other investment manager.

Assets of ERISA plans are generally held in trust and managed by trustees either named in the trust instrument or appointed by the plan's named fiduciary. Trustees have exclusive authority to manage and control plan assets, except when a plan expressly provides that (1) the trustees are subject to the direction of the named fiduciary or (2) the authority is delegated to investment managers.

One or more individuals may serve as plan trustee. In such cases, the individuals would be held to the prudent-expert rule. Unless the individuals are true experts and willing to accept personal fiduciary liability, such an idea should be approached with great trepidation. The plan sponsor may hire two types of corporate trustees: directed and discretionary. Trustees subject to the direction of the named fiduciary are called "directed trustees." Directed trustees are not liable for following the instructions of the named fiduciaries, because they have no financial decision-making authority, or discretion, over the plan investments. In such cases, the liability resides with the group calling the final shots—the plan sponsor or its retirement committee. This group retains final discretion over the investments.

Individual and Corporate Trustee Issues

Many individuals who serve as trustees do not understand the duties they must fulfill. Hiring a corporate trustee adds value to the plan because fiduciary responsibility is distributed more broadly, reducing the possibilities for potential conflicts of interest, and time-consuming administrative functions, such as preparing consolidated asset and income statements, processing receipts and disbursements, and preparing and filing tax forms, are delegated to an institution that specializes in providing these services.

If the trustee role is delegated to an institution that specializes in providing trust services, the possibility that a trust responsibility could be overlooked is significantly reduced, thereby reducing the exposure of the plan sponsor to penalties or to jeopardizing the plan's tax-qualified status. Plans with more than one hundred participants subject to the plan audit requirement may pay a lower audit fee when using a corporate trustee, because the plan may be eligible to file a limited-scope audit report and because the institution generally prepares standardized auditor's reports designed to simplify the audit process. The corporate trustee can supply an SAS 70 audit that reduces the scope of the plan audit.

The most important difference between the individual and corporate trustees, especially discretionary corporate trustees, is in the investment-management and fiduciary-liability areas. The significance of these areas should never be underestimated by the plan sponsor. At the most basic level, because a corporate trustee controls assets, plan participants receive an extra degree of protection that plan assets will be used solely to pay benefits. The corporate trustee also brings continuity to the process. And, most importantly, the corporate trustee can offer investment expertise and well-documented fiduciary reviews to enhance the outcomes of the participants and beneficiaries. This process also helps protect the plan sponsor from fiduciary liability.

Investment Responsibility Delegation

Discretionary plan trustees, except where the trustees retain an investment manager that acknowledges its ERISA fiduciary status and responsibility in writing, cannot delegate the responsibility for plan investments. An investment manager is defined under ERISA as any fiduciary (other than a trustee or named fiduciary) who:

1. has the discretionary power to manage, buy, or sell plan assets;

2. is registered as an investment advisor under the Investment Advisors Act of 1940 and is a bank or insurance company licensed to do business in more than one state; and

3. has acknowledged in writing that it is a fiduciary with respect to the plan.

Hiring an investment manager is a fiduciary act and must be a careful and well-documented process. When such an investment manager is hired by the plan, the plan trustees and fiduciaries are relieved of their fiduciary responsibilities for the assets allocated to that investment manager, as long as the fiduciaries are prudent in their selection of a manager by investigating the investment manager's background and experience with investment for similarly sized plans.

The fiduciaries should also examine the reputation, credentials (such as registration with the Securities and Exchange Commission), documented past performance with similar investments, fee structure compared with other investment managers, and type and frequency of reports to trustees. In addition the trustees must establish prudent guidelines on investments, with limits on risk, allocation, types of investments, and expected rates of return and monitor the investment manager on a regular basis to ensure the guidelines are being followed.

Directed Versus Discretionary Corporate Trustees

Considerable confusion exists among plan sponsors over the terms "directed trustee" and "discretionary trustee." Both are corporations, and both are fiduciaries to the plan in almost all circumstances. So what is the difference? The main difference and the most important difference is which group has the final say in the selection, retention, and replacement of plan investments. The key concept to keep in mind is that fiduciary risk follows discretion.

A directed trustee is a fiduciary and may even offer investment recommendations to the plan sponsor, but it is the plan sponsor (sometimes even unknowingly) that must sign off on the investments. Because the plan sponsor has the final discretion, it retains most of the fiduciary liability.

A directed trustee provides an asset custody service. Generally, directed trustees are captive trust companies for bundled recordkeeping and mutual-fund service providers; they offer little additional service relative to the bundled arrangement without trust services (e.g., if the bundled provider offers tax reporting and filing services, these services are offered whether or not the captive trust company acts as trustee). Consequently, the primary incremental value of the captive trust company stems from the perceived fiduciary liability afforded by a corporate trustee. Directed-trustee trust companies generally charge a flat annual fee for being named as plan trustee and for issuing certain trust reports. The flat fee is typically $500 to $2,000 per year.

When plan participants file lawsuits against a plan sponsor and directed trustee, the reactions of directed trustees are enlightening. In general, the directed trustee will seek to have the case dismissed under a number of defenses, usually leaving the plan sponsor out on a limb to defend itself. Often, the sponsor does not even know that it had such risk.

Nondiscretionary Cofiduciary Court Defenses Push Liability onto Plan Sponsors

It is not uncommon for directed ("cofiduciaries") to abandon the plan sponsor if problems arise. The two most common court defenses that directed trustees might use to push liability back onto plan sponsors are:

1. The directed trustee did not have or exercise the required discretion to confer fiduciary status over the plan investments under ERISA Section 3(21)(A)(iii).

2. The directed trustee did not render investment advice for a fee within the meaning of ERISA Section 21(A)(ii).

Under point 1, the plan sponsor and directed trustee may argue in court to push discretion back to the other party. Even if the plan sponsor can push some discretion back on the directed trustee, the price will be hefty legal bills for the plan sponsor. In most cases, the directed trustee will be able to show that all the final discretion belonged to the plan sponsor and will alleviate itself from the investment liability. (see Merrill Lynch Trust Company legal brief in the addendum at the end of this chapter pages 287-306) Point 2 is more straightforward. Either the directed trustee was rendering investment advice for a fee or it was not. Even if the directed trustee was rendering investment advice for a fee (rare), it almost always does so on a nondiscretionary basis.

The final liability would most likely fall to the plan sponsor, because it retained discretion. Sometimes, the directed trustee will try to fall back to ERISA Section 404(c). The directed trustee will argue that the plan participants selected their own investments and that the directed trustee is not responsible. Keep in mind that in order for 404(c) protection to work, the plan sponsor must show that the investments were prudent. The plan sponsor must also document that the numerous disclosure steps of 404(c) were met (see chapter 10).

Generally, under the terms of the plan and the trust agreement, the directed trustee is required to follow the directions as to investments given to it by the investment fiduciary, that is, the plan sponsor, and by the plan participants. Some courts may rule that the directed trustee retains sufficient discretion and even the obligation, as a directed trustee, to abide by certain duties imposed by ERISA Section 403(a). ERISA Section 403(a), the directed-trustee provision, states in part:

"All assets of an employee benefit plan shall be held in trust by one or more trustees. The trustee shall have exclusive authority and discretion to manage and control the assets of the plan, except to the extent that if the plan expressly provides that the trustee is subject to the direction of a named fiduciary who is not a trustee, in which case the trustees shall be subject to proper directions of such fiduciary which are made in accordance with the terms of the plan and which are not contrary to this chapter."

The directed trustee, therefore, is deprived of discretion to manage and control the plan's assets generally, but retains the discretion and the obligation to follow only "proper" directions of the investment fiduciary. The investment fiduciary's (plan sponsor's) directions, which are made in accordance with the terms of the plan, must not be contrary to the ERISA statute. They must be prudent.

A directed trustee is not justified in complying with directions if the trustee knows or ought to know that the holder of the power is violating his duty to the beneficiaries as a fiduciary in giving the directions. Specifically, the directed trustee is not relieved of the obligations to conform to the prudent-man standard of care, to attempt to remedy known breaches of duty by other fiduciaries, and to avoid prohibited transactions. Obviously, in such cases, the legal mess for the plan sponsor is quite a quagmire. The directed trustee will attempt to push the liability back to the plan sponsor by emphasizing, ironically, that the plan sponsor's instructions were proper.

Chart 11-1: Employer Retains Liability with Typical Directed Trustee

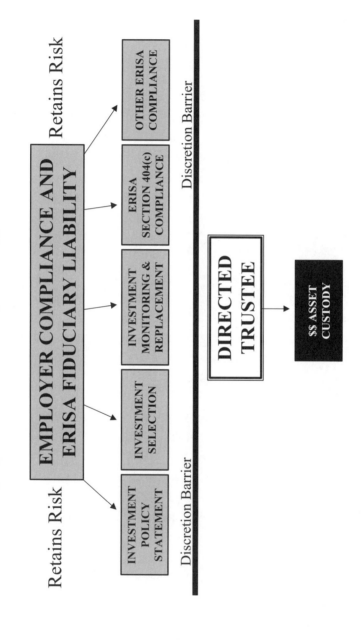

ERISA Section 404(a) Comes before Section 404(c)

Generally speaking, the directed trustee's liability protection to the plan sponsor is minimal to nonexistent. The plan sponsor does not want to end up in court fighting with the directed trustee; however, rather than worrying about the inherent weakness of a directed trustee, the plan sponsor is far better off to avoid the liability problem in the first place. The plan sponsor cannot rely upon Section 404(c) unless the investments are prudent. Rather than focus on the negative, the plan sponsor should have an excellent fiduciary process in place that will improve outcomes. ERISA Section 404(a) requires that the investments be prudent. Section 404(a) has the following requirements:

"A fiduciary shall discharge his duties with respect to a plan solely in the interest of the participants and beneficiaries and (A) for the exclusive purpose of providing benefits to participants and their beneficiaries, (B) with the care, skill, prudence, and diligence under the circumstances then prevailing that a prudent man acting in a like capacity and familiar with such matters would use in the conduct of an enterprise of a like character and with like aims; (C) by diversifying the investments of the plan so as to minimize the risk of large losses, unless under the circumstances it is clearly prudent not to do so; and (D) in accordance with the documents and instruments governing the plan."

The plan sponsor should focus on having a well-documented process in place that is prudent and that improves outcomes. So much of what is offered by financial intermediaries to "help" the plan sponsor, even in a cofiduciary but nondiscretionary role, contains no prospective outcome data to demonstrate that the process makes a difference once it is put into place. The plan sponsor has a duty to focus on processes that can improve outcomes, not just to produce a fiduciary feel-good exercise.

Discretionary Trustees

Unlike the directed corporate trustee, the discretionary trustee takes responsibility for the selection, monitoring, and retention of plan investments. There is no argument about discretion in court, as the discretionary trustee acknowledges discretion from the beginning. The hiring of a discretionary trustee is a fiduciary act, and the plan sponsor must do so prudently and document its actions. The goal of the discretionary trustee should be more than just liability protection. The goal should be to improve participant outcomes.

Under ERISA, the discretionary trustee must prudently select and monitor the participant-directed investment options in a 401(k) plan. In the preamble to the 404(c) regulations, the DOL explains these responsibilities:

"The Department emphasizes that the act of designating investment alternatives . . . in an ERISA section 404(c) plan is a fiduciary function. All of the fiduciary provisions of ERISA remain applicable to both the initial designation of investment alternatives and the ongoing determination that such alternatives remain suitable and prudent investment alternatives for the plan." That "ongoing determination," or monitoring, requires that the discretionary trustee regularly review the investment funds for issues such as investment performance, expenses, volatility, and style consistency.

When discretionary fiduciaries monitor performance, they should compare the return on the investment options against appropriate peer groups and indices. If the funds are meeting or exceeding the standards adopted by the trustee, then the plan would continue to offer those investment options. However, if a fund is under-performing its benchmark, a common step for knowledgeable discretionary trustees is to place that fund on a watch list and investigate the reason for its underperformance.

Chart 11-2: Employer Reduces Liability with a Discretionary Trustee

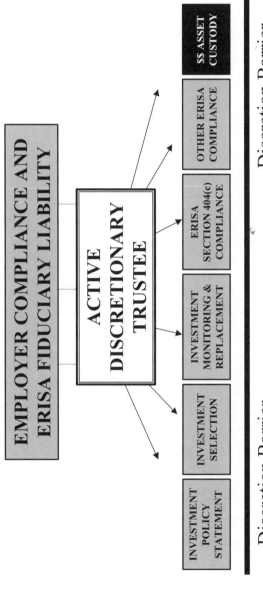

The DOL Frost and Aetna Letters

One additional and important difference exists between discretionary trustees and directed trustees. Because discretionary trustees control the investment choices, they are held to a higher standard of fee disclosure and good-faith actions than directed trustees. In essence, under the DOL Frost Letter, the discretionary trustee must return to the plan participants all revenue received from mutual funds selected by the discretionary trustee, such as 12b-1 fees, shareholder servicing fees, and other fees. These fees are returned as dollar-for-dollar fee offsets. If the revenue exceeds the discretionary trustee fees, the plan is paid a net dividend. (See chapter 17.)

Another DOL letter, commonly called the Aetna Letter, allows a directed trustee to keep the mutual-fund fees, in addition to charging other fees, as long as the information is somehow disclosed to the plan sponsor. Sometimes the mutual-fund fees are large enough to make a directed-trustee arrangement more expensive than a discretionary-trustee arrangement. This can be the case even though the discretionary trustee usually delivers far more value to the participants and to the plan sponsor.

The problem with revenue sharing, however, is that although DOL may have clarified its position for legal technicians, nothing is clear to most plan sponsors about the nature, size, use, abuse, and even existence of these payments from money managers to qualified plan vendors. Plan sponsors rarely know that these payments exist. When they know about the payments, they rarely know the amounts, who receives them, or the potential conflicts of interest thus created—all of which are items that a prudent plan sponsor (fiduciary) is expected to know about their service providers.

Addendum

UNITED STATES DISTRICT COURT
SOUTHERN DISTRICT OF NEW YORK

REPLY MEMORANDUM OF LAW
IN FURTHER SUPPORT OF MOTION BY

MERRILL LYNCH TRUST COMPANY

TO DISMISS AMENDED CONSOLIDATED MASTER
CLASS ACTION COMPLAINT

IN RE WORLDCOM, INC.
ERISA LITIGATION :
02 CIV. 4816 (DLC)

GIBSON, DUNN & CRUTCHER, LLP
1050 CONNECTICUT AVENUE, NW
WASHINGTON, D.C. 20036
ATTORNEYS FOR DEFENDANT
MERRILL LYNCH TRUST COMPANY

OF COUNSEL
WILLIAM J. KILBERG
PAUL BLANKENSTEIN
ANTOINETTE DECAMP

(Reprinted with Permission)

TABLE OF CONTENTS

TABLE OF AUTHORITIES

Cases

Koch v. Dwyer, No. 98 Civ. 5519 (RPP), 1999 WL 528181 (S.D.N.Y. July 22, 1999

Moniace v. Commerce Bank, N.A., 40 F.3d 264 (8th Cir. 1994)

Mertens v. Hewitt Associates, 508 U.S. 248, 262 (1993)

Pegram v. Herdrich, 530 U.S. 211 (2000)

Smith v. Loal 819 IBT Pension Plan, 291 F.3d 236 (2d Cir. 2002)

Sutton v. United Air Lines, Inc., 527 U.S. 471 (1999)

Statutes

29 C.F.R. § 2510.3-21(c)(1)(2002)

29 C.F.R. § 2550.404c-1(b)(3)

29 C.F.R. § 2550.404c-1(c)(4)

29 U.S.C. § 1002(21)(a)

29 U.S.C. § 1002(a)(1)

29 U.S.C. § 1002(a)(2)

29 U.S.C. § 1103(a)(1)

Rules

Fed.R.Civ.P. 12(b)(6)

I. INTRODUCTION

In its opening brief, Merrill Lynch Trust Company FSB ("Merrill Lynch") established that the Consolidated Amended Class Action Complaint ("Complaint") fails to state a claim because (1) Merrill Lynch is a directed trustee and therefore owes no fiduciary duty of prudence regarding the investment alternatives made available under the WorldCom 401(k) Salary Savings Plan (the "Plan"), (2) Merrill Lynch is not responsible for any losses sustained even if it were a fiduciary because the participants in the plan directed their own investments within the meaning of ERISA Section 4040(c), and (3) plaintiffs have not sufficiently alleged that Merrill Lynch either knew of other fiduciaries' purported breaches of fiduciary duty or, through its own alleged breaches of fiduciary duty, enabled other fiduciaries to commit their own breaches.

Plaintiffs' response consists primarily of variations on two main themes. First, plaintiffs assert that they need not do any more than recite statutory language in order to satisfy their pleading burden under the Federal Rules of Civil Procedure, and that their conclusory allegations of what Merrill Lynch purportedly "knew" or "should have known" therefore suffice to state a claim for relief. Second, plaintiffs mistakenly, yet repeatedly, contend that there is no substantive difference between the duties owned by a directed trustee and the duties owed by fiduciaries to evaluate the prudence of investments.

Plaintiffs' flawed contentions rest on faulty premises. The "notice pleading" standard does not give plaintiffs license simply to parrot statutory language in their complaint without supporting those legal conclusions with substantive factual allegations. Asserting that a defense "violated the law" hardly provides sufficient notice of the allegedly offending conduct, especially when the alleged violations sound in fraud, as plaintiff's allegation do. In order to sustain a claim against Merrill Lynch, plaintiffs must plead, at a minimum, facts which, if proved, would establish their entitlement to relief, and they must do so with particularity as to any allegations that sound in fraud. They have not done so, and nothing that plaintiffs say in their opposition relieves them of that obligation. Plaintiffs' contention that directed trustees owe the same fiduciary duties of prudence as investment fiduciaries is fundamentally unsound. Section 403(a) of ERISA creates a class of trustee – a directed trustee – that has far more limited responsibilities than a common law trustee, or an ERISA fiduciary. Plaintiffs' attempt to impose on Merrill Lynch the same duty owed by anon-directed trustee to evaluate the prudence of investment alternatives made available under the Plan completely ignores the explicit congressional intent that directed trustees such as Merrill Lynch be exempt from any such fiduciary obligations.

II. ARGUMENT

A. The Federal Rules of Civil Procedure Require Plaintiffs To Allege Facts Which, If Proved, Would Entitle Plaintiffs to Relief, And To Plead Facts With Particularity Is An Action Sounding In Fraud.

Merrill Lynch established in its opening brief that plaintiffs' allegations concerning its activities consist of nothing more than legal conclusions based on boilerplate repetition of ERISA's language. See Opening Br. at 8-9. Implicitly recognizing the conclusory nature of their allegations, plaintiffs contend that merely repeating statutory language is enough to state a claim for relief. See Plaintiffs' Br. at 4-5.

Plaintiffs are wrong. The requirement of Federal Rule of Civil Procedure 8(a) that a complaint contain an intelligible, "short and plain statement" of the claims asserted does not relieve plaintiffs of the obligations to set forth facts that, if proved, would establish their entitlement to the requested relief. As Merrill Lynch noted in its opening brief, conclusory assertions, unwarranted inferences, and legal boilerplate do not suffice. See Opening Br. at 10;

Gregory v. Daly, 243 F.3d 687, 692 (2d Cir. 2001); *First Nationwide Bank v. Gelt Funding Corp.*, 27 F.3d 763, 771 (2d Cir. 1994). Furthermore, a complaint that "sounds in fraud" must be pleaded with particularity pursuant to Rule 9(b). Plaintiffs' general discussion of the standard ona motion to dismiss (see Plaintiffs' Br. at 3-5 does not satisfactorily address this authority.

B. As A Directed Trustee, Merrill Lynch Had No Duty to Evaluate The Prudence of Plan Investments.

Plaintiffs' theory that even directed trustees must assess the prudence of investments completely ignores the carefully-constructed statutory regime in which directed trustees are exempted from duties they might otherwise owe as plan trustees. As explained below and in Merrill Lynch's opening brief, Merrill Lynch was a directed trustee within the meaning of ERISA Section 403(a), and, as such, owed no duty, fiduciary or otherwise, to assess the prudence of the decisions of the named plan fiduciaries, who are directly and explicitly charged with the responsibility to manage the investment options available under the Plan.

1. Not All Trustees are ERISA Fiduciaries.

Plaintiffs start off by broadly asserting that plan trustees are "always" and "quintessentially" fiduciaries. See Plaintiffs' Br. at 5. From this general premise Plaintiffs conclude that Merrill Lynch necessarily owed a fiduciary duty to act prudently with respect to the selection and maintenance of investment options available under the Plan. Id. at 5-7. The fatal flaw in Plaintiffs' theory is their failure to acknowledge that ERISA imposes fiduciary status – and therefore fiduciary obligations – only " to the extent" that the statutory definition of "fiduciary" is met. See 29 U.S.C. § 1002(21)(A) (defining fiduciary "to the extent" that certain conditions are met); 29 U.S.C. §1103(a)(1) (trustees are subject to direction of a named fiduciary "to the extent" that the plan documents so provide); see also *Maniace v.Commerce Bank, N.A.*, 40 F.3d 264, 267 (8th Cir. 1994) ("[A] trustee for a plan is not necessarily a fiduciary for the entire plan."). The "threshold question" in every case alleging breach of fiduciary duty under ERISA is whether the defendant was "acting as a fiduciary...when taking the action subject to complaint." *Pegram v. Herdrich*, 530 U.S. 211, 226 (2000).

ERISA expressly places outside the scope of fiduciary responsibility actions undertaken by directed trustees. Contrary to plaintiffs' contention, ERISA does not simply deprive directed trustees of "exclusive" "authority and discretion to manage and control the assets of the plan," leaving them responsible for the same conduct and to the same extent as those who direct them. See Plaintiffs' Br. at 7 n. 4; id. at 14-18. Nor does it leave with directed trustees any residual fiduciary duty to assess the prudence of the instructions they required under the terms of the plan to follow.

Instead, the statute strips a directed trustee of authority and discretion "to manage and control assets of the plan" *"to the extent that"* the plan makes the directed trustee subject to the discretions of a named fiduciary expressly charged with the discretionary authority to make investment decisions. 29 U.S.C. § 1103(a)(1) (emphasis added). In these circumstances, the directed trustee "shall be subject to proper directions of such fiduciary which are made in accordance with the terms of the Plan and which are not contrary to [ERISA]." Id. To read the phrase "and not contrary to ERISA" as reinstating for directed trustees fiduciary responsibility for the prudence of investment plan decisions would "abrogate the distinction between trustees and directed trustees clearly intended by ERISA." *Maniace*, 40 F.3d at 268. Plaintiff's contention that directed trustees nevertheless retain "residual' fiduciary duties – including the duty to assess the prudence the investment directions they receive – thus threatens to undermine the carefully-constructed allocation of responsibilities under ERISA. See generally *Connecticut Nat'l Bank v. Germain*, 503 U.S. 249, 253 (1992) (noting that "courts should disfavor interpretations of statutes that render language superfluous").In short, "to the extent" that Merrill Lynch, a directed trustee, is subject to the discretions of a named fiduciary within the meaning of Section 403(a)(1), it lacks the "discretion" or "authority" necessary to meet ERISA's definition of a fiduciary

2. Merrill Lynch Is Not A Named Fiduciary.

Astonishingly, plaintiffs next contend that Merrill Lynch was not only an ERISA fiduciary, but that it was also a "named fiduciary" within the meaning of ERISA. See Plaintiffs' Br. at 7. This contention is meritless. Significantly, this newly-minted assertion is not contained anywhere in the complaint. Plaintiffs, of course, cannot amend their Complaint by making new allegations in their brief. See, e.g., *Dawson v. Bumble & Bumble*, ___F. Supp. 2d ____, 2003WL 470341 (S.D.N.Y. Feb. 25, 2003).

Furthermore, plaintiffs' theory finds no support in the underlying Plan documents or in the text of ERISA. The term "named fiduciary," like other terms defined in ERISA, has a very specific meaning, and refers only to "a fiduciary who is named in the plan instrument" or the one who "pursuant to a procedure specified in the plan, is identified as a fiduciary …by a person who is an employer." See 29 U.S.C. §1102(a)(2). The term "plan instrument" similarly has a precise meaning: the document pursuant to which the plan is established and maintained. See 29 U.S.C.§1102(a)(1). The "plan instrument" in this case identifies WorldCom as both the Named Administrative Fiduciary and the Named Investment Fiduciary. See Plan §§1.02, 1.32, 14.03(Exhibit 1 to Kilberg Decl.). Merrill Lynch did not somehow become a "named fiduciary" through a "procedure specified in the plan' simply by having entered into an agreement with WorldCom to act as a directed trustee. In fact, the Trust Agreement recites that the Named Administrative Fiduciary and the Named Investment Fiduciary are the named fiduciaries for the Plan. See Trust Agreement §§2.01, 2.02 (Exhibit 2 to Kilberg Decl., at 102).

3. Merrill Lynch Did Not Have Or Exercise The Discretion Required To Confer Fiduciary Status Under ERISA Section 3(21)(A)(iii).

.Plaintiffs concede that they have not alleged that Merrill Lynch exercised any discretionary authority or control over the management of the Plan. See Plaintiffs' Br. at 8, n.7. They assert, however, that Merrill Lynch "*possessed* substantial discretionary authority and responsibility" sufficient to trigger fiduciary status under ERISA Section 3(21)(A)(iii). Id. at 8(emphasis added).

Once again, however, plaintiffs overlook the fact that fiduciary status is not an all-or nothing proposition. See Opening Br. at 10-11. The test is not whether a defendant had any authority or discretion whatsoever, but rather whether it had any such authority or discretion with respect to the conduct at issue. Here, the complained-of-conduct was the decision to retain WorldCom stock as an investment option in the Plan. The language plaintiffs quote from the Trust Agreement does not support their contention that Merrill Lynch had any discretion or authority to make that decision. Thus, for example, the general reference in the Trust Agreement to the obligation to act in the interests and for the benefit of plan participants and beneficiaries or Merrill Lynch's purported status as a "fiduciary" say nothing about having the authority to make decisions regarding the selection or maintenance of investment alternatives. See Trust Agreement, §§6.02, 6.03 (Kilberg Decl. Ex. 2 at 7).3 The general reference to taking action "necessary or appropriate for the protection of the Trust Fund" is likewise silent regarding any purported authority to make or cease to make available a particular investment alternative. Id. §7.02(d) (Kilberg Decl. Ex. 2 at 10).

Under the express terms of the Plan, the authority to make these decisions is vested exclusively in WorldCom as the Named Investment Fiduciary. Plan §14.05 (Kilberg Decl. Ex. 1 at 43). The Trust Agreement expressly states that Merrill Lynch, as directed trustee, "shall have no discretionary control over, nor any discretion regarding, the investment or reinvestment of any [plan] asset" and "shall invest" plan assets "as directed by the Named Investment Fiduciary." Trust Agreement, §5.01 (Kilberg Decl. Ex. 2 at 5). The powers of Merrill Lynch, as directed trustee, detailed in the Trust Agreement are ministerial in nature and designed to permit Merrill Lynch to carry out the directions of the Named Investment Fiduciary. Id. §§7.01, 7.02.

Plaintiffs' heavy reliance on the language in the Trust Agreement that allows Merrill Lynch to "limit the categories of assets in which the Trust Fund may be invested is entirely misplaced. Contrary to what plaintiffs suggest, that language merely allows Merrill Lynch to limit the investment options to those that it can administratively support. Once the parties determine the categories of administratively supportable investment alternatives, the authority to select among those alternatives belongs to WorldCom as Named Investment Fiduciary and not to Merrill Lynch as directed trustee. See Trust Agreement §5.01. Any doubt in this regard is put to rest by the fact that the immediately preceding sentence declares that Merrill Lynch "shall not have discretionary control over, nor any other discretion regarding the investment or reinvestment of any asset of the Trust." Trust Agreement, §5.01 (Kilberg Decl. Ex. 2, at 5).

In short, the provisions that plaintiffs cite are not evidence of any discretionary authority or control with regard to the conduct at issue in this complaint, but rather are ministerial powers that Merrill Lynch was given in order to carry out the directions it was instructed to execute and to protect the Trust from outside interference, such as theft, embezzlement, or claims by third parties.

Any contrary interpretation would have the effect of nullifying the specific provisions in the Trust Agreement and other plan documents that establish that Merrill Lynch had no discretion to decide what investment alternatives would or would not remain available under the Plan. See e.g., Trust Agreement, §§5.01 (Kilberg Dec. Ex. 2 at 5); Adoption Agreement #003 (Kilberg Decl. Ex. 5, at 1) (noting trustee is a non discretionary trustee). As established by settled authority plaintiffs themselves cite, plaintiffs' proposed interpretation of the Trust Agreement therefore must be rejected. *See, e.g. Galli v. Metz*, 973 F.2d 145, 149 (2d Cir. 1992) ("[A]n interpretation of a contract that has the effect of rendering at least one clause superfluous or meaningless is not preferred and will be avoided if possible.") (internal quotation and citation omitted).

4. Merrill Lynch Did Not Render Investment Advice For A Fee Within The Meaning Of ERISA Section 21(A)(ii).

Plaintiffs concede that Merrill Lynch did not have the "authority or responsibility" to render investment advice under the Trust Agreement. See Plaintiffs' Br. at 13. Nevertheless, they argue that, because they allege that Merrill Lynch did, in fact, render such advice, it is a fiduciary under ERISA Section 21(A)(ii). Id at 13-14. But, as Merrill Lynch established in its opening brief, rendering advice is not enough by itself to confer fiduciary status under ERISA Section 21(A)(ii). In order to establish fiduciary status under this provision, plaintiffs must plead facts showing that Merrill Lynch not only rendered such advice, but that it also either (1) had discretionary authority or control with respect to purchasing or selling securities or (2) rendered the advice on a regular basis. See Opening Br. at 13; 29 C.F.R. §2510.3-21(c)(1) (2002). Plaintiffs have pleaded no such facts, and make no pretense that they did. See Plaintiffs' Br. At 13-14.

5. Directed Trustees Must Be Judged By The "Clear On Their Face" Standard, Not The "Knew Or Should Have Known" Standard.

Given that Merrill Lynch has no discretionary authority over the investment alternatives available to plan participants and is obligated by the Trust Agreement to follow WorldCom's directions in that regard, the question becomes what type of residual responsibilities, if any, Merrill Lynch had a directed trustee with regard to the prudence of the investment strategies adopted by WorldCom as Named Investment Fiduciary. In its Opening Brief, Merrill Lynch established that directed trustees are not obligated to assess the prudence of the transactions they are instructed to effectuate, but rather must carry out the directions they are given unless those directions are "clear on their face" violations of ERISA or of the Plan. (Opening Br. At 15-18)

In response, plaintiffs argue that a directed trustee may follow the directions of the named fiduciary made in accordance with the terms of the plan, but may not follow those directions if to do so would violate ERISA. They then posit that because allowing and imprudent investment would violate ERISA, directed trustees are not relieved of the fiduciary duty of prudence when carrying out investment directions. See Plaintiffs' Br. At 14-19. In other words, according to plaintiffs, "liability can be imposed on directed trustees if, among other things, they follow directions that they knew or should have known were imprudent." Id. At 16. In purported support of that proposition, plaintiffs cite authority that is either clearly distinguishable or that ignores that Congress imposed or directed trustees only limited responsibilities under ERISA Section 403(a). Plaintiffs would also have the Court defer to the view of the Secretary of Labor, whose *Enron* litigation position commits the same interpretive error of treating directed trustees as full-fledged ERISA fiduciaries. They then ask the Court to imagine the horrible consequences that would result if "empty-headed" trustees were judged by the "clear on their face" standard rather than the negligence-based, "should have known" standard that plaintiffs proposed. Id. At 20-21. To begin with, the case law plaintiffs cite in support of their position is either inapplicable or unconvincing. Significantly, the ruling in *FirsTier Bank, N.A. v. Zeller*, 16 F.3d 907 (8th Cir. 1994) upon which plaintiffs so heavily rely was placed in its properly limited context by the Eight Circuit only months after *FirsTier* was decided. In *Maniace*, the Eighth Circuit confirmed that "the obligations of a directed trustee are something less than that owed by typical fiduciaries," and that a directed trustee is "not required to weigh the merits of an investment in [company] stock against all other investment options every time it was directed to purchase said stock." 40 F.3d at 268.

The court then expressly distinguished *FirsTier* on the grounds that the trustee in *FirsTier* had general fiduciary responsibility for management of all plan assets with one narrow exception. Id. "Unlike the situation in *FirsTier*," the Eight Circuit explained, the trustee in *Maniace* "had no discretion nor control with respect to [company] stock" and therefore did not "fit within the ERISA definition of a fiduciary." Id. Like the trustee in *Maniace* and unlike the trustee in *FirsTier*, Merrill Lynch did not have any discretion regarding the selection or retention of WorldCom stock as an investment alternative. The ruling in *FirsTier* is therefore inapplicable and the Court should follow the Eight Circuit's subsequent decision in *Maniace* that a directed trustee has no fiduciary obligation to examine the prudence of an investment it is directed by an investment fiduciary to make.

The positions taken by the Department of Labor do not alter the conclusion that directed trustees are not subject to the fiduciary duty of prudence regarding investment directions. There is no need to consider the views of an agency where the statute is clear and speaks directly to the issue, as it does here. *See Chevron, U.S.A., Inc. v. Natural Resources Defense Council, Inc.*, 467 U.S. 837, 842-43 (1984). The clear and unambiguous congressional determination to create different classes of trustees – ordinary trustees and directed trustees – therefore overrides any conflicting interpretation of the statute offered by the Department of Labor. *See, e.g., Sutton v. United Air Lines, Inc.*, 527 U.S. 471, 482 (1999)(rejecting "the approach adopted by the agency guidelines" as "an impermissible interpretation" of the Americans with Disabilities Act). In addition, courts need not defer to an agency's views espoused, as here, for the first time in the context of litigation. *See, e.g., Bowen v. Georgetown Univ. Hosp.*, 488 U.S. 204, 212 (1988) (refusing to grant deference to agency litigating positions that are wholly unsupported by regulations, rulings, or administrative interpretation" of the regulation).

In addition, although plaintiffs decry the purported injustice of allowing directed trustees to be "let off the hook," the "clear on their face" standard would not exculpate directed trustees who (in Plaintiffs' words) "robotically" execute directions that violate the terms of the plan or which on their face violate provision of ERISA. Instead, directed trustees would be held accountable for following facially-invalid instructions, while not being required to assess the substantive prudence of the directions they are asked to follow. The "clear on their face" standard thus reflects the proper balance between a directed trustee's obligations to follow the instructions it receives and its liberation from the responsibility of evaluating the substantive prudence of every investment it is asked to make.

There is no basis for plaintiffs' alarmist speculations regarding what would happen if directed trustees were held to owe no duty of prudence with respect to the underlying transactions. Indeed, it is plaintiffs' interpretation, not Merrill Lynch's, that would create a morass of confusion, requiring directed trustees to perform a sophisticated analysis they are either ill-equipped or not paid to perform, and creating the risk of conflict between directed trustees and the investment fiduciaries whose directions they are supposed to follow. For example, although plaintiffs assert that a directed trustee need not investigate the appropriateness of investment decision in order to be held to a "knows or should know" standard (see Plaintiffs' Br. At 18), they fail to explain how a directed trustee could be held to "know" (or have sufficient information that it "should know") that an investment. Requiring a directed trustee to undertake that analysis before it executes any order to make an investment plans an unnecessary burden on the system, and would impose on directed trustees an obligation they are not paid to assume. Investment fiduciaries exist to make exactly these types of assessments. There is no reason for directed trustees to second-guess them.

Moreover, plaintiffs fail to address what (if any) responsibility a directed trustee would bear if the directed trustee refused to carry out an instruction and the investment later increased in value. If, for example, an investment fiduciary insists that a particular mutual fund is a good investment, but the directed trustee has a good-faith belief that it is too risky and refuses to invest plan funds and directed, plaintiffs offer no answer to how that conflict could be resolved in a timely fashion, or who would be responsible for any harm to participants should the challenged investment increases in value while the parties try to sort out the prudence of the investment. Nor do plaintiffs address who would be responsible for the harm to participants (and other investors) if the stock price drops in response to directed trustees court action to prevent investment in that stock – an act that plaintiffs assert Merrill Lynch, as directed trustee, was obligated to take to avoid liability. See Plaintiffs' Br. At 28. This is no mere hypothetical example.

Plaintiffs allege that the business model of WorldCom was not viable as far back at 1998, and that the debt load it carries as of 2000 made the investment imprudent. But the open-market price of WorldCom stock increased at several points during this time period, including after the merger with MCI. See Declaration of Antoinette DeCamp, Ex.1; *see generally Ganino v. Citizens Utilities CO.*, 228 F.3d 154, 167 n.8 (2d Cir.2000) (taking judicial notice of stock prices on motion to dismiss). Plaintiffs are remarkably silent as to when between 1998 and 2002 Merrill Lynch should have overridden the Named Investment Fiduciary's decision to retain WorldCom stock as an investment option under the Plan. The regime plaintiffs propose is simply unworkable.

Fortunately, Congress carefully limited the responsibilities of directed trustees in order to avoid such questions regarding whose instructions should prevail and when. As the United States Supreme Court noted, ERISA "allocates liability for plan-related misdeeds in reasonable proportion to respective actors' power to control and prevent the misdeeds." *Mertens v. Hewitt Assocs.*, 508 U.S. 248, 262 (1993). This allocation strikes a balance between the "goal of benefiting employees and the subsidiary goal of containing pension costs." Id. At 262-63 (quotation omitted).

The fees charged by directed trustee for services rendered to a pension plan includes a component that reflects the risk of liability arising from those services. Holding directed trustees responsible for overseeing the prudence of plan investment would, in turn, increase the potential for liability, which necessarily would lead to an increase in the fees charged by directed trustees, thereby increasing pension costs. Courts must not "attempt to adjust the balance between those competing goals that the text adopted by Congress has struck."

C. Merrill Lynch Cannot As A Matter Of Law Be Held Responsible For Losses Resulting From Participants' Exercises of Discretion.

The Complaint and the documents incorporated therein by reference show that participants controlled and directed their own investments within the meaning of Section 404(c). As result, Merrill Lynch cannot be responsible for any losses to the plan even if it were some sort of a fiduciary with regard to investment decisions. See Opening Br., at 19-21.

Plaintiffs try to avoid these statutory consequences by proclaiming that the applicability of Section 404(c) cannot be considered at the pleading stage because the Section 404(c) safe harbor is a defense that must be pleaded and proved by the defendants. See Plaintiffs' Br. At 23. But even assuming that plaintiffs are correct on that point, the allocation o the burden of proof on an issue is irrelevant to a determination of whether or not the Complaint, together with the documents on which it relies, states a claim for relief. If the allegations do not support an entitlement to relief, the complaint must be dismissed, even if on a ground as to which the defendant bears the burden. *See, e.g., Johnson v. New York City Employees Income Ret. Sys. Pension Plan*, No. 00-9162. 2001 U.S. App. Lexis 11001 (2d Cir. May 25, 2001) (affirming dismissal of complaint pursuant to Rule 12(b)(6) where claims barred by statutes of limitations) cert. Denied, 534 U.S. 1091 (2002).

Here plaintiffs seek to hold Merrill Lynch responsible for failing to inform them (or the other fiduciaries) that continued investment in WorldCom stock was imprudent. They do not allege that Merrill Lynch had access to any nonpublic information. Instead, they seek in essence to hold Merrill Lynch responsible for failing to provide them with investment advice. But the regulation promulgated under Section 404(c) expressly state the plan participants need not be provided with investment advice for the statutory safe harbor to apply. See 29 C.F.R. § 2550.404c-1(c)(4).

Plaintiffs' contention that Merrill Lynch can be held accountable for imprudently offering WorldCom stock as a plan option is equally baseless. See Plaintiffs' Br. At 24. As Explained above – and as plaintiffs concede – Merrill Lynch did not have any responsibility to select investment options. See Plaintiffs' Br. At 24. Furthermore, the riskiness of an investment alternative does not preclude application of Section 404(c). The governing regulations state that in order to qualify as a Section 404(c) plan, participants must be provided a range of investment options having different degrees of risk, so that the participant can decide how to allocate his or her investments to fit his or her risk tolerance. See 29 C.F.R. § 2550.404c-1(b)(3).

D. The Complaint Fails To State A Claim For Co-Fiduciary Liability

Plaintiffs persist in asserting that Merrill Lynch's failure to fulfill its own duties "enabled" other defendants to breach their fiduciary duties, or that Merrill Lynch "participated knowingly in" or had knowledge of and failed to remedy breaches by others. But plaintiffs make almost no attempt to refute Merrill Lynch's showing that the Complaint fails to allege how Merrill Lynch "enabled" others to commit alleged breaches. They simply repeat the language of the statutes and assert that they have met its requirements. See Plaintiffs' Br. at 31-32.

The response regarding Merrill Lynch's asserted "knowing participation" or "knowledge" of others'breaches is equally ineffective, as plaintiffs do no more than point to the conclusory allegations of the Complaint and assert that they need not do any more. Indeed, in a failed attempt to bolster their contention that Merrill Lynch was an "expert" in financial matters and hand "ongoing independent analysis and rating of WorldCom [stock]" (see Plaintiffs' Br. At 24-25), plaintiffs' cited documents prepared and filed by Merrill Lynch and Co., Inc. – not defendant Merrill Lynch Trust Company. See Declaration of Derek Loeser, Exs. B, C, D, E. There is no indication anywhere that defendant Merrill Lynch Trust Company had anything at all to do with or knew of the basis for the analysis reflected in those documents. Plaintiffs' bald assertions cannot bridge the gap between two entirely separate corporate entities and make one responsible for the alleged knowledge and actions taken by the other. As discussed in Section II.A above, although plaintiffs need not prove the factual elements of their claims at this stage, they must at lease plead them.

Finally, plaintiffs cannot escape the need to plead with particularity their claims of cofiduciary liability. A claim for co-fiduciary liability, like other claims of fiduciary breach, can be based upon breach of contract or upon an alleged fraud. See Opening Br. At 23-24 and cases cited therein.

Plaintiffs here do not allege that Merrill Lynch failed to satisfy the requirements of the Trust Agreement, and therefore have not based their claim on a breach of contract theory. Instead, they have alleged that Merrill Lynch failed to speak when it had information that should have been shared with others. See, e.g., Compl. 120 (alleging that Merrill Lynch "failed to inform the other fiduciaries of the Plan or participants in the Plan" that "maintaining investments or making new investments of Plan assets in WorldCom stock was increasingly risky and potentially imprudent"); 121 (Merrill Lynch "failed to inform other fiduciaries of the Plan that maintaining investments or making new investments of Plan assets in WorldCom stock was increasingly risky and imprudent" and "failed to advise other fiduciaries of the Plan to investigate the prudence of maintaining WorldCom stock as a Plan investment"; 127 (Merrill Lynch "failed to advise fiduciaries of the Plan to investigate the prudence of maintaining WorldCom stock as a Plan investment"). Having thus attempted to plead a claim that sounds in fraud, plaintiffs must support that claim with particularized facts. *See, e.g., Koch*, 1999 WL 528181, at *6 (breach of fiduciary duty claim founded on allegations of "breach-by-omission". Because they have failed to do so, their Complaint must be dismissed.

III. CONCLUSION

For the reasons set forth above and in its opening brief, Merrill Lynch respectfully submits that the claims against it should be dismissed.

Dated: March 13, 2003 Washington, D.C.

GIBSON, DUNN & CRUTCHER LLP

By: /s/ Paul Blankenstein (PB – 8583) 1050 Connecticut Avenue N.W. Washington District of Columbia 20036 Telephone: (202) 955-8500 Facsimile: (202) 467-0539 Attorneys for Defendant Merrill Lynch Trust Company FSB

Chapter 12

The Unified Fiduciary Monitoring Index®

Chapter Summary

Successful investing requires both proper asset allocation and high asset quality. At Unified Trust Company, we focus on factors that are useful in identifying and maintaining high asset quality for each asset allocation subgroup. In order to understand which mutual-fund measurement criteria may have a predictive outcome, we have reviewed all major academic finance publications. We have compiled these predictive criteria into a single mathematical formula to create the Unified Fiduciary Monitoring Index® ("UFMI®").

The UFMI® overall composite score ranges between 1 and 100. A score of 1 is in the top 1%, a score of 10 is in the top 10%, and so on. All funds are compared with their peer groups. We now have more than 74,000 fund-years of prospective, or forward-looking, analysis data. We have found that in the aggregate, as measured across many thousands of mutual funds, the UFMI® tends to produce consistent effects that persist for twelve to twenty-four months after the fund is scored.

We have identified a useful and value-added fund management technique. The portfolio, or retirement plan, should initially select funds scoring in the top 25% (UFMI® 1–25) and replace any funds when subsequent scores are worse than those of the top 40% (UFMI® 41–100). When comparing the same peer groups (investment categories), we found in the aggregate that funds scoring in the top 25% (UFMI® 1–25) tend to outperform funds being replaced (41–100) by 2.5% to 4.6% per year in the aggregate.

The Need for Improved Outcomes

Investors need both proper asset allocation and high asset quality in each sector of their asset allocations. And every investor has been warned, as we discussed in chapter 8, that past performance does not predict future performance when it comes to picking investments. So how do investors know which asset-quality criteria are useful?

The problem that all plan fiduciaries face when they make good-faith efforts to select, monitor, and replace their investments is how to deal with the overwhelming abundance of information and how to deal with conflicting statistics. Some financial intermediaries now function as cofiduciaries (nondiscretionary) and offer investment evaluation services to plan sponsors, who must still make the discretionary decisions. Some plan sponsors use these services because the glossy brochures look helpful. Few ever ask whether they improve results. In most cases, the plan sponsor has no objective data that the purported monitoring service improves outcomes.

In chapter 8, we reviewed the academic finance studies that sought to explain investment performance in mutual funds. The studies indicate that no one measurement is infallible, but they identify certain recurring factors that have some predictive effects. Once we inventoried the important factors, we sought to answer three key questions:

1. Is it possible to further collate all the meaningful factors into a single composite measurement?

2. Is it possible to then create a bright-line test that offers a simpler way to make key fiduciary decisions concerning investment selection and replacement?

3. Most important, can such a system improve outcomes?

In an attempt to help plan fiduciaries deal with this continuing problem, we created the Unified Fiduciary Monitoring Index® ("UFMI®"). The intellectual property rights and process procedures are patent-pending.

The UFMI® is a composite percentile ranking of more than 14,000 mutual funds as compared with their peer groups (investment categories). The mathematical calculation does not look at raw investment performance, but instead incorporates several factors shown in academic studies to be somewhat predictive. For the data to be meaningful, each fund is compared with its peer group or, in other words, its investment category. The UFMI® score ranges between 1 and 100, with a score of 1 being in the top 1%, a score of 30 being in the top 30%, and so on.

The composite score takes into account previous academic studies and attempts to improve upon the results of popular rating groups, such as Lipper™ or Morningstar™. The UFMI® evaluates each fund or investment manager by using numerous relevant factors from academic research that have been taken over various rolling periods shown to be at least partly predictive. Each fund is then scored against its investment-objective category peer group in the quarter just ended. The score ranges from 1 (best) to 100 (worst). We recalculate these data every ninety days.

Most popular mutual-fund ratings systems have offered minimal value in predictive effect as measured by improved outcomes. For example, most popular rating services simply compare historical performance or some type of risk-adjusted performance. Some do not even compare the fund against its peer group. Most academic studies have found other factors, such as the fund's expense ratio, to be important partial predictors of future performance. The UFMI® takes into account a much greater number of relevant factors.

Chart 12-1: Unified Fiduciary Monitoring Index® Likelihood of Individual Fund Beating Peers in the Year after Evaluation (5 Year Average Data)

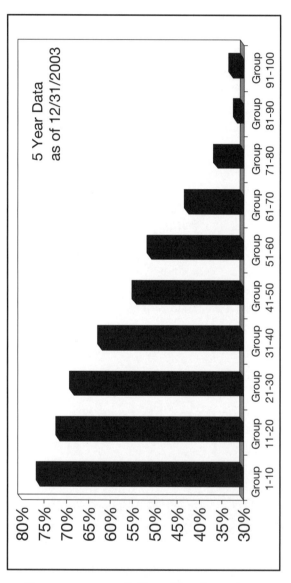

Chart 12-2: Unified Fiduciary Monitoring Index® Group Performance to Peer Group in the Year after Evaluation (5 Year Average Data)

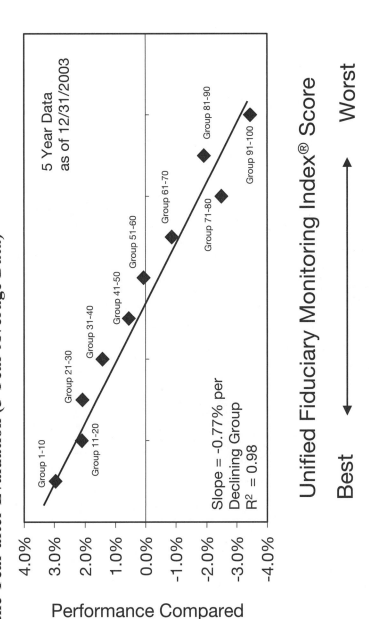

Chart 12-3: Unified Fiduciary Monitoring Index® Selection Group vs. Replacement Group in the Year after Evaluation (5 Year Average Data)

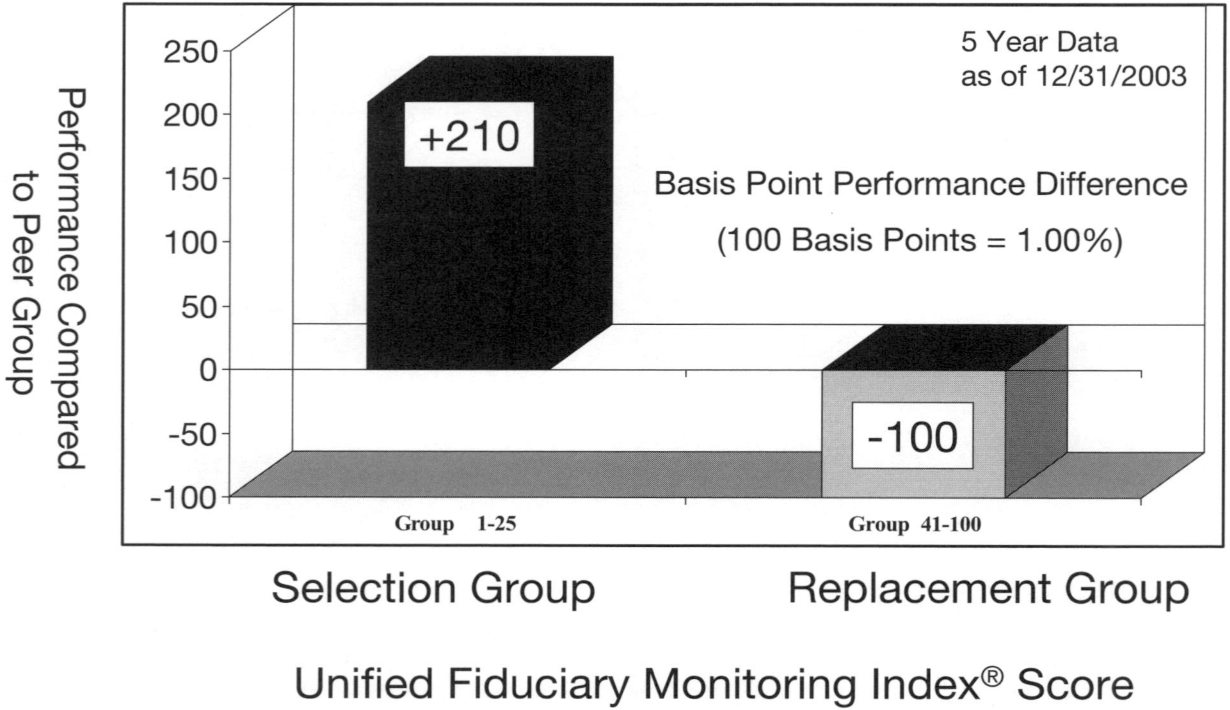

-312-

Figure 12-1: Unified Fiduciary Monitoring Index® Versus Active Sortino Ratio

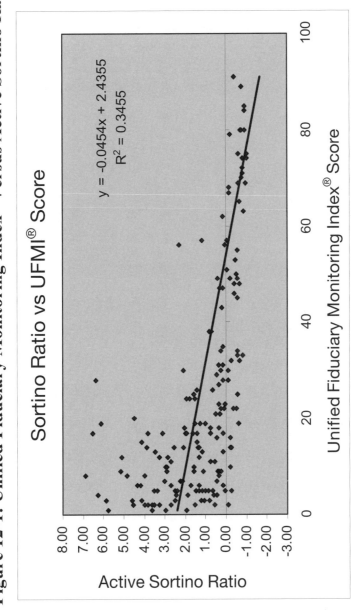

Sortino Ratio vs UFMI® Score

$y = -0.0454x + 2.4355$
$R^2 = 0.3455$

Active Sortino Ratio

Unified Fiduciary Monitoring Index® Score

An Ongoing Monitoring Tool: The 25/40 Formula

Across over 90,000 fund-years of prospective data, we have found approximately a 188- to 466-basis-point (1.88%–4.66%) prospective annual performance difference, in the aggregate, between funds scoring UFMI® 1–25 versus funds scoring worse than 40 (UFMI® 41–100). A "fund-year" is one fund measured for one year after it was scored.

Funds scoring UFMI® 1–25 have a 71%–76% probability of out-performing peers over the next year.

As chart 12-1 demonstrates, the system is not perfect, but it is the best system we have been able to identity to improve outcomes. Based upon these data, one useful decision tree is to set an initial screen of UFMI® 25 or better to select a fund or manager and to apply an ongoing retention score of UFMI® 40 or better. We call this the 25/40 Formula.

The UFMI® 1–25 score group is the selection group, and the UFMI® 41–100 score group is the replacement group.

The finalist funds undergo additional fund-selection criteria. These more subjective supplemental criteria include, but are not limited to, fund asset size, investment style (category) consistency, UFMI® score consistency, mutual-fund board of director's commitment to shareholder fairness and fiduciary oversight, Sortino Ratio, fund manager tenure, revenue sharing back to the plan sponsor, and funds employing a multi-manager approach.

For additional information about this overall fund selection and monitoring process see chapter 13 on fiduciary best practices.

Chart 12-4: Quarterly Mutual Fund Fiduciary Review Report

Unified Trust Company, NA Fiduciary Report For Columbia Acorn Z © 2003

Current UFMI® Score	3

Fund Profile

Investment Category
Small Growth

Investment Objective
The Fund seeks to provide long-term growth of capital. The Fund invests primarily in the stocks of small- and medium-sized companies. The Fund generally invests in the stocks of companies with market capitalizations of less than $2 billion at the time of purchase. The Fund invests the majority of its assets in U.S. companies, but also may invest up to 33% of its assets in companies outside the U.S. in developed markets and emerging markets.

Supplemental Fund Data

Average 4 Quarter UFMI® Score	2
Fund Assets in Millions	$5,796
Fund Expense Ratio	0.82%
Style Drift in Past 4 Quarters	No
Annual Portfolio Turnover	13%
Ticker Symbol	ACRNX
Active Sortino Ratio	2.336
Downside Risk	12.0%

Fund Performance vs. Category Average

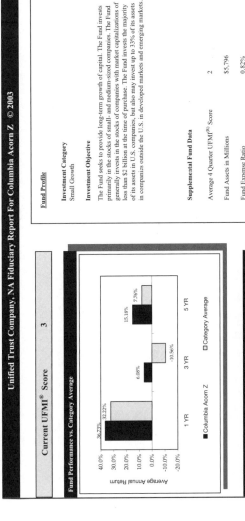

Fund Performance History As Of September 30, 2003

	Qtr	1 Yr	3 Yr	5 Yr
Columbia Acorn Z	8.95%	36.73%	6.08%	15.18%
Category Average	8.89%	32.22%	-10.56%	7.76%
Difference vs. Category	0.06%	4.51%	16.64%	7.42%
Percent Rank in Category	30	4	15

-315-

Correlation with Active Sortino Ratio

Although the two calculations are based upon entirely different methodologies, there is a correlation between the UFMI® score and the Active Sortino Ratio as illustrated in Figure 12-1. We have found that 85% of funds with a UFMI® score in the selection group (UFMI® 1-25) have a positive Active Sortino Ratio.

The Usefulness and Limitations of the System

Our fund evaluation process is designed to objectively measure asset quality. It is designed to improve outcomes. It does not affect asset allocation per se. Chapter 7 points out the importance of asset allocation. We believe that our asset-quality measurement process increases the likelihood of selecting a fund that can outperform its peer group.

The UFMI® is an essential factor to help the discretionary plan trustee decide, when designing an investment policy statement, which funds to place on the fiduciary watch list or even the fund replacement list. On a prospective basis across many thousands of funds, our methodology can help segregate choices of the same investment objective. We now have more than 90,000 fund-years of prospective (forward-looking after fund was scored) data. Though the UFMI® is valid, no quantitative system is infallible at individual choice levels, even if the data are significant at the macro level. Some plan sponsors and plan participants ask: "Does this system cause me to sell a fund at its bottom?" The answer is an emphatic no, because the index calculation does not take into account fund price. A fund could be up or down in price at the time it fails, based upon the index calculation. The data are compared with those of the fund's peer group. A failing fund is replaced with a better fund in the same investment category. Any mutual-fund tracking service can tell you which managers are on a historical winning streak. But our system tries to do something more: It takes into account prior academic research and includes fundamental factors often omitted by ratings services.

For Further Reading

Brown, K., and Harlow W. *Staying the Course: The Impact of Investment Style Consistency on Mutual Fund Performance*: University of Texas Press, (2002).

Brown, S., Goetzmann W., Ibbotson R., and Ross, S. "Survivorship Bias in Performance Studies." *Review of Financial Studies* 5, 553–580. (1992).

Brown, S., and Goetzmann W. "Performance Persistence." *Journal of Finance* 50, 679–698 (1995).

Carhart, M. "On Persistence in Mutual Fund Performance." *Journal of Finance* 52, 57–82 (1997).

Carlson, R. "Aggregate Performance of Mutual Funds, 1948–1967." *Journal of Financial and Quantitative Analysis* 5, 1–32 (1970).

Elton, E., Gruber, M., and Blake, C. "The Persistence of Risk-Adjusted Mutual Fund Performance." *Journal of Business* 69, 133–157 (1996).

Goetzmann, W., and Ibbotson, R. "Do Winners Repeat? Patterns in Mutual Fund Performance." *Journal of Portfolio Management* 20, 9–18 (1994).

Grinblatt, M., and Titman, S. "Mutual Fund Performance: An Analysis of Quarterly Portfolio Holdings." *Journal of Business* 62, 393–416 (1989).

Grinblatt, M., and Titman S. "The Persistence of Mutual Fund Performance." *Journal of Finance* 47, 1977–1984 (1992).

Grinblatt, M., and Titman, S. "Performance Measurement without Benchmarks: An Examination of Mutual Fund Returns." *Journal of Business* 66, 47–68 (1993).

Ibbotson, R., and Patel, A. "Do Winners Repeat with Style? Summary of Findings." Ibbotson Associates.
http://www.ibbotson.com/Research/papers/toc.asp (2002).

Jain, P., and Shuang Wu, J. "Truth in Mutual Fund Advertising: Evidence on Future Performance and Fund Flows." *Journal of Finance* 55, 937–958 (2000).

Kahn, R., and Rudd, A. "Does Historical Performance Predict Future Performance?" *Barra Newsletter*, (Spring 1995).

Kasten, G. "The Unified Fiduciary Monitoring Index®." Lexington, Ky.: Unified Trust Company, N.A., (2004).

Kasten, G., "Why Do Most Managed Accounts Fail?" Lexington, Ky.: Unified Trust Company, N.A., (2002).

Malkiel, Burton G. "Returns from Investing in Equity Mutual Funds, 1971–1991." *Journal of Finance* 50,, 549–572 (1995).

"Predicting Mutual Fund Performance II: After the Bear." Boston, Mass.: Financial Research Corporation, (2003).

"Fund Categories Face Increased Scrutiny: Critics Claim Definitions Need to Change." *Wall Street Journal*. (2001).

"Fund Ratings Should Be Approached with Caution." *Wall Street Journal*. (2001).

"Morningstar Study Debunks Fund World's Oldest Myth." *Wall Street Journal*. (2003).

"The Stars in the Sky Flicker, and Fund Stars Do the Same." *Wall Street Journal*. (2003).

"Three Reasons Fund Fees Are Likely to Keep Rising?" *Wall Street Journal*. (2003).

Chapter 13

Fiduciary Best Practices

Chapter Summary

The purpose of a "Best Practices" compendium is to define a prudent process for ERISA fiduciaries to improve investment outcomes for plan participants and their beneficiaries. A more important goal is to increase their retirement success probability. This chapter outlines the twenty fiduciary Best Practices employed by Unified Trust Company, N.A. It is intended to be a reference guide for trustees, directors, plan sponsors, investment committees, and their advisors. It is not designed as a "cookbook" for persons who are not familiar with ERISA procedures.

The legal requirement for prudence under ERISA is for a fiduciary to discharge its duties with, among other things, "the care, skill, prudence, and diligence under the circumstances then prevailing that a prudent man acting in a like capacity and familiar with such matters would undertake."

Although ERISA is a detailed body of law, it does not define every prudent process. A Best Practices approach allows a distinction to be made between what the law expressly requires and what represents a generally accepted practice in the investment industry. When a fiduciary follows a consistent and standardized process based on these Best Practices, the fiduciary can be confident that critical components of an investment strategy are being properly implemented. Such an approach improves participant investment outcomes.

Best Practices: Why Are They Needed?

Unified Trust Company, N.A., employs five Best Practices for each of the four major steps in the fiduciary management process, for a total of twenty Best Practices (see Chart 13-1). The purpose of a Best Practices compendium is twofold: first to establish evidence that the fiduciary is following a prudent investment process, which can minimize litigation risk, and second, to improve the investment outcomes of plan participants. Fiduciaries have the most important, most risky, yet most misunderstood role in the ERISA investment process. Any fiduciary that attempts to manage plan investments without a well-defined process will likely fail. Both case law and regulatory opinion letters reinforce this important concept.

Fiduciary liability is not determined by investment performance, but rather by whether prudent investment practices were followed.

The legal and practical scrutiny a fiduciary undergoes is tremendous. Today, the number of complaints and lawsuits alleging fiduciary misconduct is increasing. Although some of these allegations may be entirely justified, most can be avoided by following the investment practices outlined in this chapter. A fiduciary demonstrates prudence by showing the process through which investment decisions were managed, rather than by showing that investment products and techniques were chosen because they were labeled as "prudent." Few investments are imprudent on their faces. It is how they are used and how decisions about their use are made that will be examined to determine whether the prudence standard has been met. Even the most aggressive and unconventional investment can meet that standard if it is arrived at through a sound process; however, the most simple and conservative one may not measure up if a sound process is lacking.

Chart 13-1: Four Major Steps in the Fiduciary Process

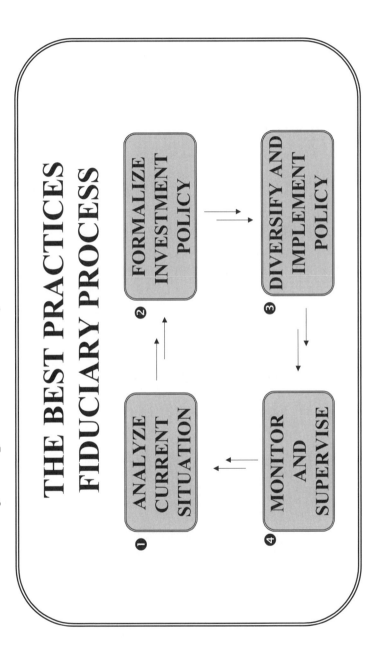

THE BEST PRACTICES
FIDUCIARY PROCESS

❶ ANALYZE CURRENT SITUATION

❷ FORMALIZE INVESTMENT POLICY

❸ DIVERSIFY AND IMPLEMENT POLICY

❹ MONITOR AND SUPERVISE

Analyze Current Situation (Best Practices 1-5)

Best Practice No. 1

Fiduciaries must always be aware of their special status, duties, and accountability.

It is not uncommon for fiduciaries to be unaware of their status. It is difficult to manage a fiduciary process unless one is aware of being a fiduciary. A fiduciary is defined as someone who acts in a position of trust for the benefit of a third party. In some cases, the status of fiduciary may be defined by statute. In other cases, it is a functional definition and is based on facts and circumstances. The issue is whether a person has discretion or influence over investment decisions.

Fiduciaries are responsible for, among other duties, the management of investments. If statutes such as ERISA and trust provisions permit, the fiduciary may delegate certain decisions to professional money managers, trustees (cofiduciaries), investment advisors, or consultants. But even when decisions have been delegated to a professional, a fiduciary can never overlook certain responsibilities. These include:

- Determining investment goals and objectives
- Choosing an appropriate asset allocation strategy
- Establishing an explicit, written investment policy consistent with the goals and objectives
- Selecting appropriate investment managers, mutual funds, or other "prudent experts" to implement the investment policy
- Monitoring the activities of the overall investment program for compliance with the investment policy
- Recommending and implementing changes to the underlying investments, asset allocation, or investment policy when indicated
- Avoiding conflicts of interest and prohibited transactions

Best Practice No. 2

The plan's investment portfolio is managed in agreement with applicable regulations, laws, the underlying trust document, and the plan's written investment policy statement.

Unified Trust Company, N.A., as discretionary trustee of the plan, is responsible for all decisions regarding the prudent management of those plan assets over which it has discretion. Within the trust company, the trust investment committee (TIC) is the body entrusted with the actual task of implementing a prudent process for the plan. The TIC generally consists of ten or more investment or ERISA specialists within the company. The TIC keeps regular minutes of every meeting and investment decision as part of its documentation of each step in the process. The trustee conducts regular reviews and educational seminars with regards to current regulations, laws, and industry standards.

The primary tool for documenting the investment process and setting clear, prudent criteria for investment selection and replacement is the investment policy statement (IPS). The IPS is, therefore, the primary tool by which the plan assets are managed and is the fiduciaries' guide to procedural prudence.

The starting point for the TIC is to analyze and review all of the documents pertaining to the establishment and management of the investments. As in managing any business decision, the fiduciary has to set definitive goals and objectives that are consistent with the portfolio's current and future resources, the limits and constraints of applicable trust documents and statutes, and in the case of individual investors, their goals and objectives. Proof that such a framework has been established presumes that written documentation exists in some form.

Best Practice No. 3

Plan service agreements and contracts are in writing and do not contain provisions that conflict with fiduciary standards of care.

In order to prudently fulfill its duties, ERISA permits a fiduciary to seek assistance from outside professionals, such as investment advisors, consultants, and money managers, if the fiduciary lacks the requisite knowledge. In addition, the fiduciary must review the plan's trust documents to ascertain whether they permit the delegation of investment responsibilities.

The fundamental duty of the fiduciary is to manage investment decisions for the exclusive benefit of the client, retirement plan participant, and/or trust beneficiary. The fiduciary should take reasonable steps to protect the portfolio from losses and to avoid misunderstandings when hiring outside professionals.

Therefore, fiduciaries should reduce any agreement of substance to writing in order to define the scope of the parties' duties and responsibilities, ensure that the portfolio is managed in accordance with the written documents that govern the investment strategy, and confirm that the parties have clear, mutual understandings of their roles and responsibilities. Legal counsel familiar with ERISA should generally review the document before execution.

The fiduciary must determine if the fees paid are reasonable; this would be difficult if the terms were not in writing. When duties are delegated to others, the agreement should be in writing so that the fiduciary and service providers have clear understandings of their respective roles and responsibilities. The agreement should contain provisions for measuring and monitoring the service provider's activities.

Best Practice No. 4

Assets are protected from self-dealing, within the jurisdiction of U.S. courts, and are safe from theft and embezzlement.

ERISA stipulates that the fundamental duty of the fiduciary is to manage the plan for the exclusive benefit of the plan participant and/or beneficiary. No one should receive a benefit simply for being a friend, business associate, or relative of the fiduciary. Fiduciaries and parties-in-interest must not be involved in self-dealing.

The fiduciary has the responsibility to safeguard entrusted assets, which includes keeping the assets within the control of the U.S. court system. This provides any regulatory agency (such as the OCC or DOL) the ability to seize the assets if, in its determination, it is in the best interests of the beneficiaries and/or participants.

ERISA requires pension plans to obtain a fidelity bond to protect the plan against theft of plan assets by fiduciaries and other plan officials. The fidelity bond covers only dishonesty and does not cover fiduciary breaches. Thus, the ERISA-required bond coverage is limited to protection against loss through fraud or dishonesty. Though not required for other fiduciaries, it's a good industry practice to maintain similar coverage against dishonesty.

In addition to bonding, it is a Best Practice that the fiduciary carry sufficient liability insurance. Fiduciary liability insurance is designed to protect plan fiduciaries that, although acting in good faith, violate the complex fiduciary rules as expressed in federal rules, regulations, and court rulings. Fiduciaries also need additional protection from liability for acts of cofiduciaries, especially where a fiduciary should have known of the breach by a cofiduciary and failed to remedy the breach.

Best Practice No. 5

The client's risk tolerance has been identified, the cash flow liabilities examined, and an expected, modeled return has been reviewed to meet investment-time-horizon objectives.

The term "risk" has different connotations, depending on the fiduciary's or the investor's frame of reference. In a participant-directed plan, the risk tolerance is determined by individuals for their personal accounts. In a trustee-directed plan, however, the trustee will use a risk tolerance questionnaire combined with the investment time horizon to determine the client's risk tolerance profile. Typically, the investment industry defines risk in terms of statistical measures, such as standard deviation, beta, or Sharpe Ratio. However, such statistical measures calculate uncertainty rather than risk. The Best Practices approach includes newer measures of downside risk, such as the Sortino Ratio.

An additional risk is cash flow risk. One of the fundamental duties of every retirement plan fiduciary is to ensure that there are sufficient liquid assets to pay bills and liabilities when they come due. The fiduciary may use the following modeling tools to help determine the likely investment return for the plan: mean variance optimization, stochastic probabilistic modeling, or Monte Carlo analysis. In this context, the term "model" means to replicate in order to determine the probable returns of an investment strategy, given current and historical information.

The fiduciary should describe the presumptions that are being used to model the probable outcomes of a given investment strategy. The fiduciary may, in some cases, compare results of analyses using both historical and projected assumptions. In one form of stochastic modeling, the fiduciary's simulations go beyond using mere historical assumptions by basing the modeling on the actual returns of each asset class.

Formalize Investment Policy (Best Practices 6-11)

Best Practice No. 6

Appropriate detail is present to implement a specific investment strategy.

The preparation and maintenance of the IPS is one of the most critical functions of the fiduciary. The IPS should be viewed as the essential management tool for directing and communicating the activities of the portfolio. It is a formal, long-range, strategic plan that allows the fiduciary to coordinate the management of the investment program in a logical and consistent framework. All material investment facts, assumptions, and opinions should be included.

The IPS should have sufficient detail that a third party would be able to implement the investment strategy and be flexible enough that it can be implemented in a complex and dynamic financial environment, yet not be so detailed that it requires constant revisions and updates. The IPS should define the duties and responsibilities of all parties involved in the investment process, thus ensuring continuity of the investment strategy when there is a change in fiduciaries and helping to prevent misunderstandings between parties, and the omission of critical fiduciary functions. The IPS should include sections on the roles of the investment committee and of any external investment consultants.

The IPS should address the information overload problem that plan fiduciaries face. It should help them select and monitor their investments, based upon objective outcome studies. In general, the primary criterion for the selection, monitoring, retention, and replacement of investment managers is the Unified Fiduciary Monitoring Index ("UFMI®"). While the UFMI® cannot be universally applied and cannot be the sole basis for investment decisions, the discretionary trustee will use it as the first step in the decision-making process.

Best Practice No. 7

The selected asset classes are consistent with the identified risk, return, and time horizon.

The fiduciary's role is to choose the combination of asset classes that optimizes the identified risk and return objectives, consistent with the portfolio's time horizon. The fiduciary's choice of asset classes and their subsequent allocation will have a significant effect on the long-term performance of the plan. The fiduciary's role is to choose a combination of assets that attempts to optimize a required return, subject to the level of acceptable risk.

In a participant-directed plan, the fiduciary must provide the minimum asset-class coverage identified below but may expand the plan's menu of investments to include funds in all permitted categories. The fiduciary should take into account the investment sophistication and knowledge of the plan participants. The fiduciary should also consider how the various asset classes would interact in various model portfolios.

Minimum Asset-Class Coverage

Coverage of the following investment categories is considered the minimum necessary to prudently diversify a participant's investment portfolio.

Cash Equivalent, or Stable Value
Intermediate Term General Bond
Large Cap Equity Growth
Large Cap Equity Value
Mid Cap Equity Blend
Small Cap Equity Blend

Permitted Categories

The discretionary trustee may make a carefully controlled number of funds available to plan participants in the participant-directed portion of the plan. The minimum number of funds is dictated by the minimum asset-class coverage described above. The fiduciary should consider that too many choices can be counterproductive to plan participants and may actually reduce their success probabilities. The investment objectives and compliance with ERISA Section 404(c) can be achieved by making available mutual funds or collective investment funds consisting of securities of domestic, global, or international issuers. The categories of funds may include the following, as determined by the trustee:

Cash Equivalent, or Stable Value
Intermediate Term General Bond
Intermediate Term Government Bond
Balanced
Lifestyle
Large Cap Equity Growth
Large Cap Equity Blend
Large Cap Equity Value
Mid Cap Equity Growth
Mid Cap Equity Blend
Mid Cap Equity Value
Small Cap Equity Growth
Small Cap Equity Blend
Small Cap Equity Value
Real Estate Investment Trusts
International Equity

The discretionary trustee will exercise caution when selecting relatively new and untested risky asset classes. Unless the IPS permits a specific category, Unified Trust Company, N.A., will generally not accept discretion, nor offer such impermissible category to the plan participants.

Best Practice No. 8

The investment policy statement provides diversification guidelines.

One of the challenges of writing a complete IPS is to create investment guidelines specific enough to clearly establish the parameters of the desired investment process, yet to provide enough latitude so as not to create an oversight burden. This is particularly true when establishing the portfolio's asset allocation and rebalancing limits.

The "art" of the trustee must lie in the methodology, based on accumulated experience of the TIC, to apply the available tools in a way that gives the highest chances for success in the widest range of possible investment environments. This art might include varying the assumptions in certain ways, changing the constraints based on asset classes in the optimization software, or simply noting when a result is not significant enough to warrant a change.

The discretionary trustee may offer multiple funds in a single category, subject to the following general guidelines:

1. When more than one fund per category is offered, the trustee should consider choosing more than one manager or mutual fund family to diversify managers.

2. The categories in which multiple funds are offered will most often be those in which a prudent asset allocation dictates the largest position. For example, large company stocks often represent a larger position in a prudent portfolio than mid cap or small cap stocks, and the plan may therefore include more large cap funds.

Best Practice No. 9

Primary due diligence criteria are derived from outcomes-based analysis for selecting and replacing investment options.

The discretionary trustee seeks to prudently manage investment policy through outcomes-based investment research. Results matter. The plan is an investment, and the ideal investment process is one that not only meets the legal requirements of procedural prudence but also delivers desirable investment results. The discretionary trustee therefore designs its investment process around insights from outcomes-based research. In other words, the trustee searches for academic studies that attempt to establish actions that may be taken to deliver predictable, desirable outcomes. Outcomes-based research attempts to answer the question, "What works?"

In selecting investment managers (funds) for the plan, the discretionary trustee will rely on the Unified Fiduciary Monitoring Index® ("UFMI®") as the primary criterion and a range of supplementary secondary criteria as well. The UFMI® is intended as a "bright line test," pass or fail, whereas the secondary criteria are less quantitative and more subjective. The discretionary trustee must exercise reasonable care, skill, and caution in selecting investment managers or mutual funds. The discretionary trustee retains the fiduciary responsibility to continually evaluate the manager's performance in light of appropriate benchmarks that are peer-group-adjusted. After the fund or manager is reviewed, reports should be prepared to document the information reviewed.

The discretionary trustee guarantees that all investments entering the plan will be in the top 25% of peer group as measured by the Unified Fiduciary Monitoring Index®.

To be retained in the plan a fund must remain in the top 40% as measured by the Unified Fiduciary Monitoring Index®.

Best Practice No. 10

Secondary due diligence criteria are considered for selecting and replacing investment options.

In addition to the primary criterion of the UFMI®, the discretionary trustee will consider the following secondary criteria in the selection and retention of funds for the plan.

Net Cost of Money Management

The fiduciary will consider funds that revenue-share. Because mutual fund revenue-sharing payments are always passed through 100% to the plan, the true cost of a fund is its total expense minus the revenue-sharing amount. In general, the fiduciary will favor funds with lower net cost.

Style Consistency

When a manager invests in different types of securities, the portfolio may drift into a different investment style, resulting in what is known as "style drift." Though the trustee does not view style drift as reason to fire a manager, it is nonetheless important to maintain control over the plan's asset-class coverage. When a manager changes styles, the portfolio risk and return characteristics may change, necessitating further change. The trustee will therefore, when selecting and retaining managers, generally prefer managers who have demonstrated style consistency over relevant trailing periods.

Manager Organization

In general, the fiduciary will compare multi-manager and single-manager funds because of the factor of management consistency. The ability of the mutual fund's board of directors to act independent of management and in the best interests of shareholders will be considered.

Manager Tenure

In general, a more experienced manager or multi-manager team is preferred to a less experienced manager. The fiduciary will not, however, implement a rigid cutoff screen to eliminate managers below a certain threshold of years managing a particular fund.

Size of Fund

The fiduciary will not hire funds with a level of assets in all share classes combined that could likely result in the following situations:

1. Maintaining an insufficient asset level whereby the fund creates a situation such that its viability is suspect or it produces a situation where the expenses charged to the shareholder are unreasonable, or
2. Maintaining an excessive asset level or sudden period of growth so that the fund becomes unwieldy and unlikely to produce its historical performance

Credit Quality

Unless it is clearly not prudent to do so, the discretionary trustee will not select bond funds or manage portfolios with average credit quality below investment grade. In general, the trustee may consider the mix of credit qualities of a fund's underlying assets when comparing similar funds.

Consistency of Results

The fiduciary will give greater consideration to funds with consistently acceptable historical UFMI® scores. In addition, the fiduciary will generally seek funds with higher performance as compared to peer group over relevant trailing periods. Such superior performance will be viewed favorably but not to the extent that higher is always viewed as better, as relative performance changes significantly year after year.

Best Practice No. 11

Procedures are in place for controlling and accounting for investment expenses.

ERISA specifically requires fiduciaries to control and account for the costs, including investment expenses, of administering an employee benefit plan. Section 404(a) requires fiduciaries of employee benefit plans to discharge their duties with respect to a plan solely in the interest of the participants and beneficiaries, and for the exclusive purpose of providing benefits to participants and their beneficiaries and defraying reasonable expenses of administering the plan [ERISA Section 404(a)(1)(A)(i) and (ii)].

The fiduciary's responsibility in connection with the payment of fees is to determine whether the fees can be paid from portfolio assets and whether the fees are reasonable in light of the services to be provided. (See also Best Practice No. 10.)

Accordingly, the fiduciary must negotiate all forms of compensation to be paid for investment management to ensure that the aggregate, as well as the individual components, provide reasonable compensation for the services rendered. The fiduciary has a duty to account for all dollars spent on investment management services, whether those dollars are paid directly from the account or through soft dollars, 12b-1 fees, or other fee-sharing arrangements.

In addition, the fiduciary has the responsibility to identify those parties that have been compensated from the fees and to apply a reasonableness test to the amount of compensation received by any party. In the case of an all-inclusive fee, sometimes referred to as a bundled-fee, or wrap-fee, investment product, the fiduciary should investigate how the total fee compares with each component purchased separately to make sure the costs are prudent.

Diversify and Implement Policy (Best Practices 12-15)

Best Practice No. 12

The plan sponsor follows applicable "safe harbor" provisions.

Several voluntary safe-harbor provisions will, if it is later determined that the plan sponsor complied with all requirements of those provisions, insulate fiduciaries from claims that they breached their fiduciary duty with regards to the plan's investments. If investment decisions are being managed by a discretionary trustee and/or by a discretionary investment advisor, there are four provisions to the safe-harbor rules:

1. Use discretionary prudent experts to make the investment decisions.
2. Demonstrate that the discretionary prudent experts were selected by following a due-diligence process.
3. Have discretionary prudent experts acknowledge their cofiduciary status.
4. Monitor the activities of discretionary prudent experts to ensure that they are performing the agreed upon tasks.

When investment decisions are participant-directed, as is often the case for defined contribution plans, there are additional provisions:

1. Plan participants must be notified that the plan sponsor intends to constitute a Section 404(c) plan.
2. Participants must be provided with at least three different investment options.
3. Participants must receive information and education on the different investment options.
4. Participants must be provided the opportunity to change their investment strategies and allocations with a frequency that is appropriate in light of market volatility.

Best Practice No. 13

The investment vehicles are appropriate for the portfolio size.

The primary focus of this Best Practices compendium is the implementation of the investment strategy with appropriate investment vehicles, specifically the proper use of mutual funds and separate account managers. A challenging question for most fiduciaries is, at what point should there be a migration from mutual funds to separate account managers? It is important for the fiduciary to be familiar with both mutual funds and separate account managers, for no one implementation structure is right for all occasions.

As discretionary trustee, Unified Trust Company, N.A., has the sole responsibility for management of those plan assets over which it has discretion and is the sole decision-maker, because this is the role delegated to it by the plan sponsor.

It is arguable that the trustee should therefore dictate which investments will be in the plan, regardless of the plan sponsor's preferences, but Unified Trust does not take this position. A prudent process may consider client preferences as long as client preferences are consistent with all other aspects of the trustee's investment process, and the trustee will make every effort to incorporate client preferences into the investment process.

In a white paper entitled "Why Most Managed Account Programs Fail," available on the company Web site, Unified Trust Company outlines reasons why a fiduciary must seriously question much of the data available on private money managers. For the reasons outlined in the paper, the trustee will favor the use of mutual funds over private managers unless clearly prudent to do otherwise.

Best Practice No. 14

A due diligence process is followed in the construction of model portfolios.

A model portfolio is a single selection of a prearranged series of mutual funds in a specific weighting designed for the plan participant's risk tolerance and needs. In a model portfolio, the plan participant directly invests in the target mutual fund portfolio with a single selection.

One theoretical advantage of the model portfolio over a mutual fund holding other mutual funds is that a potential second layer of fund fees is avoided. A second advantage is that most lifestyle funds use mutual funds from the same mutual fund company, giving a proprietary taint to the objectivity of fund selection and replacement. Model portfolios comprise mutual funds selected and monitored on an objective basis.

Since the introduction of Markowitz's mean variance optimization and the efficient frontier in the 1950s, a variety of tools has emerged to assist fiduciaries in establishing asset allocation policy. The discretionary trustee may in some cases compare results of analyses using both historical and projected assumptions.

The discretionary trustee will make available to the trust investment committee the following tools to help determine allocation policy for the plan. The committee will, however, consider the limitations of such software, including the fact that correlation coefficients between various asset classes change over time.

1. Mean variance optimization (efficient-frontier software)
2. Stochastic/probabilistic modeling software
3. Monte Carlo probability analysis software
4. Economic forecasting and asset class modeling

Best Practice No. 15

The investment strategy is implemented in compliance with the required level of prudence.

ERISA had as one of its central purposes a public policy of ensuring the adequate investment returns necessary for participants. Though based in large part on traditional principles of trust law, ERISA recognized the limitations of these principles in portfolio management and thus departed somewhat from the Prudent Man Rule by setting a standard of prudence to govern pension investments that is more attuned with economic reality and important academic developments in financial theory.

The overall investment strategy should be based upon risk and reward objectives suitable for the trust. ERISA rejects a per se rule as to imprudent investments and provides a safe harbor from liability if the fiduciary has given "appropriate consideration" to the facts and circumstances of the investment and its relationship to the needs of the pension plan. It is process-oriented rather than rule-oriented. Fiduciary law does not expressly require the use of professional money managers. However, fiduciaries will be held to the same expert standard of care, and their activities and conduct will be measured against those of investment professionals or other prudent experts.

The standard of prudence applies to the trust as a whole rather than to individual investments, with a realization that particular investments that would have been viewed as speculative on their own may be sensible, risk-reducing additions to a portfolio viewed as a whole. There is a duty to diversify, unless the trustee reasonably determines that it is in the interests of the beneficiaries not to diversify, taking into account the purposes and terms of the governing instrument. Diversification should be considered both within an asset class and across asset classes, unless it is clearly not prudent to diversify.

Monitor and Supervise (Best Practices 16-20)

Best Practice No. 16

Fees for investment management are consistent with agreements and with the law.

Under ERISA, the general obligation of a fiduciary is to discharge duties to an employee benefit plan with the requisite care, skill, and prudence required and to defray all but reasonable and appropriate expenses of the trust. ERISA requires that a prudent discretionary trustee implement procedures for controlling and accounting for expenses, including investment expenses.

The discretionary trustee has a duty to ensure that plan fees are reasonable and disclosed to the plan sponsor. Moreover, a fiduciary of an employee benefit plan is specifically prohibited from using plan assets to pay a party in interest, such as a trustee, a custodian, an investment manager, an investment advisor, or a broker, for services that are neither appropriate nor helpful in carrying out the purposes for which the plan is established or maintained, or to pay more than reasonable compensation for such services [ERISA Section 406(a)(1)(C) and 408(b)(2)].

The fiduciary has a duty to account for all dollars spent on investment management services, whether those dollars are paid directly from the account or through soft dollars, 12b-1 fees, or other fee-sharing arrangements. In addition, the fiduciary has the responsibility to identify those parties that have been compensated from the fees and to apply a reasonableness test to the amount of compensation received by any party. DOL Advisory Opinion 1997-15A, the Frost Letter, clarifies that a discretionary fiduciary with control over the investment selection for a plan may collect revenue-sharing payments on behalf of the plan but must account for each payment and pass it on 100% to the plan in the form of an expense offset or direct payment.

Best Practice No. 17

Periodic reviews are made of qualitative and organizational changes of investment decision-makers.

In general, the discretionary trustee will show a slight preference for multi-manager funds over single-manager funds due to the implied consistency of management. The trustee will evaluate from time to time the mutual fund or investment manager board of director's commitment to shareholder fairness, fiduciary oversight, and regulatory compliance.

ERISA provides that any employee benefit plan may provide that the discretionary fiduciary named by the plan to manage the plan's assets may appoint an investment manager or mutual fund to manage any assets of the plan. An investment manager or fund must be prudently selected and monitored and must satisfy the requirements of ERISA Section 3(38). If an investment manager is appointed, the named fiduciary that made the appointment has an ongoing responsibility to monitor the performance of the investment manager at reasonable intervals.

The 2003 mutual-fund trading scandal provides insight into the monitoring duties of the discretionary trustee and plan sponsor. Generally, ERISA requires a plan fiduciary to be responsible for either investing plan assets or maintaining a plan's menu of permissible investment alternatives under a participant-directed plan.

These concepts have generally been interpreted to mean that plan fiduciaries must not only be prudent in choosing to invest in or offer a particular mutual fund, but must also be prudent in deciding to maintain such investment or continue to make such fund available under the plan. Thus, plan fiduciaries, even absent a scandal, have a general fiduciary obligation to monitor plan investments and alternatives on a periodic basis to ensure that they remain prudent choices.

Best Practice No. 18

Portfolio rebalancing is reviewed and applied where necessary.

Annual or more frequent rebalancing is a simple and effective way to help plan participants improve their success rates. It is most effective if applied to plan participants' accounts using a default pathway so that the desired action does not depend on the participants' overcoming their inertia and procrastination behaviors.

Rebalancing is inherent to the element of diversification; the goal is to create a portfolio that balances appropriate levels of risk and return. That balance, once achieved, can be maintained only by periodically rebalancing the portfolio to maintain the appropriate diversification.

The rebalancing limits define the points when a portfolio should be reallocated to bring it back in line with the established asset-allocation target. The discipline of rebalancing, in essence, controls risk and forces the portfolio to move along a predetermined course. It takes gains from stellar performers or favored asset classes and reallocates them to lagging styles, without attempting to time the market.

Several methods exist by which fiduciaries may rebalance accounts. Rebalancing refers to placing trades, after periods of relative gains and losses in each category lead to inevitable changes in the actual allocation, so that the asset allocation again conforms to the target allocation. The discretionary trustee will rebalance at times determined to be best, based on the scheduled rebalancing, the deviation from target, and tactical rebalancing.

Best Practice No. 19

Periodic reports compare investment performance against an appropriate index, peer group, and IPS objectives.

The monitoring function extends beyond a strict examination of performance; by definition, monitoring occurs across all policy and procedural issues covered in this compendium. The ongoing review, analysis, and monitoring of investment decision-makers and money managers is just as important as the due diligence implemented during the manager selection process. The discretionary trustee will review model portfolios against appropriate blended benchmarks.

The discretionary trustee will deliver to the plan sponsor and the plan's advisors, if any, a quarterly fiduciary monitoring report showing the UFMI® scores of each fund in the plan, performance versus benchmarks, and performance versus IPS criteria. No investment action is required of the plan sponsor. The plan sponsor should review the report with its investment committee, board of directors, and other interested parties.

When a fund falls below the minimum retention UFMI® score or such other factors deemed important by the discretionary trustee, it is placed on the watch list. At this time, the trust investment committee will begin the process of considering a replacement fund, and the plan sponsor and advisor should take this opportunity to communicate any feedback with regard to a potential replacement.

When a fund falls below the minimum retention UFMI® score for two consecutive quarters, it is placed on the replacement list and is replaced as soon as administratively feasible in accordance with Unified Trust Company's replacement protocol.

Best Practice No. 20

Fiduciary monitoring reports are provided to the plan sponsor and appropriate advisors; meetings are held as needed.

The plan sponsor, its advisors, and the discretionary trustee should review the entire plan status to determine the likelihood of participant success. Such an evaluation should include not only the investment performance of the manager, funds, and asset allocation models related to the plan, but also the savings rate and overall funding of the participant account balances necessary for success.

In keeping with the duty of prudence, a fiduciary appointing a money manager or selecting a mutual fund must determine the frequency of the reviews necessary, taking into account such factors as the general economic conditions then prevailing, the size of the portfolio, the investment strategies employed, the investment objectives sought, and the volatility of the investments selected. The discretionary trustee may, in its discretion, place a fund on the watch list or the replacement list, based on secondary considerations in addition to the UFMI.

The fiduciary should acknowledge that fluctuating rates of return characterize the securities markets and may cause variations in performance. The fiduciary should evaluate performance from a long-term perspective and use research that shows a certain evaluation methodology can have a meaningful effect on improved outcomes.

An abbreviated example of the fiduciary investment reports that the discretionary trustee should consider making available to the plan sponsor and its advisors are shown on the following pages. These reports should be reviewed during committee meetings with the plan sponsor. The plan sponsor should permanently retain them as part of its documentation.

Figure 13-1: Fiduciary Monitoring Report Page 1

Sample Plan
RETIREMENT PLAN
FIDUCIARY MONITORING REPORT
AS OF SEPTEMBER 30, 2003

Figure 13-2: Fiduciary Monitoring Report Page 2

TABLE OF CONTENTS

Figure 13-3: Fiduciary Monitoring Report Page 3

EXECUTIVE SUMMARY

Weighted Average UFMI® Score   6

The Weighted Average UFMI® score is each fund's UFMI® score weighted by an equal amount of assets in each fund. It provides an overall snapshot of the total asset quality in your plan.

Watch List   None

The Watch List includes any fund with a failing UFMI® score for the current quarter. In your plan, a failing score is any fund with a UFMI® score no longer in the top 40% of its investment category or peer group (UFMI® 41-100).

Replacement List   None

The Replacement List includes any fund with a failing UFMI® score for two consecutive quarters. Funds on the replacement list will be replaced with a fund from the same investment category that passes fiduciary scrutiny in accordance with the Investment Policy Statement.

Plan Sponsor Action Required

For Funds on the Replacement List, please follow the Trustee's instructions for fund replacement, including prompt distribution of any required communications with participants (notices and detailed instructions sent electronically to the Plan Administrator).

For Funds on the Watch List, we will confer with you concerning any feedback or preferences you wish to pass on to Unified Trust. Note that the time for such feedback is during the "watch" period, as replacements are implemented as soon as practical once a fund appears on the Replacement List.

Figure 13-4: Fiduciary Monitoring Report Page 4

FINANCIAL MARKET REVIEW:
THE ECONOMY

Treasury Secretary Jack Snow created a stir in Washington by noting that interest rates will rise as economic growth accelerates. Specifically, in an interview with the Times of London, Mr. Snow said he'd be "frustrated and concerned if there were not some upward movement in rates." Mr. Snow was getting a political jump on the inevitable by stating that some increase in interest rates will, and indeed should, happen in the coming year. As economic growth accelerates in a recovery, so does the demand for credit. And as the demand for credit increases, the price of credit -- that is, interest rates -- tends to increase as well.

Market interest rates have already been rising for some time, as signs of strong and sustainable economic growth multiply. The Fed tends to follow the market on rates, and investors are already anticipating the day that Alan Greenspan and friends begin to lift the short-term fed funds rate they control from its current 45-year low of 1%.

The index of leading indicators designed to foreshadow movements in overall economic growth slipped in September, suggesting the U.S. economic recovery has slowed from its red-hot third-quarter pace but isn't about to stall. The Conference Board said its index fell 0.2% in September, the first decline in four months. The economy is improving although the road ahead will likely remain bumpy.

Economists estimate the economy grew at a blistering 6.1% annual rate in the third quarter ended Sept. 30, according to a survey by Macroeconomic Advisers LLC, a St. Louis forecasting firm. That would be the fastest quarterly pace in almost four years.

However, most of the expansion in economic activity took place in July and August, when the effect of tax cuts and the mortgage-refinancing boom were strongest. There are signs consumer spending cooled in September as the impact of mortgage refinancing and tax cuts faded.

The Conference Board said six of the 10 indicators in its index declined, led by the money supply, and the relationship between long-term and short-term interest rates. Positive contributors were the manufacturing workweek and stock prices. The improvement in economic performance has prompted fixed income markets to worry the Federal Reserve may start to raise interest rates sooner than expected from the current 1% federal-funds rate, which represents a 45-year low.

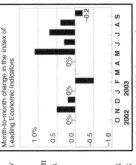

Month-to-month change in the index of Leading Economic Indicators

Figure 13-5: Fiduciary Monitoring Report Page 5

FINANCIAL MARKET REVIEW:
THE STOCK MARKET

As of September 30, 2003 the S&P 500 stood at 995, up +2.6% from a level of 974 at the end of June, and up +13.2% from 879 at the beginning of the year. Despite this recovery, the S&P 500 is still −35.8% below its peak level of 1,551 three years ago. As you can see on the chart, the stock market remains in a bullish pattern consistently above its 90-day moving average.

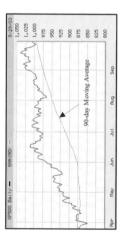

Looking back at the state of the stock market one year ago, it is striking how much times have changed. Last year at this point, investors had endured a grinding bear market for roughly 30 months, nearly three times as long as the average for such downturns. The decline was also striking in its depth, with the broad market averages losing about −45%, effectively rivaling the notorious decline of 1973-1974. For many equity investors, it was a time of despair, as there were no obvious catalysts that might pull the market out of its doldrums.

The pessimism was especially understandable given that the period saw ongoing revelations of corporate fraud, sordid tales of accounting irregularities and outright dishonesty that eroded investors' confidence. Deepening the gloom were an economy that remained stubbornly weak, a growing perception that war with Iraq might be inevitable, and repercussions from numerous routs in the bond market. The only good news seemed to be the continued decline in mortgage rates, which boosted the housing market and gave many homeowners an opportunity to reduce their mortgage payments.

Today, equity investors have enjoyed a year of excellent returns, with the largest gains coming from some of the riskiest, most volatile issues. In addition, the wide disparities in valuation (and performance) that existed 20–30 months ago between growth and value stocks and large-cap and small-cap stocks are essentially gone. In sum, the stock markets' extremes appear to be behind us.

Concerns that the U.S. economy might fall into a deflationary quagmire have almost disappeared. Overall, investors have seen the envelope stretched in several directions during the past three years, and most would welcome a less-exciting environment. However, the level of uncertainty in the global environment and the financial markets has not changed. Maintaining a broadly diversified portfolio and keeping a long-term perspective remain the keys to success for investors.

FINANCIAL MARKET REVIEW:
THE BOND MARKET

Bond investors have also seen a striking swing back toward "normal" market conditions after a tumultuous 18 months, with the yield spread between investment-grade corporate bonds and U.S. Treasury issues back to familiar levels. After a roller-coaster year in which Treasury yields fell to their lowest levels in nearly two generations, interest rates have climbed back essentially to the levels of 12 months ago.

The bond market's weakening tone toward the end of the second quarter turned into a full rout during the third quarter as yield levels spiked up significantly during the months of July and August. From a forty-year low of 3.11% reached in June, ten year Treasury yields rose by an unprecedented 149 basis points to 4.60% by early September. As yields rose bond prices fell, and for the full third quarter bond total returns (interest plus price changes) were about zero.

They have since settled back to just under 4.00% by quarter-end. As an indication of the extreme market volatility, we note that the market went from the 12 month low in yield to the 12 month high within the span of just two months. Economists estimate the economy grew at a very fast 6.1% in the third quarter. This represents the fastest quarterly growth rate in nearly four years. It is likely that stronger economic growth in late 2003-2004 will continue to drive up interest rates well into 2004.

-348-

Figure 13-6: Fiduciary Monitoring Report Page 6

KEEPING THE RIGHT INVESTMENT MIX

Several recent studies have documented the poor outcomes of most investors. One study, which looked at all mutual fund trades during the 1984-2002 time period, found that the stock market averaged +12.2%, the average stock mutual fund averaged 9.3% and *the average investor only made +2.7%*. After inflation, their real return was below zero! How can you keep this from happening to you?

As an investor, you cannot control how the financial markets perform. But here are vital variables that you can control. You can decide how much to invest. You can limit the risk in your portfolio by diversifying your holdings.

Sticking with a diversified portfolio isn't always easy. Because certain segments of the financial markets are always performing better than others—it really can't be any other way—many investors are tempted to chase performance or to speculate about when to move into or out of a particular fund or asset class. But as the past several years have demonstrated, such investment strategies can be dangerous.

That's why we believe that the best asset class to own is all of them and that the best time to own them is always. The challenge is making sure that your mix of stock funds, bond funds, and short-term investments is based on your very personal goals, financial situation, and tolerance for risk.

As you review your holdings, remember that, of the three main asset classes – equities, fixed income and cash – equity investments, or stocks, have the strongest growth potential and the best historical results over the long term.

We focus on both Asset Allocation and Asset Quality to build a sound investment foundation for you. Asset Allocation is the mix of stocks, bonds and cash in your account. Large, mid-sized and small stocks provide further diversification. We also look at styles, such as growth value, or a combination of both called blend. We use the Unified Fiduciary Monitoring Index® (UFMI®) to make sure each slice of your "pie" is of the highest Asset Quality.

The UFMI® does not tell you about the relative merits of one asset allocation piece versus another, but it will tell you about the quality of that particular piece when compared to its peers using totally objective factors shown to make a difference over time.

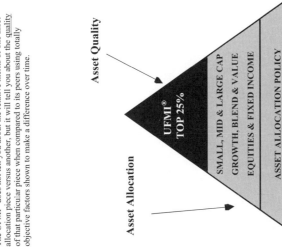

Asset Quality

Asset Allocation

UFMI®
TOP 25%

SMALL, MID & LARGE CAP
GROWTH, BLEND & VALUE
EQUITIES & FIXED INCOME

ASSET ALLOCATION POLICY

Figure 13-7: Fiduciary Monitoring Report Page 7

INVESTMENT SELECTIONS

All Returns As Of September 30, 2003

unified trust

Security Name	Investment Category	Unified Fiduciary Index Score	Ticker	Assets	% Of Plan	Tot Ret Qtr	Tot Ret 1 Yr	Notes
UTC Stable Value Fund	Stable Value	n/a	UTCSV	$3,658,079.33	18.7%	1.05%	4.54%	Passing UFMI®
Dodge & Cox Income	Intermediate-term Bond	1	DODIX	$3,785,887.30	19.4%	0.54%	7.41%	Passing UFMI®
AmCent Target 2005 Inv	Intermediate Government	1	BTFIX	$417,583.66	2.1%	-0.01%	7.04%	Passing UFMI®
Dodge & Cox Balanced	Domestic Hybrid	1	DODBX	$578,988.31	3.0%	3.78%	20.41%	Passing UFMI®
Jensen	Large Growth	12	JENSX	$2,587,478.33	13.3%	1.22%	13.17%	Passing UFMI®
Franklin Capital Gr A	Large Growth	11	FKREX	$875,887.33	4.5%	3.20%	25.00%	Passing UFMI®
Thompson Plumb Growth	Large Blend	2	THPGX	$3,598,744.30	18.4%	0.85%	34.79%	Passing UFMI®
Dodge & Cox Stock	Large Value	1	DODGX	$2,698,578.85	13.8%	5.24%	25.58%	Passing UFMI®
Scudder Dreman HiRetEqA	Large Value	7	KDHAX	$1,125,879.66	5.8%	0.77%	24.87%	Passing UFMI®
T. Rowe Price Mid Gr R	Mid-Cap Growth	14	RRMGX	$1,258,889.30	6.4%	4.08%	32.79%	Passing UFMI®
Federated Mid-Cap Index	Mid-Cap Blend	15	FMDCX	$2,475,848.87	12.7%	6.43%	25.99%	Passing UFMI®
Columbia Acorn Z	Small Growth	3	ACRNX	$2,325,879.66	11.9%	8.95%	36.73%	Passing UFMI®
Royce Low-Priced Stock	Small Blend	8	RYLPX	$987,555.66	5.1%	8.51%	36.28%	Passing UFMI®
Templeton Foreign A	Foreign Stock	8	TEMFX	$587,899.61	3.0%	9.23%	22.53%	Passing UFMI®
Average/Sum		6		$19,519,213.54	100.0%	4.06%	24.05%	

The Unified Trust Company Unified Fiduciary Monitoring Index® ("Unified Fiduciary Index") score is a relative ranking of over 14,000 mutual funds and compares each fund to its peer group. The score ranges between 1 and 100, with a score of 1 being in the top 1%, a score of 10 being in the top 10%, etc and is updated each quarter. The composite score evaluates each fund against its investment objective category (peer group) and compares numerous, and relevant, investment factors shown in published academic finance studies to be useful in an attempt to predict fund performance between funds of the same peer group or same investment category.

For more information please visit www.unifiedtrust.com.

Figure 13-8: Fiduciary Monitoring Report Page 8

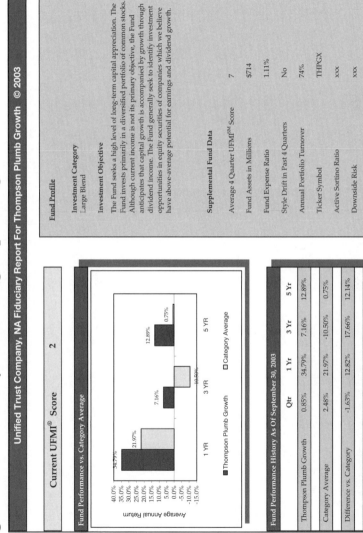

Current UFMI® Score | 2

Fund Performance vs. Category Average

- ■ Thompson Plumb Growth
- □ Category Average

	1 YR	3 YR	5 YR
Thompson Plumb Growth	34.79%	7.16%	12.89%
Category Average	21.97%	-10.50%	0.75%

(Average Annual Return axis: 40.0%, 35.0%, 30.0%, 25.0%, 20.0%, 15.0%, 10.0%, 5.0%, 0.0%, -5.0%, -10.0%, -15.0%)

Fund Performance History As Of September 30, 2003

	Qtr	1 Yr	3 Yr	5 Yr
Thompson Plumb Growth	0.85%	34.79%	7.16%	12.89%
Category Average	2.48%	21.97%	-10.50%	0.75%
Difference vs. Category	-1.63%	12.82%	17.66%	12.14%
Percent Rank in Category		2	1	1

Fund Profile

Investment Category
Large Blend

Investment Objective

The Fund seeks a high level of long-term capital appreciation. The Fund invests primarily in a diversified portfolio of common stocks. Although current income is not its primary objective, the Fund anticipates that capital growth is accompanied by growth through dividend income. The Fund generally seek to identify investment opportunities in equity securities of companies which we believe have above-average potential for earnings and dividend growth.

Supplemental Fund Data

Average 4 Quarter UFMI℠ Score	7
Fund Assets in Millions	$714
Fund Expense Ratio	1.11%
Style Drift in Past 4 Quarters	No
Annual Portfolio Turnover	74%
Ticker Symbol	THPGX
Active Sortino Ratio	xxx
Downside Risk	xxx

-351-

Figure 13-9: Fiduciary Monitoring Report Page 9

Current UFMI® Score | 1

Fund Profile

Investment Category
Large Value

Investment Objective

The Fund's primary objective is to provide shareholders with an opportunity for long-term growth of principal and income. A secondary objective is to achieve a reasonable current income. The Fund seeks to achieve its objective by investing primarily in a diversified portfolio of common stocks. Under normal circumstances, the Fund will invest at least 80% of its total assets in common stocks. The Fund invests in companies that appear to be temporarily undervalued by the stock market but have a favorable outlook for long-term growth.

Supplemental Fund Data

Average 4 Quarter UFMI℠ Score	1
Fund Assets in Millions	n/a
Fund Expense Ratio	0.54%
Style Drift in Past 4 Quarters	No
Annual Portfolio Turnover	13%
Ticker Symbol	DODGX
Active Sortino Ratio	xxx
Downside Risk	xxx

Fund Performance vs. Category Average

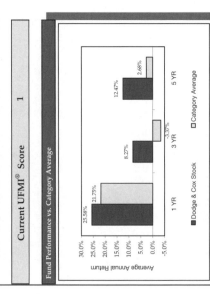

Fund Performance History As Of September 30, 2003

	Qtr	1 Yr	3 Yr	5 Yr
Dodge & Cox Stock	5.24%	25.58%	8.27%	12.47%
Category Average	2.05%	21.75%	-3.37%	2.68%
Difference vs. Category	3.19%	3.83%	11.64%	9.79%
Percent Rank in Category		24	1	1

-352-

Figure 13-10 Fiduciary Monitoring Report Page 10

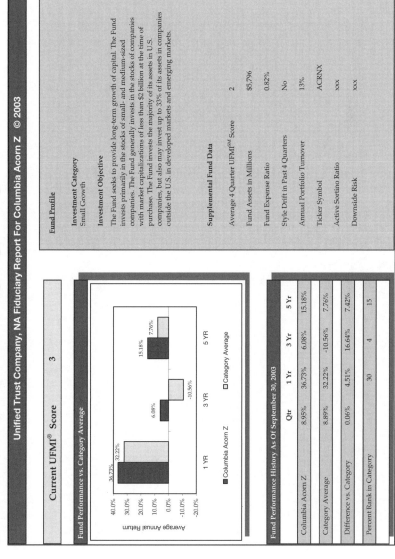

Current UFMI® Score 3

Fund Performance vs. Category Average

Average Annual Return

- Columbia Acorn Z
- Category Average

1 YR	3 YR	5 YR
36.73% / 32.22%	6.08% / -10.56%	15.18% / 7.76%

Fund Profile

Investment Category
Small Growth

Investment Objective

The Fund seeks to provide long-term growth of capital. The Fund invests primarily in the stocks of small- and medium-sized companies. The Fund generally invests in the stocks of companies with market capitalizations of less than $2 billion at the time of purchase. The Fund invests the majority of its assets in U.S. companies, but also may invest up to 33% of its assets in companies outside the U.S. in developed markets and emerging markets.

Supplemental Fund Data

Average 4 Quarter UFMI℠ Score	2
Fund Assets in Millions	$5,796
Fund Expense Ratio	0.82%
Style Drift in Past 4 Quarters	No
Annual Portfolio Turnover	13%
Ticker Symbol	ACRNX
Active Sortino Ratio	xxx
Downside Risk	xxx

Fund Performance History As Of September 30, 2003

	Qtr	1 Yr	3 Yr	5 Yr
Columbia Acorn Z	8.95%	36.73%	6.08%	15.18%
Category Average	8.89%	32.22%	-10.56%	7.76%
Difference vs. Category	0.06%	4.51%	16.64%	7.42%
Percent Rank in Category	30	4	4	15

Figure 13-11: Fiduciary Monitoring Report Page 11

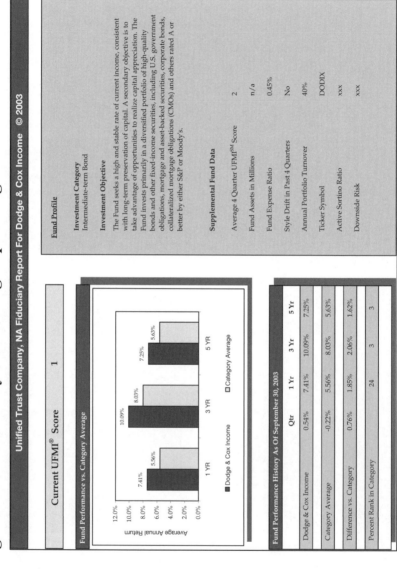

Current UFMI® Score | 1

Fund Performance vs. Category Average

(Chart: Average Annual Return)

1 YR: Dodge & Cox Income 7.41%, Category Average 5.56%
3 YR: Dodge & Cox Income 10.09%, Category Average 8.03%
5 YR: Dodge & Cox Income 7.25%, Category Average 5.63%

■ Dodge & Cox Income ☐ Category Average

Fund Performance History As Of September 30, 2003

	Qtr	1 Yr	3 Yr	5 Yr
Dodge & Cox Income	0.54%	7.41%	10.09%	7.25%
Category Average	-0.22%	5.56%	8.03%	5.63%
Difference vs. Category	0.76%	1.85%	2.06%	1.62%
Percent Rank in Category		24	3	3

Fund Profile

Investment Category
Intermediate-term Bond

Investment Objective

The Fund seeks a high and stable rate of current income, consistent with long-term preservation of capital. A secondary objective is to take advantage of opportunities to realize capital appreciation. The Fund invests primarily in a diversified portfolio of high-quality bonds and other fixed-income securities, including U.S. government obligations, mortgage and asset-backed securities, corporate bonds, collateralized mortgage obligations (CMOs) and others rated A or better by either S&P or Moody's.

Supplemental Fund Data

Average 4 Quarter UFMI℠ Score	2
Fund Assets in Millions	n/a
Fund Expense Ratio	0.45%
Style Drift in Past 4 Quarters	No
Annual Portfolio Turnover	40%
Ticker Symbol	DODIX
Active Sortino Ratio	xxx
Downside Risk	xxx

-354-

Chapter 14

Self-Directed Brokerage Accounts Reduce Success

Chapter Summary

Many employer-sponsored retirement plans now offer participants the option of self-directed brokerage accounts in addition to a core menu of mutual funds. Today, approximately 20% of all plans offer a brokerage account, but only about 6% of participants use it. The demand arose almost solely because participants pushed for more choice and because of their overconfidence in their own trading skills. In the 1990s, the bull market was in full throttle, and irrational exuberance was at its peak.

Contrary to what brokerage houses may tell plan sponsors, plan fiduciaries continue to retain significant fiduciary responsibility and liability, restricting the range of investments that may be offered in a self-directed brokerage account. The plan sponsor has a fiduciary duty of prudence in the selection and retention of investment choices, including those in self-directed brokerage accounts.

More pragmatically, the investment performance of self-directed accounts is generally inferior to model portfolios. The low performance translates into a low real rate of return and increases the probability for retirement failure. Men trade more than women because of their overconfidence, and their returns lag women's because of the extra trading activity. We have found that 72% of all self-directed brokerage accounts lag equally weighted model portfolios constructed from the core funds in the plan. The average annual underperformance was 4.70%.

Employees Want Different and More "Sexy" Investment Choices

Traditionally, employer-sponsored retirement plans offered participants a varied but limited menu of mutual funds, ranging from a handful to twenty or more, and sometimes access to company stock. But, especially with the explosion of online trading and the long bull market of the 1990s, some participants began pushing for more choices, so more employers began offering the option of self-directed brokerage accounts.

Under this arrangement, participants open an account with a brokerage firm of their choosing or through a single brokerage-firm plan window coordinated with the plan's trustee or record keeper. The notion of a self-directed brokerage account is not new or revolutionary. It represented one of the first forms of employee direction in profit-sharing and money purchase plan accounts.

Long a staple of programs established for law firms or medical practices, these brokerage programs survived for many years primarily due to the hard work of bank trust departments—and the insistence of the law partners and doctors who picked the providers. Eventually, more powerful computer technology began to tear down some of the barriers that initially restricted such offerings.

In the mid-1990s, another event pushed the idea to the forefront. In 1996, the Department of Labor issued its proposed regulations on ERISA's Section 404(c)—the so-called dividing line between education and advice. The ruling did not specifically shed any light on brokerage accounts; however, it did remind plan sponsors and providers that there was a level of fiduciary liability for restricting investment choices. More choice meant less liability, or so the thinking went. The idea was then heavily promoted to plan sponsors (fiduciaries) by brokerage houses (nonfiduciaries).

The shift in thinking coincided nicely with two other factors: By 1996, the bull market was in full throttle, and irrational exuberance was at its peak. If ever there was a time when participants felt ready—and eager—to transcend the dozen or so mutual fund choices of their 401(k) plan, this was it.

For most 401(k) plans, a brokerage account is the medium for offering the widest range of investments to plan participants. These self-directed brokerage accounts offer a broad range of investments, including listed and over-the-counter stocks, fixed-income instruments, money market funds, and many mutual funds. In this way, in theory, plan participants can customize their retirement portfolios, and plan sponsors can satisfy their employees' desire for more investment alternatives.

There are some ERISA limitations, however. Plan participants with self-directed brokerage accounts may not be able to invest in all of the investment vehicles that are available in retail brokerage accounts. They cannot hold investments that are prohibited under ERISA or invest in municipal bonds. They cannot generally buy options or futures, commodities, or derivatives, and they cannot margin or sell short. They cannot conduct investment maneuvers that might cause them to lose more than their total account value.

Over the past ten years, more 401(k) plan service providers have permitted plan sponsors to augment their plans with self-directed brokerage accounts. In a predictable response to the customer demand, the percentage of 401(k) service providers who can offer this option has grown from virtually zero in 1993 to more than 90% today.

As with plan sponsors, many service providers remained unconvinced of the prudence or practicality of the option. However, having found themselves eliminated from one search after another because they did not offer the option, most now have figured out a way to say yes.

The impetus for this change did not arise from plan sponsors, industry consultants, fiduciaries, or service providers. The driving force was the employees themselves. Plan sponsors contemplated implementing self-directed options because of employee pressure. For example, a 2001 survey of large-plan sponsors by Hewitt Associates found that some 12% of plan sponsors offered brokerage accounts, compared with 7% in 1999. In 2003, Hewitt's research found that more than half the employers surveyed either had a brokerage option in place or were considering adding a self-directed brokerage account within the next eighteen months. Of this group, 75% cited employee demand as the primary driver for the additional option.

The surge in interest shows that employers are responding to employee demand for ultimate investment choice and control. The plan sponsor hopes that the brokerage option will take pressure off the employer to continually be adding the next "hot fund" or investment category. In theory, a self-directed brokerage window allows employers to focus a plan's core investments around the needs of a broad participant base while meeting the fund requests of other employees.

Only a handful of employees use the service when it is offered. Of the plans that now offer brokerage options, only about 6% of participants use the feature. In general, these employees tend to be more sophisticated and more highly paid employees. However, under the ERISA rules, the option must be made available to everyone in the plan.

The brokerage-house sales pitches claim that a self-directed brokerage account can protect fiduciaries even more than a traditional 404(c) plan, because it removes almost all restrictions on investment options. Some employers have been told that the more investment options or strategies that are offered, the less fiduciary liability. This is a myth. The fact is that more investment options create greater fiduciary responsibilities to educate, communicate, and evaluate retirement-plan investment options.

Brokerage Accounts Do Not Eliminate Fiduciary Liability Concerns

We discussed ERISA fiduciary liability risk in detail in chapter 12. However, several points are worth reviewing, because they are particularly applicable to self-directed brokerage accounts. At first blush, self-directed brokerage accounts are attractive, because they appear to offer two advantages: (1) the plan sponsor has been told that the individual investments do not need to be prudently selected and monitored, and (2) if the twenty-plus DOL 404(c) requirements are met, the fiduciaries are not responsible for the investment allocation decisions of the participants.

Compliance with ERISA section 404(c) protects plan fiduciaries only from losses that result from plan participants' exercise of control over the assets in their accounts. An employer's designation or limitation of investment options is a fiduciary function. Plan fiduciaries have not only the obligation to prudently select investment choices, but also the residual obligation to evaluate the performance of these vehicles to determine whether they should remain available under the plan.

Thus, there is more risk to self-directed brokerage accounts than meets the eye. ERISA imposes an overriding responsibility on plan fiduciaries to act prudently and for the exclusive purpose of providing benefits for participants. A plausible interpretation of that general requirement is that plan fiduciaries must decide whether it is prudent to offer brokerage accounts to participants.

DOL officials have opined that fiduciaries must consider the nature of the workforce in selecting 401(k) investments. That is, they must decide whether the participants have the education, experience, and ability to make intelligent buy-and-sell decisions about individual stocks. If they do not, offering brokerage accounts in a 401(k) plan could be a breach of fiduciary duty. Keep in mind that when fiduciaries limit investment options to a specific number—whether it be five or fifty—those options are designated, and as a result, they must be prudently selected, periodically monitored, and removed from the plan when they are no longer prudent and suitable for the participants.

The legislative history, statutory construction, and labor regulations make it clear that plan fiduciaries continue to retain significant fiduciary responsibility and liability, restricting the range of investments that may be offered in self-directed brokerage accounts. The plan sponsor has a fiduciary duty of prudence in the selection and retention of investment choices, including those in self-directed brokerage accounts.

The preamble to the DOL regulations makes it clear that the plan sponsor needs to review the investments that are purchased in the self-directed brokerage account. It would appear that prudent fund selection and retention duties continue to apply, even if the plan sponsor places no limits on the investment universe of the account.

The common-law concept of investment prudence, codified by ERISA, would appear to require fiduciaries—that is, trustees, plan sponsors, retirement committees, or other decision-makers—to review the entire portfolio of each self-directed brokerage account.

The plan sponsor needs to have a procedure to conduct periodic reviews to ensure that inappropriate investment options are eliminated in a self-directed brokerage account. The plan sponsor's investment policy should establish criteria for the selection and ongoing due diligence of the investment vehicles under such accounts.

The plan sponsor should make certain that the self-directed brokerage account provider is liable for the consequences of its failure to satisfy any agreed-upon limitation on permitted investment vehicles. Although some plan sponsors would like to reserve self-directed accounts for participants who are sophisticated investors by establishing a minimum account balance, the use of such thresholds may discriminate in favor of highly compensated employees. Such discrimination would jeopardize the tax qualification and tax exemption of the plan and trust.

The educational challenges alone are significant. Studies show that most people have trouble managing a mutual fund portfolio. The problems that plan participants have with picking individual stocks are even greater. For example, a recent national survey of 401(k) plan participants commissioned by Northern Trust Retirement Consulting suggests that even sophisticated investors with access to self-directed brokerage accounts need more targeted education to take full advantage of this flexible benefit.

In Northern Trust's survey of more than 450 randomly selected, prequalified 401(k) plan participants ranging in age from eighteen to sixty-five, more than a third of respondents indicated that they do not know how to invest or do not know anything about the stock market. Another 9% indicated that they would be better off trusting investment professionals. The survey also found that even participants most likely to take advantage of a self-directed brokerage account—those who tend to be more aggressive and confident in their retirement plan management— are reluctant to use this tool.

As a result, 401(k) brokerage accounts should be approached with caution. In deciding whether to offer the option, plan fiduciaries should consider, among other issues, the investment sophistication of the workforce, the scope and effectiveness of the investment education programs, whether investment advice is made available to the participants, and the communication needed to inform the participants of the risks.

Section 404(c) Safe-Harbor Provisions

ERISA mandates significant fiduciary requirements for 401(k) plan sponsors in order to protect employees who depend on these plans for their retirement. However, ERISA Section 404(c) offers plan sponsors a "safe harbor" from their fiduciary responsibilities in cases where participants have decision-making power over their account investments. Section 404(c) relieves plan sponsors from liability for any loss that is a "direct and necessary" result of a participant's exercise of control.

In order for Section 404(c)'s safe-harbor provision to take effect, plans must meet certain procedural and substantive requirements. Procedurally, the plan must make certain disclosures to participants. Substantively, the plan must offer a range of investment options. Generally, a plan must offer a minimum of three investment options, each of which must be diversified and each of which must have materially different risk and return characteristics.

Though most plan core offerings address the investment needs of most participants, a brokerage window ensures that all participants will be able to create portfolios that are appropriate for all levels of risk and return. Ensuring that a plan qualifies for safe harbor under Section 404(c) could be important in declining markets, especially if disgruntled investors search for scapegoats.

Most fiduciaries do not understand their duties, or they understand them but don't have time to fulfill them. Self-directed brokerage accounts add another layer of complexity and exposure to plan sponsors. Most plan sponsors should know that an essential aspect of Section 404(c) compliance is fulfilling its disclosure requirements. The primary disclosure requirements relate to providing participants with the information needed to make informed decisions in exercising control over their accounts.

Section 404(c) imposes a series of disclosure requirements on both designated and non-designated investment alternatives. A brokerage account offering mutual funds or other securities would be categorized as a non-designated investment alternative under a 401(k) plan and would have to provide the following information to plan participants:

- A general description of the brokerage account, including the investment alternatives available

- An explanation of the circumstances under which participants may give investment instructions in the brokerage account

- A description of the transaction fees and expenses of the brokerage account

- The name, address and phone number of the person responsible for providing disclosures, which are required to be provided upon request

- The distribution of a prospectus to participants in connection with their initial investment in a mutual fund or other registered security

- A description of proxy voting materials, if proxy voting is passed through to participants for the investment

- Prospectuses, financial statements, reports, and other materials relating to mutual funds offered under the brokerage account, provided upon request

As an added measure of protection, plan sponsors may also require participants who want to invest through brokerage accounts to read and sign documents indicating that they understand the risks of this approach and assume responsibility for their decisions.

Administrative Fees and Cost Issues

As part of its fiduciary duties, the plan sponsor should determine whether the self-directed brokerage arrangement would increase its record-keeping and plan-audit fees. The DOL recently conducted a study of 401(k) plan fees and found that in some instances, the fees paid by a typical 401(k) plan compared unfavorably with retail investments. In some cases, the higher fees paid could be explained—additional services were provided to the plans—and in some cases, they could not. The study further concluded that participants are likely to pay most or all fees charged for investment management and increasingly likely to pay administrative fees as well.

A quarterly report from Charles Schwab Corporate Services found that a surprisingly large number of participants—nearly half (43%)—use brokerage accounts to purchase stock mutual funds. Unfortunately, in many cases, the plan participants were purchasing funds of lower fiduciary quality than the core choices in their plan in the same category.

Another problem is that purchasing no-load mutual funds through a self-directed brokerage window can increase the overall costs to the plan. Following the Frost Model DOL opinion letter, one of the key concepts today in retirement-plan cost control is mutual-fund revenue-sharing. Not all provider groups do this, but some trustees will fully disclose, collect, and then rebate certain fees to the plan sponsor.

Various internal fees from the no-load funds, such as 12b(1) fees, shareholder servicing fees, finders fees, and sub T/A fees, are collected by the plan's trustee and returned to the plan as dollar-for-dollar fee offsets. In most self-directed brokerage accounts, the mutual-fund-trail fees are retained by the brokerage house and not returned to the plan sponsor, eliminating any revenue share possibility from the self-directed brokerage assets and typically raising the overall fee level of the plan.

Overconfidence

One of the major contributions of academic behavioral finance is that it provides insights into investor behavior where such behavior sometimes appears to be irrational and counterproductive. Probably the most prevalent behavioral trait of investors using self-directed brokerage accounts is overconfidence.

It is difficult to reconcile the volume of trading observed in equity markets with the trading needs of rational investors. Rational investors make periodic contributions and withdrawals from their investment portfolios and rebalance their portfolios. The high level of ongoing trading—about 78% annual turnover on average—far exceeds these basic needs.

Overconfidence is the most simple and powerful explanation for high levels of trading on financial markets. Human beings are overconfident about their abilities, their knowledge, and their future prospects. Studies have shown that overconfident investors trade more than rational investors and that doing so lowers their expected returns. Greater overconfidence leads to greater trading and to lower expected returns.

A direct test of whether overconfidence contributes to excessive market trading is to separate investors into those more and those less prone to overconfidence. Psychologists find that in areas such as finance, men are more overconfident than women. This difference in overconfidence yields two predictable outcomes: (1) men will trade more than women, and (2) the performance of men will be hurt more by excessive trading than the performance of women.

Chart 14-1: Comparison of Annual Trading Rates

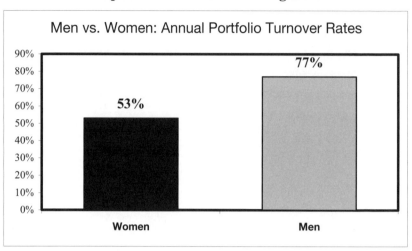

When compared with the portfolios they had in place at the beginning of the year, both men and women earned net monthly returns that were lower than those earned by the portfolio they held at the beginning of the year. Men earned returns lower than women and in direct proportion to their increased trading activity.

Other studies have shown the same trend. Two finance professors, Brad Barber and Terrance Odean, studied the performances of 66,465 households with discount brokerage accounts. Households that traded actively earned 6.7% less on their investments each year than the households that seldom traded.

Odean also found that investors had a strong tendency to chase past performance. On average, the stocks they bought had higher returns over the previous two years than the stocks they sold. Investors also were more likely to sell stocks with positive two-year track records than to sell stocks with negative returns. Investors tended to buy stocks with above-average volatility. Yet returns were below market average. So the average investor underperformed the market by an even larger margin on a risk-adjusted basis.

The Unified Trust Company Study of 401(k) Self-Directed Brokerage Accounts

Unified Trust sought to determine whether the generally poor outcome of self-directed brokerage accounts is also applicable to the ERISA market subsegment. We found that 72% of self-directed brokerage accounts underperformed a model portfolio. The average account underperformed by 4.72%.

The primary goal of this study was to identify whether participants using self-directed brokerage account options in qualified retirement plans were exceeding or lagging the performance of the core options in their plans. A secondary goal was to determine the extent of asset class diversification achieved by each participant. Sixty-one brokerage accounts were examined with a collective market value of $12.5 million during the 2002–2003 period. Because we have generally discouraged this approach, self-directed brokerage assets represent less than 2% of all assets of the trust company. But the sample size is large enough to draw meaningful conclusions and does represent 100% of the Internet-driven participant-directed brokerage accounts that Unified Trust Company maintains for ERISA plans.

Account Demographics

- Although the plan sponsors offered the self-directed brokerage account to all participants, virtually 100% of users were highly compensated and highly educated professionals.

- Accounts ranged in size from $1,100 to $1,300,865.

- The median account value was $75,952.

- Most users were between the ages of thirty-five and forty-eight.

Asset Allocation

- Most participants managed their accounts either very aggressively or very conservatively.

- Ninety-eight percent of assets consisted of equities (stocks or stocks funds) plus cash.

- The overall asset allocation was 68% equities and 30% cash.

- Fifty-five percent of accounts held at least 75% of the portfolio in equities.

- Thirty-one percent of accounts held at least 90% of the portfolio in equities and 22% of accounts held at least 80% of the portfolio in cash.

Investment Performance

- Seventy-six percent of account returns were below the S&P 500 return.

- Sixty-three percent of account returns were below a blended return of 68% stocks, 30% cash, and 2% bonds—the overall asset allocation of the accounts.

- Seventy-two percent of account returns were below the core fund model portfolio for their plan (equivalent asset allocation).

- Larger portfolios tended to fare worse than smaller portfolios.

- Compared with model portfolios constructed from the plan's core funds, the overall asset-weighted performance lag was 4.70%, and accounts greater than $250,000 lagged by 5.18%.

Chart 14-2: Number of Accounts Underperforming Benchmarks

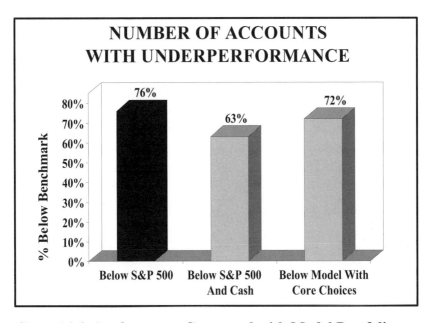

NUMBER OF ACCOUNTS WITH UNDERPERFORMANCE

Chart 14-3: Performance Compared with Model Portfolios

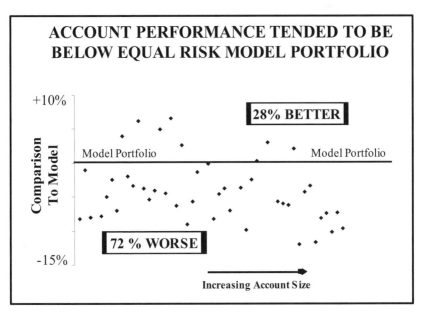

ACCOUNT PERFORMANCE TENDED TO BE BELOW EQUAL RISK MODEL PORTFOLIO

For Further Reading

Bajtelsmit, V., and Bernasek, A. "Why Do Women Invest Differently Than Men?" *Financial Counseling and Planning* 7 (1996).

Bajtelsmit, V., and Vanderhei, J. "Risk Aversion and Pension Investment Choices." In *Positioning Pensions for the Twenty-first Century*. Edited by Michael S. Gordon, Olivia S. Mitchell, and Marc M. Twinney. Philadelphia: University of Pennsylvania Press, (1997).

Barber, B., and Odean, T. *Boys Will Be Boys: Gender, Overconfidence, and Common Stock Investment.*, President and Fellows of Harvard College and the Massachusetts Institute of Technology, (2000).

Barber, Brad M., and Terrance Odean. "Trading Is Hazardous to Your Wealth: The Common Stock Investment Performance of Individual Investors." *Journal of Finance* 15, no. 2 (April 2000).

Deaux, K., and Emswiller, T. "Explanations of Successful Performance on Sex-linked Tasks: What Is Skill for the Male Is Luck for the Female." *Journal of Personality and Social Psychology* 29 (1974).

Deaux, K., and Farris, E. "Attributing Causes for One's Own Performance: The Effects of Sex, Norms, and Outcome." *Journal of Research in Personality* 11 (1977).

Griffin, D., and Tversky, A. "The Weighing of Evidence and the Determinants of Confidence." *Cognitive Psychology* 24 (1992).

Grinblatt, M., and Titman, S. "Performance Measurement without Benchmarks: An Examination of Mutual Fund Returns." *Journal of Business* 66 (1993).

Hinz, R., McCarthy, D., and Turner, J. "Are Women Conservative Investors? Gender Differences in Participant-directed Pension Investments." *In Positioning Pensions for the Twenty-first Century* (2000).

Jensen, M. "Risk, the Pricing of Capital Assets, and Evaluation of Investment Portfolios." *Journal of Business* (1969).

Lewellen, W., Lease R., and Schlarbaum, G. "Patterns of Investment Strategy and Behavior among Individual Investors." *Journal of Business* (1977).

Odean, T. "Do Investors Trade Too Much?" *American Economic Review* (1999).

Odean, T., "Volume, Volatility, Price, and Profit When All Traders Are Above Average." *Journal of Finance* (1998).

Papke, L. "Individual Financial Decisions in Retirement Savings Plans: The Role of Participant Direction." Working paper, Michigan State University, (1998).

Reish, F., Ashton, B., and Reich, G. "Is It Prudent to Offer Brokerage Accounts to 401(k) Participants?" Reish, Luftman, Reicher, and Cohen, (2001).

Schultz, C., "Fiduciary Liability of Individually Directed Accounts in Defined Contribution Plans." Lawson & Chambers, (2000).

Chapter 15

Model Portfolios Are Superior to Lifestyle Funds

Chapter Summary

Earlier chapters pointed out the importance of asset allocation and asset quality. However, even when participants' plans contain funds of high asset quality, many participants do not understand or apply effective asset-allocation policies. This is in stark contrast to successful defined benefit plans, where virtually every plan has a detailed asset-allocation investment policy managed by specialists who are hired by the plan sponsor.

We examined lifestyle funds and model portfolios to determine which of these choices give the best asset allocation and asset quality. We conclude that a model portfolio is superior on both counts. A model portfolio is more likely to improve participant retirement success.

A model portfolio is a single selection of a prearranged series of high-quality mutual funds in a specific weighting designed for the plan participant's risk tolerance and needs. It can be automatically rebalanced without any action on the part of the plan participant. Annual rebalancing is a simple and effective tool that can help plan participants improve their success rates. It is most effective when it is applied to the plan participant's account via a default success pathway with model portfolios.

Which Is Better for Participant Success: Lifestyle Funds or Model Portfolios?

Many retirement plan experts and commentators recommend that plan sponsors provide a comprehensive investment solution, which can be delivered either as a single fund or a single choice. Taking into account participants' inertia and procrastination behaviors, the more the solution can be delivered via a default pathway, the more likely it is to be successful. A lifestyle fund seeks to deliver this comprehensive solution in a single fund; a model portfolio seeks to deliver it in a single choice.

The comprehensive investment solution should provide features that will help solve the following participant investment problems:

1. Participant inertia and desire for professional oversight. Extensive observations of participant behavior reveal that most retirement plan participants are relatively unengaged, yet such participants desire to benefit from professional oversight. A comprehensive solution that provides professional management while requiring limited engagement by plan participants can meet this goal.

2. Choice overload. Studies show that investors are overwhelmed by too many choices in their retirement plans and that they make less than optimal decisions. A comprehensive solution eliminates the choice overload that results from too many options.

3. Participant knowledge. Despite repeated attempts at education, studies reveal that most retirement plan participants have limited knowledge of basic investment concepts. Typically, investors do not understand, for example, bond market risk or how to use effective tools to optimize asset allocation. A comprehensive solution requires little or no investment expertise.

4. Participant attitudes. Research has shown that many plan participants maintain a short attention span concerning investment issues. For a sizable number, anxiety is a factor. The participant perceives the subject as too difficult and finds just thinking about it stressful. A comprehensive solution will appeal to plan participants who are simply not interested in monitoring their investments, even if they understand how important this is to their financial well-being. As we have mentioned earlier, awareness does not translate into appropriate action.

The concept of lifestyle funds and model portfolios arose from the observation that many experts believed it a serious mistake to allow 401(k)s to offer narrow industry funds, such as biotech or housing stocks. From time to time, these sectors blow up themselves and their investors. Experience has shown that most investors enter the hot sector late. During the boom times, to many plan participants, diversification simply meant three different large-cap growth funds, even though the participants' portfolios had ineffective asset allocation.

Most plans, if not all plans, should offer a comprehensive solution. The discretionary trustee should study the same types of plan data that are used to decide on other investment options in a plan. The participant population should be examined to gauge investment knowledge and sophistication. Employee demographics, such as age, education level, savings rates, and risk profile, should provide insight into these areas. The strongest indicator of overall knowledge and motivation is participant behavior.

Many commentators now recommend that plans give more thought to single-choice portfolios. A single-choice portfolio can be in the form of a lifestyle fund or a model portfolio. Participants get a specific mix of stocks and bonds that work for people of a certain age and risk-tolerance attitude. An investment committee adjusts the fund or fund mix from time to time so that it always tracks its original investment goal.

A lifestyle fund is a distinct mutual fund or collective investment fund that invests in a portfolio of underlying stock and bond mutual funds in a specific asset allocation. In other words, a lifestyle fund is usually a fund of funds. A model portfolio is a single selection of a prearranged series of mutual funds in a specific weighting designed for the plan participant's risk tolerance and needs. In a model portfolio, the plan participant directly invests in the target mutual-fund portfolio with a single selection.

So far, lifestyle funds haven't proved overwhelmingly popular with employees. Despite the good intention, lifestyle funds have had little effect in improving participant success. This may be because they were not well explained or because participants simply did not understand how to utilize them.

Studies reveal that only about one in three plan participants use lifestyle funds when they are offered. Of those who do, a majority combine the lifestyle fund with other funds and defeat its purpose.

One theoretical advantage of the model portfolio over a mutual fund holding other mutual funds is that a potential second layer of fund fees is avoided. A second advantage is that most lifestyle funds use mutual funds from the same mutual fund company—giving a proprietary taint to the objectivity of fund selection and replacement.

With a lifestyle fund, the plan sponsor is stuck with every fund that is part of the lifestyle fund portfolio. There is no opportunity to replace an individual fund that is of low asset quality. In contrast, a model portfolio is made up of mutual funds that are selected and monitored on an objective basis. An individual fund within a model portfolio can be replaced.

Simply offering several lifestyle funds in addition to regular funds does not solve the choice overload many plan participants face. The more choices participants have, the more comparisons they need to make and the more information they have to process. Paradoxically the addition of lifestyle funds can exacerbate the choice-overload problem that they were designed to solve. Model portfolios, particularly along default pathways, do not produce choice overload and help participants deal with too many choices in an effective way.

The problem of plan participants defeating the purpose of lifestyle funds by combining them with other funds can be solved. Using a model-portfolio approach, the plan can allow a participant to select only a single model portfolio. By allowing participants to invest in just one model portfolio, the participants will always have diversification and proper asset-allocation strategies. Such an approach is vastly superior to simply offering a smattering of lifestyle funds mixed with other funds and relying upon participants to build their own asset allocations.

In addition to offering several model portfolios, the plan should provide at least two default model portfolios for participants who make no investment selections. (see Figure 15-1) For example, the plan could offer a 40:60 stock:fixed-income asset-allocation model portfolio for participants over the age of fifty and a 60:40 stock:fixed-income asset allocation for participants under the age of fifty. The plan sponsor should be aware that it is possible that the plan may not be able to rely upon ERISA Section 404(c) protection under such an approach. However, the discretionary trustee would be prudent in the selection, monitoring, and replacement of investments as well as diversification of plan assets under ERISA Section 404(a).

Unified Trust Company offers six model portfolios. The six are: Ultra Conservative 100, Conservative 20 80, Balanced 40 60, Balanced 60 40, Aggressive 80 20 and Ultra Aggressive 100. Each portfolio is comprised of funds with acceptable UFMI® scores, usually in the top 25% of their peer group.

Table 15-1: Key Differences between Model Portfolios and Lifestyle Funds

PARAMETER	MODEL PORTFOLIO	LIFESTYLE FUND
Participant Can Select Multiple Choices	No	Yes
Default Pathway "Ease of Use"	Yes	No
Participant Can View Underlying Funds	Always	Difficult
Underlying Fund Asset Quality	Yes	No
Replacement of Failing Underlying Fund	Yes	No
"Best Of Class" Underlying Funds	Yes	No- Single Family
Monitored Against Benchmarks	Always	Sometimes
Likelihood of Success	Very High	Usually Low

Figure 15-1: Model Portfolio Default Pathway

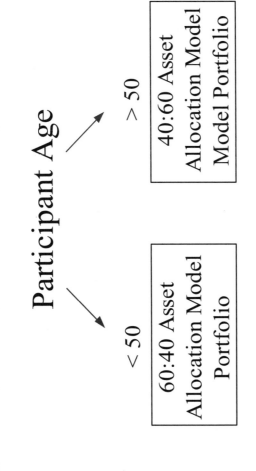

Participant Age

< 50

> 50

60:40 Asset Allocation Model Portfolio

40:60 Asset Allocation Model Model Portfolio

Model Portfolio Asset Allocation

The discretionary trustee will construct a series of six risk-adjusted asset-allocation model portfolios for the retirement plan. Plan participants can easily select their models by making a single selection. Participants can make their selections by completing the enrollment form during the retirement meetings, by calling the customer care center, or by going online to the Unified Retirement Counselor^{SM} Web site (www.unifiedtrust.com). A significant advantage of the model portfolios is that participants can see the underlying funds that the model holds. This helps participants understand the importance of diversification.

Since the introduction of Dr. Markowitz's mean variance optimization and the efficient frontier in the 1950s, a variety of tools has emerged to assist fiduciaries in establishing asset allocation policy. The discretionary trustee may in some cases compare results of analyses using both historical and projected assumptions. The discretionary trustee will make available to the trust investment committee the following tools to help determine allocation models for the plan:

1. Mean variance optimization (efficient frontier software)

2. Stochastic/probabilistic modeling software

3. Monte Carlo probability analysis software

The fiduciary's choice of asset classes and their subsequent allocation will have a significant effect on the long-term performance of the plan. Each underlying mutual fund in the model must pass its own fiduciary monitoring process to ensure asset quality. In selecting investment funds for the models, the discretionary trustee will rely on the UFMI$^{®}$ as the primary criterion and on a range of secondary criteria to supplement. In general, only funds scoring in the top 25% will be selected for the model portfolio.

Figure 15-2 Model Portfolio Report Page 1 Using Sortino Downside Risk Analysis

Analysis Based Upon Model Asset Allocation and Market Index Returns for Each Class

Portfolio Name	Portfolio Return	MAR Benchmark Return	Active Excess Return	Active Sortino Ratio	U-P Ratio	Upside Potential	Upside Probability	Downside Risk	Average Under Performance	Downside Probability	99th Percentile	Number of Bootstrapped Years
Ultra Conservative 100 Model	7.47%	6.14%	1.34%	0.42	1.08	3.47%	65.50%	3.20%	-2.45%	34.50%	-7.30%	1000
Conservative 20 80 Model	8.21%	7.19%	1.03%	0.26	1.04	4.04%	59.20%	3.87%	-3.02%	40.80%	-8.63%	1000
Balanced 40 60 Model	9.95%	8.24%	1.71%	0.23	0.96	7.01%	58.90%	7.29%	-5.71%	41.10%	-16.69%	1000
Balanced 60 40 Model	10.95%	9.31%	1.64%	0.16	0.95	10.04%	55.80%	10.56%	-8.36%	44.20%	-23.90%	1000
Aggressive 80 20 Model	12.20%	10.38%	1.82%	0.13	0.98	13.97%	56.80%	14.31%	-11.33%	43.20%	-32.83%	1000
Ultra Aggressive 100 Model	13.14%	11.46%	1.68%	0.09	0.88	16.64%	56.50%	18.91%	-15.04%	43.50%	-44.17%	1000

Analysis Based Upon Model Asset Allocation and Underlying Mutual Fund Returns for Each Class

Portfolio Name	Portfolio Return	MAR Benchmark Return	Active Excess Return	Active Sortino Ratio	U-P Ratio	Upside Potential	Upside Probability	Downside Risk	Average Under Performance	Downside Probability	99th Percentile	Number of Bootstrapped Years
Ultra Conservative 100 Model	9.60%	6.14%	3.46%	1.37	1.82	4.60%	85.20%	2.52%	-1.93%	14.80%	-4.72%	1000
Conservative 20 80 Model	9.99%	7.19%	2.80%	0.94	1.55	4.61%	74.30%	2.97%	-2.32%	25.70%	-6.57%	1000
Balanced 40 60 Model	11.39%	8.24%	3.14%	0.48	1.23	8.08%	66.20%	6.59%	-5.21%	33.80%	-15.86%	1000
Balanced 60 40 Model	12.40%	9.31%	3.09%	0.28	1.01	11.24%	58.90%	11.14%	-8.78%	41.10%	-25.09%	1000
Aggressive 80 20 Model	13.48%	10.38%	3.10%	0.23	1.01	13.45%	60.70%	13.26%	-10.70%	39.30%	-29.58%	1000
Ultra Aggressive 100 Model	14.25%	11.46%	2.78%	0.16	1.04	18.61%	58.60%	17.85%	-14.08%	41.40%	-42.13%	1000

Figure 15-3 Model Portfolio Review Report Page 2

Summary of Model Portfolio Holdings

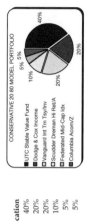

ULTRA CONSERVATIVE 100 MODEL PORTFOLIO

Security Name	UFMI[R] Score	Investment Category	% Allocation
UTC Stable Value Fund	n/a	Stable Value	60%
Dodge & Cox Income	1	Intermediate-term Bond	20%
Vanguard Int Tm Tsy/Inv	1	Intermediate Government	20%

CONSERVATIVE 20 80 MODEL PORTFOLIO

Security Name	UFMI[R] Score	Investment Category	% Allocation
UTC Stable Value Fund	n/a	Stable Value	40%
Dodge & Cox Income	1	Intermediate-term Bond	20%
Vanguard Int Tm Tsy/Inv	1	Intermediate Government	20%
Scudder Dreman Hi Ret/A	7	Large Value	10%
Federated Mid-Cap Idx	13	Mid-Cap Blend	5%
Columbia Acorn/Z	4	Small Growth	5%

BALANCED 40 60 MODEL PORTFOLIO

Security Name	UFMI[R] Score	Investment Category	% Allocation
UTC Stable Value Fund	n/a	Stable Value	20%
Dodge & Cox Income	1	Intermediate-term Bond	20%
Vanguard Int Tm Tsy/Inv	1	Intermediate Government	20%
Scudder Dreman Hi Ret/A	7	Large Value	20%
Federated Mid-Cap Idx	13	Mid-Cap Blend	10%
Columbia Acorn/Z	4	Small Growth	10%

Figure 15-4 Model Portfolio Review Report Page 3

Summary of Model Portfolio Holdings

BALANCED 60 40 MODEL PORTFOLIO

Security Name	UFMI[R] Score	Investment Category	% Allocation
UTC Stable Value Fund	n/a	Stable Value	20%
Dodge & Cox Income	1	Intermediate-term Bond	20%
Scudder Dreman Hi Ret/A	7	Large Value	15%
Vanguard Gr Idx/Inv	10	Large Growth	15%
Federated Mid-Cap Idx	13	Mid-Cap Blend	10%
Columbia Acorn/Z	4	Small Growth	10%
Royce Opport/Inv	2	Small Value	10%

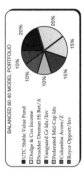

BALANCED 60 40 MODEL PORTFOLIO

- UTC Stable Value Fund — 20%
- Dodge & Cox Income — 20%
- Scudder Dreman Hi Ret/A — 10%
- Vanguard Gr Idx/Inv — 10%
- Federated Mid-Cap Idx — 10%
- Columbia Acorn/Z — 15%
- Royce Opport/Inv — 15%

AGGRESSIVE 80 20 MODEL PORTFOLIO

Security Name	UFMI[R] Score	Investment Category	% Allocation
UTC Stable Value Fund	n/a	Stable Value	10%
Dodge & Cox Income	1	Intermediate-term Bond	10%
Scudder Dreman Hi Ret/A	7	Large Value	20%
Vanguard Gr Idx/Inv	10	Large Growth	20%
Federated Mid-Cap Idx	13	Mid-Cap Blend	20%
Columbia Acorn/Z	4	Small Growth	10%
Royce Opport/Inv	2	Small Value	10%

AGGRESSIVE 80 20 MODEL PORTFOLIO

- UTC Stable Value Fund — 10%
- Dodge & Cox Income — 10%
- Scudder Dreman Hi Ret/A — 10%
- Vanguard Gr Idx/Inv — 20%
- Federated Mid-Cap Idx — 20%

ULTRA AGGRESSIVE 100 MODEL PORTFOLIO

Security Name	UFMI[R] Score	Investment Category	% Allocation
Scudder Dreman Hi Ret/A	7	Large Value	15%
Vanguard Gr Idx/Inv	10	Large Growth	15%
SSgA S&P 500 Index	5	Large Blend	20%
Federated Mid-Cap Idx	13	Mid-Cap Blend	20%
Columbia Acorn/Z	4	Small Growth	15%
Royce Opport/Inv	2	Small Value	15%

ULTRA AGGRESSIVE 100 MODEL PORTFOLIO

- Scudder Dreman Hi Ret/A — 15%
- Vanguard Gr Idx/Inv — 15%
- SSgA S&P 500 Index — 15%
- Federated Mid-Cap Idx — 20%
- Columbia Acorn/Z — 20%

Figure 15-5 Model Portfolio Review Report Page 4

Model Portfolio Performance Comparison

	Return Qtr	Avg Return 1 Yr	Avg Return 3 Yr	Avg Return 5 Yr
ULTRA CONSERVATIVE 100 MODEL PORTFOLIO				
Recommended Portfolio	0.77%	4.35%	6.52%	6.17%
Blended Benchmark	0.14%	1.73%	3.91%	4.50%
Performance Above Benchmark	0.63%	2.62%	2.61%	1.67%
CONSERVATIVE 20 80 MODEL PORTFOLIO				
Recommended Portfolio	3.44%	10.62%	6.46%	6.78%
Blended Benchmark	2.54%	7.33%	2.71%	3.72%
Performance Above Benchmark	0.89%	3.29%	3.76%	3.06%
BALANCED 40 60 MODEL PORTFOLIO				
Recommended Portfolio	6.10%	16.89%	6.41%	7.39%
Blended Benchmark	4.95%	12.94%	1.50%	2.94%
Performance Above Benchmark	1.16%	3.96%	4.91%	4.44%
BALANCED 60 40 MODEL PORTFOLIO				
Recommended Portfolio	8.99%	26.03%	5.72%	7.41%
Blended Benchmark	7.35%	18.54%	0.29%	2.16%
Performance Above Benchmark	1.64%	7.49%	5.43%	5.24%
AGGRESSIVE 80 20 MODEL PORTFOLIO				
Recommended Portfolio	11.35%	31.34%	4.56%	7.08%
Blended Benchmark	9.76%	23.34%	-2.36%	0.50%
Performance Above Benchmark	1.58%	8.01%	6.92%	6.58%
ULTRA AGGRESSIVE 100 MODEL PORTFOLIO				
Recommended Portfolio	14.00%	39.08%	3.91%	7.33%
Blended Benchmark	12.17%	28.67%	-4.05%	-0.57%
Performance Above Benchmark	1.83%	10.41%	7.96%	7.90%

(1) Returns longer than 1 year are annualized. Past performance does not guarantee future results. Not Covered by FDIC Insurance. A fund may be worth more or less when sold. See attached sheets for additional disclosures.

Figure 15-6 Model Portfolio Review Ultra Conservative 100 Report

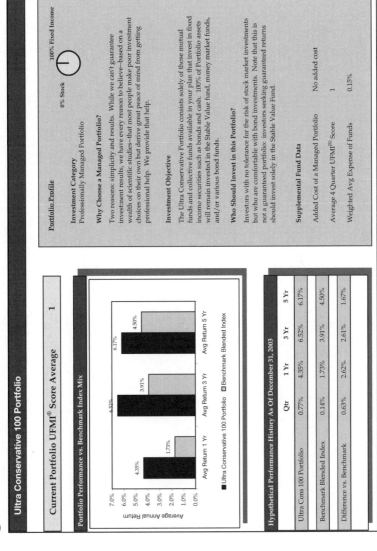

Ultra Conservative 100 Portfolio

Current Portfolio UFMI® Score Average 1

Portfolio Performance vs. Benchmark Index Mix

Average Annual Return

	Avg Return 1 Yr	Avg Return 3 Yr	Avg Return 5 Yr
Ultra Conservative 100 Portfolio	4.35%	6.52%	6.17%
Benchmark Blended Index	1.73%	3.91%	4.50%

■ Ultra Conservative 100 Portfolio ☐ Benchmark Blended Index

Hypothetical Performance History As Of December 31, 2003

	Qtr	1 Yr	3 Yr	5 Yr
Ultra Cons 100 Portfolio	0.77%	4.35%	6.52%	6.17%
Benchmark Blended Index	0.14%	1.73%	3.91%	4.50%
Difference vs. Benchmark	0.63%	2.62%	2.61%	1.67%

Portfolio Profile

0% Stock 100% Fixed Income

Investment Category
Professionally Managed Portfolio

Why Choose a Managed Portfolio?

Two reasons: simplicity and results. While we can't guarantee investment results, we have every reason to believe—based on a wealth of scientific studies—that most people make poor investment choices on their own but derive great peace of mind from getting professional help. We provide that help.

Investment Objective

The Ultra Conservative Portfolio consists solely of those mutual funds and collective funds available in your plan that invest in fixed income securities such as bonds and cash. 100% of Portfolio assets will remain invested in the Stable Value fund, money market funds, and/or various bond funds.

Who Should Invest in this Portfolio?

Investors with no tolerance for the risk of stock market investments but who are comfortable with bond investments. Note that this is not a guaranteed portfolio: investors seeking guaranteed returns should invest solely in the Stable Value Fund.

Supplemental Fund Data

Added Cost of a Managed Portfolio	No added cost
Average 4 Quarter UFMI® Score	1
Weighted Avg Expense of Funds	0.15%

Figure 15-7 Model Portfolio Review Conservative 20 80 Report

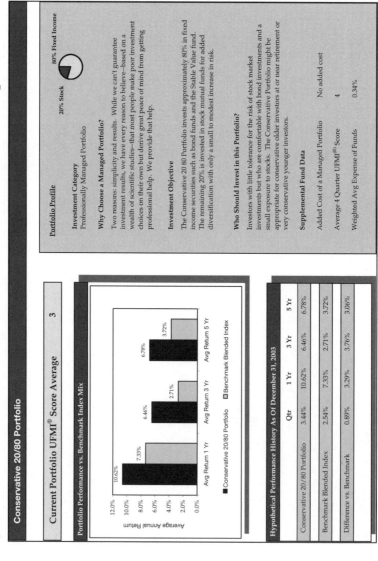

Conservative 20/80 Portfolio

Current Portfolio UFMI® Score Average   3

Portfolio Performance vs. Benchmark Index Mix

Average Annual Return

- 10.62% / 7.33% — Avg Return 1 Yr
- 6.46% / 2.71% — Avg Return 3 Yr
- 6.78% / 3.72% — Avg Return 5 Yr

■ Conservative 20/80 Portfolio   ■ Benchmark Blended Index

Hypothetical Performance History As Of December 31, 2003	Qtr	1 Yr	3 Yr	5 Yr
Conservative 20/80 Portfolio	3.44%	10.62%	6.46%	6.78%
Benchmark Blended Index	2.54%	7.33%	2.71%	3.72%
Difference vs. Benchmark	0.89%	3.29%	3.76%	3.06%

Portfolio Profile

20% Stock   80% Fixed Income

Investment Category
Professionally Managed Portfolio

Why Choose a Managed Portfolio?

Two reasons: simplicity and results. While we can't guarantee investment results, we have every reason to believe—based on a wealth of scientific studies—that most people make poor investment choices on their own but derive great peace of mind from getting professional help. We provide that help.

Investment Objective

The Conservative 20 80 Portfolio invests approximately 80% in fixed income securities such as bond funds and the Stable Value fund. The remaining 20% is invested in stock mutual funds for added diversification with only a small to modest increase in risk.

Who Should Invest in this Portfolio?

Investors with little tolerance for the risk of stock market investments but who are comfortable with bond investments and a small exposure to stocks. The Conservative Portfolio might be appropriate for conservative older investors at or near retirement or very conservative younger investors.

Supplemental Fund Data

Added Cost of a Managed Portfolio	No added cost
Average 4 Quarter UFMI® Score	4
Weighted Avg Expense of Funds	0.34%

-386-

Figure 15-8 Model Portfolio Review Balanced 40 60 Report

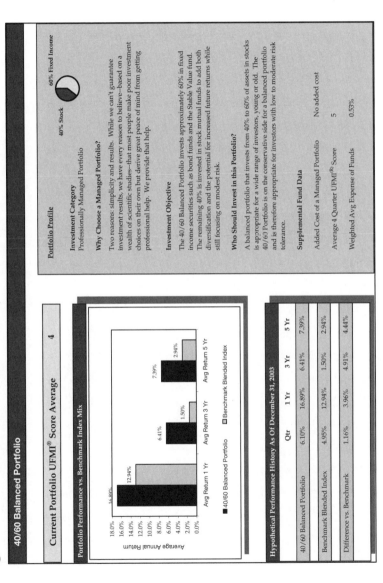

Figure 15-9 Model Portfolio Review Balanced 60 40 Report

60/40 Balanced Portfolio

Current Portfolio UFMI® Score Average   6

Portfolio Performance vs. Benchmark Index Mix

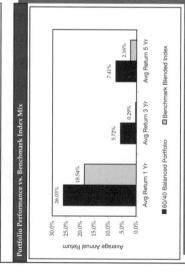

Average Annual Return

- ■ 60/40 Balanced Portfolio
- □ Benchmark Blended Index

Avg Return 1 Yr	Avg Return 3 Yr	Avg Return 5 Yr
26.03% / 18.54%	5.72% / 0.29%	7.41% / 2.16%

Hypothetical Performance History As Of December 31, 2003

	Qtr	1 Yr	3 Yr	5 Yr
60/40 Balanced Portfolio	8.99%	26.03%	5.72%	7.41%
Benchmark Blended Index	7.35%	18.54%	0.29%	2.16%
Difference vs. Benchmark	1.64%	7.49%	5.43%	5.24%

Portfolio Profile

60% Stock   40% Fixed

Investment Category
Professionally Managed Portfolio

Why Choose a Managed Portfolio?
Two reasons: simplicity and results. While we can't guarantee investment results, we have every reason to believe—based on a wealth of scientific studies—that most people make poor investment choices on their own but derive great peace of mind from getting professional help. We provide that help.

Investment Objective
The 60/40 Balanced Portfolio invests approximately 40% in fixed income securities such as bond funds and the Stable Value fund. The remaining 60% is invested in stock mutual funds to add both diversification and the potential for increased future returns with moderate risk.

Who Should Invest in this Portfolio?
A mix of 60% stocks and 40% fixed income is a common asset mix for large pension funds and is just as appropriate for individual investors, of all ages, as it is for large institutions. Investors must be comfortable investing over half of their money in stocks and committed to leaving it there long term.

Supplemental Fund Data

Added Cost of a Managed Portfolio	No added cost
Average 4 Quarter UFMI® Score	8
Weighted Avg Expense of Funds	0.56%

Figure 15-10 Model Portfolio Review Aggressive 80 20 Report

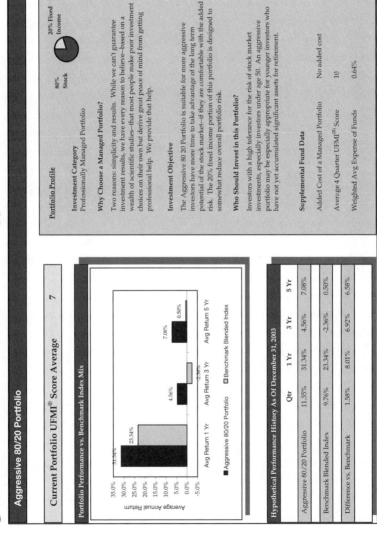

Figure 15-11 Model Portfolio Review Ultra Aggressive 100 Report

Ultra Aggressive 100 Portfolio

Current Portfolio UFMI® Score Average	7

Portfolio Performance vs. Benchmark Index Mix

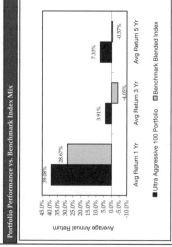

Average Annual Return

45.0%
40.0%
35.0%
30.0%
25.0%
20.0%
15.0%
10.0%
5.0%
0.0%
-5.0%
-10.0%

Avg Return 1 Yr — 39.08% / 28.67%
Avg Return 3 Yr — 3.91%
Avg Return 5 Yr — 7.33% / -0.57%

- ■ Ultra Aggressive 100 Portfolio
- □ Benchmark Blended Index

Hypothetical Performance History As Of December 31, 2003

	Qtr	1 Yr	3 Yr	5 Yr
Ultra Aggressive 100 Portfolio	14.00%	39.08%	3.91%	7.33%
Benchmark Blended Index	12.17%	28.67%	-4.05%	-0.57%
Difference vs. Benchmark	1.83%	10.41%	7.96%	7.90%

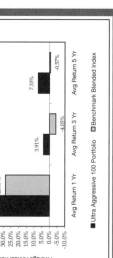

100% Stock

Portfolio Profile

Investment Category
Professionally Managed Portfolio

Why Choose a Managed Portfolio?
Two reasons: simplicity and results. While we can't guarantee investment results, we have every reason to believe—based on a wealth of scientific studies—that most people make poor investment choices on their own but derive great peace of mind from getting professional help. We provide that help.

Investment Objective
The Ultra Aggressive 100 Portfolio consists solely of those mutual funds and collective funds available in your plan that invest in stocks. 100% of Portfolio assets will remain fully invested in stock funds.

Who Should Invest in this Portfolio?
Investors with a high tolerance for the risk of stock market investments who seek the highest possible long term returns and are comfortable taking on added risk. An all stock portfolio is suitable mostly for younger investors who have not yet accumulated significant retirement assets.

Supplemental Fund Data

Added Cost of a Managed Portfolio	No added cost
Average 4 Quarter UFMI® Score	11
Weighted Avg Expense of Funds	0.65%

For Further Reading

Balzer, L. "Measuring Investment Risk: A Review." *Journal of Investing* 3, no. 3 (1994).

Brinson, G., L. and Beebower, G. "Determinants of Portfolio Performance." *Financial Analysts Journal* 42, no. 4, 39–48 (1986).

Brinson, G., L. and Beebower. "Determinants of Portfolio Performance II: An Update." *Financial Analysts Journal* 47, no. 3 40–48 (1991).

Gibson, R. "Asset Allocation: Balancing Financial Risk." New York: Irwin Professional Publishing, (1996).

Hensel, C., Ezra C., and Ilkiw, J. "The Importance of the Asset Allocation Decision." *Financial Analysts Journal* 47, no. 4,65–72 (1991).

Ibbotson, R., and Kaplan, P. "Does Asset Allocation Policy Explain 40, 90, or 100 Percent of Performance?" *Financial Analysts Journal* 29, no. 7, 26–32 (2000).

Kasten, G. *Optimizing Investment Outcomes for Retirement Plan Participants.* Lexington, Ky.: Unified Trust Company, N.A., (2002).

Quinn, J. "Burned! Why We Need to Fix the 401(k)." *Newsweek,* (August 19, 2002).

Lucas, W. "Study Finds Participants Don't Understand Lifestyle Funds." *Employee Benefit News*, IMG Media, (November 10, 2000).

Chapter 16

Investment Advice Is Superior to General Education

Chapter Summary

Most efforts to influence participants in workplace-based retirement plans to take full advantage of the investment benefits that are available to them have limited impact. Despite years of educational initiatives, retirement success probability for most Americans remains low. Retirement success requires the triad of adequate savings, proper asset allocation, and high asset quality.

Some plan sponsors now seek to do more than educate their participants about generally accepted diversification and investment principles. Today, many plan sponsors, under the complex legal constraints of ERISA, are looking for outside experts to provide fiduciary-level investment advice to plan participants. In addition, the DOL has recently issued a favorable opinion letter detailing how to offer plan participants investment advice.

Advice moves beyond education. Advice is participant-specific, and it helps participants build portfolios for their individual situations. Advice includes specific recommendations concerning which mutual funds to invest in and in what proportions. Advice-driven asset allocation can be maintained through the use of model portfolios. In its role as discretionary trustee, Unified Trust Company uses the UFMI® to measure and maintain asset quality. Advice can be delivered in person, online, or over the telephone to individual participants. Default pathways are the preferred medium

Plan Participants Need Investment Advice Rather Than General Education

Any program that produces for most participants performance in line with or above appropriately equity/fixed income benchmarks is a superior program. For most of the past decade, plan sponsors and other fiduciaries have attempted to provide educational programs to their plan participants. For the most part, these educational programs have not been successful in producing defined-contribution-plan participants with investing skills similar to the experts employed to manage defined benefit plans. The savings rates, investment performance, and appropriate real rates of return have been insufficient to produce retirement success for most participants, with most earning negative real rates of return.

Some commentators raised questions about the investing skills of plan participants during the 1991–1999 bull market for stocks. The worldwide bear market in equities during 2000–2002 has taken its toll on retirement plan investors, with more than $1 trillion lost in retirement plans. Some experts have questioned the very premise of participant-directed 401(k) plans versus traditional pension plans. After the stock market dive and the Enron disaster, a disturbing question has bubbled up: How capable is the American public of managing these enormous sums?

During the equity market bubble years, investing looked like a piece of cake. But just when Americans thought they were headed for easy street and early retirement, the deepest bear market since the late 1930s slammed them. After the market decline, plan participants were hundreds of billions of dollars behind with no road map for catching up. ERISA Section 404(c) requires that participants be given sufficient education to make investment choices. ERISA does not require plans to offer investment advice to participants who have the right to direct the investment of their accounts, but under the general prudence standard of

ERISA, it may be imprudent for a plan not to offer investment advice to its participants.

The DOL has specifically addressed the connection between 404(c) "education" and investment advice in Interpretive Bulletin 96-1, noting that participant investment advice and education are not required to obtain the relief afforded by 404(c). ERISA Section 404(a)(1)(B) requires that plan fiduciaries discharge their duties "with the care, skill, prudence and diligence under the circumstances then prevailing that a prudent man acting in a like capacity and familiar with such matters would use in the conduct of an enterprise of a like character and with like aims."

In a participant-directed plan, a key role of the plan fiduciary is to select and monitor prudently the investment options made available to participants. But, DOL regulations under section 404(c) specifically state that fiduciaries have no duty to provide investment advice to participants under a 404(c) plan. However, there may be an additional duty under the "circumstances then prevailing." For example, if the plan sponsor knows that the workforce is unsophisticated about investing, what would a knowledgeable and prudent person do in a similar situation? Although we are not aware of any case law or regulatory pronouncement that would impose a requirement for providing investment advice to participants, under the general prudence rule, an argument could be made that plan fiduciaries cannot fulfill their duty to act prudently if they do not make investment advice available.

Even if there is no requirement that a plan provide investment advice, fiduciaries may want to make investment advice available as a method to improve participant retirement success. The true fiduciary goal of the plan sponsor should be to have a system in place that will allow the participants to have a high probability of meeting the retirement goals. In addition, if advice is available and the participants make use of it, either the investment results will be superior, or the fiduciaries may have an

Chart 16-1: Investment Performance of Plan Participants Lags Inflation, the Average Mutual Fund, and Market Benchmarks

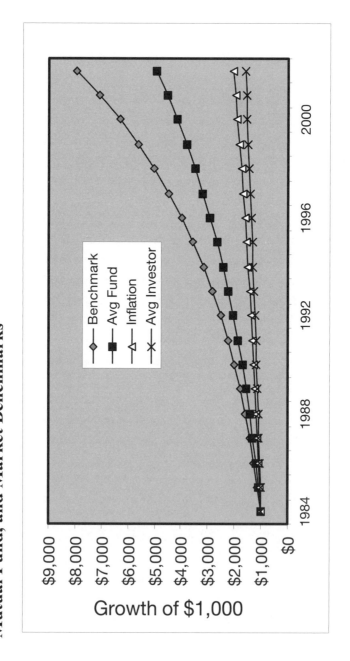

additional line of defense against participant claims and the fiduciaries could assert that they had selected and monitored prudently the investment advisor. Conversely, if the participants fail to take advantage of the advice available to them, the fiduciaries may be able to defend against participant claims on the basis that the fiduciaries took prudent steps to assist the participants in making investment choices by offering a qualified investment advisory service, but that the participant(s) failed to take advantage of the opportunity.

As with any designation of a service provider to a plan, the designation of a person to provide investment advice to plan participants and beneficiaries is an exercise of discretionary authority or control with respect to management of the plan; therefore, persons making the designation must act prudently and solely in the interest of plan participants and beneficiaries, both in making the designation and in continuing such designation. In addition, the designation of an investment advisor to serve as a fiduciary may give rise to cofiduciary liability if the person making and continuing such designation fails to act prudently and solely in the interest of plan participants and beneficiaries, or knowingly participates in, conceals, or fails to make reasonable efforts to correct a known breach by the investment advisor.

The DOL also has noted that a plan sponsor or fiduciary would have no fiduciary responsibility or liability with respect to the actions of a third party selected by a participant or beneficiary to provide education or investment advice where the plan sponsor or fiduciary neither selects nor endorses the educator or advisor, nor otherwise makes arrangements with the educator or advisor to provide such services. However, the DOL has noted that, in the context of an ERISA section 404(c) plan, neither the designation of a person to provide education nor the designation of a fiduciary to provide investment advice to participants and beneficiaries would, in itself, give rise to fiduciary liability for loss, or with respect to any breach of ERISA, that is the direct and necessary result of a participant's or beneficiary's exercise of independent control.

Specific Advice Can Improve Outcomes

Investment success requires both asset allocation and asset quality. The plan sponsor, discretionary trustee, retirement committee, and other fiduciaries have a duty under ERISA to monitor investments to maintain asset quality. In its role as discretionary trustee, Unified Trust Company, N.A., uses the UFMI to measure and maintain asset quality. In addition, the plan sponsor must educate participants about asset allocation and other generally accepted investment principles. However, education is not advice. Advice is much more specific and helps participants build portfolios for their individual situations. Advice includes specific recommendations concerning which mutual funds to invest in and in what proportion.

Topics Covered by Investment Advice

1. An assessment of the individual participant's needs and risk tolerance
2. An assessment of the individual participant's funding level
3. Recommendation of a specific asset allocation model for the participant via model portfolios
4. Recommendation of a specific selection of mutual funds for the participant
5. Demonstration of the recommended portfolio's historical performance against appropriate risk-adjusted market benchmarks
6. Implementation of the recommended asset allocation model and specific mutual funds for the participant
7. Annual or more frequent rebalancing of the participant's asset allocation model to align the account to the recommended asset-allocation percentages
8. Calculation of the participant's retirement success probability both before and after implementation of the investment advice
9. Ongoing monitoring of the individual mutual funds to make sure that the funds are performing appropriately and are prudent choices

Data from a national study demonstrate the effectiveness and outcome improvement of professional investment advice. After an advice program was initiated, participants steadily increased their use of the online advice program. Use was especially strong when the plan sponsor promoted the program. When participants had Internet access, their use of advice rose from 25% the first year to 51% the second year and 74% the third year.

The data demonstrated that 86% of advised portfolios outperformed non-advised portfolios. The performance improvement was 1.48% in bull markets and 3.12% in bear markets. Participants using advice raised their savings rates from 6% to 10%. Finally, participants receiving advice in the age-sixty-five-and-older category reduced their overall risk exposures. The proliferation of investment options combined with the bursting of the stock market bubble increased risks for retirement plan participants. The result is a growing need for more sophisticated and robust investment advice that is participant-specific.

Chart 16-2: Performance Improvement from Investment Advice

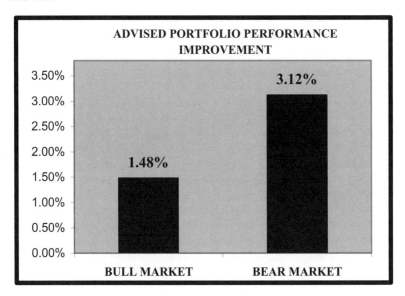

For Further Reading

Bollen, N., and Busse, J. On the Timing Ability of Mutual Fund Managers." *Journal of Finance* 56, 1075–1094 (2001).

Brown, K., Harlow, V. "Staying the Course: The Impact of Investment Style Consistency on Mutual Fund Performance." Dallas: University of Texas Press, (2002).

Brown, S., and Goetzmann, W. "Performance Persistence." *Journal of Finance* 50, 679–698 (1995).

"Department of Labor Advisory Opinion 2001-09A." U.S. Department of Labor, (December 14, 2001).

Feinberg, P. "401(k) Participants Sniff at Internet Advice Tools." *Pensions & Investments, New York*, (March 8, 2004).

"From High Tech to High Touch." Plan Sponsor Inc., (2003).

IOMA's Report on Managing 401(k) Plans. "How Motorola Rolled Out Online Advice for Its 401(k) and DB Plans." New York: Institute of Management and Administration, (July 2002).

"How Fast Do 401(k) Participants Warm Up to Online Advice?" *IOMA's Report on Managing 401(k) Plans.* New York: Institute of Management and Administration, (July 2002).

Jacobius, W. "Retirement Assets' Huge Drop over the Past Two Years." *Pensions & Investments, New York*, (June 10, 2002).

Jain, P., and Shuang Wu, J. "Truth in Mutual Fund Advertising: Evidence on Future Performance and Fund Flows." *Journal of Finance* 55, 937–958 (2000).

Kasten, G. "Optimizing Investment Outcomes for Retirement Plan Participants." Lexington, Ky.: Unified Trust Company, N.A., (2002).

Lucas, W. "Study Finds Participants Don't Understand Lifestyle Funds." *Employee Benefit News*, IMG Media, (November 10, 2000).

Quinn, J. "Burned! Why We Need to Fix the 401(k)." *Newsweek*, (August 19, 2002).

Saliterman, V., and Sheckley, B. "Adult Learning Principles and Pension Participant Behavior." Pension Research Council, University of Pennsylvania, (2003).

"A Guide to Fixing Your 401(k)." *Wall Street Journal*, (2003).

"The Emperor's New Mutual Funds." *Wall Street Journal*, (2003).

"Fundholder's Lament: All Bear Market, No Bull Market." *Wall Street Journal*, (2002).

"Morningstar Study Debunks Fund World's Oldest Myth." *Wall Street Journal*, (2003).

"Once High-Flying 401(k)s Pale beside Payouts from Pensions." *Wall Street Journal*, (2002).

"Retirement Plans Reduce Choices." *Wall Street Journal*, (2003).

"The Stars in the Sky Flicker, and Fund Stars Do the Same." *Wall Street Journal*, (2003).

Chapter 17

Revenue Sharing Reduces Costs

Chapter Summary

Revenue sharing is a well-kept secret in the retirement industry. This practice has created an environment that makes it hard for employers and employees to understand the true cost of their retirement services. As a fiduciary, the plan sponsor has an obligation to make sure that all expenses are appropriate and reasonable. The plan sponsor has a duty to understand the true net costs of all investment vehicles offered to plan participants. Many times service providers do not fully disclose the internal costs of the underlying investments and hide potential sources of revenue sharing that may offset some or all plan servicing costs.

Plan sponsors often mistakenly select the highest-cost vendor, because revenue-sharing payments mask the true cost of the plan. Plan sponsors are not required to select the lowest-cost vendor, but as fiduciaries, they are required to make sure that all fees paid are reasonable. A modestly higher-cost plan should have a higher level of service and improved outcomes for participants; otherwise, the fees are not reasonable. In other words, plan participants should be getting their money's worth for all fees that they pay. A discretionary trustee must disclose all revenue sources and offset any revenue received from plan investments against the discretionary trustee's fees. However, a directed trustee is not required to offset revenue received from plan investments against the directed trustee's fees. Thus, another major difference exists between directed trustees and discretionary trustees.

Plan Sponsors Must Understand and Account for Revenue-Sharing Payments

Revenue sharing is a well-kept secret in the retirement industry. This practice has created an environment that makes it hard for employers and employees to understand the true cost of their retirement services. Gross inequities can exist for plan sponsors and participants alike. As a fiduciary, the plan sponsor is obligated to make sure that all expenses are appropriate and reasonable. The plan sponsor has a duty to understand the internal costs of all investment vehicles offered to the plan participants. Service providers often do not fully disclose the internal costs of the underlying investments and potential sources of revenue sharing that may offset some or all of plan servicing costs.

> **A discretionary trustee must disclose all revenue sources and offset any revenue received from plan investments against the discretionary trustee's fees.**

> **A directed trustee is not required to offset revenue received from plan investments against the directed trustee's fees.**

Revenue sharing is a blanket term for the practice of transferring "soft" dollars between mutual funds and administration service providers who support 401(k) and other types of defined contribution plans. Until recently, there has not been a comprehensive source of objective information about the sources and uses of revenue from mutual funds in support of retirement programs that use mutual funds and related investment products. Most plan sponsors, even sophisticated, middle-market companies, do not have the information technology, skills, tools, or time to fully understand and manage the expense and revenue realities of their 401(k) plans. Most software programs have been inadequate to track and record revenue-sharing monies owed to the plan.

A Review of the Rules

ERISA Section 404(a)(1)(a): The Exclusive Benefit Rule. Fiduciaries must act in the exclusive interests of plan participants and beneficiaries. In other words, fiduciaries may not even consider the size of their own compensation in making investment decisions for the plan; they may consider only what is best for participants.

ERISA Section 406(b): A broad prohibition against fiduciary self-dealing in a variety of forms. In the case of revenue sharing, fiduciaries are prohibited from receiving compensation of any sort that might influence the decision-making process. As a .50% payment by Fund A might influence a fiduciary to choose Fund A over Fund B, which only pays .25%, the receipt of such payments is a prohibited transaction. Overall, fiduciaries may not "receive any consideration from any party dealing with a plan in connection with a transaction involving plan assets," although specific exemptions exist.

DOL Advisory Opinion 1997-16A: The Aetna Letter. In the Aetna letter, the DOL clarifies that a nondiscretionary nonfiduciary can keep revenue-sharing payments. More importantly, however, the Aetna Letter provides a crucial insight: that plan fiduciaries have an obligation to discover the full amounts of compensation from whatever source derived, including revenue-sharing payments. In other words, the DOL believes that plan fiduciaries are expected to discover the existence and amounts of revenue-sharing payments to all vendors. Considering that the available disclosure is limited, proper discovery can be quite difficult.

DOL Advisory Opinion 1997-15A: The Frost Letter. In the Frost Letter, the DOL clarifies that a fiduciary with control over the investment selection for a plan may collect revenue-sharing payments on behalf of the plan but must account for each payment and pass it on 100% to the plan in the form of an expense offset or direct payment. The problem with the Frost Letter is that it goes further; it suggests that even an

ERISA investment advisor or other fiduciary who does not have discretion is also bound by the prohibition against keeping the revenue-sharing payments. Thus, a directed trustee, a fiduciary with no discretion over plan assets, could be prohibited from accepting revenue-sharing payments, contrary to the existing practice of many directed trustees and other vendors. This concern led ABN/AMRO to seek clarification, which the DOL provided in 2003-09A.

DOL Advisory Opinion 2003-09A: The ABN/Amro Letter. In this letter, the DOL solved the problem created by the language in the Frost Letter by clarifying that a directed trustee with no discretion over plan assets could keep revenue-sharing payments. Thus, those vendors who offer cofiduciary services under various labels but do not accept true discretion over plan assets avoid the problem of not being permitted to continue accepting revenue-sharing payments.

Because most plan platforms are predicated on such payments, a different ruling from the DOL would have had immediate and far-reaching consequences for the industry. In the ABN/Amro case, ABN/Amro serves as plan trustee, but as a directed trustee, not a discretionary trustee, and even though a trustee is always a fiduciary—which would seem to require conformance with the Frost Letter—this ruling agreed with ABN/Amro that it could keep the revenue-sharing payments. Over the last several years, several significant cases have been brought claiming breaches of fiduciary responsibility based upon 401(k) plan investment-fund selection, in some cases related to retail (through a broker) versus institutional (without broker involvement) fund use. In one such case, a substantial amount was paid (more than $25 million) as part of a negotiated settlement. Others are still pending. Though three or four high-visibility court cases do not represent a tidal wave of litigation, some observers suggest that in the current environment, more may be expected, which may affect the decisions of other retirement plan fiduciaries.

The Frost Model: An Acid Test of Fiduciary Status

The Frost model, in which a discretionary trustee passes through 100% of all revenue-sharing payments, is in many ways an acid test of fiduciary status. Vendors that offer to serve as plan fiduciaries but keep revenue-sharing payments either are not accepting discretion—and therefore liability—or have fallen behind in their reading. Vendors that accept full discretion and fiduciary status over plan assets, however, are bound by the Frost Letter and are generally liable in the plan sponsor's place for prudent management of plan assets—at least to the extent specified in the vendor's contract or trust agreement.

Why is this test useful? Because most plan sponsors do not understand the distinction between directed and discretionary, or between a cofiduciary who is responsible for only a small part of the plan and a cofiduciary with full responsibility for plan assets. It might therefore be unclear to sponsors that vendors offering to serve in a fiduciary capacity come in all shapes and sizes and that some accept more responsibility and liability than others. The only way to be certain of the extent of a vendor's responsibilities is to study the trust or service agreement, but noncompliance with the Frost model is a simple, useful indicator.

We have seen many instances where plan sponsors can misperceive the extent of a vendor's fiduciary responsibility. For example, recently a vendor was offering to serve as "plan fiduciary," a feature that the director of human resources found very appealing. The vendor was offering a passive, directed-trustee service—custodial only—yet the plan sponsor clearly was under the impression that the vendor was accepting full liability for the plan. As the vendor followed the Aetna model, not the Frost model, with respect to revenue-sharing payments, it was not difficult to set the client straight.

Understanding the Internal Expenses of Mutual Funds and Other Investment Vehicles

Under DOL regulations, expenses must be "reasonable" for plan sponsors to meet their obligations. Compensation in excess of amounts ordinarily paid for such services by similar enterprises under like circumstances is not reasonable compensation. Studies show that more than 90% of plan sponsors cite cost as the key consideration in selecting outsourcing vendors for plan administration, but research shows that plan sponsors are unable to determine plan costs. Unified Trust Company, N.A., believes that plan sponsors and participants should receive full disclosure of mutual fund fees and expenses. A fund's fees and expenses are required by law to be clearly disclosed to investors in a standardized fee table at the front of the fund's prospectus. The fee table breaks out the fees and expenses shareholders can expect to pay when purchasing fund shares and allows investors to easily compare the cost of investing in different funds.

Direct Shareholder Fees

? **Sales charge.** A sales charge may be attached to the purchase or sale of mutual fund shares. This fee compensates financial professionals for their services.

? **Redemption fee**. This fee is paid to a fund to cover the costs, other than sales costs, involved with a redemption.

? **Exchange fee**. This fee may be charged when an investor transfers money from one fund to another within the same fund family.

? **Annual account maintenance fee**. This fee may be charged by some funds, for example, to cover the costs of providing service to low-balance accounts.

Annual Fund Operating Expenses

These fees and expenses reflect the normal costs of operating a fund. Unlike shareholder fees, these expenses are not charged directly to an investor but are deducted from fund assets before earnings are distributed to shareholders. They are a significant determinant of fund performance over time.

? **Management Fee.** This is a fee charged by a fund's investment advisor for managing the fund's portfolio of securities and providing related services.

? **Shareholder Servicing Expenses.** These expenses include, for example, fees paid to a fund's transfer agent or other groups for providing fund shareholder services, such as toll-free phone communications, help centers, computerized account services, Web site services, recordkeeping, printing, and mailing.

? **Distribution (12b-1) Fee.** This fee, if charged, is deducted from fund assets to compensate sales professionals for providing investment advice and ongoing services to mutual fund shareholders and to pay fund marketing and advertising expenses. Rule 12b-1 of the U.S. Securities and Exchange Commission allows a mutual fund, under specified circumstances, to use fund assets to pay for distribution expenses. The size of the annual 12b-1 fee can vary from 0.05% of assets to 1.00% of assets. Since the adoption of the rule in 1980, mutual funds have used 12b-1 fees, often in combination with contingent-deferred sales charges, as an alternative to front-end sales loads for compensating sales professionals for assistance provided to purchasers of fund shares. Other uses of 12b-1 fees have included advertising, sales materials, and activities involving the marketing of fund shares to new investors. Finally, mutual funds have used 12b-1 fees to pay for administrative services provided by third parties to existing fund shareholders. According to recent industry surveys, covering the costs of compensating broker-dealers for the sale of fund shares and related expenses is the most important use of 12b-1 fees. Expenses related to this type of distribution activity accounted for 63% of 12b-1 fees.

Subtransfer Agent Fees

These fees represent a portion of the compensation normally paid to fund transfer agents diverted to those performing shareholder recordkeeping, recording daily activity and handling all shareholder servicing, from issuing account statements, confirmations, and tax statements to maintaining customer service departments on behalf of the funds. Most of these duties fall to the plan's administration provider in a participant-directed, defined contribution plan, and the administrator can be compensated for taking over this function if arrangements are made and contracts negotiated. Such revenues take the form of asset-based fees, fixed fees on a per-participant basis, or a combination of both.

When paid as a per-participant fee, payment formulas for subtransfer agent fees have a broad range. Annual compensation varies from $3 per participant position (owning shares in a fund) in a given fund family to as much as $23 per position. Some funds compensate for all positions; others cap at, say, three positions within the family for any given participant. Hybrid approaches, intended to reduce exposure to adverse selection, have formulas that pay, for example, $10 per position capped at 10 basis points (0.10%) on total plan assets. Some families pay higher amounts, if the plan participant's personal information is shared by the record-keeper, on a sliding scale (for example, $3, if participant head counts only are provided; $12, if home addresses and social security numbers are provided).

Finders' Fees

Some mutual fund groups pay a one-time finder's fee for the placement of the money. Over the past decade, the number of mutual fund families paying finders' fees has diminished. Finders' fees represent an attractive revenue-sharing vehicle for plan sponsors and participants, because they are paid for by the mutual fund group. In addition, new contributions to the fund also qualify for the finder's fee. The mutual fund may pay a 1.00% finder's fee and yet have an annual expense ratio below 0.75%. Finders' fees create opportunities for plan sponsors to reduce expenses without reducing services or to increase services without increasing fees. Many plans operate with the finders' fees secretly retained by the investment broker, but a discretionary trustee must provide full disclosure of the finders' fees and the services provided. This is consistent with the DOL Frost National Bank DOL letter (U.S. Department of Labor Advisory Opinion 1997-15A-see Appendix).

Multiple Share Classes

Multiple share classes were introduced as an alternative to front-end load sales charges to compensate distribution and service firms. Shareholders pay the costs based, generally, on whether they are retail or institutional customers, their tolerance for front- or back-end sales charges, or the level of service required. A typical fund family may offer six share classes, each with a different expense ratio and revenue-sharing payment stream:

- Institutional class
- Investor class:
- "A" class (retail):
- "B" class (retail):
- "C" class (retail):
- "R" class (retirement)

Fee Transparency Often Difficult to Obtain

When plan sponsors hire independent consultants to conduct due-diligence reviews of their 401(k) plans, it is not uncommon to unearth numerous fee "surprises." As an example, Unified Trust Company, N.A., recently discovered more than $41,000 in excessive, or "hidden," charges, amounting to 52% of total plan expenses, when the company conducted a due-diligence review for a prospective client. There were enough monies from the subsequent reallocation of the plan assets to greatly enhance investment advice for the plan's roughly 125 participants, with $4.9 million in assets under management.

A surprising number of plan sponsors, about one-third, do not know the true fees they are paying. From a liability perspective, plan sponsors have a fiduciary obligation to police fund expenses periodically. But doing so involves examining much more than cost. A plan can have reasonable fees based on averages, but its value may be low, and the plan sponsor may not be getting what it is paying for. By simply benchmarking fees, the plan sponsor may be missing the opportunity to use excess dollars for the benefit of participants.

Deciphering the true cost of 401(k) services is not easy, given a highly complex value chain that involves at least one hundred combinations of cost structure and a multilayered array of administration, money management, and distribution systems. It is a bewildering task for the average HR person to know what to look for and where to look and to compile this information. This is even more the case when a vendor search is conducted once every five years. Key internal staffers in small or midsize companies that have their share of other manpower challenges typically do not have enough time, after having absorbed cutbacks, to devote to these intricate issues. Under such circumstances, plan sponsors must hire competent, independent consultants to produce total fee transparency.

Unified ERISA Revenue Tracker^{SM} Software

There are numerous inherent difficulties in tracking fees and revenue-sharing payments from mutual funds and other investment groups. Unified Trust Company, N.A., created the Unified ERISA Revenue Tracker^{SM} software system to provide several key functions:

Calculation of Revenue Receivable

The first step in the calculation process is to understand the revenue that each mutual fund owes the plan sponsor. Most mutual funds calculate their fees bill on average daily balance, but each fund family has a different method to calculate average daily balance. For example, some may actually calculate a balance every day, while others may calculate an average balance based upon the value of the fund on the first day of the month and on the last day of the month. In order to match the revenue to the plan, the receivable must be calculated in a manner consistent with the mutual-funds calculation methodology.

Verification of Revenue Payment

The next step is to verify that the mutual fund payment received is correct when compared to the amount owed to the plan. It is not uncommon for mutual fund families to make mistakes, and only the verification process can ensure that the correct amount is credited to the plan sponsor. In addition, mutual fund families sometimes change their revenue contractual agreements, and these changes must be examined to make sure that plan sponsors receive the revenue they are due.

Crediting of Revenue to Individual Plan Sponsors

Most mutual fund assets are held in omnibus accounts rather than plan-level accounts. Mutual fund revenue-sharing payments are typically at the omnibus level and must then be broken down to the plan level. At the individual plan level, the correct revenue payment is credited to the plan sponsor as a direct fee offset under the Frost model.

Benefiting from Revenue Sharing

The first step in reaping the potential benefits from revenue sharing is to find out how this element may apply to your retirement and savings plans, either now or potentially.

In short, as a fiduciary, the plan sponsor's job is to understand and document the full details of the fees your plan pays, including all investment management fees and other asset-based fees. This is the case whether your plan uses mutual funds, collective trust instruments, separate investment management accounts, brokerage accounts, an insurance contract, or any other form of funding instrument.

The practice of revenue sharing in the retirement and investment management businesses is most likely here to stay. As a fiduciary of a qualified retirement or savings plan, your obligation is to be completely aware of the fees associated with the operation of your plan. These are the steps to take:

Step 1: Require complete disclosure from all plan service providers. Require a disclosure letter for your files, signed by each investment management firm and service provider, attesting to each one's fee amount and form of compensation, including any portion of that fee paid to another party. Require a disclosure of potential conflict from each service provider. This will help to identify any parties who may be receiving or providing revenue sharing in any other form.

Step 2: Audit for the presence of revenue sharing. Read the fine print in every prospectus, with an eye toward expense items.

Step 3: Identify all services provided to your plan by any firm or individual. Measure the amount of fees each service provider receives from all sources involved in your plan.

Step 4: You are now in a position to evaluate each service provided to your plan in the context of economic benefit received for those services. There may be no misalignment. Or there may be opportunities to reduce costs or identify capacity for additional services with no added expenses to your plan.

Managing and Auditing the Process

Tracking the various revenue-sharing components can be an arduous task. Unified Trust Company, N.A., has created a revenue-sharing accounting system to track all aspects of this process. Each step of the process must be measured and verified. For example, the actual 12b(1) due from each mutual fund is calculated to verify that the amount paid by the mutual fund company matches the amount due to the plan.

Our experience has shown that many fund groups incorrectly calculate the fee and remit an incorrect payment. Once each piece of revenue share is calculated and properly accounted for, Unified Trust Company credits the fee to the plan. The plan sponsor receives regular detailed reporting illustrating all sources of revenue share and credits to the plan. An example of the billing invoice and revenue credit reporting form given to the plan sponsor is shown on the following page.

Figure 17-1: Basic Revenue Sharing Calculation

Discretionary Trustee Fee
+ Plan Administration Fee
+ Mutual Fund Trading Fee Cost
- Revenue Share (100% Pass Through)
_____

Net Billed Amount

Figure 17-2: Revenue Sharing Invoice

2353 Alexandria Drive · Suite 100 · Lexington, KY 40504

XYZ CLIENT
MAIN STREET
ANYWHERE, USA

Account Number: 000125677
Invoice Number: 1733
Invoice Date: July 02, 2003

Average Daily Balance $1,406,616.06

Fees
Recordkeeping Fee $250.00
Discretionary Trustee Fee $1,878.11

Total Fees   **$2,128.11**

Revenue Credits
12b-1 Revenue $(307.74)
Shareholder Serving Fees $(1,218.96)

Total Revenue   **$(1,526.70)**

Amount Due This Quarter: **$601.41**

Under the DOL Frost Letter, Unified Trust Company, N.A., offsets your fees with any revenue credits from the underlying investments. You may pay any net amount due directly. If not paid directly, any remaining amount due will be deducted from plan assets as described in your Plan Services Agreement.

For Further Reading

"An Example Set for Fiduciaries." *Pensions & Investments*, New York (April 15, 2002).

U.S. Department of Labor Advisory Opinion 1997-15A.

U.S. Department of Labor Advisory Opinion 1997-16A.

U.S. Department of Labor Advisory Opinion 1997-19A.

U.S. Department of Labor Advisory Opinion 2003-09A.

U.S. Department of Labor Model Fee Disclosure, www.dol.gov (under "DOL Agencies—EBSA" as "401(k) Plan Fees Disclosure Tool").

Levin, D., and Ferrera., T. *ERISA Fiduciary Answer Book*. 4th ed. (New York: Panel Publishers, 2001).

Kasten, G. "Revenue Sharing Aspects of Qualified Retirement Plan Management." www.unifiedtrust.com ("library" section), (2002).

"Revenue Sharing Report, Revenue Sharing in the 401(k) Marketplace: 'Whose Money Is It?'" McHenry Consulting Group, media@mchenryconsulting.com. (2003)

Swisher, P. "The Legality of Kickbacks: Understanding Revenue Sharing after Advisory Opinion 2003–09." www.unifiedtrust.com ("library" section), (2002).

"Some Mutual-Fund Fees Face the Smell Test." *Wall Street Journal*, (2003).

Chapter 18

Participant Communication Focusing on Retirement Success

Chapter Summary

The image of defined-contribution participant reports has improved dramatically over the past decade. Ten years ago, most plan participants received only an annual statement in black-and-white text. Today most vendors have substantially improved the presentation format and the content and now send colorful, multiple-page quarterly statements to participants, either by regular mail or over the Internet.

However, today's retirement success rates are no higher despite all the efforts to improve participant reports. With all the bells and whistles, they may actually be lower than ten years ago, when participants received simple black-and-white reports.

As we have said, retirement success can be defined as holding a sufficient level of assets at the beginning of retirement to give a 75% or higher probability that an appropriate lifestyle can be maintained in retirement. We have combined the savings rate and the real rate of investment return, the two most important factors of retirement success, to determine the SR+RR Index. Through the use of supplemental reporting, we demonstrate to participants how using the SR+RR Index can accurately predict and improve their retirement success rates.

Revamped Reporting Formats Have Not Improved Success Rates

Participant reports have improved dramatically over the past decade. Ten years ago, most plan participants received only an annual statement in black-and-white text. The annual statement contained only basic information such as beginning balance, contributions, earnings, ending balance, and vested balance. Most plans at that time used balance-forward accounting rather than daily administration accounting, so the annual participant statement would often arrive three or four months after the close of the plan year.

Today most vendors have substantially improved both the presentation format and the content. Most daily valuation plans now send quarterly statements to participants, either by regular mail or electronically. Timeliness has improved such that most participants receive their statements within two or three weeks of the close of the quarter. Statements today are in color and contain additional information, such as mutual fund performance and the individual participant's account performance. The statements provide information in text form and often include graphics, such as asset-allocation pie charts. Moreover, the statements often contain general investment information and educational articles.

Plan sponsors today place a great deal of emphasis on the image portrayed by the statement and the delivery speed. They may select as their next vendor a group who promises to deliver statements three days earlier than the current vendor. Or they may select a vendor based upon the statement graphics.

Despite all the effort made in improving participant reports, participant retirement-success probability rates are no higher today and may actually be lower than ten years ago. The reporting format improvements over the last ten years have been mostly cosmetic and have not contributed to any meaningful improvement in participant success rates.

At Unified Trust Company, N.A., we believe that participant reports should have a meaningful impact on improving success outcomes. The report should give participants a realistic look at the likelihood of their success probabilities. If the success probability is low, methods must be in place to improve the success without making the participant feel like the situation is hopeless. As we have pointed out throughout this book, inertia and procrastination dominate the activities of most participants. Thus, any solution that is going to have a meaningful effect on success must deal with inertia and procrastination.

Despite the glossy new 401(k) reports, for practical effects geared toward participant success, there really are no "defined contribution" plans. Every 401(k) plan must be operated as a series of tiny defined benefit plans, one for each plan participant. This means that actuarial calculations, periodic review and assessment of adequate funding, ongoing mutual fund evaluation, investment manager reviews, and so forth must be provided to the individual participants, because they cannot do these tasks themselves.

Supplemental Participant Reports That Improve Success Rates

Earlier we demonstrated that the two most important factors of retirement success are savings rate and real rate of investment return. Real rate of investment return is determined by asset allocation and asset quality. We demonstrated that using the SR+RR Index could accurately predict and improve retirement success rates for participants of all ages. Supplemental participant statements should include "Success Factor" information to improve the success rate.

Figure 18-1: Success Factors

Savings Rate	Real Rate of Investment Return
Total Current Savings Rate %	Current Asset Allocation
SMarT™ Participation	Model Portfolio Participation
Current Deferral %	Model Portfolio Selected
Deferral Increase %	Model Performance
Deferral Increase Date	Model Performance vs. Benchmark
Employer Match %	Asset Quality (UFMI®)
Employer Other %	Automatic Rebalancing
	Individual Fund Performance

The participant's SR+RR Index is also reported. For example, if the overall savings rate is 8% and the real rate of return is 3%, the SR+RR Index would be 11%. The Unified Trust Company reporting format, showing the participant's overall success probability, is shown on the next page. If a participant has a low success probability, suggestions are made to improve it. The best formula for success is to have participants in an auto-pilot (default pathway) program to improve their SR+RR Indexes and their chances for success.

Focusing on both his real rate of return and savings rate will enhance his success. If he can enter a long-term program to raise his savings rate from 8% to 11%, then he only needs to earn 5% on a real basis for a high probability of success. In most cases, the savings rate is the more certain way to increase the SR+RR Index. To facilitate this process, Unified Trust Company has developed the Unified Retirement Counselor[SM] online advice and retirement planning tool for our retirement plan clients. The Web address is www.unifiedtrust.com.

Figure 18-2: Success Projection Report

◢◣ **Retirement Success Projection**

For XYZ Participant
October 10, 2003

Your current probability of Retirement Success | 54%

Your Savings Rate + Real Return Index (SR+RR) | 11

Your current Savings Rate	(SR)	8%
Estimated long-term real return	+(RR)	3%
	= SR+RR	11%

The SR+RR You Need for a 75% Chance of Success | 16

The Savings Rate you need	(SR)	11%
Estimated long-term real return	+(RR)	5%
	= SR+RR	16%

Retirement Success Defined as retiring with enough money to replace 70% of your current income for the rest of your life.

SR+RR Index — The percentage of your current pay that you save (Savings Rate, or SR) plus an estimated real return on your money (RR) after inflation. Your savings rate includes your own payroll deferrals and your employer's contributions.

Retirement Success Probability — To calculate your chances of success, we run tens of thousands of calculations that ask "What If?" Each "what if" scenario is a possible series of future returns for your investments. The success probability is the percentage of "what if" scenarios in which you do not run out of money.

Estimated Long Term Real Returns — How will your investments perform over the next five, ten, or twenty years *after inflation*? Historically a return of 2% to 7%, net of inflation and fees, is a reasonable range. To be safe, don't plan your retirement based on something you can't control—the markets. Assume a conservative 3-4% real return as we do for this Retirement Success Projection.

Figure 18-3: Success Factor Report

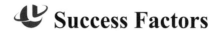

Success Factors

For XYZ Participant
October 10, 2003

Savings Rate

Total Current Savings Rate %	11.0%
SMarT™ Participation	Yes
Current Deferral %	6.0%
SMarT™ Deferral Increase %	2.0%
SMarT™ Deferral Increase Date	July 1, 2004
Employer Match %	4.0%
Employer Other %	1.0%

Real Rate Of Investment Return

Model Portfolio Participation	Yes
Model Portfolio Selected	60:40 Equity:Fixed Income
Model Performance 1 yr	+19.88%
Model Performance 3 yr	+3.08%
Model Performance 5 yr	+9.73%
Model Performance 1 yr vs Benchmark	+3.37% above Benchmark
Model Performance 3 yr vs Benchmark	+6.02% above Benchmark
Model Performance 5 yr vs Benchmark	+6.59% above Benchmark
Automatic Rebalancing	Yes
Asset Quality (UFMI®)	Average UFMI® = 9

(UFMI® score range is 1-100, with 1 being best and 100 being worst)

All results as of 09/30/2003. For additional information, please refer to the quarterly Fiduciary Monitoring Report issued by Unified Trust Company, NA for your plan. The report provides details about your plan investments and asset allocation model portfolios.

Chapter 19

Unified Success Pathway™ Retirement Program

Chapter Summary

At the beginning of this book, we observed that the more a defined contribution plan operated in principle like a sophisticated defined-benefit plan, the more likely the retirement success of the participants.

The Unified Success Pathway™ is the process of taking an ordinary defined contribution plan and bringing in all of the professional managerial elements that contribute to the success of a sophisticated defined-benefit plan. The Unified Success Pathway™ makes a significant improvement in the SR+RR Index and retirement success.

The Unified Success Pathway achieves this through a sophisticated series of default steps that produce a vastly improved participant outcome. Unless participants opt out of the default steps, they automatically travel the success pathway. The default steps enhance the overall savings rate and the investment return. Only discretionary trustees can offer this complete program in a series of default pathways. Directed trustee arrangements must rely upon the participants to "get it right" on their own, which they seldom do.

In addition, Unified Trust Company has produced a proprietary software package that makes the SMarT™ increased annual savings program easy for employers to administer. By automating both the initial and the ongoing payroll changes, the Unified Savings Manager™ eliminates much of the complexity and workload of administering SMarT™ for the employer.

Offering the Plan Participant a Retirement Success Pathway

Far too many retirement plan sponsors do not manage their retirement plans with the goal of participant success. Instead, they get bogged down with minutia that will have little if any meaningful effect on participants' retirement success. Unified Trust Company believes that the measure of a retirement plan's success or failure is the ability of its participants to retire with enough money to last them for the rest of their lives. So the most basic question is, how do most plans measure up?

The 80/20 Rule: Unless Something Changes, Most Plans Will Fail

The Goal: Improve Outcomes

- The point of a retirement plan is to help people retire

- The odds of the average participant retiring successfully from most employers are very small

- Our job is to *improve your participants' chances for successful retirement*

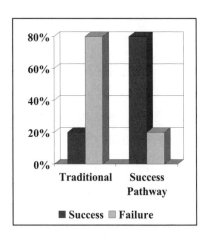

The typical 401(k) plan, in which proper funding and investment management are left largely to the discretion of participants, has less than a 20% chance of success as measured by current funding levels and historical ranges of real investment returns. That means 80% of plan participants will fail. We must take everything we learned in this book up till this point and create a retirement success pathway for participants.

The Unified Success Pathway™: Applying the Three A's for Successful Retirement as a Default Pathway

*A*dequate Savings

➤ Automatic enrollment
➤ Annual Savings increases
➤ **Unified Savings Manager**SM
➤ Regular Retirement
  Success illustrations
  Online Retirement
  Success calculators
➤ Defaults defined by the **Unified**
  Success Pathway™
➤ Targeted Success Pathway
  Communication materials

*A*sset Quality

➤ **Unified Fiduciary Monitoring Index**®
➤ Thoroughly tested Investment Policy
➤ An open platform for investments
➤ Objective selection
➤ Transparent fees
➤ Quarterly scrutiny with changes
  made for the participant
➤ A Plan Trustee that accepts full
  discretion and responsibility for
  investments

*A*sset Allocation

➤ Investment Advice
➤ Professional Model Portfolios
➤ **Unified Retirement Counselor**SM
➤ Regular/automatic rebalancing
➤ Avoid recent, return-chasing, knee-
  jerk reactions, and other costly
  behavioral mistakes
➤ Allocations designed with the help of
  mean variance optimization, Monte
  Carlo analysis, and other tools
➤ Targeted Success Pathway
  Communication materials

Figure 19-1: The Unified Success Pathway™

Choose Your Path to Retirement

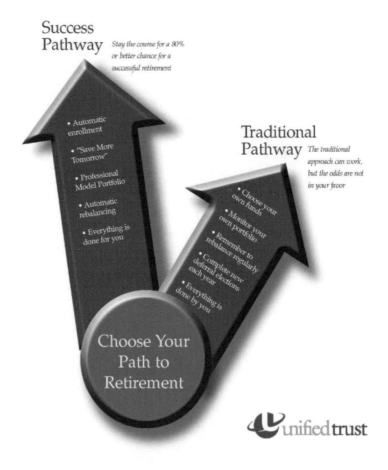

The Path of Least Resistance: The Unified Success Pathway™

People do what is easiest—they follow the path of least resistance. Unfortunately, most retirement plans are structured so that the path of least resistance is the wrong path. Action is required to participate, action is required to increase savings, action is required to oversee and manage the investments, and action is required to rebalance periodically. Yet behavioral finance research tells us that people not only fail to do the things they should, they often do the opposite—following the worst possible course.

Why not make the default path for participants the one that is most likely to lead to success? We know that the following works for employees:

- ✓   Join the plan.
- ✓   Increase the amount saved every year.
- ✓   Choose a professionally managed, prudent asset allocation based on a diversified portfolio.
- ✓   Receive investment advice.
- ✓   Have the portfolio automatically rebalanced periodically.
- ✓   Maintain a very high portfolio asset quality.
- ✓   Employ discretionary trustee fiduciary Best Practices.
- ✓   Understand the success rate probability.
- ✓   Receive additional Success Pathway contributions

We also know that we cannot rely on people to do these things for themselves. So instead of fighting human nature, Unified Trust Company uses inertia and procrastination to the participant's advantage by making these steps the default for the plan. Instead of choosing to join, participants are automatically enrolled and must opt out if they choose not to participate. Instead of having to discipline themselves to increase savings every year, their savings increase automatically each year unless they take action to do otherwise.

The default investment is a diversified model portfolio, prudently managed by investment professionals, and rebalancing is handled automatically. Everything is done for the participants unless they opt out. By doing nothing and allowing inertia to take over, participants will now be far more certain of success.

Only a Discretionary Trustee Can Give You the Unified Success Pathway™

Model portfolios with automatic rebalancing may pose a potentially serious fiduciary-liability threat to the plan sponsor, because they most likely constitute "investment advice" as defined in DOL Interpretive Bulletin 96-1. Sponsors may lose fiduciary liability protection under ERISA Section 404(c). Few sponsors are willing to forgo this protection. But with Unified Trust Company serving as the plan's discretionary trustee, the full delegation of discretionary fiduciary responsibility for plan assets means that the plan sponsor has no added liability from the offering of investment advice.

Positive Changes Seen in Plans Adopting the Unified Success Pathway™

1. Plan participation increased from < 60% to > 95%

2. Average deferral rates increased from 4.0% to 6.5%

3. SMarT™ program participation of > 95%

4. SMarT™ program annual deferral increase of 2.25%

5. Usage of model portfolios > 95%

6. Portfolio investment performance improvement > 3.4%

7. SR+RR Index plan average improvement from 8.5 to 15.7

The Success Pathway Contribution

It is important to encourage all employees, especially those who are not highly compensated, to remain on the default pathway. The Success Pathway contribution is an additional (usually 2%) employer contribution given to those employees who remain on the default pathway. This contribution is calculated as part of the overall employer contribution. An example of the calculation is shown below.

Beginning of Year Total Employer Estimated Contribution	**4.5%**
Estimated Fraction of Employees on the Default Pathway	**90%**
Estimated Cost to Employer for the Success Pathway Contribution (0.9 x 2.0%)	**1.8%**
Estimated Remaining Employer Contribution for Every Employee (4.5% -1.8%)	**2.7%**

Based on the above example, the program would work as follows. First, all employees would receive an employer contribution of 2.7%. Second, the employees participating in the default pathway would receive an additional employer contribution of 2.0%. The overall employer contribution costs would be 4.5%. If we assume that through both automatic enrollment and automatic annual savings increases the default employee is deferring 8.0% of pay, that employee would receive a total contribution of 12.7%. Such a savings rate would be a rate far above the national average. As employee retirement success is related to both the savings rate and the real rate of investment return, at least half the battle is won. The real rate of investment return is improved by maintaining proper asset allocation and high asset quality.

The plan could be set up in several different ways to make the success pathway contribution effective. The most common would be to provide the Success Pathway contribution at the end of the plan year when it was known exactly how many employees had remained in the default pathway during the plan year. Keep in mind that employees can opt out of the default pathway at any time. In order to qualify for the Success Pathway contribution at the end of the year, three key default pathway activities must be maintained by the employee:

1. The employee must participate in the plan.
2. The employee must take advantage of automatic annual savings-rate (deferral) increases, up to a preset maximum.
3. The employee must utilize a model portfolio.

Each year, the plan would undergo ordinary compliance testing to ensure that coverage between highly compensated employees and those who are not highly compensated was acceptable per IRS rules. Thus, it is possible that, under very unusual circumstances, the Success Pathway contribution could not be made as originally planned. Because the default pathway usually covers non-highly compensated employees, the plan generally passes the various IRS benefit coverage tests. In fact, passing IRS coverage tests is almost always much easier than normal under the default pathway because of the higher participation and deferral rates of employees who are not highly compensated

In addition to the higher savings rate, the real rate of investment return for participants should improve. The default pathway provides participants with a discretionary trustee, quarterly fiduciary monitoring, appropriate asset allocation through model portfolios, high asset quality, periodic rebalancing, and investment advice. For participants who fail to select a model portfolio, the default pathway solves this problem. Generally, participants over age fifty who do not select a portfolio are given the 40:60 model portfolio. Participants under fifty are given the 60:40 model portfolio as their default.

The Unified Savings Manager^{SM}

Unified Trust Company, N.A., has produced a proprietary software package that makes the SMarT™ increased annual savings program easy for employers to administer. By automating both the initial and ongoing payroll changes, the Unified Savings Manager^{SM} ("USM") virtually eliminates the complexity and workload of administering SMarT™ for the employer.

Instituting the SMarT™ program means employees' chances for maintaining sufficient savings rates improve exponentially, whereas without the SMarT™ program, employees are likely to fail in most traditional 401(k)s. Yet the SMarT™ program imposes an administrative burden on the employer to track and remember an ever-changing set of data over a period of many years. And because accuracy of the company payroll is of paramount importance for many reasons, not the least of which is liability, the system must be all but foolproof. Here is a sampling of the tasks that are imposed on a company's payroll or HR department when it institutes the SMarT™ program:

1. Gather and file initial elections
2. Make initial payroll election in payroll system
3. Create and manage a "tickler system" to update elections annually
4. Manually, accurately add each year's additional deferral to the existing deferral and enter the new deferral amount
5. Alternatively, create a spreadsheet or custom computer program to generate these data entries automatically
6. Keep pristine records as required for any payroll operation
7. Accommodate midyear participant changes, new hires, and terminations.

The USM works through an online interface and is part of the employer contingent's regular payroll process. It simplifies and automates the payroll process by first, reducing the error rate, and second, easing the administrative workload of the employer.

1. New hires, terminations, and changes are processed as usual, and the updated SMarT data is simply included in the regular payroll file.

2. Once a year or at any interval the employer prefers, their HR manager simply prints or downloads a report of payroll changes that need to be entered. For example, if all employees elect a 3% annual increase in their deferral SMarT^{TM} program, the USM computes the new deferral percentage and creates a report showing the changes for entry into the employer's payroll system.

3. The USM automatically archives each participant's payroll elections, SMarT^{TM} status, and deferral percentage changes. The employer can retrieve these records at any time.

4. The savings rate for each participant is tracked on the recordkeeping system and is used in the SR+RR Index calculation. The SR+RR Index is the heart of the retirement success projection shown to each participant with each quarterly statement.

5. Tools for participants on the Web site allow initiation of election changes and viewing of current deferral/ SMarT^{TM} elections.

The Unified Success Pathway™ partial booklet and basic enrollment forms are shown on the following pages. These forms are supplemented with face-to-face meetings including more detailed informational brochures in the meetings, call center support, and internet advice.

Figure 19-2: Unified Success Pathway™ Booklet

Applying The Three A's of
Successful Retirement

1. Adequate Savings

- Automatic enrollment
- SMarT
- Unified Savings Manager
- Regular Retirement Success illustrations
- Online Retirement Success calculators
- Defaults defined by the Success Pathway
- Targeted Success Pathway Communication materials

2. Asset Quality

- Unified Fiduciary Monitoring Index^{SM}
- Thoroughly tested Investment Policy
- An open platform for investments
- Objective selection with transparent fees
- Quarterly scrutiny with changes made for you
- A Plan Trustee that accepts full discretion and responsibility for investments

3. Asset Allocation

- Professional Model Portfolios
- Unified Retirement Counselor
- Regular/automatic rebalancing
- Avoid recency, return-chasing, knee-jerk reactions, and other costly behaviors at all costs
- Allocations designed with the help of mean variance optimization, monte carlo analysis, and other tools
- Targeted Success Pathway Communication materials

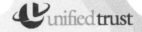

Figure 19-3: Unified Success Pathway™ Booklet

The purpose of your retirement plan is to allow you to retire. The result you want is successful retirement. Successful retirement simply means retiring with enough money to support yourself. It sounds simple, and it is simple — but it's not easy. The goal of Unified Trust's approach to your retirement savings is to make it easy for you to succeed. We do this by helping you make the right choices on the three elements you control — The Three A's of Successful Retirement.

The Three A's of Successful Retirement

Adequate Savings...*Invest* enough of every paycheck...

Asset Quality...*Invest* in the right funds

Asset Allocation...*Invest* in the right proportions.

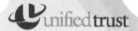

Figure 19-4: Unified Success Pathway™ Booklet

Adequate Savings— Save 8% to 15% of your paycheck from an early age and enjoy a comfortable retirement. Wait too long to start and you may never have enough. Follow two simple rules: start now, and save as much as you can. Unfortunately, the evidence is overwhelming that most people fail to save, even after they have announced the intention to do so. We are all human, we put things off, and years go by without progress. But without adequate savings, you will fail to retire successfully. No magic investment bullet will save you. To help overcome the very human tendency to put things off, therefore, we have a special program we strongly suggest you enter: the SmaRT Program.

MOST PEOPLE FAIL TO INCREASE THEIR SAVINGS OVER TIME

Most of us know we need to save more, but saving money is hard. The real problem, however, is not that people have trouble saving but that they fail to increase their savings over time, even when they are ready to do so. In one study, ...(data on Greg's study about participants failing to increase savings). In short, even those of us who are ready to save more somehow fail to make it happen. Most of us need a very easy way to implement the decision to save more over time.

THE SmaRT PROGRAM

Perhaps you can only save 3% or 6%—or less—of your pay today, but what if you increase that number a little bit every year for a few years? For example, suppose you save 5% today, and add 1% to that number every year for ten years, like this:

Year 1   Save 5%
Year 2   Save 6%
Year 3   Save 7%
....
Year 10 Save 15%.

There may be no earthly way you could save 15% today, but if your pay goes up by as little as 2% per year, your paycheck will still grow over time, yet your savings rate will triple! This is important, because without adequate savings you cannot retire successfully. By allowing you to gradually increase your savings over a number of years—without having to think about it or take any further action—you take a huge step toward a successful retirement.

-437-

Figure 19-5: Unified Success Pathway™ Booklet

Asset Quality—To help increase your chances for a successful retirement, choose only the very best investments available in the world of investments. The problem is how to know which funds are "right." While there is no crystal ball to help us pick only winners, we do have an advanced process based on our investment policy and the Unified Fiduciary Monitoring Index℠. Judge our performance for yourself every quarter when we publish our latest fiduciary monitoring data as well as your personalized rate of return for your portfolio.

INVESTING WITH THE UNIFIED FIDUCIARY MONITORING INDEX℠

We guarantee that no fund will enter your plan unless it scores in the top 25% of its peer group on our Unified Fiduciary Monitoring Index℠, and funds must generally maintain a score of 40% or better to remain in your plan. In short, we guarantee that the funds in your plan will be as good as we can possibly make them, though no one, including Unified Trust, can guarantee or predict the future performance of any one investment.

NO HOME RUNDS, JUST SINGLES

Any investor who expects to radically "beat the market" will almost certainly be disappointed. By definition a diversified portfolio is built to reduce risk and, therefore, the likelihood of "home runs." The statistics in support of our Unified Fiduciary Monitoring Index℠ are strong and we believe the quality of the assets in your plan to be very high. If you understand both the strengths and limitations of the system and begin with reasonable expectations, you are well-positioned to reap the long-term benefits of the UFMI℠.

For a more detailed discussion of the UFMI℠, visit our website (www.unifiedtrust.com) or ask for one of our free brochures—Advanced Fiduciary Management for the Prudent Investor.

Figure 19-6: Unified Success Pathway™ Booklet

A̲sset Allocation—Invest the right percentage of your assets in the appropriate categories and rebalance periodically. Research tells us that most plan participants are poor asset allocators and do better when they get professional help. Delivering that help—and making it stick—is a major focus for Unified Trust and your Plan Advisor. You can get help choosing your asset allocation in three ways:

- Choose a model portfolio. Let us pick an asset allocation—at no added charge to you—using one of the model portfolios available in the plan.
- Use the Unified Retirement Counselor (URC), our online advice tool that guides you through the process of completing a basic retirement plan.
- Talk to your Plan Advisor—each advisor is an experienced financial professional and can help you create and implement a personal financial strategy. In most cases you can personally call or meet with an advisor at no added charge for help with the basics.

WHAT YOU DON'T KNOW CAN HURT YOU

According to a growing number of studies, most plan participants make poor investment decisions and do better when they get professional help.

These studies should not surprise us. While investing involves much that is uncontrollable, we do know a great deal about what works and what doesn't. Investment experts generally agree that allocating your money across a variety of asset classes and rebalancing periodically is a strategy likely to succeed over time. The problem is that this strategy—diversifying your portfolio and leaving it alone except to rebalance—is exactly what most people don't do.

How many people understand even the basics of investing? The popular press suggests that investors can do it all themselves, and so they can, but the question is, can you do it yourself? More importantly, should you do it yourself? Do you have the time, inclination, and discipline to study the science of investing and apply what you learn without fail? If you are like most Americans, the answer is no.

MODEL PORTFOLIOS—YOUR PERSONAL INVESTMENT MANAGER

When you choose a model portfolio, you ask Unified Trust to pay attention to your portfolio for you. You decide what level of risk you can accept and match that risk level with one of six model portfolios, and we do the rest. You get a portfolio consisting of the investment funds available in the plan in proportions that make sense for your age and temperament. Combine a model portfolio with a savings rate that you increase over time, and you have every reason to expect—as we do—that your odds of retirement success will soar.

Figure 19-7: Unified Success Pathway™ Booklet

Summary—What We Do For You

- Manage the plan—and your account—in accordance with a formal Investment Policy Statement (IPS) representing the most advanced investment science available.
- Select the funds—only the top 25% based on our Unified Fiduciary Monitoring Index℠ can be selected for your plan, and each must maintain a score of 40 or better (top 40%) to remain.
- Monitor the funds—every quarter we monitor the funds in your plan and ensure they meet the criteria we set in the Investment Policy Statement. Funds that fall below the minimum score are promptly replaced with funds scoring in the top 25%.
- Choose the asset allocation—based on every advanced tool that modern investment science has given us, such as portfolio optimization and "monte carlo" analysis.
- Monitor the asset allocation—and make changes if appropriate, though we expect the core allocation to change only little over time. You are notified of changes as they occur and whether any action is required to take advantage of the new allocation.
- Rebalance your portfolio—if you simply "check the box" indicating that you would like us to automatically rebalance your account, we will do so once per year (or at any other interval you specify, though we recommend one year), or in accordance with the IPS.

PERHAPS THE SIMPLEST WAY TO EXPLAIN WHAT UNIFIED TRUST COMPANY DOES FOR YOU IS THAT WE PAY ATTENTION TO YOUR MONEY:

1. We pay attention to the funds in your plan, selecting only the top quality funds in each category and firing funds that do not continue to meet our standards quarter after quarter.
2. We pay attention to asset allocation through our model portfolios and online advice tools.
3. We pay attention to your savings rate by making it easy to increase your savings over time.

THREE EASY STEPS TO SUCCESS

1. Start by deferring as much of your pay as you are able.
2. Enroll in the SmarT Program to ensure your savings rate increases over time.
3. Choose a model portfolio with automatic rebalancing.

AND LEAVE THE REST TO US.

Figure 19-8: Unified Success Pathway™ Enrollment Form Page 1

Part 1 INVESTMENT DIRECTION SECTION--SELECTION OF MODEL PORTFOLIO

Instruction: Use this section to advise the Trustee of the manner in which newly contributed funds are to be invested for your account under the Plan. Important--You may only select one (1) model. If no instruction is received the Balanced 40 60 Model Portoflio will be the default investment if you are over age 50 and the Balanced 60 40 Model portfolio will be the default investment if you are age 50 or younger.

_____ **ULTRA CONSERVATIVE 100 MODEL PORTFOLIO**

The Ultra Conservative 100 Portfolio consists solely of those mutual funds and collective funds available in your plan that invest in fixed income securities such as bonds and cash. 100% of Portfolio assets will remain invested in the Stable Value fund, money market funds, and/or various bond funds.

Security Name	Investment Category	% Allocation
UTC Stable Value Fund	Stable Value	60%
Dodge & Cox Income	Intermediate-term Bond	20%
Vanguard Int Tm Tsy/Inv	Intermediate Government	20%

_____ **CONSERVATIVE 20 80 MODEL PORTFOLIO**

The Conservative 20 80 Portfolio invests approximately 80% in fixed income securities such as bond funds and the Stable Value fund. The remaining 20% is invested in stock mutual funds for added diversification with only a small to modest increase in risk.

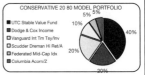

Security Name	Investment Category	% Allocation
UTC Stable Value Fund	Stable Value	40%
Dodge & Cox Income	Intermediate-term Bond	20%
Vanguard Int Tm Tsy/Inv	Intermediate Government	20%
Scudder Dreman Hi Ret/A	Large Value	10%
Federated Mid-Cap Idx	Mid-Cap Blend	5%
Columbia Acorn/Z	Small Growth	5%

_____ **BALANCED 40 60 MODEL PORTFOLIO**

The Balanced 40 60 Portfolio invests approximately 60% in fixed income securities such as bond funds and the Stable Value fund. The remaining 40% is invested in stock mutual funds to add both diversification and the potential for increased future returns while still focusing on modest risk.

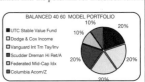

Security Name	Investment Category	% Allocation
UTC Stable Value Fund	Stable Value	20%
Dodge & Cox Income	Intermediate-term Bond	20%
Vanguard Int Tm Tsy/Inv	Intermediate Government	20%
Scudder Dreman Hi Ret/A	Large Value	20%
Federated Mid-Cap Idx	Mid-Cap Blend	10%
Columbia Acorn/Z	Small Growth	10%

_____ **BALANCED 60 40 MODEL PORTFOLIO**

The Balanced 60 40 Portfolio invests approximately 40% in fixed income securities such as bond funds and the Stable Value fund. The remaining 60% is invested in stock mutual funds to add both diversification and the potential for increased future returns with moderate risk.

Security Name	Investment Category	% Allocation
UTC Stable Value Fund	Stable Value	20%
Dodge & Cox Income	Intermediate-term Bond	20%
Scudder Dreman Hi Ret/A	Large Value	15%
Vanguard Gr Idx/Inv	Large Growth	15%
Federated Mid-Cap Idx	Mid-Cap Blend	10%
Columbia Acorn/Z	Small Growth	10%
Royce Opport/Inv	Small Value	10%

unified trust
COMPANY, N. A.

Figure 19-9: Unified Success Pathway™ Enrollment Form Page 2

PARTICIPATION AGREEMENT
Unified Trust Client Retirement Plan ("The Plan")

_____ **AGGRESSIVE 80 20 MODEL PORTFOLIO**

The Aggressive 80 20 Portfolio is suitable for more aggressive investors have more time to take advantage of the long term potential of the stock market--if they are comfortable with the added risk. The 20% fixed income portion of this portfolio is designed to somewhat reduce overall portfolio risk.

Security Name	Investment Category	% Allocation
UTC Stable Value Fund	Stable Value	10%
Dodge & Cox Income	Intermediate-term Bond	10%
Scudder Dreman Hi Ret/A	Large Value	20%
Vanguard Gr Idx/Inv	Large Growth	20%
Federated Mid-Cap Idx	Mid-Cap Blend	20%
Columbia Acorn/Z	Small Growth	10%
Royce Opport/Inv	Small Value	10%

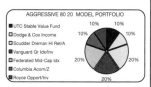

_____ **ULTRA AGGRESSIVE 100 MODEL PORTFOLIO**

The Ultra Aggressive 100 Portfolio consists solely of those mutual funds and collective funds available in your plan that invest in stocks. 100% of Portfolio assets will remain fully invested in stock funds.

Security Name	Investment Category	% Allocation
Scudder Dreman Hi Ret/A	Large Value	15%
Vanguard Gr Idx/Inv	Large Growth	15%
SSgA S&P 500 Index	Large Blend	20%
Federated Mid-Cap Idx	Mid-Cap Blend	20%
Columbia Acorn/Z	Small Growth	15%
Royce Opport/Inv	Small Value	15%

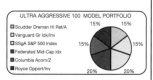

Part 2 SELECTION OF INDIVIDUAL FUNDS

ALLOCATION MUST TOTAL 100%, AND MUST BE IN WHOLE NUMBERS.

Important--If you selected a Model Portfolio in Part 1 you may NOT select individual funds. If you select both a Model Portfolio and individual mutual funds, the Model Portfolio you selected will be your choice.

UTC Stable Value Fund	_____%	Artisan Mid Cap Fund	_____%
Dodge & Cox Income	_____%	Federated Mid-Cap Idx	_____%
Vanguard Int Tm Tsy/Inv	_____%	PIMCO:PEA Renaissance	_____%
Amer Cnt Infltn Bond/Inv	_____%	Columbia Acorn/Z	_____%
Dodge & Cox Balanced	_____%	Royce Opport/Inv	_____%
Jensen Portfolio	_____%	Templeton Foreign Fd/A	_____%
Vanguard Gr Idx/Inv	_____%		
SSgA S&P 500 Index	_____%		
Scudder Dreman Hi Ret/A	_____%		
T Rowe Price Eq Inc/Ad	_____%		

Part 3 AUTOMATIC REBALANCING OF ACCOUNT INSTRUCTIONS:

Use this section to advise the Trustee of the manner in which to rebalance your account. I hereby authorize Unified Trust Company, N.A. to create recurring rebalance transactions according to my current election at the time of the rebalance. **If no other instructions are received Unified Trust Company, N.A. will rebalance your account on an annual basis**. I understand that the rebalance will occur on the 10th day of the month.

I want Unified Trust Company, N.A. to rebalance my account twice per year: _____

I do not want Unified Trust Company, N.A. to rebalance my account: _____

Figure 19-10: Unified Success Pathway™ Enrollment Form Page 3

PARTICIPATION AGREEMENT
Unified Trust Client Retirement Plan ("The Plan")

Part 4 INFORMATION ABOUT YOURSELF

Instruction: To enroll in the Plan, complete the Investment Direction Section, sign and date the form at the bottom of the form and deliver it to the Plan Administrator. To change a prior authorization, complete the Participant Change Request form. (Please Print)

Employee Name: _____ Social Security Number: _____

Street Address: _____

City: _____ State: _____ Zip: _____

Home Phone: (_____)_____ Mothers Maiden Name: _____

E-Mail: _____

Date of Birth: _____ Original Hire Date: _____

If you have been rehired please provide: Date of Termination _____ Date of Rehire: _____

Marital Status: (circle one) Single   Married   Widowed   Divorced

Part 5 PAYROLL DEDUCTION

☐   The Unified Success Pathway™ Election

I hereby authorize the deduction from my compensation of an amount equal to:

        3%   5%   7%   (circle one) of my gross pay for each payroll period

I choose to sign up for the Unified Success Pathway™ Election. I understand that I can opt-out of the Unified Success Pathway™ Election at any time. Each year on January 1, I authorize my employer to automatically increase my savings rate into the retirement plan by:

        1%   2%   3%   (circle one) increase of my deferral rate each January 1

☐   **I hereby opt out of The Unified Success Pathway™ Election and choose The Traditional Pathway Election**

I hereby authorize the deduction from my compensation of an amount equal to:

        _____% Of my gross pay for each payroll period.

Any percentage you elect above will be stopped when you reach the total legal maximum for the year. All amounts so withheld shall be delivered to the funding agent of this Plan for credit to my elective deferral account under the Plan.

Part 6 YOUR SIGNATURE

I have been given the opportunity to obtain and read the prospectus for each of these funds before making my selection(s). I understand that I can change my investment selections at anytime by means of a Voice Response Unit, Internet, or Customer Service Center. The instruction set forth herein shall remain in full force until revoked or modified through the Trustee.

I understand that this Plan is a "404(c)" plan, which means that it intends to be in compliance with Section 404(c) of the Employee Retirement Income Security Act of 1974, as amended. That Section states that in a plan in which employees can select the investments for their account(s), the plan's fiduciaries will not be liable for any losses resulting from an employee's selections. I have been given the Plan's 404(c) materials.

_____   _____
        Signature   Date

unified trust
COMPANY, N. A.

-443-

Chapter 20

How to Prudently Review a Proposal for ERISA Services

Chapter Summary

Reviewing and comparing multiple ERISA service proposals is quite difficult for most plan sponsors. Most of the time the plan sponsor does not know which questions to ask, nor how to sift through reams of information to find the right answers. Typically the focus is on details that have no impact on participant success. Most of the time participant success is not even considered in the proposal review process.

Proposal review and analysis can be broken into two parts. The first is relatively easy, if the plan sponsor knows which questions to ask. The easy part deals with objective analysis such as total plan costs, investment quality and performance analysis. The second is more subjective and more difficult to analyze, but equally important to the to the overall goal of participant retirement success. The challenge for the plan sponsor is to prudently analyze both parts of the equation.

To solve this problem, we created the Unified Proposal Evaluation System^{SM}. This system properly analyzes both the objective and the subjective parts of an ERISA proposal. It allows the plan sponsor to weight different categories according to their preferences, and by categories having the greatest impact on success. It provides an overall score of basis points spent for each unit of overall value added. Our unique approach allows a true "apples to apples" cost/value comparison between different proposals that typically have somewhat different costs and vastly different levels of services.

Plan Sponsors Often Change Vendors but Seldom Conduct a Prudent Search

Fiduciaries responsible for their company's qualified retirement plan face numerous difficult decisions when selecting plan service vendors. As technologies change, and as plan sponsors seek to shift additional responsibilities to external vendors, the complexity of the assignment increases. It has been our observation that few plan sponsors have the appropriately trained and experienced internal personnel to adequately conduct a vendor search. All too often the HR department or retirement plan committee focuses on details that have no impact on participant success. In fact most of the time participant success, or the lack thereof, is not even considered in the proposal process.

In selecting providers for the plan, each vendor's direct fees, total plan fees, capabilities and experience must be assessed in each of several key areas, including:

1. Administrative and recordkeeping capabilities;
2. Discretionary fiduciary services, including trustee services, investment advice and significant fiduciary oversight;
3. Access to high quality funds;
4. Ability to insulate the plan sponsor and other company employees from fiduciary liability; and
5. Employee communications and investment advice capabilities.

Many plan sponsors make frequent changes to their service vendors. A recent survey shows that in 1999 alone, nearly one-half (47%) of 401(k) plan sponsors intended to change at least one service provider. Overall, 64% of plan sponsors will retain a selected provider for five years or less. This high turnover suggests that many plan sponsors have unmet expectations. Sponsor expectations, often very unrealistic expectations, are generally created during the service provider's sales process.

Distinguishing "Sales Claims" from True Service Capability

One conclusion that might be drawn from these high turnover statistics is that too many plan sponsors adopt a flawed vendor selection process. The DOL ERISA Advisory Council seemed to agree with our conclusion. In their 1996 Report of the Working Group on Guidance in Selecting and Monitoring Service Providers, the Advisory Council wrote:

"Many of the problems with respect to service providers arise because the responsible plan fiduciary either does not understand his role and responsibility in the selection and monitoring of service providers or exercises poor judgment because he does not have experience or an appropriate source of information concerning legal requirements and industry practices. The Working Group heard testimony that many of the cases also involve an element of self-dealing."

We have observed that flawless plan administration is a particularly "oversold" capability. Plan sponsors are often frustrated with their current level of administration, and want to believe the next new vendor is going to provide almost perfect service. Plan administration is extremely important and detail oriented. However, the notion that one group will provide almost flawless service is extremely unrealistic.

Instead, the plan sponsor should take an attitude of; "It's not if, but when" in terms of whether or not an administration problem will crop up. It is far more important that the vendor constantly be on the lookout for administration problems and then correct them as soon as possible. Documented evidence of a proactive approach from the vendor is what the plan sponsor should be seeking, rather than perfection. Perfection in the plan administration business does not exist!

Developing a Prudent Vendor Selection Process

Selecting a new vendor and moving a plan is more complicated than most plan sponsors realize. The plan sponsor must endure a never-ending learning process that accompanies the 401(k) plan world. The plan sponsor must not only ask a large number of questions, they must know how to ask the right questions. Once the right questions are asked, the plan sponsor can be confident that they have prudently chosen a provider who will be a partner in ensuring their employees' retirement success.

Bundled or Unbundled?

One of the key decisions that the plan sponsor faces is whether to bundle all plan services with a single provider, or to separately engage specialist providers for each required plan function. There are advantages and disadvantages with each approach. Recently, more plan sponsors seem to be choosing the bundled approach. Recent surveys have indicated about 60% of defined contribution plans the end of 1996 were fully bundled, up from 50% in recent from a recent at the end of 1991.

Characteristics of the Bundled Arrangement:

The chief advantage of the bundled arrangement is "one-stop shopping." The bundled arrangement is a combination of trustee, recordkeeping, and investment management services from a single group. It usually includes a relatively structured set of available plan provisions, recordkeeping reports, funds, etc. In an integrated arrangement, the bundling vendor provides all services; in a contracted arrangement third parties may render some administrative services.

The bundled arrangement may require some or all of the investment choices be products of the bundled provider. However some bundled arrangements, including those offered by Unified Trust Company, NA do not limit the plan sponsor to the investments of any one particular group.

Characteristics of the Unbundled Arrangement:

The unbundled arrangement features separate trustee, recordkeeper, and investment management vendor(s). The plan sponsor, or more, commonly a plan consultant, selects all vendors separately. Theoretically the unbundled arrangement features maximum flexibility for the sponsor in designing plan provisions and selecting and replacing service providers, but may not provide streamlined administration. It may be more difficult for the plan sponsor to prudently select and monitor numerous providers. The unbundled arrangement may result in communication difficulties between disparate companies.

Fiduciary Responsibility for Vendor Selection

Vendor selection is a fiduciary responsibility under ERISA. Fiduciaries are responsible for operating the plan solely for the benefit of plan participants and beneficiaries, and can be sued by participants, beneficiaries and the DOL for not adequately fulfilling their fiduciary responsibilities. In selecting vendors for their plans, plan fiduciaries face two potential problems:

1. Poor or inadequately documented selection of investment providers; and

2. Lack of appropriate distinction between administrative service pricing and capabilities, and investment management pricing and capabilities.

Both problems tend to occur because of the fact that most plan sponsors focus on selecting a specific provider too early in the process. Most large bundled providers have aggressive sales executives who are eager to demonstrate their organization's capabilities. Subsidization of plan administrative services has developed to the extent that for many vendors in the mid- and large plan market, the perceived out-of-pocket price for recordkeeping, administrative, and directed (nondiscretionary) trustee services is near zero. With the opportunity to eliminate most or all out-of-pocket costs, and to take advantage of the latest service package offered by the bundled providers, many sponsors jump immediately from basic fact finding to vendor selection. All too often little analytical review is done to answer the most basic question of whether or not the new vendor will have any meaningful impact on improving participant retirement success.

Fiduciary liability is significant when visible administration fees drive the vendor selection decision.

Completely or partially closed menu investment structures in some bundled service arrangements present plan fiduciaries with the greatest potential exposure to fiduciary litigation. Generally, in these arrangements the only funds available to the plan are funds managed by the investment provider that also delivers administrative services. In some cases a limited menu of outside funds with unknown fiduciary characteristics are available to plan sponsor. The plan sponsors generally are unaware that the vendor typically included such funds because of the extra revenue payments they are paying to the nondiscretionary vendor.

Typically funds cannot be selected or replaced for the plan, unless they are available through the investment provider. Although these plans tend to have relatively low "hard dollar" administrative costs, they often bear significantly higher than average investment expenses. In addition such funds typically have mediocre to poor fiduciary characteristics when evaluated objectively. Few (if any) investment providers offer solid fund options in every asset class. Thus, in selecting the bundled service provider using proprietary investments, the plan fiduciaries may implicitly select less than optimal funds for their plan. Often they have no objective analysis and documentation of their investment selection process and leave themselves vulnerable under ERISA.

There is a good rule of thumb for actual 401(k) costs in a closed menu typical bundled, "one-stop shopping" approach for both proprietary investments and administration services from the same company:

In general a closed menu bundled approach will, at a minimum, double the employees' cost for every 25% reduction in the plan sponsor's out-of-pocket plan administration fees.

Many plan fiduciaries fail to distinguish between a vendor's administrative service pricing and capabilities, and their investment management pricing and capabilities. There are several reasons for this confusion, including that investment fees are generally paid directly from fund assets, through an implicit reduction in the fund's Net Asset Value (NAV), while administrative fees are generally paid by the plan sponsor, and hence receive greater scrutiny. In addition investment performance and costs are often difficult to evaluate, due to varying performance measurement approaches and fee schedules buried deep in the prospectus. Administrative services and related fees are generally easier to evaluate objectively. Often the HR department responsible for the vendor evaluation will work most closely with the selected provider, and will rely on the vendor for administrative support which should for functions such as distributing participant statements, processing benefit payments, etc.

If administrative services are deficient, the fiduciary will receive numerous complaints and questions from disgruntled plan participants. Although these reasons appear legitimate, ERISA makes fiduciaries responsible for ensuring that participants have the opportunity to invest in high quality funds. Keep in mind the SR+RR Index requires both an acceptable savings rate and investment return for retirement success. Thus the investment results will also have a significant impact on a participant's ability to retire at a suitable and sustainable standard of living.

The Unified Proposal Evaluation System^{SM}

The first step the plan sponsor should undertake is to calculate an overall success probability calculation for each plan participant based upon the formulas we outlined earlier in this book. Only after the current success probability is known is the plan sponsor in a position to improve the success by prudently selecting a new vendor. The new vendor should be selected in a prudent and well-documented process.

Selecting a new vendor prudently is best accomplished through a formal Request for Proposal ("RFP") process, using the Unified Proposal Evaluation System^{SM} where a cross section of service providers are asked to respond to a standardized set of questions. Our proposal system allows the plan sponsor to weight different categories according to their preferences, and also focus the weighting on areas most important for participant success. It also provides the ability to accurately compare different proposals for cost and value by dividing the plan costs (in basis points) by the overall value score.

For example, assume the plan sponsor is considering three proposals that range in total cost from 96 to 155 basis points. At first glance the 96 basis point proposal ("XYZ") looks best. However when the overall value is considered, XYZ costs 1.78 basis points per unit of overall value. On the other hand, ABC only costs 1.19 basis points per unit of overall value and is the best choice for the plan participants.

Table 20-1: Cost per Unit of Value Delivered

Vendor	Total Plan Costs	Overall Value Score	Basis Points Spent Per Unit of Value
ABC	115	97%	1.19
DEF	135	67%	2.01
JKL	120	52%	2.31
QRS	155	37%	4.19
XYZ	96	54%	1.78

The Unified Proposal Evaluation System^{SM}

Categories Evaluated

- ✓ Outcome Analysis
- ✓ Investment Platform
- ✓ Investment Management
- ✓ Asset Quality
- ✓ Fiduciary Responsibility
- ✓ Potential Conflicts of Interest
- ✓ Asset Safety
- ✓ 404(c) Compliance Responsibility
- ✓ Plan Cost Analysis
- ✓ Participant Investment Advice
- ✓ Education and Communication
- ✓ Service Quality
- ✓ Recordkeeping
- ✓ Plan Administration

- ✓ Overall Score

- ✓ Basis Points Spent Per Unit of Overall Value Received

Figure 20-1: Proposal Score Summary

ERISA Services Proposal Analysis Summary

Prepared for The Acme Corporation Board of Directors

January 10, 2004

By Unified Trust Company, NA

RFP CATEGORY	POSSIBLE SCORE	ACTUAL SCORE	% OF POSSIBLE SCORE	CATEGORY WEIGHT
Investment Platform	100	95	95%	3.0%
Investment Management	100	100	100%	5.0%
Asset Quality	100	100	100%	10.0%
Fiduciary Responsibility	100	100	100%	15.0%
Conflicts of Interest	100	100	100%	10.0%
Asset Safety	100	100	100%	6.0%
404(c) Compliance	100	100	100%	5.0%
Plan Cost Analysis	100	100	100%	5.0%
Participant Investment Advice	100	100	100%	10.0%
Education and Communication	100	100	100%	5.0%
Service Quality	100	95	95%	5.0%
Recordkeeping	100	93	93%	3.0%
Plan Administration	100	100	100%	3.0%
RFP Totals	1400	1383	99%	

WEIGHTED OVERALL SCORE	99.34%

Basis Points Spent Per Unit Of Overall Value	1.19

Chart 20-1: Overall Score Per Category Summary

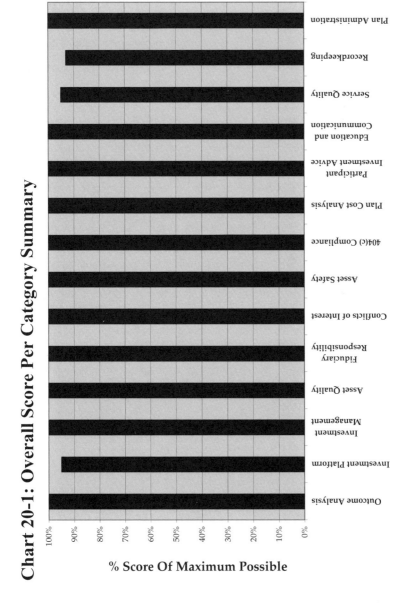

% Score Of Maximum Possible

Categories (top to bottom): Plan Administration, Recordkeeping, Service Quality, Education and Communication, Participant Investment Advice, Plan Cost Analysis, 404(c) Compliance, Asset Safety, Conflicts of Interest, Fiduciary Responsibility, Asset Quality, Investment Management, Investment Platform, Outcome Analysis

Axis: 0%, 10%, 20%, 30%, 40%, 50%, 60%, 70%, 80%, 90%, 100%

Figure 20-2: Outcome Analysis Data

		1. OUTCOME ANALYSIS		
Proposal Points	Proposal Answer	**Investment Performance Monitoring** (select all that apply)	Possible Points	Percent Weighting
10	Yes	1. Vendor has examined its investment monitoring system prospectively for outcome effects	10	
15	Yes	2. Vendor has determined its monitoring system adds value prospectively	15	
10	Yes	3. Vendor will share prospective outcome data with plan sponsor	10	
35	Total Actual Points	Total Possible Points	**35**	**35%**
Proposal Points	Proposal Answer	**Employee Plan Participation and Savings Rates** (select all that apply)	Possible Points	Percent Weighting
10	Yes	4. Vendor has examined its educational system prospectively for outcome effects on employee participation and savings rates	10	
15	Yes	5. Vendor has determined its programs improve employee participation and savings prospectively	15	
10	Yes	6. Vendor will share program outcome data with plan sponsor	10	
35	Total Actual Points	Total Possible Points	**35**	**35%**
Proposal Points	Proposal Answer	**Retirement Success and Default Pathways** (select all that apply)	Possible Points	Percent Weighting
15	Yes	7. Vendor has developed a program to quantify both the individual employee's success probability and aggregate plan retirement success probability	15	
15	Yes	8. Vendor utilizes default pathways to improve both the individual employee's success probability and aggregate plan retirement success probability	15	
30	Total RFP Actual Points	Total Possible Points	**30**	**30%**
100	Outcome Analysis Grand Total Proposal Actual Points		**100** Total Possible	**100%**
100%	Outcome Analysis Proposal Actual % of Possible Total Points			

Figure 20-3: Investment Platform Analysis Data

		2. INVESTMENT PLATFORM			
Proposal Points	**Proposal Answer**	**Access to Investments** (select one)		**Possible Points**	**Percent Weighting**
20	Yes	9. Open architecture		20	
0	n/a	10. If not open architecture, number of investment options offered by vendor (n/a = 0 points) (select one from drop down list)	1-5 Options 6-10 Options 11-20 Options 21-30 Options >30 Options	3 5 8 10 5	
20	Total Actual Points		Total Possible Points	**20**	**20%**
Proposal Points	**Proposal Answer**	**Self Directed Brokerage Accounts** (select all that apply)		**Possible Points**	**Percent Weighting**
10	Yes	11. Self directed brokerage account available		10	
0	No	12. Plan sponsor may choose multiple vendors		2	
10	Total Actual Points		Total Possible Points	**12**	**12%**
Proposal Points	**Proposal Answer**	**Proprietary Investments** (select one)		**Possible Points**	**Percent Weighting**
0	No	13. Non-proprietary investments only		20	
25	Yes	14. Proprietary investments available, not required		25	
0	No	15. Proprietary investments partially required		5	
0	No	16. Proprietary investments only options		0	
25	Total Actual Points		Total Possible Points	**25**	**25%**
Proposal Points	**Proposal Answer**	**Types of Pooled Investment Vehicles** (select all that apply)		**Possible Points**	**Percent Weighting**
15	Yes	17. Mutual Funds		15	
5	Yes	18. Collective Investment Trusts		5	
0	No	19. Insurance Company Separate Accounts		3	
5	Yes	20. Institutional Money Managers		5	
25	Total Actual Points		Total Possible Points	**28**	**28%**
Proposal Points	**Proposal Answer**	**Trading** (select one)		**Possible Points**	**Percent Weighting**
0	No	21. No daily trading ability		0	
15	Yes	22. Daily valuation trading, T+0 execution		15	
0	No	23. Daily valuation trading, T+1 execution		12	
15	Total Actual Points		Total Possible Points	**15**	**15%**
95	Investment Platform Grand Total Proposal Actual Points			**100**	**100%** Total Possible
95%	Investment Platform Proposal Actual % of Possible Total Points				

Figure 20-4: Investment Management Analysis Data

		3. INVESTMENT MANAGEMENT		
Proposal Points	Proposal Answer	**Investment Policy Statement (IPS")** (select one)	Possible Points	Percent Weighting
20	Yes	24. Vendor is responsible for IPS drafting and maintenance	20	
0	No	25. Vendor provides tools, but plan sponsor is responsible for IPS as fiduciary	10	
0	No	26. Vendor provides no IPS assistance	0	
20	Total Actual Points	Total Possible Points	20	20%
Proposal Points	Proposal Answer	**Fiduciary Responsibility For Plan Asset Monitoring** (select one)	Possible Points	Percent Weighting
20	Yes	27. Vendor is responsible for asset monitoring as a fiduciary	20	
0	No	28. Vendor provides tools, but plan sponsor is responsible for asset monitoring as fiduciary	10	
0	No	29. Vendor provides no monitoring assistance	0	
20	Total Actual Points	Total Possible Points	20	20%
Proposal Points	Proposal Answer	**Fiduciary Responsibility For Fund Replacement** (select one)	Possible Points	Percent Weighting
20	Yes	30. Vendor is responsible for fund replacement as a fiduciary	20	
0	No	31. Vendor provides tools, but plan sponsor is responsible for fund replacement as fiduciary	10	
0	No	32. Vendor provides no fund replacement help	0	
20	Total Actual Points	Total Possible Points	20	20%
Proposal Points	Proposal Answer	**Frequency of Fiduciary Monitoring** (select one)	Possible Points	Percent Weighting
10	Yes	33. Quarterly	10	
0	No	34. Semi-Annual	5	
0	No	35. Annual	3	
0	No	36. No set schedule or definitive process	0	
10	Total Actual Points	Total Possible Points	10	10%
Proposal Points	Proposal Answer	**Plan Level Monitoring Reports** (select all that apply)	Possible Points	Percent Weighting
10	Yes	37. Reports compare investment results vs. IPS	10	
10	Yes	38. Reports show "Watch List" investments	10	
10	Yes	39. Reports show "Replacement List" investments	10	
30	Total Actual Points	Total Possible Points	30	30%
100		Investment Management Grand Total Proposal Actual Points	100	100% Total Possible
100%		Investment Management Proposal Actual % of Possible Total Points		

Figure 20-5: Asset Quality Analysis Data

		4. ASSET QUALITY		
Proposal Points	Proposal Answer	Unified Fiduciary Monitoring Index® Score (select one)	Possible Points	Percent Weighting
40	Yes	40. All funds currently held score in top 25%	40	
0	No	41. All funds currently held score in top 40%	20	
0	No	42. All funds currently held score in top 50%	10	
0	No	43. Some funds currently held score in bottom 50%	0	
40	Total Actual Points	Total Possible Points	40	40%
Proposal Points	Proposal Answer	Investment Performance Monitoring (select one)	Possible Points	Percent Weighting
30	Yes	44. All investments are mutual funds, or AIMR audited money managers	30	
0	No	45. Vendor offers some investment managers not AIMR audited, but AIMR compliant	20	
0	No	46. Vendor offers some investment managers neither AIMR audited, nor AIMR compliant	10	
30	Total Actual Points	Total Possible Points	30	30%
Proposal Points	Proposal Answer	Unbiased Assessment of Proprietary Funds (if any) (select one)	Possible Points	Percent Weighting
30	Yes	47. Vendor subjects its proprietary funds to same fiduciary criteria as external funds	30	
0	No	48. Vendor subjects its proprietary funds to lessor or no fiduciary criteria as external funds	0	
30	Total Actual Points	Total Possible Points	30	30%

100	Asset Quality Grand Total Proposal Actual Points		100	100% Total Possible
100%	Asset Quality Proposal Actual % of Possible Total Points			

Figure 20-6: Fiduciary Responsibility Analysis Data

5. FIDUCIARY RESPONSIBILITY

Proposal Points	Proposal Answer	Trustee Status (select one)	Possible Points	Percent Weighting
15	Yes	49. Vendor functions as a discretionary trustee	15	
0	No	50. Vendor functions as a directed trustee	5	
0	No	51. Vendor is not a trustee	0	
15	Total Actual Points	Total Possible Points	**15**	**15%**

Proposal Points	Proposal Answer	Vendor Fiduciary Status (select one)	Possible Points	Percent Weighting
15	Yes	52. Vendor accepts discretion and full fiduciary liability in writing	15	
0	No	53. Vendor does not accept discretion, but does accept full fiduciary liability in writing	10	
0	No	54. Vendor does not accept discretion, but does accept partial fiduciary liability in writing	5	
0	No	55. Vendor does not accept discretion, and does not accept any fiduciary liability in writing	0	
15	Total Actual Points	Total Possible Points	**15**	**15%**

Proposal Points	Proposal Answer	Vendor's Accepted Fiduciary Responsibilities: (select all that apply)	Possible Points	Percent Weighting
5	Yes	56. Drafting Investment Policy Statement ("IPS")	5	
5	Yes	57. Asset custody	5	
5	Yes	58. Investment management	5	
5	Yes	59. Model portfolio management	5	
5	Yes	60. Establishment of prudent criteria for plan investment selection	5	
5	Yes	61. Selection of plan investments or investment managers	5	
5	Yes	62. Establishment of prudent criteria for plan investment retention	5	
5	Yes	63. Monitoring of plan investments vs IPS	5	
5	Yes	64. Creation of fiduciary monitoring reports for plan sponsor's corporate records	5	
5	Yes	65. Automatic replacement of assets not meeting IPS criteria	5	
50	Total Actual Points	Total Possible Points	**50**	**50%**

Proposal Points	Proposal Answer	Named Fiduciary (select all that apply)	Possible Points	Percent Weighting
10	Yes	66. Vendor serves as Named Fiduciary of plan	10	
10	Yes	67. Vendor serves as Named Fiduciary for ERISA 404(c) purposes and notices	10	
20	Total Actual Points	Total Possible Points	**20**	**20%**

100	Fiduciary Responsibility Grand Total Proposal Actual Points	100	100% Total Possible
100%	Fiduciary Responsibility Proposal Actual % of Possible Total Points		

Figure 20-7: Potential Conflicts of Interest Analysis Data

6. POTENTIAL CONFLICTS OF INTEREST

Proposal Points	Proposal Answer	Proprietary Investments (select one)	Possible Points	Percent Weighting
30	Yes	68. Proprietary investments available, but not required	30	
0	No	69. Proprietary investments partially required	10	
0	No	70. Proprietary investments only options	0	
30	**Total Actual Points**	**Total Possible Points**	30	30%

Proposal Points	Proposal Answer	Compensation Disclosure (select one)	Possible Points	Percent Weighting
20	Yes	71. Vendor is paid fees or commissions for its services, with full disclosure to plan sponsor	20	
0	Yes	72. Vendor is paid fees or commissions for its services, without full disclosure to plan sponsor	0	
20	**Total Actual Points**	**Total Possible Points**	20	20%

Proposal Points	Proposal Answer	Sources of Compensation (select one)	Possible Points	Percent Weighting
30	Yes	73. Vendor is revenue neutral, meaning that any selection of an investment does not change vendor's compensation	30	
0	Yes	74. Vendor receives additional potential fees from changes in investments, mutual funds or third party service providers, such as soft dollar fees	0	
30	**Total Actual Points**	**Total Possible Points**	30	30%

Proposal Points	Proposal Answer	Referral Fees (select all that apply)	Possible Points	Percent Weighting
20	Yes	75. Has vendor paid a referral fee to a third party in exchange for referrals or business?	20	
0	No	76. Have full amounts of referral fees, and name of the referring group been disclosed to plan sponsor?	0	
20	**Total Actual Points**	**Total Possible Points**	20	20%

100	Potential Conflicts of Interest Grand Total Proposal Actual Points		100	100% Total Possible
100%	Potential Conflicts of Interest Proposal Actual % of Possible Total Points			

Figure 20-8: Asset Safety Analysis Data

		7. ASSET SAFETY		
Proposal Points	**Proposal Answer**	**Trustee Charter** (select one)	**Possible Points**	**Percent Weighting**
0	Yes	77. Trustee is an individual	0	
0	No	78. Trustee is State chartered	5	
10	Yes	79. Trustee is Federally chartered	10	
10	Total Actual Points	**Total Possible Points**	10	10%
Proposal Points	**Proposal Answer**	**Trustee Financial Status** (select all that apply)	**Possible Points**	**Percent Weighting**
10	Yes	80. The most recent income statement and balance sheet for the trustee have been provided, and deemed acceptable	10	
10	Yes	81. Trustee has provided evidence of in force Errors & Omission insurance, and deemed adequate	10	
5	Yes	82. Trustee has provided evidence of in force fidelity bonding, and deemed adequate	5	
5	Yes	83. The most SAS 70 audit report for the trustee has been provided, and deemed acceptable	5	
30	Total Actual Points	**Total Possible Points**	30	30%
Proposal Points	**Proposal Answer**	**Interest Bearing Account Risk Assessment** (select all that apply)	**Possible Points**	**Percent Weighting**
5	Yes	84. Vendor offers GIC, Stable Value Fund, or other such fixed interest bearing deposit like investment	5	
10	Yes	85. Is investment principal protected from claims by vendor's creditors?	10	
5	Yes	86. Is principal guaranteed?	5	
5	Yes	87. Is guarantee by group other than vendor?	5	
5	Yes	88. If account is guaranteed by vendor, is vendor's third party credit status review investment grade?	5	
5	Yes	89. If account is guaranteed by group other than vendor, is such outside group's credit rating by independent third part review investment grade?	5	
5	Yes	90. Is the account without surrender charge at the participant level?	5	
40	Total Actual Points	**Total Possible Points**	40	40%
Proposal Points	**Proposal Answer**	**Named Fiduciary** (select all that apply)	**Possible Points**	**Percent Weighting**
10	Yes	91. Has vendor operated without any type of regulatory sanction in past two years?	10	
10	Yes	92. Has vendor operated without any type of material lawsuit in past two years?	10	
20	Total Actual Points	**Total Possible Points**	20	20%
100	Asset Safety Grand Total Proposal Actual Points		100	100% Total Possible
100%	Asset Safety Proposal Actual % of Possible Total Points			

Figure 20-9: 404(c) Compliance Analysis Data

8. 404(c) COMPLIANCE RESPONSIBILITY

Proposal Points	Proposal Answer	Participant Investment Direction (select one)	Possible Points	Percent Weighting
15	Yes	93. Is plan participant directed?	15	
15	Total Actual Points	Total Possible Points	15	15%

IF ANSWER TO #93 IS "NO", OMIT REMAINDER OF THIS SECTION

Proposal Points	Proposal Answer	404(c) Notice to Participants (select one)	Possible Points	Percent Weighting
20	Yes	94. Vendor provides notice	20	
0	No	95. Vendor provides assistance to plan sponsor, but plan sponsor is responsible	10	
0	No	96. Vendor provides no assistance	0	
20	Total Actual Points	Total Possible Points	20	20%

Proposal Points	Proposal Answer	404(c) Ongoing Compliance Responsibility (select one)	Possible Points	Percent Weighting
15	Yes	97. Vendor is responsible	15	
0	No	98. Plan sponsor is responsible	0	
15	Total Actual Points	Total Possible Points	15	15%

Proposal Points	Proposal Answer	404(c) Workflow (select all that apply)	Possible Points	Percent Weighting
10	Yes	99. Vendor has written 404(c) compliance policy	10	
10	Yes	100. All investment instructions are delivered to the Named Fiduciary listed in the Notice to Participants	10	
20	Total Actual Points	Total Possible Points	20	20%

Proposal Points	Proposal Answer	Investment Advice and/or Model Portfolios (select all that apply)	Possible Points	Percent Weighting
10	Yes	101. Vendor accepts, in writing, fiduciary responsibility and discretion for investment advice	10	
10	Yes	102. Vendor accepts, in writing, fiduciary responsibility and discretion for managing models	10	
20	Total Actual Points	Total Possible Points	20	20%

Proposal Points	Proposal Answer	404(c) Ongoing Compliance Responsibility (select one)	Possible Points	Percent Weighting
10	Yes	103. Vendor is responsible for prospectus delivery	10	
0	No	104. Plan sponsor is responsible for prospectus delivery	0	
10	Total Actual Points	Total Possible Points	10	10%

100	404(c) Compliance Responsibility Grand Total Proposal Actual Points	100 100% Total Possible

100%	404(c) Compliance Responsibility Proposal Actual % of Possible Total Points

Figure 20-10: Plan Cost Analysis Data

9. PLAN COST ANALYSIS				
Proposal Points	**Proposal Answer**	**Fee and Cost Disclosure** (select all that apply)	**Possible Points**	**Percent Weighting**
10	Yes	105. Cost illustrations submitted in DOL Model Fee Disclosure format	10	
10	Yes	106. Vendor has provided easy-to-understand breakdown of costs showing exact amounts of compensation for each party	10	
10	Yes	107. Vendor has provided comprehensive fee schedules that include all pertinent costs, such as asset-based fees, surrender charges, and event processing fees	10	
5	Yes	108. Vendor guarantees rates for at least two years	5	
15	Yes	109. Vendor tracks revenue sharing payments at the plan level, and reports plan specific data to the plan sponsor no less than annually participant level?	15	
50	**Total Actual Points**	**Total Possible Points**	50	50%
Proposal Points	**Proposal Answer**	**Revenue Sharing DOL Model Letter Framework** (select one)	**Possible Points**	**Percent Weighting**
0	No	110. Vendor has not disclosed or will not disclose the full dollar amounts of all revenue sharing payments it collects ("Aetna Model")	0	
20	Yes	111. Vendor provides full disclosure of all revenue sharing payments it collects ("Frost Model")	20	
20	**Total Actual Points**	**Total Possible Points**	20	20%
Proposal Points	**Proposal Answer**	**Revenue Sharing Fee Offset** (select one)	**Possible Points**	**Percent Weighting**
0	No	112. Vendor provides offset of fees with some of the revenue sharing payments received, but any excess revenue payments are retained by vendor	10	
30	Yes	113. Vendor provides offset of fees with 100% of the revenue sharing payments received, and any excess revenue payments are rebated back to the plan participants.	30	
30	**Total Actual Points**	**Total Possible Points**	30	30%
	Proposal Data	**Plan Cost Data** (enter plan data for first four fields)		
	125	114. Total number of participants		
	$1,750,000	115. Total plan assets		
	$4,400	116. Total estimated recordkeeping costs		
	$16,300	117. Total estimated asset based costs (direct & indirect)		
	$20,700	118. [Sum] estimated all inclusive plan costs (dollars)		
	118	119. [Sum] estimated all inclusive plan costs [basis points (100 = 1.0%)]		

100	Plan Cost Analysis Grand Total Proposal Actual Points	100	100%
100%	Plan Cost Analysis Proposal Actual % of Possible Total Points		**Total Possible**

Figure 20-11: Participant Investment Advice Analysis Data

10. PARTICIPANT INVESTMENT ADVICE

Proposal Points	Proposal Answer	Availability of Participant Investment Advice (select one)		Possible Points	Percent Weighting
10	Yes	120. Vendor provides specific investment advice, and accepts fiduciary liability in writing		10	
0	No	121. Vendor provides "near advice", but does not accepts fiduciary liability in writing		5	
10	Total Actual Points		Total Possible Points	10	10%

Proposal Points	Proposal Answer	Investment Advice Fee Structure (select one from drop down list)		Possible Points	Percent Weighting
15	0.00%	121. Additional charge for advice	0.00%	15	
		of investment options offered	up to 0.25%	10	
		by vendor	0.25% to 0.50%	5	
			0.50% to 1.00%	2	
			more than 1.00%	0	
15	Total Actual Points		Total Possible Points	15	15%

Proposal Points	Proposal Answer	Advice Delivery Channels from Vendor (select all that apply)	Possible Points	Percent Weighting
5	Yes	123. Internet investment advice	5	
5	Yes	124. Internet investment "near advice"	5	
5	Yes	125. Suggested portfolio models (paper)	5	
10	Yes	126. Actively managed model portfolios	10	
5	Yes	127. One on one personal counseling (call center)	5	
10	Yes	128. One on one personal counseling (in person)	10	
40	Total Actual Points	Total Possible Points	40	40%

Proposal Points	Proposal Answer	Model Portfolio Analysis (select all that apply)	Possible Points	Percent Weighting
5	Yes	129. Manager accepts fiduciary status and discretion in writing for model management	5	
5	Yes	130. Model performance shown against appropriate stock:bond benchmark mix	5	
5	Yes	131. Model portfolios are comprised of non-proprietary funds only	5	
5	Yes	132. IPS for model management is provided/available	5	
20	Total Actual Points	Total Possible Points	20	20%

Proposal Points	Proposal Answer	Model Portfolio Advice Fee Structure (select one from drop down list)		Possible Points	Percent Weighting
15	0.00%	133. Additional charge for advice	0.00%	15	
		concerning model portfolios	up to 0.25%	10	
		by vendor	0.25% to 0.50%	5	
			0.50% to 1.00%	2	
			more than 1.00%	0	
15	Total Actual Points		Total Possible Points	15	15%

100	Participant Investment Advice Grand Total Proposal Actual Points	100	100% Total Possible
100%	Participant Investment Advice Proposal Actual % of Possible Total Points		

Figure 20-12: Education and Communication Analysis Data

		11. EDUCATION AND COMMUNICATION		
Proposal Points	Proposal Answer	Enrollment Materials (select all that apply)	Possible Points	Percent Weighting
5	Yes	134. Vendor provides instructions for enrolling and participating in the plan	5	
5	Yes	135. Vendor provides guidance to help participants determine their risk tolerance	5	
5	Yes	136. Vendor provides guidance for participants to decide on their asset allocation	5	
5	Yes	137. Vendor provides all necessary forms	5	
20	Total Actual Points	Total Possible Points	20	20%
Proposal Points	Proposal Answer	Online Tools and Content (select all that apply)	Possible Points	Percent Weighting
5	Yes	138. Vendor provides online account information	5	
5	Yes	139. Vendor provides online account trading	5	
5	Yes	140. Vendor provides online articles on financial topics	5	
5	Yes	141. Vendor provides information on the plan, benefits of participating and other basic retirement topics	5	
5	Yes	142. Vendor provides online retirement calculator	5	
10	Yes	143. Vendor provides online advice service	10	
5	Yes	144. Vendor provides online fiduciary reviews of plan investment choices for participants	5	
5	Yes	145. Vendor provides plan level information online for the plan sponsor	5	
45	Total Actual Points	Total Possible Points	45	45%
Proposal Points	Proposal Answer	Enrollment and Education Meetings (select all that apply)	Possible Points	Percent Weighting
5	Yes	146. Vendor provides onsite *group* meetings with vendor's staff, or with investment professionals representing or working in conjunction with vendor	5	
5	Yes	147. Vendor provides *group* teleconferences with vendor's staff, or with investment professionals representing or working in conjunction with vendor	5	
15	Yes	148. Vendor provides onsite *one-on-one* meetings with vendor's staff, or with investment professionals representing or working in conjunction with vendor	15	
10	Yes	149. Vendor provides call center for one-on-one interactions with vendor's staff	10	
35	Total Actual Points	Total Possible Points	35	35%
100	Education and Communication Grand Total Proposal Actual Points		100 Total Possible	100%
100%	Education and Communication Proposal Actual % of Possible Total Points			

Figure 20-13: Service Quality Analysis Data

		12. SERVICE QUALITY			
Proposal Points	Proposal Answer	Experience (Years in ERISA Business) (select one from drop down list)		Possible Points	Percent Weighting
15	more than 15	150. Years vendor has offered ERISA services to its clients	> 15 Years	15	
			10-15 Years	10	
			5-10 Years	5	
			< 5 Years	2	
			Unknown	0	
15	Total Actual Points		Total Possible Points	15	15%
Proposal Points	Proposal Answer	Experience (Number of Plans Serviced) (select one from drop down list)		Possible Points	Percent Weighting
5	250-500	151. Total number of plans serviced	> 1,000	10	
			500-1000	8	
			250-500	5	
			< 250	2	
			Unknown	0	
5	Total Actual Points		Total Possible Points	10	10%
Proposal Points	Proposal Answer	Quality Philosophy (select all that apply)		Possible Points	Percent Weighting
10	Yes	152. Vendor has adopted formal "Best Practices" method of quality management		10	
10	Yes	153. Vendor has a formal quality improvement process		10	
10	Yes	154. Vendor's quality/process improvement program is documented and vendor is willing to permit plan sponsor to inspect documentation		10	
10	Yes	155. Vendor follows written policies/procedures for most major functions and is willing to permit plan sponsor to inspect policies/procedures		10	
40	Total Actual Points		Total Possible Points	40	40%
Proposal Points	Proposal Answer	Installations and Conversions (select all that apply)		Possible Points	Percent Weighting
10	Yes	156. Vendor maintains dedicated installation or conversion specialists		10	
10	Yes	157. Vendor maintains formal, written transition plan with timeline and checklists)		10	
10	Yes	158. Vendor promptly communicates any changes in timeline to the plan sponsor as a matter of policy		10	
5	Yes	159. Vendor's normal blackout time period length is equal to or less than industry average		5	
35	Total Actual Points		Total Possible Points	35	35%
Proposal	Proposal	Model Portfolio Advice Fee Structure		Possible	Percent
95	Service Quality Grand Total Proposal Actual Points			100 Total Possible	100%
95%	Service Quality Proposal Actual % of Possible Total Points				

Figure 20-14: Recordkeeping Analysis Data

13. RECORDKEEPING

Proposal Points	Proposal Answer	Number of Participants Serviced (select one from drop down list)		Possible Points	Percent Weighting
13	10000 to 100000	160. Total number of plan participants serviced by vendor	> 100,000	15	
			10,000 to 100,000	13	
			1,000 to 10,000	10	
			< 1,000	5	
			Unknown	0	
13	Total Actual Points		Total Possible Points	**15**	**15%**

Proposal Points	Proposal Answer	Participant Call Center Activity (select all that apply)	Possible Points	Percent Weighting
10	Yes	161. Participants have a toll-free number to call to receive live assistance	10	
0	No	162. Call center hours of operation are 24 x 7 x 365	5	
5	Yes	163. Spanish language support	5	
10	Yes	164. Written confirmations follow trades placed through call center	10	
25	Total Actual Points	Total Possible Points	**30**	**30%**

Proposal Points	Proposal Answer	Employee Workload (select one from drop down list)		Possible Points	Percent Weighting
25	less than 50	165. Number of plans per recordkeeping employee	< 50	25	
			50 to 75	20	
			75 to 100	15	
			> 100	0	
			Unknown	0	
25	Total Actual Points		Total Possible Points	**25**	**25%**

Proposal Points	Proposal Answer	Installations and Conversions (select all that apply)	Possible Points	Percent Weighting
5	Yes	166. Vendor accepts contributions by wire	5	
5	Yes	167. Vendor accepts contributions by check	5	
5	Yes	168. Vendor accepts contributions by ACH	5	
5	Yes	169. Vendor accepts payroll data via email	5	
5	Yes	170. Vendor accepts payroll data by paper	5	
5	Yes	171.Vendor accepts payroll data from payroll service	5	
30	Total Actual Points	Total Possible Points	**30**	**30%**

Proposal	Proposal	Model Portfolio Advice Fee Structure	Possible	Percent
93	Recordkeeping Grand Total Proposal Actual Points		100	100%
				Total Possible
93%	Recordkeeping Proposal Actual % of Possible Total Points			

Figure 20-3: Plan Administration Analysis Data

14. PLAN ADMINISTRATION				
Proposal Points	**Proposal Answer**	**Plan Administration Staff Credentials** (select all that apply)	**Possible Points**	**Percent Weighting**
20	Yes	172. Vendor has in house ERISA legal counsel to answer plan sponsor technical and legal questions	20	
10	Yes	173. Vendor's employees have special certification generally accepted by the employee benefits industry in their field of work	10	
30	Total Actual Points	Total Possible Points	30	30%
Proposal Points	**Proposal Answer**	**Plan Design Expertise** (select all that apply)	**Possible Points**	**Percent Weighting**
5	Yes	174. Includes standardized pension and profit sharing plans (including 401k)	5	
10	Yes	175. Includes non-standardized pension and profit sharing plans (including 401k)	10	
10	Yes	176. Includes safe harbor 401(k) plans	10	
10	Yes	177. Includes age weighted plans	10	
10	Yes	178. Includes new comparability plans	10	
5	Yes	179. Includes defined benefit plans	5	
10	Yes	180. Vendor will prepare IRS filings, including all determination letter requests	10	
60	Total Actual Points	Total Possible Points	60	60%
Proposal Points	**Proposal Answer**	**Vendor Administration Relationships** (select one)	**Possible Points**	**Percent Weighting**
10	Yes	181. Vendor provides plan administration services with in house staff	10	
0	No	182. Vendor provides plan administration services through a third party, and the vendor-third party relationship has been in place at least five years	10	
0	No	183. Vendor provides plan administration services through a third party, and the vendor-third party relationship has been in place less than five years	5	
10	Total Actual Points	Total Possible Points	10	10%
100	Plan Administration Grand Total Proposal Actual Points		100 Total Possible	100%
100%	Plan Administration Proposal Actual % of Possible Total Points			

Appendix

Important Department of Labor Advisory Opinions

Advisory Opinion 97-15A

This opinion ("Frost Letter") sets forth the DOL views concerning under what circumstances a discretionary trustee may receive fees from mutual funds recommended by the trustee. When the discretionary trustee controls the mutual fund menu, the discretionary trustee must offset any mutual fund fees received as a dollar for dollar offsets against the trustee's reasonable fees. Pages 472-480.

Advisory Opinion 97-16A

This opinion ("Aetna Letter") sets forth the DOL views concerning under what circumstances a non-discretionary fiduciary may receive fees from mutual funds and retain such fees without offset. Pages 481-491.

Advisory Opinion 2001-09A

This opinion ("SunAmerica Letter") sets forth the DOL views concerning under what circumstances a fiduciary may be exempt from the prohibited transaction restrictions of Section 406 of ERISA, with respect to a asset allocation program under which SunAmerica would render certain discretionary and nondiscretionary investment services to participants in ERISA-covered plans. Pages 492-504.

Advisory Opinion 2003-09A

This opinion ("ABN AMRO Letter"). sets forth the DOL views concerning under what circumstances a nondiscretionary fiduciary offering limited investment advice may be exempt from the prohibited transaction restrictions of Section 406 of ERISA. Pages 505-515.

Advisory Opinion   97-15A

May 22, 1997

Mark S. Miller
Fulbright & Jaworski, LLP
1301 McKinney, Suite 5100
Houston, Texas 77010-3095
ERISA SEC.
406(b)(3)

Dear Mr. Miller:

This is in response to your request for an advisory opinion regarding the prohibited transaction provisions of the Employee Retirement Income Security Act of 1974 (ERISA). In particular, you ask whether the payment of certain fees by a mutual fund in which an employee pension benefit plan has invested to a bank serving as the plan's trustee would violate sections 406(b)(1) and 406(b)(3) of ERISA.

You represent that Frost National Bank (Frost) serves as trustee to various employee pension benefit plans (the Plans). As trustee of the Plans, Frost's duties may include one or more of the following functions, pursuant to instructions from the Plan sponsor or participants: opening and maintaining individual participant accounts; receiving contributions from the Plan sponsor and crediting them to individual participant accounts; investing contributions in shares of a mutual fund and reinvesting dividends and other distributions; redeeming, transferring, or exchanging mutual fund shares; providing or maintaining various administrative forms in making distributions from the Plan to participants or beneficiaries; keeping custody of the Plan's assets; withholding amounts on Plan distributions; making sure all Plan loan payments are collected and properly credited; conducting Plan enrollment meetings; and preparing newsletters and videos relating to the administration of the Plan.

In connection with its Plan-related business, Frost has entered into arrangements with one or more distributors of, or investment advisors to, mutual fund families pursuant to which Frost will make the mutual fund families available for investment by the Plans. Frost will periodically review each such mutual fund family to determine whether to continue the arrangement, and will reserve the right to add or remove mutual fund families that it makes available to the Plans.

As part of Frost's arrangements with the mutual fund families, Frost may provide shareholder services to, and receive fees from, some of the individual mutual funds in which Plan assets are invested. The shareholder services may include, e.g., providing mutual fund recordkeeping and accounting services in connection with the Plans' purchase or sale of shares, processing mutual fund sales and redemption transactions involving the Plans, and providing mutual fund enrollment material (including prospectuses) to Plan participants. The fees paid by the mutual funds to Frost will generally be based on a percentage of Plan assets invested in each mutual fund, and will be paid pursuant to either a distribution plan described in Securities and Exchange Commission (SEC) Rule 12b-1, 17 C.F.R. 270.12b-1 (a 12b-1 plan), or a "subtransfer agency arrangement."1

You further represent that, with respect to some of the Plans, Frost will recommend to the Plan fiduciary the advisability of investing in particular mutual funds offered pursuant to Frost's arrangements with the mutual fund families. In addition, Frost will monitor the performance of the individual mutual funds selected by the Plan fiduciary and, as it deems appropriate, will make further recommendations regarding additional or substitute mutual funds for the investment of Plan assets.

With respect to other Plans, Frost will not make any recommendations concerning the selection of, or continued investment in, particular mutual funds. Rather, the responsible Plan fiduciary will independently select, from the mutual fund families made available by Frost, particular mutual funds for the investment of Plan assets, or for designation as investment alternatives offered to participants under the Plan.

In both instances, whether or not Frost makes specific investment recommendations, you represent that, before a Plan enters into the arrangement, the terms of Frost's fee arrangements with the mutual fund families will be fully disclosed to the Plans. In addition, Frost's trustee agreement with a Plan will be structured so that any 12b-1 or subtransfer agent fees received by Frost that are attributable to the Plan's investment in a mutual fund will be used to benefit the Plan. Pursuant to the particular agreement with each Plan, Frost will offset such fees, on a dollar-for-dollar basis, against the trustee fee that the Plan is obligated to pay Frost or against the recordkeeping fee that the Plan is obligated to pay to a third-party recordkeeper; or Frost will credit the Plan directly with the fees it receives based on the investment of Plan assets in the mutual fund.2 The trustee agreement will provide that, to the extent that Frost receives fees from mutual funds in connection with the Plan's investments that are in excess of the fee that the Plan owes to Frost, the Plan will be entitled to the excess amount.

You request an opinion that Frost's receipt of fees from the mutual funds under the circumstances described would not constitute a violation of ERISA section 406(b)(1) or (b)(3).3 You have asked us to assume for the purpose of your request that the arrangements between Frost and the Plans satisfy the conditions of ERISA section 408(b)(2).4

Section 406(b)(1) of ERISA prohibits a fiduciary with respect to a plan from dealing with the assets of the plan in his or her own interest or for his or her own account. Section 406(b)(3) prohibits a fiduciary with respect to a plan from receiving any consideration for his or her personal

account from any party dealing with the plan in connection with a transaction involving the assets of the plan.5

Under section 3(21)(A) of ERISA, a person is a "fiduciary" with respect to a plan to the extent that the person (i) exercises any discretionary authority or control respecting management of the plan or any authority or control respecting management or disposition of its assets, (ii) renders investment advice for a fee or other compensation, direct or indirect, with respect to any moneys or other property of the plan, or has any authority or responsibility to do so, or (iii) has any discretionary authority or responsibility in the administration of the plan.

Frost, as trustee, is a fiduciary with respect to the Plans under section 3(21)(A) of ERISA. See 29 C.F.R. 2509.75-8, D-3 (the position of trustee of a plan, by its very nature, requires the person who holds it to perform one or more of the functions described in ERISA section 3(21)(A)).6

When the Trustee Advises

You have indicated that, with respect to some of the Plans, Frost will advise the Plan fiduciary regarding particular mutual funds in which to invest Plan assets.7 It also appears from your submission that, under Frost's arrangements with various mutual fund families, Frost may receive fees from some of the mutual funds as a result of a Plan's investment in the mutual funds recommended by Frost. In the view of the Department, advising that plan assets be invested in mutual funds that pay additional fees to the advising fiduciary generally would violate the prohibitions of ERISA section 406(b)(1).

You represent, however, that before entering into an arrangement with a Plan, or recommending any particular mutual fund investments, Frost will disclose to the Plan fiduciary the extent to which it may receive fees from the mutual fund(s). Furthermore, you represent that the trustee agreement between Frost and the Plan will expressly provide that any fees received by Frost as a result of the Plan's investment in such a mutual fund will be used to pay all or a portion of the compensation that the Plan is obligated to pay to Frost, and that the Plan will be entitled to any such fees that exceed the Plan's liability to Frost.8 To the extent the Plan's legal obligation to Frost is extinguished by the amount of the offset, it is the opinion of the Department that Frost would not be dealing with the assets of the Plan in its own interest or for its own account in violation of section 406(b)(1).

With respect to the prohibition of section 406(b)(3), Frost's contract with a Plan, as described above, will provide that Frost's receipt of fees from one or more mutual funds in connection with the Plan's investment in such funds will be used to reduce the Plan's obligation to Frost, will in no circumstances increase Frost's compensation, and thus will benefit the Plan rather than Frost. Accordingly, it is the opinion of the Department that in these circumstances Frost would not be deemed to receive such payments for its own personal account in violation of section 406(b)(3).

When the Trustee is Directed

With respect to Plans for which Frost does not provide any investment advice, it appears that the Plan fiduciary, and in some instances the Plan participants, will select the mutual funds in which to invest Plan assets from among those made available by Frost. Generally speaking, if a trustee acts pursuant to a direction in accordance with section 403(a)(1) or 404(c) of ERISA and does not exercise any authority or control to cause a plan to invest in a mutual fund that pays a fee to the trustee in connection with the plan's investment, the trustee would not be dealing with the assets of the plan for its own interest or for its own account in violation of section 406(b)(1).

Similarly, it is generally the view of the Department that if a trustee acts pursuant to a direction in accordance with section 403(a)(1) or 404(c) of

ERISA and does not exercise any authority or control to cause a plan to invest in a mutual fund, the mere receipt by the trustee of a fee or other compensation from the mutual fund in connection with such investment would not in and of itself violate section 406(b)(3). Your submission indicates, however, that Frost reserves the right to add or remove mutual fund families that it makes available to Plans. Under these circumstances, we are unable to conclude that Frost would not exercise any discretionary authority or control to cause the Plans to invest in mutual funds that pay a fee or other compensation to Frost.9

However, because Frost's trustee agreements with the Plans are structured so that any 12b-1 or subtransfer agent fees attributable to the Plans' investments in mutual funds are used to benefit the Plans, either as a dollar-for-dollar offset against the fees the Plans would be obligated to pay to Frost for its services or as amounts credited directly to the Plans, it is the view of the Department that Frost would not be dealing with the assets of the Plans in its own interest or for its own account, or receiving payments for its own personal account in violation of section 406(b)(1) or (b)(3).

Finally, it should be noted that ERISA's general standards of fiduciary conduct also would apply to the proposed arrangement. Under section 404(a)(1) of ERISA, the responsible Plan fiduciaries must act prudently and solely in the interest of the Plan participants and beneficiaries both in deciding whether to enter into, or continue, the above-described arrangement and trustee agreement with Frost, and in determining which investment options to utilize or make available to Plan participants or beneficiaries. In this regard, the responsible Plan fiduciaries must assure that the compensation paid directly or indirectly by the Plan to Frost is reasonable, taking into account the trustee services provided to the Plan as well as any other fees or compensation received by Frost in connection with the investment of Plan assets. In this connection, it is the view of the Department that the responsible Plan fiduciaries must obtain sufficient information regarding any fees or other compensation that

Frost receives with respect to the Plan's investments in each mutual fund to make an informed decision whether Frost's compensation for services is no more than reasonable. The Plan fiduciaries also must periodically monitor the actions taken by Frost in the performance of its duties, to assure, among other things, that any fee offsets to which the Plan is entitled are correctly calculated and applied.

This letter constitutes an advisory opinion under ERISA Procedure 76-1 (41 Fed. Reg. 36281, August 27, 1976). Accordingly, it is issued subject to the provisions of that procedure, including section 10 thereof regarding the effect of advisory opinions.

> Sincerely,
> Bette J. Briggs
> Chief, Division of Fiduciary
> Interpretations
> Office of Regulations and
> Interpretations

1 A "subtransfer agency fee" is typically a fee paid for recordkeeping services provided to the mutual fund transfer agent with respect to bank customers.

2 We assume for purposes of this opinion that each Plan's governing documents provide that the Plan will pay costs and expenses for trustee services necessary to the operation and administration of the Plan.

3 For a discussion of related issues involving receipt of fees by a record-keeper offering a program of investment options and services to plans, see also Advisory Opinion 97-16A, May 22, 1997.

4 We offer no opinion herein as to whether such conditions have been satisfied; nor does this opinion address the application of any other provisions of ERISA.

5 Under Reorganization Plan No. 4 of 1978, effective December 31, 1978, the authority of the Secretary of the Treasury to issue interpretations regarding section 4975 of the Internal Revenue Code of 1986 (the Code) has been transferred, with certain exceptions not here relevant, to the Secretary of Labor, and the Secretary of the Treasury is bound by interpretations of the Secretary of Labor pursuant to such authority. Therefore, references in this letter to specific sections of ERISA should be read to refer also to the corresponding sections of the Code.

6 Section 403(a) of ERISA establishes that, in general, a trustee of a plan must have exclusive authority and discretion to manage and control the plan's assets. Under section 403(a)(1), when the plan expressly so provides, the trustee may be subject to the proper directions of a named fiduciary which are made in accordance with the terms of the plan and not contrary to ERISA. Nevertheless, a directed trustee has residual fiduciary responsibility for determining whether a given direction is proper and whether following the direction would result in a violation of ERISA. Accordingly, it is the view of the Department that a directed trustee necessarily will perform fiduciary functions.

7 We assume for the purposes of your request that Frost will provide investment advice within the meaning of ERISA section 3(21)(A)(ii) and 29 C.F.R. 2510.3-21(c)(1)(i) and (ii)(B) with respect to these Plans.

8 We express no opinion herein as to the propriety of such a pass-through of fees under Federal securities laws. Questions concerning the application of the Federal securities laws are within the jurisdiction of the SEC.

9 See, in this regard, the Department's position as expressed in the preamble to the final regulation regarding participant-directed individual account plans (ERISA section 404(c) plans), 57 Fed. Reg. 46906, 46924 n. 27 (Oct. 13, 1992):

In this regard [a fiduciary is relieved of responsibility only for the direct and necessary consequences of a participant's exercise of control], the Department points out that the act of limiting or designating investment options which are intended to constitute all or part of the investment universe of an ERISA 404(c) plan is a fiduciary function which, whether achieved through fiduciary designation or express plan language, is not a direct or necessary result of any participant direction of such plan.

Advisory Opinion   97-16A

May 22, 1997

Stephen M. Saxon
Groom & Nordberg
1701 Pennsylvania Avenue, N.W.
Washington, DC 20006
ERISA SEC.
406(b)(3)

Dear Mr. Saxon:

This is in response to your request for an advisory opinion concerning the application of section 406(b)(3) of the Employee Retirement Income Security Act (ERISA) to the receipt of certain fees by the Aetna Life Insurance and Annuity Company (ALIAC), an indirect subsidiary of Aetna Insurance Company, Inc. (Aetna). In particular, you request an opinion that ALIAC's receipt of fees from mutual funds that are unrelated to Aetna for recordkeeping and other services in connection with investments by employee benefit plans in the unrelated funds does not violate section 406(b)(3) under the circumstances described in your request.

ALIAC is a life insurance company domiciled in Connecticut, as well as a registered broker-dealer and a registered investment adviser. You represent that ALIAC sponsors and manages the Aetna Mutual Funds 401(k) Program (the 401(k) Program), which offers sponsors (other than Aetna) of participant-directed defined contribution plans (Plans): a) a volume submitter plan document; b) recordkeeping and related administrative services through Aetna 401 Retirement Plan Services (ARPS), ALIAC's business unit; c) investment options selected by ALIAC consisting of no-load or low load mutual funds from various fund families that are unrelated to Aetna (Unrelated Funds), Aetna Series

Funds (a series of mutual funds within a diversified open-ended investment company registered under the Investment Company Act of 1940 (ICA)), and group annuity contracts (GACs) issued by Aetna Life Insurance Company (ALIC), an affiliate of ALIAC;1 and d) directed trustee or custodial services provided by a bank that is unrelated to Aetna (the Bank). You represent that Unrelated Funds from three different mutual fund families are currently available and that additional families may be added in the future. You further represent that, in the future, Unrelated Funds may also pay fees to ALIAC for "marketing services.2

Plan fiduciaries who are independent of and unrelated to ALIAC, ALIC, and their affiliates are responsible for selecting the investment options to be offered to Plan participants from among the Unrelated Funds, Aetna Series Funds, and several options under the GACs. You further represent that neither ALIAC, ALIC, nor any other affiliate of Aetna (or any of its employees) provides investment advice or recommendations, within the meaning of ERISA section 3(21)(A)(ii), to Plan fiduciaries or participants regarding the advisability of either selecting any of the investment options for the Plans, or investing in any of the investment options that are available under the Plans.

ARPS, ALIAC's business unit, will, pursuant to a plan services agreement, provide some or all of the following services to Plans:

1) one-time installation services, which may include assistance in preparation of Plan documents, participant communication materials, and government filings, and installation of Plan and participant level records into the ARPS recordkeeping systems;

2) basic non-discretionary administrative and recordkeeping services, e.g., (a) enrolling participants, (b) maintaining participant and Plan-level account records, (c) balancing and allocating contributions, loan repayments, and forfeitures among accounts, (d) processing distributions and withdrawals, (e) reconciling Plan and participant activity on a daily

basis, (f) preparing periodic account activity statements for participants and Plan fiduciaries, (g) providing participant communication materials, (h) providing toll-free telephone access permitting participants to obtain current balance and investment information, change investment elections, and initiate loans, withdrawals and terminations, (i) performing certain tax qualification testing on a semi-annual basis, and (j) preparation of certain tax reporting forms;

3) recordkeeping and administrative support services for an employer stock fund, or for existing non-convertible GICs held by a Plan pending maturity (which are not associated with the GACs); and

4) optional services, e.g., (a) processing of participant loans, rollovers, lump sum and installment distributions, and qualified domestic relations orders, (b) additional tax qualification testing, (c) assistance in preparation of Plan-level government filings, and (d) recordkeeping and administrative support services for an employer stock fund and/or non-convertible GICs.

You represent that ARPS is not a "plan administrator" as defined in ERISA section 3(16)(A).

You indicate that the 401(k) Program service charges are fully disclosed in the marketing materials describing the 401(k) Program that are provided to Plan fiduciaries. Plans entering into the 401(k) Program pay ARPS a one-time charge for installation services, and annual charges for standard administrative and recordkeeping services, based on the number of participants. Additional services are available on a fee-for-service basis, at the election of the Plan fiduciary. Either party may terminate the arrangement without penalty on 60 days written notice. ALIC receives fees for administration and management of the GACs, including the separate accounts maintained in connection with the GACs. ALIAC receives advisory and administrative fees for investment management and related services provided to the Aetna Series Funds, pursuant to agreements between the Aetna Series Funds and ALIAC, which you represent are standard in the mutual fund industry.3

ALIAC has entered into various contracts with the Unrelated Funds (or their advisers or distributors) pursuant to which shares issued by the Unrelated Funds are purchased on behalf of Plans from the distributors of the Unrelated Funds or directly from the Unrelated Funds. Pursuant to these agreements, ALIAC receives from the Unrelated Funds (or their advisers or distributors) payments in consideration of (1) ARPS's provision of shareholder services (including participant-level recordkeeping) and other administrative services in connection with Plan investments in the Unrelated Funds, and (2) reductions in the Unrelated Funds' shareholder servicing and other administrative expenses (e.g., transfer agency fees) made possible by ARPS's provision of such services. These payments are based on a percentage of Plan assets invested in each Unrelated Fund through the 401(k) Program, and are paid either as administrative expenses by an Unrelated Fund (or by a servicing agent, adviser, or distributor from which the Unrelated Fund obtains its administrative services), or pursuant to a written plan described in Securities and Exchange Commission (SEC) Rule 12b-1, 17 C.F.R. 270.12b-1 (a 12b-1 Plan). The total administrative expenses paid by Unrelated Funds, including fees paid pursuant to 12b-1 Plans, are described to shareholders in prospectus materials. ALIAC discloses its receipt of fees from the Unrelated Funds (or their investment managers or other affiliates) in marketing and other disclosure materials provided to Plan fiduciaries. In particular, ALIAC will provide existing and prospective Plan customers a statement disclosing that ALIAC receives, or may receive, fees from many, but not all, of the Unrelated Funds, their managers or other affiliates (described as a percentage of assets under management with the Unrelated Funds). The statement will enumerate the services that ALIAC provides to the mutual funds and the rate of fees paid. The statement will also provide a toll-free telephone number to request more detailed information concerning which funds pay fees and an estimate of how much ALIAC may receive or has received during a particular time period. ALIAC will update the disclosure whenever there is any material change.

ALIAC reserves the right to modify the agreement with the Plan, including the list of Unrelated Funds available for investment, by giving 60 days written notice to the Plan's named fiduciary. If ALIAC decides to delete or replace an Unrelated Fund, ALIAC will notify the fiduciary of each Plan affected by the change. This notice would generally be sent by first class mail or fax. The notice would: (1) explain the proposed modification to the Unrelated Funds menu; (2) fully disclose any resulting changes in the fees paid to ALIAC by the Plan, or by any other entity with respect to Plan assets invested in the affected Funds; (3) identify the effective date of the change; (4) explain the Plan fiduciary's right to reject the change or terminate the agreement; and (5) reiterate that, pursuant to the contract provisions agreed to by the Plan fiduciary, failure to object will be treated as consent to the proposed change.

In addition, ALIAC may, depending on the facts and circumstances, send the notice by certified mail, include additional information and notice of the proposed deletion or substitution in other mailings to the Plan fiduciary (e.g., in periodic newsletters, in materials provided to assist the Plan fiduciary in notifying participants of the change, or in an invoice), or follow up its notice of a Fund deletion or substitution by telephone or other contact with the Plan fiduciary. Any or all of these procedures might be taken with respect to a particular Plan or implemented for all Plans affected by a deletion or substitution of a Fund.

You represent that if a Plan fiduciary rejects the proposed deletion or substitution, ALIAC would not be authorized to make the proposed deletion or substitution effective with respect to that particular Plan. In such circumstances, upon written notice of termination, the Plan fiduciary is afforded an additional 60 days to convert the Plan to another service provider. You represent, however, that in most cases ALIAC would seek to avoid terminating the agreement and losing a customer by negotiating to address the concerns of a Plan fiduciary that has rejected a proposed modification to the Unrelated Funds menu.

You also represent that ALIAC may determine, based on the particular facts and circumstances, to provide more than the minimum 60 days notice of the proposed change, waive some or all of the agreement's 60-day period for notice of termination by a Plan, and/or, if administratively feasible, agree to continue to provide services to a particular Plan beyond the 60-day termination period without deleting or substituting any Unrelated Funds pending the Plan's conversion to a new service provider if additional time is required to complete a conversion. Any of these or other measures might be taken with respect to particular Plans, or implemented for all Plans affected by a deletion or substitution of an Unrelated Fund. You thus represent that a Plan fiduciary will have a reasonable period of time within which to convert to a new service provider.

You have requested an opinion that the receipt of fees by ALIAC from the Unrelated Funds would not violate ERISA section 406(b)(3).4 Section 406(b)(3) provides that:

A fiduciary with respect to a plan shall not receive any consideration for his own personal account from any party dealing with such plan in connection with a transaction involving the assets of the plan.

The Department has taken the position that if a fiduciary does not exercise any authority or control to cause a plan to invest in a mutual fund, the mere receipt by the fiduciary of a fee or other compensation from the mutual fund in connection with the plan's investment would not in and of itself violate section ERISA 406(b)(3) (See, Advisory Opinion 97-15A, May 22, 1997).

Whether the receipt of such fees by ALIAC involves violations of section 406(b)(3) turns first on whether ALIAC is a fiduciary with respect to the investing Plans. ALIAC receives fees from an Unrelated Fund for its own account that are based on a percentage of the Plan assets invested in the Unrelated Fund. Such fees are paid to ALIAC by the Unrelated Fund or a related party in connection with a transaction (the purchase and sale of securities issued by the Unrelated Fund) involving the assets of the Plans.

The circumstances under which ALIAC provides recordkeeping and administrative services to Plans, you believe, would not cause ALIAC to be considered a fiduciary. You seek assurance, however, that ALIAC will not be deemed to be a fiduciary with respect to a Plan merely because ALIC, an affiliate under common control with ALIAC, may be considered a fiduciary of the Plan by virtue of providing investment management services for Plan assets invested in an ALIC separate account.

ERISA section 3(21)(A) provides that a person is a fiduciary with respect to a plan to the extent that he/she (i) exercises any discretionary authority or control respecting management of the plan or exercises any authority or control respecting management or disposition of its assets, (ii) renders investment advice for a fee or other compensation, direct or indirect, with respect to any moneys or other property of the plan, or has any authority or responsibility to do so, or (iii) has any discretionary authority or responsibility in the administration of the plan. Section 3(21)(B) provides that neither an investment company registered under the ICA, nor its investment adviser or principal underwriter shall be deemed to be fiduciaries or parties in interest with respect to a plan solely by reason of the plan's investment in securities issued by the investment company, unless the plan covers employees of the investment company, investment adviser or principal underwriter.

Interpretive Bulletin 75-8 (IB 75-8, 29 C.F.R. 2509.75-8) provides additional guidance concerning what types of functions will make a person a fiduciary with respect to a plan. In particular, question-and-answer D-2 states that a person who performs purely ministerial functions, such as preparation of employee communications material, preparation of government reports, and preparation of reports concerning participants' benefits, among others, within a framework of policies, interpretations, rules, practices and procedures made by other persons is not a fiduciary because such person does not have or exercise any discretionary authority or control regarding the management of the plan or its assets.

Pursuant to these provisions, a determination of whether a person is a fiduciary with respect to a plan requires an analysis of the types of functions performed and actions taken by the person on behalf of the plan to determine whether particular functions or actions are fiduciary in nature and therefore subject to ERISA's fiduciary responsibility provisions. As a result, the question of whether ALIAC is a "fiduciary" within the meaning of section 3(21)(A) of ERISA is inherently factual and will depend on the particular actions or functions ALIAC performs on behalf of the Plans.

You represent that ALIAC is not a trustee or administrator of the Plans, and provides only non-discretionary administrative and recordkeeping services pursuant to detailed administrative guidelines described in the Plan services agreement. Based on this representation, it would appear that, in most respects, ALIAC would not be a fiduciary with respect to Plans that are a party to such service agreements. ALIAC, however, retains some authority over the investment options selected by the Plans under the 401(k) Program in that it may, in its discretion, delete or substitute Unrelated Funds. In such instances, you represent that, before implementing a change in Funds with respect to any given Plan, ALIAC will provide advance notice to the appropriate Plan fiduciary regarding the change, including any changes in the fees to be received by ALIAC. If the Plan is permitted to maintain its investments in a deleted or replaced Fund, the advance notice will disclose any increased charges attributable to the retention by the Plan of the deleted or replaced Fund. In connection with this notice, you represent that Plan fiduciaries are afforded up to 120 days, or more, to reject the change and terminate ALIAC's services without penalty.

It is the view of the Department that a person would not be exercising discretionary authority or control over the management of a plan or its assets solely as a result of deleting or substituting a fund from a program of investment options and services offered to plans, provided that the appropriate plan fiduciary in fact makes the decision to accept or reject the change. In this regard, the fiduciary must be provided advance notice of the change, including any changes in the fees received, and afforded a reasonable period of time within which to decide whether to accept or reject the change and, in the event of a rejection, secure a new service provider. On the basis of your representations that ALIAC provides the appropriate Plan fiduciary advance notice of the deletion or substitution of Funds and a reasonable period of time following receipt of the notice (here, at least 120 days) within which to reject the change in Funds and secure a new service provider,5 as described in your letter, it is the view of the Department that ALIAC would not become a fiduciary solely as a result of deleting or substituting an Unrelated Fund under such circumstances, provided that the actual decision to accept or reject the change in Funds is made by the Plan fiduciary.

You have assumed that ALIC, an affiliate under common control with ALIAC, is a fiduciary with respect to the Plans by virtue of exercising authority or control over Plan assets invested in separate accounts maintained by ALIC. There is nothing, however, in your submission to indicate that ALIAC is in a position to (or in fact does) exercise any authority or control over those assets. Accordingly it does not appear that ALIAC would be considered a fiduciary merely as a result of its affiliation with ALIC.

Finally, it should be noted that ERISA's general standards of fiduciary conduct also would apply to the proposed arrangement. Under section

404(a)(1) of ERISA, the responsible Plan fiduciaries must act prudently and solely in the interest of the Plan participants and beneficiaries both in deciding whether to enter into, or continue, the above-described arrangement with ALIAC, and in determining which investment options to utilize or make available to Plan participants and beneficiaries. In this regard, the responsible Plan fiduciaries must assure that the compensation paid directly or indirectly by the Plan to ALIAC is reasonable, taking into account the services provided to the Plan as well as any other fees or compensation received by ALIAC in connection with the investment of Plan assets. The responsible Plan fiduciaries therefore must obtain sufficient information regarding any fees or other compensation that ALIAC receives with respect to the Plan's investments in each Unrelated Fund to make an informed decision whether ALIAC's compensation for services is no more than reasonable.

This letter constitutes an advisory opinion under ERISA Procedure 76-1 (41 Fed. Reg. 36281, August 27, 1976). Accordingly, this letter is issued subject to the provisions of the procedure, including section 10 relating to the effect of advisory opinions.

> Sincerely,
> Bette J. Briggs
> Chief, Division of Fiduciary
> Interpretations
> Office of Regulations and
> Interpretations

1 You represent that ALIC utilizes several separate accounts in connection with the GACs, and have assumed for purposes of the advisory opinion request that the assets of these separate accounts would be deemed to be plan assets pursuant to the Department's regulation at 29 CFR 2510.3-101.

2" The Department does not express any opinion concerning the effect, if any, of the receipt by ALIAC of fees for marketing services that may be added in the future.

3 In this letter the Department expresses no opinion regarding the fees paid by the Aetna Series Funds to ALIAC.

4 Under Reorganization Plan No. 4 of 1978, effective December 31, 1978, the authority of the Secretary of the Treasury to issue interpretations regarding section 4975 of the Internal Revenue Code of 1986 (the Code) has been transferred, with certain exceptions not here relevant, to the Secretary of Labor, and the Secretary of the Treasury is bound by interpretations of the Secretary of Labor pursuant to such authority. Therefore, references in this letter to specific sections of ERISA should be read to refer also to the corresponding sections of the Code.

5 What constitutes a "reasonable period" within which to terminate an arrangement and change service providers will depend on the particular facts and circumstances of each case. There may be situations in which a time period shorter than 120 days may constitute a "reasonable period."

Advisory Opinion 2001-09A

December 14, 2001

Mr. William A. Schmidt
Mr. Eric Berger
Kirkpatrick & Lockhart LLP
1800 Massachusetts Avenue, NW, 2nd Floor
Washington, DC 20036-1800
ERISA Sec. 406(b)

Dear Messrs. Schmidt and Berger:

This is in response to your application, on behalf of SunAmerica
Retirement Markets, Inc. (SunAmerica), for an exemption from the
prohibited transaction restrictions of section 406 of the Employee
Retirement Income Security Act of 1974, as amended (ERISA), with
respect to a program (the Program) under which SunAmerica would
render certain discretionary and nondiscretionary asset allocation
services to participants in ERISA-covered plans (Plans). On the basis of
the facts and representations contained in your submission, it is the view
of the Department that, for the reasons discussed below, the transactions
with respect to which you have requested exemptive relief would not, to
the extent executed in a manner consistent with such facts and
representations, violate the provisions of section 406(b) of ERISA.
Accordingly, we have determined that the appropriate response to your
request is an advisory opinion, rather than an exemption under ERISA
section 408(a).(1)

Your submission contains the following facts and representations.
SunAmerica is an indirectly wholly owned subsidiary of SunAmerica
Inc., and is one of a group of companies wholly owned by SunAmerica,
Inc. that provide a broad range of financial services. SunAmerica's

affiliate, SunAmerica Asset Management Corp., is a registered investment adviser under the Investment Advisers Act of 1940. SunAmerica intends to offer the Program to individual account plans described in section 3(34) of ERISA. It is anticipated that virtually all of these Plans will be designed or administered in a manner intended to comply with the provisions of section 404(c) of ERISA.(2) Under the Program, asset allocation services may be rendered to Plan participants(3) either through the "Discretionary Asset Allocation Service" or the "Recommended Asset Allocation Service" (collectively, Services; singly, Service). Through the Discretionary Asset Allocation Service, a specific Model Asset Allocation Portfolio will be implemented automatically with respect to a participant's account (Account). Through the Recommended Asset Allocation Service, a specific Model Asset Allocation Portfolio will be recommended to a participant for investment of his or her Account and the participant then may choose to implement the advice, or to disregard the recommendation and invest in a manner that does not conform to the Model Asset Allocation Portfolios.(4) The Plan fiduciary who causes a Plan to participate in the Program will select the Service (or Services) that will be available to participants and the manner by which participants will authorize such Service (or Services). Model Asset Allocation Portfolios will be based solely on the investment alternatives available under the Plan, which your application refers to as "Core Investments," but which we refer to herein as "Designated Investments."(5) In this regard, it is anticipated that the Plans will offer, exclusively or in addition to other vehicles, collective investment vehicles to which SunAmerica or an affiliate of SunAmerica provides investment advisory services (SunAmerica Funds).(6)

According to your submission, while SunAmerica will be making the Program, as well as other services, available to Plans, the Model Asset Allocation Portfolios offered under the Program will, in fact, be the product of a computer program applying a methodology developed, maintained and overseen by a financial expert who is independent of SunAmerica (the Financial Expert). The Model Asset Allocation

Portfolio produced under the Program with respect to a particular participant, therefore, will reflect the application of the methodologies developed by the Financial Expert to the Designated Investments, taking into account individual participant data, as provided by the participant, Plan sponsor or recordkeeper.

You represent that, with respect to a Plan's initial participation in the Program, a Plan fiduciary (i.e., a fiduciary independent of SunAmerica and its affiliates) will be provided detailed information concerning, among other things, the Program and the role of the Financial Expert in the development of the Model Asset Allocation Portfolios under the Program. In addition, the Plan fiduciary will be provided, on an on-going basis, a number of disclosures concerning the Program and Designated Investments under the Plan, including information pertaining to performance and rates of returns on Designated Investments, expenses and fees of SunAmerica Funds that are Designated Investments, and any proposed increases in investment advisory or other fees charged under a SunAmerica Fund.

You represent that, with respect to the development of the Model Asset Allocation Portfolios, the Financial Expert, using its own methodologies, will construct strategic "asset class" level portfolios. Using generally accepted principles of Modern Portfolio Theory, the Financial Expert will evaluate and determine its strategic asset class level portfolio recommendations. The Financial Expert then will construct each Model Asset Allocation Portfolio by combining Designated Investments so that the total asset class exposures of those Designated Investments equals the desired strategic asset class portfolio weight.(7) The Model Asset Allocation Portfolios will have different risk and return characteristics. In order for these methodologies to be employed, the Designated Investments of a participating Plan must provide a minimum exposure to a certain number of asset classes. SunAmerica will inform the Plan fiduciary who causes a Plan to participate in the Program of the asset classes that must be available for operation of the Program,(8) and will inform the Plan fiduciary whether this requirement has been satisfied, as solely determined by the Financial Expert, with respect to a particular selection of an investment alternative.

SunAmerica may assist the Financial Expert by providing certain background information for the development of the Model Asset Allocation Portfolios. Specifically, SunAmerica may supply the Financial Expert with algorithms, studies, analytics, research, models, papers and any other relevant materials. The Financial Expert also may seek the assistance of other entities in developing the Model Asset Allocation Portfolios. You represent that in all cases, the Financial Expert retains the sole control and discretion for the development and maintenance of the Model Asset Allocation Portfolios.

With regard to the computer programs utilized by the Financial Expert to select the specific Model Asset Allocation Portfolio provided to a participant, you represent that any programmers who are retained to formulate those programs will have no affiliation with SunAmerica, and that neither SunAmerica nor any of its affiliates will have any discretion regarding the output of such programs. You further represent that these computer programs require an input of minimum participant data that will be determined by the Financial Expert. The Financial Expert also will create a worksheet (the Worksheet) for gathering information from individual participants. The Worksheet will consist of a series of questions designed primarily to assess the participant's retirement needs, and will provide the participant an opportunity to designate specific investments other than Designated Investments, or to place constraints on investments in and among Designated Investments, if available under the Plan. Also, with respect to the Discretionary Asset Allocation Service, subsequent to initial participation in the Program, at least once each calendar quarter, a "Facilitator" will contact each participant to whom services are provided to obtain any new or different information requested on the Worksheet. This information may lead the Financial Expert to implement a new Model Asset Allocation Portfolio for the participant. The Facilitators will be employees of SunAmerica, independent contractors of SunAmerica's affiliates, or independent contractors or employees of broker-dealers not affiliated with SunAmerica. Facilitators will not provide services to participants who receive the Recommended Asset Allocation Service, and will not choose or recommend a Model Asset Allocation Portfolio in connection with the Discretionary Asset Allocation Service.

The Model Asset Allocation Portfolios (or any other Asset Allocation Portfolio) implemented will be reviewed regularly and "rebalanced." You explain that participant Account or Asset Allocation Portfolio rebalancing is the process of moving the assets in an Account or Asset Allocation Portfolio asset class exposures toward its strategic target. This process seeks to reduce the relative performance risk associated with moving the asset class exposures away from what was intended in the strategic asset allocation. You represent that the rebalancing procedures will not involve any discretion on the part of SunAmerica or its affiliates, and that the Financial Expert will develop a mechanical formula to rebalance the relative value of the assets in each Account on a predetermined basis.

With regard to amounts paid by a Plan under the Program, you represent that SunAmerica will receive a fixed percentage of assets of the Plan invested in the Designated Investments up to 100 basis points (the Program Fee). In addition, SunAmerica may receive reimbursements, not to exceed a fixed percentage of Plan assets invested in the Designated Investments up to 25 basis points, for Facilitator fees and "direct expenses" within the meaning of 29 C.F.R. section 2550.408c-2 in connection with the operation of the Program paid by SunAmerica to unaffiliated third persons for goods and services provided to SunAmerica. SunAmerica, or any affiliate, will not be precluded from receiving fees from the SunAmerica Funds.

The Program Fee and any reimbursements payable to SunAmerica, and any compensation payable to the Facilitators under the Program, will not vary based on the asset allocations made or recommended by the Financial Expert, except that the Program Fee and any such reimbursements will be based on Designated Investments only and will be reduced if an Account invests in other than the Designated Investments. The compensation of the Financial Expert in connection with the Program will not be affected by the decisions made by the participants regarding investment of the assets of their Accounts in accordance with any Asset Allocation Portfolio.

With regard to the Financial Expert, you represent that the Financial Expert will receive compensation from SunAmerica for its services as the Financial Expert. You represent that fees to be paid by SunAmerica to the Financial Expert will not exceed 5 percent of the Financial Expert's gross income on an annual basis. In addition you represent that the fees paid to the Financial Expert by SunAmerica will not be affected by investments made in accordance with any Asset Allocation Portfolio under the Program. For example, neither the choice of the Financial Expert by SunAmerica nor any decision to continue or terminate the relationship shall be based on the fee income to SunAmerica that is generated by the Financial Expert's construction of the Model Asset Allocation Portfolios. You further represent that there have not been, nor will there be, any other relationships between SunAmerica and the Financial Expert that would affect the ability of the Financial Expert to act independent of SunAmerica and its affiliates. Your submission indicates that by providing discretionary asset management services and investment advice to participants, SunAmerica may be acting as a fiduciary with respect to the Plans.

Your submission further indicates that implementation of a Model Asset Allocation Portfolio, whether automatically or at the direction of a participant, may result in the receipt of increased investment advisory fees by SunAmerica or an affiliated entity. At issue, therefore, is whether, under the circumstances described in your submission, the receipt of such fees resulting from the asset allocation services rendered to Plan participants under the Program violates the prohibitions of section 406(b) of ERISA.

Section 3(21)(A) of ERISA defines the term fiduciary as a person with respect to a plan who (i) exercises any discretionary authority or discretionary control respecting management of such plan or exercises any authority or control respecting management or disposition of its assets, (ii) renders investment advice for a fee or other compensation, direct or indirect, with respect to any moneys or other property of such plan, or has any authority or responsibility to do so, or (iii) has any discretionary authority or discretionary responsibility in the administration of such plan. Regulation 29 C.F.R. section 2510.3-21(c)(1) states that, as a general matter, a person will be deemed to be rendering investment advice within the meaning of section 3(21)(A)(ii) if two criteria are met. First, pursuant to regulation section 2510.3-21(c)(1)(i), the person must render advice to the plan with regard to the value of securities or other property, or make recommendations as to the advisability of investing in, purchasing or selling securities or other property. Second, pursuant to regulation section 2510.3-21(c)(1)(ii), a person performing this type of service must either (A) have discretionary authority or control with respect to purchasing or selling securities or other property for the plan, or (B) render such advice on a regular basis pursuant to a mutual agreement, arrangement or understanding, written or otherwise, with the plan that the plan or a fiduciary with respect to the plan will rely on such advice as a primary basis for investment decisions with regard to plan assets. Although the question of whether an entity is a fiduciary by reason of providing services generally depends on the particular facts and circumstances of each case, we are assuming, for purposes of the discussion that follows in this advisory opinion, that the totality of services provided by SunAmerica causes it to be a fiduciary with respect to plans and participants to which it renders services. In this regard, we note that section 404 of ERISA generally provides that fiduciaries shall discharge their duties with respect to a plan prudently and solely in the interest of the participants and beneficiaries.

While section 406(a)(1)(C) of ERISA proscribes the provision of services to a plan by a party in interest, including a fiduciary, and section 406(a)(1)(D) prohibits the use by or for the benefit of, a party in interest, of the assets of a plan, section 408(b)(2) of ERISA provides a statutory exemption from the prohibitions of section 406(a) of ERISA for contracting or making reasonable arrangements with a party in interest, including a fiduciary, for office space, or legal, accounting, or other services necessary for the establishment or operation of the plan, if no more than reasonable compensation is paid.

Section 406(b)(1) of ERISA provides that a fiduciary with respect to a plan shall not deal with plan assets in his or her own interests or for his or her own account. Section 406(b)(3) provides that a fiduciary with respect to a plan shall not receive any consideration for his or her own personal account from any party dealing with such plan in connection with a transaction involving the assets of the plan.

With respect to the prohibitions in section 406(b), regulation 29 C.F.R. section 2550.408b-2(a) indicates that section 408(b)(2) of ERISA does not contain an exemption for an act described in section 406(b) of ERISA (relating to conflicts of interest on the part of fiduciaries) even if such act occurs in connection with a provision of services which is exempt under section 408(b)(2).(9) As explained in regulation 29 C.F.R. section 2550.408b-2(e)(1), if a fiduciary uses the authority, control, or responsibility which makes it a fiduciary to cause the plan to enter into a transaction involving the provision of services when such fiduciary has an interest in the transaction which may affect the exercise of its best judgment as a fiduciary, a transaction described in section 406(b)(1) would occur, and that transaction would be deemed to be a separate transaction from the transaction involving the provision of services and would not be exempted by section 408(b)(2). Conversely, the regulation explains that a fiduciary does not engage in an act described in section 406(b)(1) if the fiduciary does not use any of the authority, control, or responsibility which makes such person a fiduciary to cause a plan to pay additional fees for a service furnished by such fiduciary or to pay a fee for a service furnished by a person in which such fiduciary has an interest which may affect the exercise of such fiduciary's best judgment as a fiduciary.

In general, the provision of investment advice for a fee is a fiduciary act. On the basis of the foregoing, it is the view of the Department that SunAmerica would be acting as a fiduciary with respect to both the discretionary and nondiscretionary asset allocation services provided to plans and plan participants and, as such, would be subject to the fiduciary responsibility provisions of ERISA, including sections 404 and 406. In this regard, SunAmerica would be responsible for the prudent selection and periodic monitoring of its investment advisory services consistent with the requirements of ERISA section 404.(10)

With respect to the prohibitions in section 406(b) of ERISA, it is the view of the Department that, based on the facts and representations contained in your submission, the individual investment decisions or recommendations (i.e., Asset Allocation Portfolios) provided or implemented under the Program would not be the result of SunAmerica's exercise of authority, control, or responsibility for purposes of section 406(b) and the applicable regulations. This conclusion is premised on the following facts. First, Plan fiduciaries responsible for selecting the Program are fully informed about, and approve, the Program and the nature of the services provided thereunder, including the role of the Financial Expert. Second, the investment recommendations provided to, or implemented on behalf of, participants are the result of methodologies developed, maintained and overseen by a party (the Financial Expert) that is independent of SunAmerica and any of its affiliates.(11) The Financial Expert (an independent party) retains sole control and discretion over the development and maintenance of the methodologies.

Any computer programmers engaged to formulate the computer programs used by the Financial Expert will have no affiliation with SunAmerica. Recommendations provided to, or implemented on behalf of, participants by SunAmerica will be based solely on input of participant information into computer programs utilizing methodologies and parameters provided by the Financial Expert and neither SunAmerica, nor its affiliates, will be able to change or affect the output of the computer programs. SunAmerica will exercise no discretion over the communication to, or implementation of, investment recommendations provided under the Program. Third, the arrangement between SunAmerica and the Financial Expert preserves the Financial Expert's ability to develop Model Asset Allocation Portfolios solely in the interests of the plan participants and beneficiaries. Neither the Financial Expert's compensation from SunAmerica, nor any other aspect of the arrangement between the Financial Expert and SunAmerica, is related to the fee income that SunAmerica or its affiliates will receive from investments made pursuant to the Portfolios.

It is the view of the Department, therefore, that, to the extent that SunAmerica follows the Program as structured in relation to an investment of Plan assets in SunAmerica Funds, there would not be a per se violation of section 406(b)(1) or (3) of ERISA solely as a result of SunAmerica's, or any affiliate's, receipt of increased investment advisory fees resulting from such investments.

In view of this letter, the Department believes that no further action is necessary with respect to your exemption application. Accordingly, your exemption application is closed without further action. This letter constitutes an advisory opinion under ERISA Procedure 76-1, 41 Fed. Reg. 36281 (Aug. 27, 1976). Accordingly, this letter is issued subject to the provisions of that procedure, including section 10 thereof, relating to the effect of advisory opinions.

Sincerely,
Louis Campagna
Chief, Division of Fiduciary Interpretations
Office of Regulations and Interpretations

Footnotes

Under Reorganization Plan No. 4 of 1978, 43 Fed. Reg. 47713 (Oct. 17, 1978), the authority of the Secretary of the Treasury to issue rulings under section 4975 of the Internal Revenue Code (Code) has been transferred, with certain exceptions not here relevant, to the Secretary of Labor. Therefore, the references in this letter to specific sections of ERISA also refer to the corresponding sections of the Code.

The Department expresses no views herein, and no views should be implied, concerning the application of ERISA section 404(c) to the Program or any participating Plan or participant.

The asset allocation services under the Program also may be available to beneficiaries who, under the terms of their Plan, have the power to direct the investments in their account balances. For purposes of convenience, we refer only to participants.

You represent that the Program and Services will impose no limit on the frequency with which a participant may change his or her investment election. However, there may be limits concerning such frequency under the terms of a participating Plan.

You explain that, with respect to the Recommended Asset Allocation Services, under circumstances where a participating Plan permits participant input such as direction to invest in assets other than

Designated Investments or to place ceilings or floors on the percentages, or amounts, of Designated or non-Designated Investments, the methodologies followed by the Financial Expert, as described below, may result in a portfolio, other than a Model Asset Allocation Portfolio, that includes non-Designated Investments. You refer to such portfolios, along with the Model Asset Allocation Portfolios, generally as "Asset Allocation Portfolios."

As described below, an independent Plan fiduciary will determine the investments that will be available under the Plan.

You explain that the assets underlying the Designated Investments may fall into more than one asset class, and that in constructing a Model Asset Allocation Portfolio, the Financial Expert will employ a statistical method to determine the asset class exposure to a participant of a Designated Investment's investment approach.

You note that this process may be completed in a summary manner where SunAmerica offers the Program along with a range of SunAmerica Funds that will constitute the Designated Investments. You also represent that under no circumstances, except for Plans maintained by SunAmerica and its affiliates, will SunAmerica select investment alternatives to be made available under a Plan. This letter addresses only participation by Plans that are not maintained by SunAmerica and/or its affiliates.

We express no opinion as to whether the requirements of section 408(b)(2) of ERISA would be satisfied with respect to the Program.

The Department notes that, with regard to the selection and monitoring of the Financial Expert and SunAmerica's investment advisory services, any consideration of the effect of investment recommendations, or methodologies upon which such recommendations are based, on the fees or other compensation of SunAmerica or any of its affiliates, would, in the view of the Department, be inconsistent with a fiduciary's obligations under section 404 of ERISA.

Whether a party is "independent" for purposes of the subject analysis will generally involve a determination as to whether there exists a financial interest (e.g., compensation, fees, etc.), ownership interest, or other relationship, agreement or understanding that would limit the ability of the party to carry out its responsibility beyond the control, direction or influence of the fiduciary. In this regard, we note there have been other contexts in which the Department dealt with this issue. Under Prohibited Transaction Class Exemption 84-14, relief from section 406(a) of ERISA was provided for transactions between plans and parties in interest if approved by a qualified professional asset manager (QPAM). The party in interest could not be "related" to the QPAM - meaning such party in interest (or person controlling, or controlled by, the party in interest) could not own a five percent or more interest in the QPAM; or the QPAM (or person controlling, or controlled by, the QPAM) could not own a five percent or more interest in the party in interest. Further, the plan with respect to which the person was a party in interest could not represent more than 20% of the assets that the QPAM had under management at the time of the transaction.

Advisory Opinion 2003-09A

June 25, 2003
ERISA Sec. 406(b)(1), 406(b)(3)

Gary W. Howell
Gardner, Carton & Douglas
191 North Wacker Drive, Suite 3700
Chicago, IL 60606

Dear Mr. Howell:

This is in response to your request for guidance under the Employee Retirement Income Security Act of 1974 (ERISA). In particular, you ask whether a trust company's receipt of 12b-1 and subtransfer fees from mutual funds, the investment advisers of which are affiliates of the trust company, for services in connection with investment by employee benefit plans in the mutual funds, would violate section 406(b)(1) and 406(b)(3) of ERISA when the decision to invest in such funds is made by an employee benefit plan fiduciary or participant who is independent of the trust company and its affiliates.

You write on behalf of ABN AMRO Trust Services Company (AATSC), a state-chartered trust company. You represent that AATSC is a wholly owned subsidiary of Alleghany Asset Management Company (Alleghany), which is a wholly owned subsidiary of ABN-AMRO North America Holding Company, a bank holding company (ABN-AMRO).(1)

Alleghany is also the parent organization of several institutional investment advisers (Advisers), including some that have entered into investment advisory contracts with mutual funds registered under the Investment Company Act of 1940. You refer to those mutual funds with which such Advisers have investment advisory contracts as 'Proprietary

Funds.' All other mutual funds are referred to as 'Non-Proprietary Funds.'

You represent that AATSC provides directed trustee and 'non-fiduciary' services to participant-directed and other defined contribution pension plans (Client Plans) through 'bundled service' arrangements. You represent that these services (Plan Services) provided by AATSC through bundled service arrangements include, but are not limited to, custodial trustee services, participant level recordkeeping, participant communications and educational materials and programs, voice response system access to accounts for participants, plan documentation, including prototype plans, summary plan descriptions and annual reports, tax compliance assistance, administrative assistance in processing plan distributions and loans, and a facility for plan investment options.

In connection with the Client Plan-related business, AATSC has entered into shareholder service arrangements with distributors of, or investment advisers to, mutual fund families pursuant to which AATSC will make mutual fund families available for investment by Client Plans. Among the investment advisers with which AATSC enters into such arrangements are those Advisers with investment advisory contracts with Proprietary Funds.

You represent that neither AATSC, nor any other bundled service provider of which AATSC is aware, engages in arrangements where just Plan Services are provided. You represent that, because the true cost of Plan Services would exceed any amount that could be charged in the competitive bundled service market with regard to a Client Plan's engagement of AATSC as a bundled service provider, all bundled service arrangements between AATSC and a Client Plan are predicated on a Client Plan's offering of one or more Proprietary Funds as an investment option.

You represent that disclosures with regard to Proprietary Funds will enable the fiduciaries of potential Client Plans to make an informed decision regarding whether to engage AATSC in a bundled service arrangement. Included in every proposal made by AATSC to a potential Client Plan are the following disclosures regarding each Proprietary Fund offered:

the total number of actively-managed mutual funds in the same category as the Proprietary Fund (based on fund classifications by Lipper, Morningstar, or some other generally recognized mutual fund analytical service);

the investment advisory fee, 12b-1 fee (if any) and other fees paid by the Proprietary Fund, as well as the aggregate fees paid by such Proprietary Fund; and

the same fee information described in (b) with respect to the highest-fee, lowest-fee, median-fee, and average-fee fund in the same category as the Proprietary Fund.

You represent that participant-directed and other defined contribution pension plans become Client Plans through a process of presentation and negotiation. Typically, a plan sponsor, on behalf of a potential Client Plan, either directly, or through a third-party consultant, will ask AATSC to respond to a 'request for proposal' to provide a bundle of services for the plan, such as recordkeeping, directed trusteeship, participant investment education, participant loan and distribution processing and investment vehicles. You represent that a potential Client Plan will typically ask other bundled service providers also to respond to a request for proposal.

Client Plan fiduciaries select the funds in which the Client Plans will invest. AATSC does not restrict the mutual funds that a Client Plan may utilize, beyond requiring, as a condition of engagement, that a Client

Plan select at least one Proprietary Fund to offer as an investment option. AATSC will, if requested, provide a list of investment funds for the Client Plan to consider. The Client Plan fiduciaries are free to select funds other than those listed by AATSC. Your representations indicate that AATSC, under the terms of a bundled service arrangement, will not be able to assert any influence with respect to selection of other investment options in which Client Plans will invest or the particular Proprietary Fund in which the Client Plan elects to invest.

Potential Client Plan fiduciaries are free to accept, reject or further negotiate a bundled service arrangement from AATSC. Based upon such flexibility on the part of a potential Client Plan with respect to negotiation of the terms surrounding engagement of AATSC to provide Plan Services, you represent that engagement of AATSC results from arm's length negotiations between a potential Client Plan and AATSC.

You represent that a Client Plan's choice of investment vehicles affects the cost of engaging AATSC to provide Plan Services. AATSC estimates the amounts that a potential Client Plan would likely invest in Proprietary Funds based on the amount of the Client Plan's assets and the number of Proprietary Funds selected. This estimate affects the price at which AATSC offers to perform Plan Services. For example, if Client Plan fiduciaries may direct investment into three Proprietary Funds, Plan Services would cost less than if Client Plan fiduciaries may direct investment into two Proprietary Funds. Similarly, Client Plan fiduciaries that may direct investment into only one Proprietary Fund would be quoted a higher price for bundled services, because AATSC would expect to cover less of the cost of providing Plan Services from asset management revenue.

As a directed trustee, AATSC takes direction from Client Plans regarding their selection of investment options. You assert that, because AATSC does not restrict the mutual funds that a potential Client Plan may utilize, the preparation and furnishing of a list offering an array of mutual fund choices does not constitute discretion to add or delete mutual fund families in which Client Plans may invest.

You represent that if a Client Plan decides to remove a Proprietary Fund as an investment option, AATSC's total anticipated revenue from the Client Plan and Proprietary Fund would be affected, leaving less asset management revenue with which to provide Plan Services. In such a situation, you represent that AATSC would invite the Client Plan fiduciaries to consider one or more other Proprietary Funds to replace non-Proprietary Fund investment options. If the plan fiduciaries do not choose to offer another Proprietary Fund as an investment option, AATSC would continue to provide Plan Services pursuant to the bundled services arrangement, but would evaluate such arrangement, as follows.

If AATSC determines that a bundled service arrangement is no longer profitable, AATSC can withdraw or make an offer to the Client Plan fiduciaries to renegotiate the fees for AATSC's provision of Plan Services. You represent that AATSC's bundled service arrangements generally include a provision whereby AATSC may propose a fee adjustment upon sixty days' written notice. In addition, either party can terminate a bundled service arrangement without cause, upon at least thirty days' advance written notice. Upon termination of a bundled service arrangement, funds are transferred on the effective date of appointment of a successor trustee.

You represent that AATSC has the systems and administrative capability to provide investment facilities to a Client Plan for any mutual fund that accepts investments from pension plans. You represent that the majority of mutual funds are traded by AATSC on the National Securities Clearing Corporation (NSCC) 'platform' for processing transactions in mutual funds. Mutual fund transactions processed through NSCC's 'Fund/SERV' service are made on its standard, highly automated platform that links approximately 2,000 key providers in the mutual fund industry, including AATSC. For those few funds utilized by Client Plans that do not participate in NSCC, generally because of their small size or low volume of trades, you represent that AATSC processes trades manually, in a manner consistent with industry practice.

You ask whether AATSC's receipt of 12b-1 and subtransfer agency fees from mutual funds, including those Proprietary Funds the investment advisers of which are affiliates of AATSC, for services in connection with investment by employee benefit plans in the mutual funds, would violate section 406(b)(1) and 406(b)(3) of ERISA when the decision to invest in such funds is made by an employee benefit plan fiduciary who is independent of AATSC and its affiliates.(2)

Section 3(14)(A) and (B) of ERISA provides that a party in interest means, as to an employee benefit plan, any fiduciary, including a trustee, of an employee benefit plan or a person providing services to a plan. ERISA section 3(21)(A) provides that a person is a fiduciary with respect to a plan to the extent that it (i) exercises any authority or control respecting management or disposition of its assets, (ii) renders investment advice for a fee or other compensation, direct or indirect, with respect to any moneys or other property of the plan, or has any authority or responsibility to do so, or (iii) has any discretionary authority or responsibility in the administration of the plan. Accordingly, as directed trustee of Client Plans, AATSC will be a party in interest and a fiduciary.

Section 406(a)(1)(C) of ERISA proscribes the provision of services to a plan by a party in interest, including a fiduciary, and section 406(a)(1)(D) prohibits the use by or for the benefit of, a party in interest, of the assets of a plan. However, section 408(b)(2) of ERISA provides an exemption from the prohibitions of section 406(a) of ERISA for contracting or making reasonable arrangements with a party in interest, including a fiduciary, for office space, or legal, accounting, or other services necessary for the establishment or operation of the plan, if no more than reasonable compensation is paid.

29 CFR 2550.408b-2 provides, with respect to a reasonable contract or arrangement, that no contract or arrangement is reasonable within the meaning of section 408(b)(2) and 29 CFR 2550.408b-2(a)(2) if it does not permit termination by the plan without penalty to the plan on reasonably short notice under the circumstances to prevent the plan from becoming locked into an arrangement that has become disadvantageous. Your representations indicate that, pursuant to the Client Plan's arrangement with AATSC and consistent with 29 CFR 2550.408b-2(c), the Client Plan may terminate a bundled service arrangement without cause and without penalty, upon at least thirty days' advance written notice.(3)

Section 406(b)(1) of ERISA prohibits a fiduciary with respect to a plan from dealing with the assets of the plan in its own interest or for its own account. Section 406(b)(3) of ERISA prohibits a fiduciary with respect to a plan from receiving any consideration for its own personal account from any party dealing with the plan in connection with a transaction involving the assets of the plan.

With respect to the prohibitions in section 406(b), regulation 29 CFR 2550.408b-2(a) indicates that section 408(b)(2) of ERISA does not contain an exemption for an act described in section 406(b) of ERISA (relating to conflicts of interest on the part of fiduciaries) even if such act occurs in connection with a provision of services which is exempt under section 408(b)(2). As explained in regulation 29 CFR 2550.408b-2(e)(1), if a fiduciary uses the authority, control, or responsibility which makes it a fiduciary to cause the plan to enter into a transaction involving the provision of services when such fiduciary has an interest in the transaction which may affect the exercise of its best judgment as a fiduciary, a transaction described in section 406(b)(1) would occur, and that transaction would be deemed to be a separate transaction from the transaction involving the provision of services and would not be exempted by section 408(b)(2). Conversely, the regulation explains that a fiduciary does not engage in an act described in section 406(b)(1) if the fiduciary does not use any of the authority, control, or responsibility which makes such person a fiduciary to cause a plan to pay additional fees for a service furnished by such fiduciary or to pay a fee for a service furnished by a person in which such fiduciary has an interest which may affect the exercise of such fiduciary's best judgment as a fiduciary.

You assert that principles previously expressed by the Department in Advisory Opinion 97-15A(4) would apply here. In Advisory Opinion 97-15A, the Department opined that if a trustee acts pursuant to a proper direction in accordance with sections 403(a)(1) or 404(c) of ERISA and does not exercise any authority or control to cause a plan to invest in a mutual fund that pays a fee to the trustee in connection with the plan's investment, then the trustee would not be dealing with assets of the plan for its own interest or for its own account in violation of section 406(b)(1) of ERISA and the trustee would not be receiving consideration for itself from a third party in connection with a transaction involving plan assets in violation of section 406(b)(3).

The arrangement about which you request the Department's guidance differs from the facts of Advisory Opinion 97-15A. In that letter, the trustee had reserved the right to add or remove mutual fund families that it made available to its client plans. The trustee also agreed to apply any fees it received from the mutual funds to the benefit of the plans. You represent that, once a Client Plan enters into a bundled service arrangement with AATSC, the Client Plan fiduciary possesses authority to make decisions regarding investment fund choices and any modifications to the menu of investment fund choices available for investment of plan assets.

In Advisory Opinion 97-16A,(5) the Department expressed the view that a person would not be exercising discretionary authority or control over the management of a plan or its assets solely as a result of deleting or substituting a fund from a program of investment options and services offered to plans, provided that the appropriate plan fiduciary in fact makes the decision to accept or reject the change. In this regard, the Department went on to opine that the plan fiduciary must be provided advance notice of the change, including disclosure of record-keeper fee information and must be afforded a reasonable amount of time in which to accept or reject the change. Such advance notice ensured that the fiduciary would maintain independence with respect to selection of investment options offered. Similar to the arrangement described in Advisory Opinion 97-16A, here a Client Plan sponsor or other fiduciary shall, independent of AATSC, maintain complete control with respect to the selection of funds in which the Client Plan will invest. AATSC itself has no role with respect to selection of investment options beyond requiring, as a condition of initial engagement of AATSC as a bundled service provider, that at least one Proprietary Fund is offered by a Client Plan for investment.

You represent that when a Client Plan engages AATSC to provide bundled services, a Client Plan fiduciary, independent of AATSC or its affiliates, will select the Client Plan's investment options. We note, however, that if, with respect to a particular Client Plan, AATSC provides 'investment advice' within the meaning of regulation 29 CFR 2510.3-21(c), AATSC would engage in a violation of section 406(b)(1) of ERISA in causing the Client Plan to invest in a Proprietary Fund (or any mutual fund that pays a fee to AATSC or its affiliates).

It is the view of the Department that AATSC's receipt of 12b-1 or subtransfer fees from mutual funds, including those Proprietary Funds the investment advisers of which are affiliates of AATSC, for services in connection with investment by employee benefit plans in the mutual funds, under the circumstances described above, would not violate section 406(b)(1) or 406(b)(3) of ERISA when the decision to invest in such funds is made by a fiduciary who is independent of AATSC and its affiliates, or by participants of such employee benefit plans.

Finally, it should be noted that ERISA's general standards of fiduciary conduct also would apply to the proposed arrangement. Section 403(c)(1) of ERISA provides that the assets of a plan shall never inure to the benefit of any employer and shall be held for the exclusive purposes of providing benefits to participants and beneficiaries and defraying reasonable expenses of administering the plan. Under section 404(a)(1) of ERISA, the responsible plan fiduciaries must act prudently and solely in the interest of the plan participants and beneficiaries both in deciding whether to enter into, or continue, arrangements with AATSC and in determining the investment options in which to invest or make available to plan participants and beneficiaries in self-directed plans.

This letter constitutes an advisory opinion under ERISA Procedure 76-1, 41 Fed. Reg. 36281 (Aug. 27, 1976). Accordingly, it is issued subject to the provisions of that procedure, including section 10 thereof relating to the effect of advisory opinions.

Sincerely,
Louis Campagna
Chief, Division of Fiduciary Interpretations
Office of Regulations and Interpretations

Footnotes

In your initial submission, you wrote on behalf of The Chicago Trust Company (TCTC). Since the date of submission, TCTC has been renamed AATSC, effective January 1, 2002. This change is in name only and was effected without any legal change in the individual corporate status of TCTC. AATSC continues as a state-chartered trust company under the original charter and corporate status granted by the state to the former TCTC, and remains in the same legal relationship, by way of ownership, to Alleghany and ABN-AMRO.

Consistent with Prohibited Transaction Exemption 96-74, granted to TCTC, TCTC will never receive any 12b-1 or subtransfer agency fees from its Proprietary Funds in connection with the conversion of certain collective investment fund units into shares of Proprietary Funds. Furthermore, you represent that AATSC relies upon Prohibited Transaction Class Exemption 77-4 to cover situations where AATSC may serve as a fiduciary to a Client Plan with authority to select investments, including Proprietary Funds. In Advisory Opinions 93-12A and 93-13A, the Department expressed the view that it was unable to conclude that PTE 77-4 would be available for plan purchases and sales of mutual fund shares if a 12b-1 fee is paid to the fiduciary or its affiliate with regard to that portion of the mutual fund's assets attributable to the plan's investment.

The Department expresses no view as to whether the conditions contained in section 408(b)(2) of ERISA would be satisfied with respect to any arrangement between AATSC and a Client Plan.

Index